JESUS IN CONTEXT

JESUS IN CONTEXT
Power
People, &
Performance

Richard A.
Horsley

Fortress Press
Minneapolis

JESUS IN CONTEXT
Power, People, and Performance

Cover image: *Jesus Wept*, by Daniel Bonnell. Photo © www.iocproject.com.
Used by permission.
Cover design: Micah Thompson
Book design: Amy Anderson

Library of Congress Cataloging-in-Publication Data

Horsley, Richard A.
Jesus in context : power, people and performance / Richard A. Horsley.
    p. cm.
Includes bibliographical references and index.
ISBN 978-0-8006-6312-4 (alk. paper)
1. Bible. N.T. Mark—Social scientific criticism. 2. Q hypothesis
(Synoptics criticism) 3. Christian sociology—History—Early church, ca.
30-600. I. Title.
 BS2585.52.H67 2008
 226'.06—dc22

2008017545

The paper used in this publication meets the minimum requirements of American
National Standard for Information Sciences-Permanence of Paper for Printed Library
Materials, ANSI Z329.48-1984.

Manufactured in the U.S.A.

12   11   10   09   08   1   2   3   4   5   6   7   8   9   10

Contents

Part III: Social Memory

Part IV: Moral Economy and the Arts of Resistance

Introduction

One of the most significant developments in New Testament studies in the last generation or so has been the separation of Gospel studies and the study of the historical Jesus into distinct subfields. Each of these then split by special approach or particular perspective. Young American scholars in particular who were just entering New Testament studies in the 1970s and 80s, seeking alternatives to the already established "criticisms" (form, source, and redaction criticism, for example), pursued sociological analysis or one or another form of literary analysis. Serious challenges to standard assumptions and concepts by Black, Feminist, and Latin American liberation theologies and pioneering works in rhetorical and ideological criticism then further complicated approaches to Jesus and the Gospels.[1]

While interest in the "theology" of particular Gospels continues, various kinds of literary analysis have become increasingly sophisticated. Much of this has consisted of adapting what is done in the study of modern literatures to the Gospels as narrative literature. In investigating and reconstructing the historical Jesus, the "liberals" of the Jesus Seminar, building on form criticism, have developed a highly sophisticated "scientific" analysis focused primarily on the sayings of Jesus, and have located Jesus in a cosmopolitan Hellenistic culture. Meanwhile, more "conservative" scholars, placing greater trust in the historical reliability of the canonical Gospels, have found Jesus to be more continuous with Israel and the "Old Testament" / Hebrew Bible.

Emerging Puzzles and Unanticipated Challenges

Despite the splintering in the field, however, most interpreters in these subfields tend to accept the standard assumptions, approaches, and conceptual apparatus of established New Testament studies. Gospel scholars proceed by interpretation of written texts, which are assumed to be religious in character and focus. Many of the questions asked of the texts, and the very way interpretation is conceived, derive from the concerns of Christian theology, either explicitly or implicitly. The texts are assumed to be produced by at least literate "compilers" and, more recently, by literate "authors." Moreover, the Gospels as religious texts are assumed to have been "written" in an epoch-making process in which a new (and at least relatively more cosmopolitan) religion, "Christianity," emerged and separated from an old (and relatively more parochial) religion, "Judaism," which was struggling to define itself in the wider "Hellenistic" culture. Whether as the promised "Messiah" in the Gospels or as the historical figure of a teacher, Jesus is the key, the revealer-figure in the decisive break with "Judaism."

The following brief review of the standard assumptions, approaches, and concepts in Gospel studies and Jesus studies over the last few decades will show both "where we are coming from" and ways in which these constructions are proving inappropriate to the very texts we have been trying to interpret.

Religion, Yes: But What about the People?

The academic study of the New Testament originally developed as an integral division of theological studies, whose purpose was to provide an educated clergy. The New Testament professoriate took its place among the cultural elite in western societies. In the nineteenth and early twentieth centuries, the field developed a critical perspective to keep pace in the post-Enlightenment universities. Christian theological agendas and concepts, however, continued to dominate discourse in the field. A Christian construction of "Judaism" was the key framework against which to interpret Jesus and the Gospels. According to this framework, "Judaism" consisted mainly of four "sects," the four "philosophies" described by the Judean historian Flavius Josephus. The Pharisees represented "normative" Judaism, whose views were fleshed out from the debates of the Rabbis, their supposed successors. Their supposed obsession with the Law, especially the ritual laws, provided the foil for Jesus' preaching of the gospel. Although NT scholars are now more sensitive about the traditional anti-Judaism of the field, the old contrast of "Jesus vs. the Law / the Pharisees" persists in recent constructions of Jesus as the teacher of a "non-conventional" or "counter-cultural" ethic. Similarly, the older generalization that, in contrast with Jewish "parochialism" "Christianity" (or Jesus himself) included "Gentiles" appears to underlie some literary interpretation of the Gospels: for example, when Jesus' journeys back and forth across the Sea in Mark are read as a mediation between the "Jewish" side and the "Gentile" side.

The Christian theological construction of Jesus/Christianity vs. Judaism is problematic for at least two major reasons.

First, the construction of a monolithic "Judaism," the principal representatives of which were the elite scribal "parties" or "philosophies" of Pharisees, Sadducees, Essenes, and the "Fourth Philosophy" (which was previously collapsed, anachronistically, into "the Zealots"), left the vast majority of people out of consideration. Josephus offers accounts of *many* movements and revolts among the people who lived in hundreds of villages in the Palestinian countryside. He also identifies them according to different districts: the Judeans (*hoi Ioudaioi*) in Judea, the Samaritans in Samaria, and the Galileans in Galilee. Similarly, the assumption that the rituals and festivals in the Temple were the core of "common Judaism"[2] is also problematic because it does not take into account the attitudes and actions of the vast majority of the people. For example, again according to Josephus, villagers who made the pilgrimage to Jerusalem for Passover, a festival that celebrated the people's liberation from a foreign ruler (Pharaoh), often took the occasion to protest the High Priesthood's cooperation with Roman rule.[3]

Second, it is difficult to find in the Gospels the Christian theological scheme of Jesus versus the Jewish Law or Jewish convention, once we examine them more closely. To the contrary, Jesus himself is the "conventional" teacher, insisting on observance of the basic commandment of God over against the Pharisees' "traditions of the elders" (Mark 7:1-13). Nor is Mark's Jesus opposed to "the Jews." The only occurrence in Mark of the term "the Judeans"(*hoi Ioudaioi*), other than the Romans' reference to the condemned Jesus as "the king of the Judeans," is clearly a regional reference in this same episode (as it is for Josephus). As for the "Jewishness" of Jesus himself, Mark's Jesus appears reluctant to respond to the entreaty of a Syrophoenician woman (who is also identified as a "Greek") until she embarrasses him into it (7:24-30). In appointing the Twelve, in healing a woman hemorrhaging for twelve years and a twelve-year old girl (5:21-43), in carrying out sea crossings and feedings in the wilderness, and in appearing with Moses and Elijah on the mountain, Mark's Jesus is clearly spearheading a renewal of Israel (as a prophet like Moses or Elijah), not seeking a break or departure from "Judaism" and the Law. The opposition is not Jesus vs. Judaism or "conventional" Jewish teachings, but Jesus and the crowds in Galilee vs. the Roman and high priestly rulers in Jerusalem.[4]

This can be seen by reading Mark in terms of elementary principles of literary analysis of a narrative, that is, characters, setting, and plot (Literature 101). Jesus works mainly in the villages of Galilee and nearby territories. The scribes and Pharisees come "down" from Jerusalem to Galilee to oppose him (Mark 3:22; 7:1). The plot comes to a climactic conflict when Jesus marches "up" to the capital city of Jerusalem to engage in a sustained confrontation of the chief priests and their representatives in the Temple. The disciples (and, indirectly, the readers) are directed to go back down to Galilee, where Jesus would meet them after he is arrested and tried by the Jerusalem rulers and crucified by the Roman governor, Pilate. In Mark's Gospel, Jesus is carrying out a renewal of Israel against the rulers that Rome has appointed over Israel. Matthew presents the same picture, only more elaborately and explicitly, showing Jesus even more clearly in the role of the new Moses.

Many recent critical studies of the historical Jesus and literary analyses of Gospels still rely on the standard theological scheme, *Jesus vs. Judaism,* failing to recognize that the associated constructs do not fit the texts being interpreted. Clearly we will need to adopt a new perspective and a new approach if we want more appropriately to represent life in Judea and Galilee at the time of Jesus, and to account for the story of Jesus himself and for the particular ways the Gospels represent him and the popular response to him.

Written Texts, Yes: But What if People Could Not Read and Write?

Almost by definition, Gospel studies, like biblical studies generally, focus on the interpretation of written texts that have long been considered sacred. Since the Gospels are almost our only sources for Jesus, investigations of the historical Jesus, too, at least begin with the written texts.

For two or three decades now, however, at least some Gospel scholars have recognized two related aspects of ancient life that pose a challenge to conventional assumptions in biblical studies. First, literacy in antiquity was limited. Second, even when texts existed in writing, they were almost always performed orally before a group.[5] Some scholars have also been intrigued by the possibility that a text such as the Gospel of Mark might have been what specialists in oral literature would call an "oral derived text," that is, a text that would have been performed orally before it was preserved in writing. On the assumption that the Gospels, like other ancient texts, might have been performed orally to communities, it makes sense to explore how they might have functioned as oral performance.[6]

Since seeing the Gospels as orally performed, and even more as texts originally composed orally, posed a threat to some of the most fundamental assumptions and approaches in biblical studies, there has been strong resistance in the field to such exploration. Some scholars insisted that whether or not the Gospels were ever *recited* orally to groups, they were *composed* in writing, and therefore their texts would have been stable.[7] It seemed important to reaffirm that conclusion, since the whole enterprise of biblical interpretation had previously been premised on having a stable written text. Especially where the written texts in the Bible are regarded as "the word of God," the particular words of Scripture are of utmost importance. Established modern biblical studies has accordingly spent considerable energy in *establishing* the precise wording of the books of the Bible, conceived as the "best" or even the "original" text. The resulting text could then be translated into modern languages by carefully selected committees of scholarly experts, and their translations could become the versions officially recognized as authoritative by the mainline churches.[8] This whole enterprise of establishing, translating, and presenting the holy writ is premised upon assumptions that derive from modern print culture, where identical printed texts are mass-produced.

Very recently, however—although only a few scholars have noticed—the very text critics on whom the whole enterprise of biblical studies depended for the establishment of these stable texts have been shaking the foundations of that enterprise. They have pointed out that for many centuries prior to the invention of the printing press, the Gospels and other scriptural texts were cultivated in manuscript and memory. The religious elites—monks, bishops, and scholars—

had access to manuscripts (in which the text was by no means identical from copy to copy). But they had also memorized the texts, and recited and interpreted the texts from memory. Further, these text critics observe, in the process of copying texts, memory often trumped manuscript. The transmission and reproduction of the written texts of the Gospels were most unstable precisely at the earliest stages.[9] There are many more variations among second- and third-century manuscripts (which are often fragmentary) than in later manuscripts. In fact, there are sometimes greater variations among early manuscripts of the same Gospel than between manuscripts where different Synoptic Gospels contain parallel passages! These data strongly suggest that *various versions of each Gospel existed from as early as can be traced in their written transmission.* This further suggests that establishing an "original" text of Mark or Matthew may be a chimera of the modern scholarly print-cultural imagination.

Related, but independent research into the culture of antiquity has only compounded the threat from recent text-criticism. The general sense that literacy was limited has been confirmed by extensive studies that have documented that in Jewish Palestine, for example, literacy was limited to the cultural elite, who used it to wield power over ordinary people who could not read or write.[10] It has long been recognized that, with the possible exception of Luke, the Gospels are texts about, and deriving from among the common people, in "common" Greek. But it is not just the language that gives away their common origins. The composition of Mark, for example, appears to have relied on the popular tradition, in contrast to the elite tradition, of which only the scribes had accurate knowledge. At the outset of the Gospel of Mark (1:2-3), for example, some lines from Malachi (3:10) are identified as coming from Isaiah (40:3). Similarly, when Mark's Jesus throws a "proof-text" into the face of the Pharisees, he has confused a story from 2 Samuel (15:35) with one from 1 Samuel (21:1-6; Mark 2:23-28). Presumably elite scribes would have known which books particular prophecies, stories, and figures came from!

So, what if the expert text-critics cannot establish the "original," or even the "best" texts of the Gospels? And what if the people among whom the Gospels first functioned could not read and write? In oral story-telling the words change, but the main plot remains more or less the same. Is it the overall story of a Gospel, and not the particular wording, that was important for the original audiences? And if the Gospels existed in periodic performances before communities of people, and not as documents in an historical archive, then how should this change the way we understand the Gospels as sources for the investigation and reconstruction of history? To use an old cliché, we are entering a whole new ball-game. Clearly, in continuing to interpret the Gospels and to use them as sources for the historical Jesus, we need to understand the relationship between orality and literacy better. We need to appreciate how texts worked in oral performance.

Oral, Then Written Transmission: But What about Social Interaction and Memory?

In Gospel studies, as in biblical studies in general, we have been trained to think of "books" that were composed in writing by literate "authors," who used written sources and drew upon and "quoted" from other written texts. Scholars have usually admitted that *some* Jesus-materials were carried in an "oral tradition" (or "*the* oral tradition"!) prior to being included in written texts. But the Gospels, it has generally been assumed, were written by authors who quoted texts that they found written in books of the "Old Testament"/Jewish Scripture. When biblical scholars began to notice the extensive interrelationships among texts, it was understandable that, deeply rooted as these scholars were in print-culture, they conceived of these relationships in terms of what they called "*intertextuality*." That is, they spoke as if written texts interacted with one another, *text to text,* without passing through the mediation of society, or even through a teacher-to-student learning process. Here is yet another expression of a contemporary cultural elite projecting its own scholarly practices and assumptions onto ancient "authors" and (biblical) books. For example, a distinguished Gospel scholar could declare confidently that

> Mark's Gospel . . . was composed at a desk in a scholar's study lined with texts. . . . In Mark's study were chains of miracle stories, collections of pronouncement stories in various states of elaboration, some form of Q, memos on parables and proof texts, the scriptures, including the prophets, written materials from the Christ cult, and other literature representative of Hellenistic Judaism.[11]

But there was no print in antiquity! In Judea, as elsewhere, scrolls were extremely cumbersome, very expensive, and difficult to read without already knowing the text. They were generally impossible to consult—usually laid up in the Temple or kept in a scribal circle, such as the dissidents that withdrew to Qumran in the wilderness by the Dead Sea. In addition to the sorts of "errors" of "citation" in Mark noted above, we may also note that the episode of Jesus' entry into Jerusalem makes no more than an allusion to the prophecy in Zechariah 9:9; the line that we can read in Psalm 118:26 was apparently part of a Hallel psalm customarily sung at Passover time, evidently from memory (that is, no one had to "look it up"; Mark 11:1-10). Moreover, Matthew's Gospel, which makes the reference to Zechariah's prophecy explicit, does not appeal to its authority as "written," but as "*spoken* through the prophet" (Matt 21:4-5)—as is the case in most of the other supposed "formula quotations" in the Gospel.

These examples suggest that not only do the Gospels understand authoritative texts as *oral*: they make allusions or quotations *from memory*, not from written texts. Further, in the case of Jesus' "triumphal entry" in both Mark and Matthew, memory led to and informed *protest* (as it did in Josephus' accounts of pilgrims' volatile celebrations of Passover in Jerusalem). Is it possible that in a largely oral communications environment, Passover sacrifices and family meals carried foundational social memories more effectively than written texts did? In fact, New Testament scholars have long acknowledged in principle that in their origins, texts were in close interrelationship with community practices (the premise of form criticism). We have usually just assumed that the "last supper" episode in Mark reflects a regular celebration of the Lord's Supper.

In the critical investigation of the teachings of Jesus, more liberal interpreters focus on isolated sayings of Jesus as artifacts—little nuggets of wisdom or revelation. The aim is to work backwards, reconstructing how those nuggets may have been transmitted from one disciple to another until written down for preservation in a text, so that the original or earliest available form of the saying can be discerned and its meaning-in-itself determined. Jesus' individual sayings are thus understood—like the written texts we have assumed Mark used in writing his Gospel—to have by-passed any significant mediating effect from social interaction and communication, being simply "transmitted" from person to person. Admittedly, memory is involved, but this is memory understood at a very superficial level, not memory embedded in culture or in social interaction. More conservative historical Jesus scholars, on the other hand, have been inclined to use a similarly superficial concept of memory, but in an almost opposite way. They place great trust in the reliability of the Gospel accounts of Jesus' teaching and actions, even arguing (in the most extreme recent form of this approach) that the Gospels consist largely of eye-witness testimony from Jesus' followers.[12]

In older historical Jesus studies, the standard criterion for what can be determined as coming from Jesus himself, the criterion of "double dissimilarity," fits the same understanding of *memory as mere transmission*. Few scholars today would defend this criterion in its classic formulation, that is, that only those sayings can be from Jesus himself that are both dissimilar to standard Jewish sayings, on the one side, *and* to what must be attributed to early Christianity's faith in Jesus as the resurrected Lord, on the other. But this double criterion is very resilient, and continues to operate today (if less blatantly) when scholars seek to differentiate Jesus' "unconventional" sayings from "conventional" Jewish teachings. The effect is a Jesus who appears as a teacher of individual disciples, but who seems to float through Galilee without any genuine social interaction or cultural roots. In effect, Jesus, thus constructed as a wisdom teacher or revealer, *has no memory*. The connections with Israelite tradition evident, for example, in the Gospels' portrayals of Jesus' acting as the new Moses or Elijah, or speaking prophecies of God's judgment that resemble those of the Israelite prophets, are explained (and dismissed) as the later interpretation of early Christians.

But a figure construed as having no memory, no deep interaction with the culture in which he lived, taught, acted, and was ultimately executed, can hardly be taken seriously as a concrete human being. Moreover, the Gospels clearly involve memory not derived from written texts. In dealing with both the Gospels and with Jesus as a historical human being, we clearly need to understand what in other fields is called the *social* or *cultural memory* in which human communication and social interaction are inevitably rooted. To state the problem another way: if communication in ancient Galilean and Judean society was predominantly oral, then how did culture, including the transmission and composition of texts, work?

Religion, Economics, and Politics Were Inseparable; Political Protest Could Be Subtle

Not only do conventional Gospel studies and Jesus studies focus on the emergence of one religion (Christianity) from another (Judaism), they also define the Gospels as *religious texts* and Jesus as *a religious figure*. In this they accord with modern western intellectual culture in general. Think about the academic division of labor into separate disciplines (or departments in a college or university): the disciplines of political science and history deal with politics, which is defined as a separate realm from economics, which is studied in economics departments, and from religion, which is investigated in religion departments and separate theological schools. This is further reinforced in countries like the United States by what we call the "separation of church and state." Texts, movements, and institutions are divided into these separate realms for study. The conceptual apparatus that have become standard in these separate fields have been developed to deal with separate areas of life. But this academic arrangement reinforces the perception that these dimensions of life were separate in antiquity. And that, we know, is an anachronism.

The Jerusalem Temple, the high priests who headed it, the tithes and offerings they collected, the Pharisees, Jesus himself, his proclamation of "the kingdom of God," the Gospels, the disciples—all these are categorized as *religious*. The Roman emperor, the tribute to Caesar, and revolts against Roman rule, on the other hand, are categorized as *political*. In some scholarship, moreover, these categories are heavily valorized as good and acceptable or bad and unacceptable. In Gospel and Jesus studies, religious matters are basically good, while political matters are basically bad. (The only thing worse than being political is to be involved in a kind of politics motivated by a religious fanaticism.)[13] The result is that Jesus, or one or another Gospel, is defined as *religious* to the exclusion of the political. If an interpreter suggests that Jesus' teachings and actions had political implications, the response from other scholars is often to insist that Jesus must have been one or the other, and that it is unacceptable to Christian faith that he could have been political. The only radicalism that can be entertained is individualistic, merely cultural, and politically innocuous, such as the liberal construction of Jesus as an "itinerant charismatic" or a "hippie-like" Cynic philosopher.[14]

The problem is that Jesus' teachings and actions in the Gospels, like so much in his historical context, *are inseparably religious, political, and economic.* The Temple was the central political-economic as well as religious institution of Judean society, its High Priest (e.g., Caiaphas) was appointed by the Roman governor (e.g., Pontius Pilate), and the high priestly officers were responsible for collection of the tribute to Rome. The scribes and Pharisees were representatives of the temple-state. Tithes and offerings were taxes. Jesus declared that "the kingdom of God," the direct political-economic-religious rule of God, was coming for the poor and hungry—that is, for people suffering economic dearth. In the Lord's Prayer, Jesus taught the people to petition for bread and for cancellation of their debts, the most fundamental of economic matters for poverty-stricken peasants. When Jesus charged the scribes and Pharisees who "came down from Jerusalem" to Galilee with violating "the commandment of God" to honor father and mother by urging the people to devote the produce of their land to the Temple (Mark 7:1-13), he construed the commandment as pertaining to economics. The dedication of land or produce to the Temple that the Pharisees advocated was economic support elicited through religious motives. In a similar charge, Jesus condemned the scribes for "devouring widows' households" or livings (Mark 12:38-40). Again, Jesus' forcible demonstration against the Temple was clearly not a mere ritual "cleansing." The tribute that Caesar demanded was clearly a political-economic matter, but it was also just as clearly a religious-political issue: according to the first and second commandments, it was "unlawful" to submit to or to serve (with one's produce and labor) any god other than the God of Israel, who was alone Israel's King and Lord.[15]

Related to the inseparability of religion, politics, and economics in ancient Judea are the modes in which political and religious conflict was played out. Some of these modes seem more volatile and brazen, others more subtle and indirect than we are familiar with in modern western democracies. Think, for example, of the way Jesus marched up into the Temple complex in Jerusalem (Mark 11:1-19 par.). How, we might ask, would someone posing as an insurrectionary ruler, leading a large number of followers, storm into a complex of government buildings without immediately being taken into custody (by the military at the disposal of the Roman governor, and/or by the high priests who controlled Jerusalem especially tightly during festival time)? Surely, we might be tempted to conclude, there was nothing "political" about Jesus' action. But the analogy is false. Rulers of pre-industrial cities often let protests and riots run their course, knowing that brutal repression might well evoke an escalation of the protest.

On the other hand, although his demonstration in the Temple involved some exertion of force, in his confrontation with the rulers in Jerusalem Jesus generally does not do or say anything directly against them. He does not declare directly to their faces, "God has condemned you." Rather, he tells the parable of the tenants who kill the son of their landlord. This parable in effect holds up the mirror to the rulers in Jerusalem. Since they are probably absentee landlords themselves, they can easily recognize themselves as analogous to the tenants in Jesus' parable, and God as analogous to the landlord who will take action against them (Mark 12:1-12 & par). Again: in response to the question about paying the tribute to Caesar—a question that Jesus realizes is an attempt to entrap him, since the direct answer, "no, don't pay it," would have been incitement to insurrection—he offers an indirect answer instead. But everyone listening to his clever response would have known that, according to Israel's Covenant with God, "the things that are Caesar's" are precisely nothing, since "the things that are God's" are everything (Mark 12:13-17 and par). Here are political (religious) confrontations in a form more subtle and indirect than we are accustomed to recognize. There were apparently more possibilities in Jesus' context than are allowed by our standard dichotomy, *either* a political revolutionary *or* a politically innocuous teacher of religious truths.[16]

Since there was no separation of the religious and the political-economic in antiquity, we need a new approach. We need to appreciate how power relations work when our modern western separation of political and religious categories does not fit, and indeed may obscure the dynamics of religio-political conflict. Since political opposition could take a range of forms, moreover, we require an approach that can discern the subtler forms. And, since economic matters seem so central to Jesus' teaching, we need an approach that discerns how economic concerns meshed with religio-political concerns in the Gospels.

New Directions

The chapters below, organized into four parts, explore these interrelated issues. Insofar as these essays are elementary and provisional, they are as much as anything *invitations* to join in exploration of new approaches to questions and challenges that better-established approaches did not anticipate. The longer-range project for interpretation will be to bring these explorations together in a richer appreciation of the Gospels and of the role(s) and significance of Jesus.

The extent to which these chapters inevitably overlap indicates the ways in which the new approaches discussed intersect. I place the chapters on people's history first because, while they depend on and explore implications of the other approaches, they also provide a provisional reconstruction of the historical context of the texts and historical figures explored throughout the rest of the book. In subsequent chapters, the discussion of each approach leads directly to the next: appreciation of texts in oral performance requires an understanding of social memory, and the function of social memory, particularly among non-literate ordinary people, invites recognition of the popular "hidden transcript" in which subtle and not-so-subtle forms of resistance are rooted.

People's History

At first glance "people's history" seemed somewhat new to me. But colleagues in history departments pointed out that my own earlier work on popular movements among the Judean and Galilean peasants in late Second-Temple times paralleled explorations by others into people's history and popular culture in medieval and early modern Europe, and elsewhere.[17] People's history also turns out to be parallel to the "subaltern studies" on the part of Indian historians, and feminist investigations of women's history. Peasants and other ordinary people had been, like women, "hidden from history." This was largely because only the literate elite left literary sources, and their focus fell on the life and exploits of the wealthy and powerful.   Yet the elite did occasionally mention ordinary people–usually when the latter disrupted the dominant order. A parade example is the Judean historian Flavius Josephus. He is a very "hostile witness" as far as the common people are concerned, but we can "cross-examine" his accounts for good historical information. We also have some direct sources in the Gospels, which are unusual among world literatures insofar as they give us direct sources for ordinary people, evidently from the people's point of view.

From Josephus and other sources, we can derive a far more precise understanding of late Second-Temple Judean and Galilean society than the synthetic and monolithic construction of "Judaism" current in older, more established New Testament scholarship. This is true in two important and interrelated respects. First, instead of describing a long-standing, widespread, and monolithic movement under the heading "the Zealots" or "Jewish nationalism," we can now recognize that the Judean and Galilean populations produced *a variety* of protests and movements, some of them clearly resembling movements remembered in Israelite tradition (as we know it through the books of the Hebrew Bible). Second, we can now recognize that the primary division in the societies of the eastern Roman empire was not an imagined religious-cultural divide between "Judaism" and "Hellenism," but a political-economic divide between the wealthy and powerful rulers and the vast majority, the people who supplied the rulers with tribute, taxes, tithes, and rents.

It has been easy enough for Gospel and Jesus studies to assimilate the first point. Gradually, books on Jesus and introductory textbooks in New Testament[18] have relied less and less on an artificial construction of "the Zealots" as the foil against which an apolitical, non-resistant Jesus could be contrasted. Instead we find increasing recognition of distinctively Israelite "messianic" and "prophetic" movements and periodic protests and strikes throughout the Second-Temple period.[19] The second point has been more difficult to take in. Like western academics in other fields, many interpreters of the Gospels and Jesus seem reluctant to recognize and discuss the division between ordinary people and their wealthy and powerful rulers. It seems particularly difficult to grasp that this division was cultural-religious as well as political-economic. In explaining how the popular "messianic" and "prophetic" movements in Galilee, Samaria, and Judea were informed by the social and cultural memory of Israelite tradition, I have adapted the anthropological concept of the "little tradition," cultivated among ordinary people, parallel to the "great tradition" of the political-cultural elite.[20] This cultural-religious divide means that texts produced by elite circles cannot be used as direct sources for popular attitudes and beliefs.[21] Further exploration of social memory and of the relations between written texts and oral communication, however, may help us develop critical principles for using elite texts as *indirect* sources for popular attitudes.[22]

Other recent studies help us to fill in a more precise history of late Second-Temple times, including the regional differences between Galilee and Judea and the rapid "development" of Galilee during Jesus' lifetime carried out by Herod Antipas. Appointed by Rome to rule the territory, Antipas established two new cities there. By pulling together information from a variety of sources, including later rabbinic texts, archaeological digs, and scattered references to control and use of land, it has been possible to generate a far clearer picture of the Galilean context of Jesus' work in Galilee and the rise of the Jesus movements.[23] Attention to the fundamental forms of family and village in Galilean society lets us read Gospel representations of Jesus' mission and teaching with new eyes. We begin to see the societal basis for Jesus' activity in catalyzing a popular renewal of local communities, something that has been impossible on more individualistic assumptions about Jesus' relation with "followers." Fuller knowledge about the social-economic circumstances in mid-first-century Galilee—in particular, how the multi-generational family and the village community were threatened with disintegration—lets us understand better how Jesus' mission would have resonated with poor, hungry, and desperate people.

Oral Performance

As with people's history, so the exploration of the Gospels as oral performance combines research initiatives with theoretical reflection. The chapters below apply this combination to what are commonly regarded as the earliest written texts of the Jesus tradition. The Gospel of Mark is widely believed to have been the first narrative Gospel composed. Many scholars, although by no means all, believe that Matthew and Luke, besides following Mark, also used a collection of Jesus' teachings called "Q" (short for the German term *Quelle*). Whether or not these texts existed already in written form, they would presumably have been the earliest texts performed. Understanding them in oral performance also has implications for our understanding of Matthew and Luke, who drew upon both.

The starting point in these chapters is the recognition of the limits and functions of literacy in antiquity, and of how writing was embedded in oral communication.[24] We have now moved well beyond older dichotomies between oral and literate cultures, toward an understanding of the close relationship between orality and literacy, the different kinds of writing, and what was involved in producing oral and written texts. In Judea and Galilee, the line between literacy and non-literacy corresponded closely with the political-economic division between the rulers and their scribal retainers on the one hand, and the common people on the other.[25] Since I first wrote the chapters below, very recent research has explored how Judean and other ancient Near Eastern scribes learned and cultivated texts by oral recitation, in addition to making written copies of them.[26] That even literate scribes cultivated the texts of the official tradition *orally* suggests that orality was all the more dominant in communication and in the cultivation of the popular tradition among the people.

Literary criticism taught us to understand the Gospels as sustained narratives, and not mere collections of originally separate stories and sayings. It thus prepared the way for us to appreciate the Gospels as oral performance. But unless we imagine, anachronistically, that Mark and John are modern short stories (like the objects of much modern literary criticism), we must learn how oral communication works, particularly in the telling of longer narratives. For this I have found most helpful the theory of John Miles Foley, who brings together insights from a variety of fields related to oral performance, such as ethnography and sociolinguistics. Communication by performance involves several interrelated components: the text performed, the audience, and the context of the particular performance. The performed text then resonates with the hearers by referencing the cultural tradition shared by performer and audience. Examining the interrelationships of these components thus leads us right back into people's history as the broader context of performance, and requires that we investigate the particular social memory of a people with which the performed text resonates.

Comparative studies of oral performance dramatically change the focus of our appreciation of the Gospels as (performed) texts. While the wording of an epic song or story may vary according to the context and audience, the basic plot or principal events of the narrative will remain relatively constant from performance to performance. This suggests that in appreciating the Gospels as recited stories, it is not the meaning of individual words or sayings or "pericopes" (episodes) that matter, but the story as a whole. This also has important implications for the use of the Gospels as sources for the historical Jesus. The standard approach among critical liberal scholars has focused on isolating Jesus' sayings, reading them as particular artifacts supposedly containing meaning within themselves. But no one communicates in such isolated aphorisms! And Jesus *must* have communicated with people in order to have become a historically significant figure. He cannot have simply tossed out pithy aphorisms that were only later "transmitted" and still later collected. Approaching our texts as oral performances leads us to recognize that the Jesus traditions survived only as genuine social communication, and not as mere objects of "transmission" from one individual to another.

Exploring the Gospel narratives as performance also enables us to appreciate the patterns behind or underneath the fuller narrative. For example, stories of "acts of power," such as sea crossings, exorcisms, healings, and wilderness feedings, went together in "chains," which later came to provide the structure for a whole narrative sequence in Mark's Gospel (4:35—8:26). Jesus' teachings that are parallel in Matthew and Luke but are not in Mark and hence were supposedly part of "Q" consisted not of a mere collection of individual sayings, but of *speeches* on several different issues, speeches that contained their own inherent argumentative structures. In these ways and more, recognizing Gospel materials as oral communication leads us to a more fully relational approach both to the Gospels and to the historical Jesus. What matters in a performed text is not so much what it means on its own, as the work it does on and in the community of hearers.

Social Memory

The explorations of people's history and of oral performance lead directly to the need for a better understanding of social memory, which forms a direct link between history and performance. The theory of oral performance clarifies how performed texts resonated with their audience by drawing on their cultural tradition—their social memory. That cultural tradition is what the life of families and communities is rooted in.

As with orality and literacy, the pioneer in exploration of cultural memory as well has been Werner Kelber.[27] Over against the more superficial understanding of "transmission" posited by the fathers of form criticism, Kelber has recognized that Jesus' teachings continued to be cultivated because they resonated in concrete social contexts. Kelber shows how memory was instrumental in the composition of the plotted narrative of a Gospel. Now younger scholars as well, including Alan Kirk and Tom Thatcher, have introduced the leading theorists of social memory to biblical scholarship.[28]

It is impossible to summarize social memory theory succinctly because it is geared to particular historical situations, figures, and events, and is multi-disciplinary. Adapting social memory studies to Gospel and Jesus studies requires finding analogous instances in which shared memory has influenced, informed, or perhaps even been shaped by particular texts. Corresponding to the important differences between elite (and partly written) tradition and popular (and always oral) tradition mentioned above, social memory theory distinguishes between memory used to dominate people and memory that enables some people to resist domination.

I find social memory theory helpful in interpreting the Gospels at three different levels. First, focusing broadly, fuller awareness of Israelite social memory enables us to recognize that the main plot of Mark and Matthew is the renewal of the people Israel over against Israel's Roman and Roman-imposed rulers. Social memory studies can then offer new insights into how the composition of the Gospels drew on, adapted, and transformed Israelite popular tradition.

At an intermediate level, social memory studies help us recognize broader patterns in Israelite culture. Whereas scholarship on Jesus and the Gospels have previously been fairly narrowly focused on words, sayings, and "miracle stories," social memory studies can help us discern the same broader cultural patterns in the Jesus tradition and the Gospels as well. What are usually seen as separate individual sayings belong together in larger patterns of meaning, as in the covenant renewal speech in "Q" discussed in chapter 3 below. Attention to salient cultural patterns—what some social memory theorists call "frames"—might help us understand the resilience, in Israelite social memory at the time of Jesus, of the figures of Moses, prophetic leader of the exodus, or Joshua, the leader in the taking of the land, or the young David, the popularly "anointed" king who led the people against the Philistine invaders. These "frames" informed popular prophetic and messianic movements;[29] they appear also to supply the "frame" for Mark's portrayal of Jesus.[30] Might the interaction between Jesus and his first "followers" also have been informed by one or more of these "frames?"

Third, narrowing our focus, social memory theory also suggests ways we might rethink the "history of the Synoptic tradition." Once we recognize that the Synoptic tradition involved not mere transmission but genuine communication, the next step would surely be to determine what the minimum units of communication were. As noted above, no one communicates in isolated sayings. Social memory studies help to cure us of the illusion that there could ever have been an "original form" of an individual saying of Jesus. Even individual tales about Jesus' acts of power (often called "miracle stories") may be too small to constitute units of communication. It is easier to imagine that the speeches in Q, such as the covenant renewal speech in Q/Luke 6:20-49 or the mission discourse in Q/Luke 10:1-16, could have been free-standing units of communication. Considerations like these should enable us to realize that Jesus' communication with Galileans and others, and its development in what has been called the "Synoptic Gospel tradition," was far more complex, patterned, and embedded in Israelite social memory than can be approached through form criticism.

Hidden Transcripts, the Arts of Resistance, and Moral Economy

Investigations of the popular movements among the Judean and Galilean peasants at the time of Jesus in the 1970s suggested that our study of the Gospels and of Jesus himself would benefit immensely from comparative study of peasant life and social movements in agrarian societies. The research, groundbreaking reflection, and highly suggestive theorizing of political scientist James C. Scott may not completely fill the void, but it does provide numerous insights and evokes ideas for new analysis and interpretation of the Gospels and Jesus. Scott's analysis is based both on fieldwork in Southeast Asian villages and on numerous historical and anthropological studies of peasant societies across Europe and Asia. Scott's work helps us understand the relationship between the religious-cultural and the political-economic dimensions of pre-industrial life, appropriate to ancient Galilee and Judea. His work also helps us build on the other new approaches sketched above with greater subtlety.

Recognizing how biblical studies have often focused narrowly on the religious dimension, some scholars have sought to compensate by emphasizing the material dimension of poverty and exploitation of peoples. Scott shows how the religious-cultural dimension and the political-economic aspects of peasant life are inseparable. For example, the inability of peasants to provide a decent burial for a parent, or to feed guests at a child's wedding, compounded their embarrassment and indignity. In response, villagers in many societies develop ways of affirming their own dignity despite their circumstances. Their shared *indignation* eventually generates forms of resistance to those circumstances.

When earlier scholars gave attention to popular resistance and revolt, they often concluded that in general "all was quiet" among the people, except when they suddenly and unexpectedly erupted into violent rebellion. Scott's investigations showed that resistance is virtually endemic to the peasants' situation, though often in hidden forms. The indignities suffered by villagers tend to simmer in their communities, undetected by their superiors living in urban mansions. Scott points out that peasants' acquiescence under domination stems from their rulers' monopoly on coercive power. Peasants do not dare disobey their superiors, or refuse to "render to Caesar." They must act out the "public transcript" dictated by the rulers. But they may not accept the ideology of the powerful. In fact, when subject people are "offstage"—back in their own village communities, out of earshot of their superiors—they cultivate a "hidden transcript." In such sequestered sites, the people's "raw" anger can be transformed into a "cooked" indignation. One result, among first-century Galileans, was the proliferation of visions of a renewal of Israel under the direct rule of God.

Other scholars whose work I have adapted for the analysis of ancient Palestine at the time of Jesus, especially historian Eric Hobsbawm and political scientist John Kautsky, have argued that in traditional agrarian societies, peasants do not really participate in politics (which is monopolized by the aristocratic rulers). Scott, however, relying on his broad knowledge of peasant societies, discerns that subject people generate different forms of political discourse, ranging from insisting that their superiors live up to their own ideology to active resistance. The cultivation of a "well-cooked" hidden transcript provides the basis for acts of protest that are indirect, disguised, and/or anonymous, and for much riskier efforts to "speak truth to power." All of these can be detected in the way Mark and the other Gospels portray Jesus' mission, first in the village assemblies (*synagōgai*) in Galilee and then in his confrontation with the high priests in Jerusalem.

Scott's earlier work focused on the "moral economy of the peasant." This work is highly suggestive for understanding the economic aspects of Jesus' teaching in the Gospels. Scott teases out the fundamental values evident in many peasant societies, according to which (for example) families in traditional village communities will give priority, not to expanding the individual family's possessions, but to sharing their produce in order to keep *all* families economically viable. Villagers with enough to share cooperate in various mechanisms to aid other families in need. Scott's accounts of how the "moral economy" works among various peasantries immediately brings to mind the mechanisms mentioned in the Hebrew Bible to aid the impoverished, such as liberal lending, the prohibition of interest, and sabbatical cancellation of debts. Just these seem to be what Jesus seeks to renew in the "Lord's Prayer," the covenantal speech, and other speeches in Q.

Convergences

Even before the exploration of oral performance and social memory came to the fore, it had become evident to some of us that the standard critical approach to the historical Jesus—mainly through form criticism—was seriously problematic. Among other fatal flaws, it simply did not take the realities of human communication into account. After all, historians would not attempt to research and reconstruct the life of another significant historical figure, such as Abraham Lincoln or Martin Luther King Jr., by focusing primarily on his or her sayings deliberately isolated from their context in life! A figure becomes historically significant through interaction with other people, usually in a significant social or political role or office, and usually in responding to some circumstantially specific historical crisis. If we were to approach the historical Jesus the same way, our approach would therefore have to be fully relational and contextual. We would have to consider at least five interrelated historical aspects or factors: (1) In the particular historical conditions that had created a crisis for the Judean and Galilean peoples in the first century C.E., (2) working out of the Israelite cultural tradition in which those people, and he, were rooted, (3) Jesus emerged as a leader (4) by adapting a particular social role(s) inherent in Israelite tradition (5) in interaction with particular others who formed a movement (or movements) that became historically significant.[31] We cannot investigate Jesus in isolation, that is, without understanding and working through *the response to Jesus* represented in the movements that produced the Gospels (canonical and non-canonical) and are reflected in them. (To remind myself of this, in the chapters that follow I occasionally will write "Jesus-in-movement.")

It is now evident that the new approaches sketched above, which will be explored in the chapters that follow, will reinforce one or more aspects of the relational and contextual approach I have just described. People's history and an application of James C. Scott's work will contribute to (1) and (5). Attention to oral performance and to the Gospels-in-performance will help us understand (5). Social memory studies will help us understand (2) and (4).

The new approaches discussed here suggest that a similarly broad contextual and relational approach is necessary for the Gospels themselves. Once we are aware that oral communication was dominant, and that our "critical editions of the New Testament" do not give us the "best," much less the "original" text of the Gospels, we come closer to realizing that the Gospels were stories of Jesus' mission that emerged in various performance contexts. Gospel studies would not necessarily include the investigation of the historical Jesus—the division of subfields mentioned at the beginning of this introduction might well continue. But Gospel studies would necessarily include attention to the process by which the Gospels came to be composed and continued to develop in continuing oral performance, and that attention would necessarily entail serious consideration of the social context(s) around Jesus and the Jesus movement(s).

On the other hand, investigation of the historical Jesus necessarily includes study of the Gospels. In fact, historians of Jesus would have to understand the Gospels in ways different from Gospel studies based on the assumptions of print-culture. We would have to understand how performed texts can be used as historical sources. And that would require an understanding of how oral performance, social memory, and the "hidden transcript" of subordinate groups interrelate.

Using This Book in the Classroom

A number of colleagues in other colleges, graduate schools, and seminaries have mentioned that they have used one or more of the following chapters in their courses. This makes sense. These chapters are almost all elementary explorations of one or another important new approach to Jesus and the Gospels.

The Parts are arranged in more or less "logical" or "pedagogical" order. The chapters on people's history in Part I are introductory: they provide general orientation to the first-century context of the Jesus movement(s). These chapters presuppose and, to a degree, summarize the other new approaches that follow. Both chapters on oral performance in Part II provide information and orientation to the predominantly oral communication situation in antiquity, and discuss where writing fit into that situation. The theory of oral performance presented in those chapters leads explicitly and directly into the consideration of social memory in Part III. Finally, the chapters in Part IV, drawing on the work of James C. Scott, lead to further complication and, hopefully, sophistication in understanding both texts and contexts.

All of the chapters could be used in courses specifically focused on the historical Jesus or on Mark and Q, supposedly the earliest sources for Jesus. But several chapters would also be highly relevant to courses discussing the background and composition of Matthew and Luke. The chapters in Part I, on people's history, and two chapters in Part II, on oral performance, address Mark and Q. Of the chapters on social memory, Part III, chapter 5 covers the Synoptic Gospel tradition generally, chapter 6 is pertinent especially to the Q speeches, and chapter 7 focuses specifically on Mark. In Part IV, chapter 8 pertains to Jesus and the Gospels generally, chapter 9 focuses on Mark, and chapter 10 on Q.

The approaches discussed here have to date been applied primarily in exploration of the historical Jesus and the Gospels. In very recent years, however, elementary steps have been taken to extend these approaches to the letters of Paul and the assemblies (ekklēsiai) in which he worked. They also seem highly applicable to Johannine literature and its particular social history and traditions, the apocalyptic vision of John on Patmos and the communities he addresses, and so on. For that reason these chapters may serve well in other New Testament courses where instructor might invite students to explore one or more of these new approaches. Finally, insofar as Christian theology engages the historical Jesus, the chapters below, which locate Jesus squarely in a social-political context very different from that of the industrialized, urbanized West, may bring a suggestive stimulus to courses on theology and Christology.

Part I: People's History

Chapter
One

"People's History" and Gospel Studies

Until recently, a people's history of Christianity—particularly in the New Testament period—would have been considered a contradiction in terms, according to the canons of standard history. There are two reasons for this, the first having to do with the "people," and the second with "Christianity." First, history has been focused almost entirely on the ruling elites who were involved in significant events, particularly "kings and wars," the statesmen and generals who "made history." Since those who wrote history were intellectuals employed by the dominant classes, moreover, historical accounts were written in the interests of and from the perspective of the elites. The meaning of history, furthermore, turned out to be the meaning for the elites. Ordinary people simply were not a subject worthy of historical investigation, according to established historians.

Since at least the French Revolution, however, ordinary people have adamantly insisted on their own interests and rights. In fact, they were so brazen as to make history themselves in ways that could not be suppressed. In recent decades, colonized peoples, Latin American *campesinos* and Southeast Asian peasants, African Americans, and women's groups around the world have taken significant historical action that elites could no longer effectively suppress, much less ignore. In response, a younger generation of professional historians finally gave ever-widening attention to the history of ordinary people.

The second reason that a people's history of Christianity would have been considered an oxymoron is rooted in the Enlightenment origins of what is usually understood as history. The Enlightenment thinkers who determined the subject matter, methods, and criteria for what constitutes history were struggling to get out from under the authoritarian dogma of established Christianity. Accordingly, they defined religion in restrictive ways, as something irrational (to be suppressed) or as a matter of individual belief (to be tolerated). As an irrational or essentially private matter, religion was excluded from history proper. History came to mean primarily the story of politics, national and international. The exclusion of religion from history was reinforced by the separation of church and state in many Western societies.

The result has been the development of smaller fields of history such as the history of Christianity and, for the period of the origins of Christianity, the overlapping field of New Testament studies. The modern developers of these interrelated fields, moreover, accepted both the standard focus of history on the elite and the separation of religion from history proper as focused on political affairs. This meant that the history of Christianity concentrated on the bishops, theologians, and church councils (which corresponded to "kings and wars"). And it meant that the field of New Testament studies focused on the origin of what was defined as a religion, as if it could be separated from the broader concrete historical context. As both a goal and a result of interpretation of New Testament and related texts, New Testament studies focused on the origins of the Christian sacraments (baptism and the Lord's Supper), creeds, Christology, and church order. The only people who mattered were the apostles, such as Peter and Paul, and the evangelists, such as Matthew and John, and primarily for their faith and theology. The principal distinction made among people was between the Jews, among whom the new religion had its background, and the Gentiles, among whom the religion flourished and expanded.

For the New Testament period, in particular, there is considerable irony that a people's history of Christianity would have been considered a contradiction in terms. For in the period of their origins, the communities and movements that were later called Christianity consisted of *nothing but* people's history. We must therefore rethink many of the basic assumptions, approaches, and conceptual apparatus that previously were standard fare in the fields of New Testament and Christian origins.

First, we must recognize that Christianity did not yet exist in the New Testament period as an identifiable religion. Similar to the period of colonization of the Atlantic seaboard that preceded the origins of the United States, the New Testament period was a time of origins of parallel movements and communities, some of which later became identified as Christian. Most books in the New Testament have no reference to Christians, let alone to Christianity. The people who produced and used the Gospels according to Mark, Matthew, and John, for example, understood themselves as renewal movements or an extensions of the people of Israel. Somewhat similarly, Paul seems to think even of the non-Israelite assemblies he helped to organize as an extension of Israel's blessings to other peoples, in fulfillment of the promises to Abraham. Certainly there is no Christianity over against Judaism in most books of the New Testament.

This means that the people involved in these communities and movements were not yet defined as non-elite members of something called Christianity. They were not the ordinary laity as distinct from the bishops, popes, theologians, and church councils. Rather, they were very small groups among the diverse peoples in the provinces and cities of the Roman Empire, such as Galilee or Judea, Antioch or Corinth. They were to be located in the lowest classes, subject to the wealthy and powerful imperial elite and their aristocracies.

Once we recognize that the communities and movements associated with New Testament literature had not (yet) developed into what was later identified as Christianity, it should be easier not to restrict them to the category of religion. Religion as separate from politics and economics is a peculiar modern Western concept and phenomenon. In the ancient Roman Empire, as in most other times and places, religion was inseparable from political-economic life. The diverse communities and movements represented in the New Testament almost certainly understood themselves as more than what modern Westerners would think of as religious. Insofar as these communities and movements emerged among peoples subject to the Roman Empire, whose rulers were intensely suspicious and repressive of any disturbance of the imperial order, they often developed in conflict with the Roman imperial elite and its culture. In fact, it could be that a principal reason that they developed into what we now call religion is that the Roman imperial order blocked them from continuing as anything more than religion, in some cases as an alternative society.

Insofar as the people involved in the communities and movements of the New Testament period were acting without the leadership of any Christian elite and were almost always acting in conflict with the elites who controlled the Roman imperial order, they were making history. The people who formed these communities took various initiatives that eventually resulted in the wider, more diverse movements that would become an important historical force in the late Empire.[1]

In writing the history of the Roman Empire, historians have almost always focused on the triumphs of the Roman warlords and emperors. The aristocratic ancient Judean historian Josephus focuses on the relations of the Roman imperial elite and the Herodian and high priestly rulers of Judea and Galilee. Yet one cannot read very far into his accounts without realizing that it was the popular movements, and particularly the popular protests and revolts by the Judean and Galilean peasantry, that drove events in Palestine during the time of Jesus. The rulers were repeatedly in a reactive posture, trying to respond to initiatives taken by the Judean and Galilean people. These communities and movements therefore cannot be consigned to a marginalized history of religion in the ancient world, but must be understood as those who made history in a more general sense, including the conflicts of power and politics.

A people's history of the New Testament period, therefore, presents a challenge to the usual understanding of history, particularly as practiced by modern

Western historians. Western historians of India, for example, virtually ignored the significance of peasant movements in the anticolonial struggle because they were defined as religious. In premodern and non-Western societies, however, not only is religion inseparable from political-economic life, but adherence to traditional religion and culture can inspire historical movements. It is thus important, in response to the modern Western separation of religion from politics, to explain how religious phenomena are factors in historical movements, and hence in the making of history. Established New Testament scholars, apparently embarrassed by demon possession and exorcism and people swept up in ecstatic spiritual behavior, have given such phenomena little attention, even downplayed them. Yet Spirit-possession, prophecy, healings, and similar spiritual experiences may be precisely what catalyzed community solidarity and the motivation for the formation of alternative communities and resistance to the dominant order.

The task before us is to explore the ways in which ordinary people whose lives were determined by the Roman imperial order formed communities and movements, movements that expanded into a significant historical factor later in antiquity. Of particular interest are a number of interrelated factors in what were complex and varied historical developments, depending on local conditions and cultures: the interrelationship of problematic circumstances, discontented people, distinctive leaders, messages, and organizations that resulted in movements and communities with the solidarity and staying power to survive and expand. Our aim will be both to discover and reconstruct significant historical communities and movements and to explain them.[2] While this will often involve investigations into local conditions and cultures, it requires attention to events in the wider imperial world, since nearly all of the areas into which these movements spread were directly or indirectly subject to Rome. And since ordinary people are almost invariably subject to various layers of the wealthy and powerful, the key to understanding may often be particular relations of power.

Soundings in people's history could thus be compared with standard studies in history in several basic respects:[3]

	People's History	Standard History
Focus:	Ordinary people	Elites: "kings and war"
Scope:	All aspects of life	Mainly political events at the top
View:	From below	From above
Sources:	Archaeology, texts, comparative studies	Written texts, archives
Approach:	Interdisciplinary	The discipline of history

Investigating people's history raises new questions about New Testament and other already familiar materials, and involves looking again at less familiar sources, questioning old assumptions, and working critically toward new conceptual tools more appropriate to how ordinary people made history. The initiative to explore these materials in terms of people's history just happens to come at a time when recent research is forcing us to rethink assumptions about and approaches to people of the ancient Mediterranean world. Even more, our investigations of people's history will lead us beyond the standard assumptions, approaches, and agenda of traditional New Testament studies in several basic respects:

	People's History	New Testament Studies
Focus:	Reconstruction of people's history	Interpretation of texts
Scope:	All aspects of life	Mainly religion and meaning
Basic division:	Rulers versus ruled	Judaism versus Hellenism
Issues:	People's circumstances and actions	Christian theological questions
Media:	Oral communication in communities	Writings by authors
Culture:	Popular tradition versus elite culture	Stable Scripture
Agenda:	People in their own circumstances	Bridging the distance from text to today

At the risk of oversimplifying historical complexities, we can sketch some basic factors and issues involved.

Events That Set the Conditions

Certain major events and developments in the wider history of the ancient Mediterranean world helped set up the conditions in which a small number of ordinary people formed movements focused on Jesus of Nazareth.

The movements that gathered around Jesus as their martyred prophet (or messiah) originated among the peasants of Galilee and spread quickly among Judeans and Samaritans. These were all descendants of the ancient Israelites. In their Passover meal they celebrated the ancestors' escape from foreign rulers in the exodus from hard labor under the Egyptian Pharaoh, led by the great prophet Moses. They also cultivated the memory of resistance that the prophet Elijah had offered to the oppressive rule of King Ahab.

Just before Jesus was born, Galilean, Samaritan, and Judean peasants lived under the rule of the military strongman Herod, who had been installed by the Roman Senate as king of the Judeans (40–4 B.C.E.). Herod, in turn, kept intact the Jerusalem temple-state, headed by a priestly aristocracy. Herod's oppressive rule of the Judeans, Galileans, and Samaritans was a decisive stage in a long history of conflict between Israelite peoples and their rulers, one that set the stage for the Jesus-movements.

The Jerusalem temple-state had been set up by the Persian Empire in the sixth century B.C.E. It served several purposes simultaneously: it institutionalized an indigenous people's service of their own God, it established a ruling priestly aristocracy that owed their position to the imperial regime, and it set up a Temple administration to secure revenues for the imperial court as well as itself. The Hellenistic empires established by the successors of Alexander the Great in the third century B.C.E. imposed the Greek language and Greek political forms on much of the ancient Near East. But they left the high priesthood in control of the Temple in Jerusalem, where Judean villagers continued to deliver their tithes and offerings.

An attempt by ambitious figures in the priestly aristocracy to transform Jerusalem into a Hellenistic city-state, more integrated into the dominant imperial cultural order, evoked resistance by scribal teachers, including those who produced the visions of future restoration of the people's independence in the book of Daniel. The imperial regime's military enforcement of the changes in the people's traditional way of life touched off a popular insurgency led by Judas "the Maccabee" ("Hammer"), from an ordinary priestly family, the Hasmoneans. After several years of guerrilla warfare, the Judean peasants and ordinary priests managed to fight the imperial armies and their war elephants to a standoff.

In the ensuing vacuum of imperial power, successive Hasmonean brothers negotiated with rival imperial rulers to take over the high priesthood in Jerusalem. Depending increasingly on mercenary troops, the Hasmonean regime in Jerusalem proceeded to expand its power over other traditional Israelite territories. After conquering Samaria and destroying the Samaritan Temple on Mount Gerizim, they finally took over Galilee as well in 104 B.C.E. and required the inhabitants to live "according to the laws of the Judeans." About a hundred years before the generation of Jesus, Galileans were thus brought together with other Israelite people under the Temple and high priesthood. But in contrast to their Israelite cousins in Judea, they would not have been accustomed to rule and taxation by the Jerusalem temple-state.

The Roman takeover of Palestine in 63 B.C.E., and their imposition of Herod as king in 40 B.C.E., meant that the Galilean, Samaritan, and Judean peasants were suddenly subject to three layers of rulers and their respective demands for revenues: tribute to Rome, taxes to Herod, and tithes and offerings to the Temple and priesthood. With military fortresses and highly repressive measures,

Herod maintained tight control of the people. At his death, however, revolts erupted in every major district of his realm, most of them led by popular leaders whom their followers acclaimed as king, or in Israelite parlance, "messiah."

The Romans reconquered Galilee and Judea with typically vengeful destruction of villages, slaughter and enslavement of the inhabitants, and crucifixion of hundreds of combatants to further terrorize the populace. They installed Herod's Rome-educated son Antipas as ruler of Galilee. After ten years of ineffective rule by Archelaus, Judea and Samaria were placed under a Roman governor, who governed through the priestly aristocracy. Galileans now for the first time in their history had their ruler living in Galilee itself. In fact Herod Antipas not only rebuilt the town of Sepphoris as his fortress-capital but within twenty years built yet another capital city on the shores of the Sea of Galilee, named Tiberias, after the new emperor in Rome. One can imagine that collection of the taxes necessary to fund these massive building projects was suddenly far more efficient in Galilee than under distant rulers. It may be significant to note that after only a hundred years under Jerusalem jurisdiction, Galileans were no longer under Jerusalem control during the lifetime of Jesus and figures like Peter or Mary Magdalene.

Both Galilee and Judea experienced increasing political-economic turmoil from around the time of Jesus' mission until widespread revolt erupted in the summer of 66 C.E. (as we know from the accounts of the Judean historian Josephus, who witnessed many of the events first hand). The epidemic and escalating social banditry may be a good barometer of the steady disintegration of village life under the accumulating economic pressures. A series of popular prophetic movements that anticipated replays of the exodus led by Moses and the battle of Jericho led by Joshua arose in the Samaritan and Judean countryside during the 30s to the 50s. The increasingly predatory high priestly families who were building ever more luxurious mansions for themselves in Jerusalem gradually lost authority among the people and, eventually, had virtually no social control over Judean society. Eventually, some of the very Pharisees and other scribal intellectuals who served the temple-state as retainers organized a terrorist group of "dagger-men" (*sicarii*) to assassinate high priestly figures who collaborated too closely in imperial rule. Repressive measures taken by the Roman governors seemed only to exacerbate the popular protests and resistance. This is precisely the historical context in which movements focused on Jesus were spreading from Galilee to Samaria, Judea, and beyond to the villages and towns of Syria, such as Damascus.

Polarization and Power

It is difficult for Americans and Europeans who live in societies of mainly middle-class people to appreciate the dramatic divide that separated the dominant elite and the ordinary people in most ancient and medieval societies.[4] The Roman Empire, under which what became Christianity developed in diverse communities, was dominated by a numerically tiny but extremely wealthy elite who owned or controlled most of the land as well as large numbers of slaves. The imperial, provincial, and city elites monopolized the civil-religious offices such as the civic and imperial priesthoods. The vast majority of people (roughly 90 percent) were peasants living at subsistence levels in villages and towns. In some areas of the Empire peasants may have retained control over their ancestral land and village communities. But many had sunk to the status of sharecroppers or landless laborers, vulnerable to wealthy absentee landlords. A much smaller percentage of ordinary people eked out a subsistence living in the cities as artisans and laborers. In certain areas of the Roman Empire, the estates of the wealthy were worked by gangs of slaves taken in various conquests of subject peoples. The large urban households and country villas of the elite were staffed by more domestic slaves, the more educated of whom served as tutors, readers, and managers. There were a very few people in between who served as agents or clients of the ruling aristocracies. But there was no middle class in either an economic or a political sense under the Roman Empire.

Given the political-economic polarization, it is not surprising that there were deep social divisions and significant cultural differences between the elite and powerful and the subordinate. Peasants were often of different ethnic and cultural heritage from their urban landlords and rulers. Villagers had little contact with the wealthy and powerful families in the cities, except for the agents sent to collect rents, taxes, and tribute. Especially where the peasantry continued on ancestral lands, villages were semi-independent communities, with their own local assemblies (called "synagogues" in the Gospels) and even distinctive local customs and rituals.

In Galilee, where the Jesus movements arose, there is little or no evidence of villagers' interaction with the new cities that Herod Antipas had built, presumably in Roman style—other than being taxed and perhaps laboring in the construction. The Judean historian Josephus, however, does emphasize the popular attacks on Sepphoris in 4 B.C.E. and the regularly threatened peasant attacks on the pro-Roman elites in both Sepphoris and Tiberias during the great revolt in 66–67 C.E. In Judea, villagers rendered up offerings as well as tithes to the Temple and priesthood, and supposedly participated in the pilgrimage festivals centered in the Temple. The Judean peasantry, however, far from simply acquiescing to these mediating rituals, mounted periodic movements of independence from or direct attack on Jerusalem rule. They found in the pilgrimage festivals occasions for protest against Roman as well as aristocratic domination. Josephus claims that the Pharisees had influence among the people (did he mean the Judean peasantry or only the Jerusalemites?). But he portrays them as agents and representatives of the Hasmonean, Herodian, and high priestly regimes. There is no evidence of the Pharisees or other scribal circles having made common cause with any peasant groups. When a "teacher" named Menahem and his scribal followers attempted to set themselves at the head of the revolt in the summer of 66, the Jerusalemites themselves attacked and killed him.

Popular Culture in Interaction with Elite Culture

People's movements are usually rooted in popular culture distinct from high culture. That should not be surprising since peasants are often of different ethnic background from their lords and often live in semi-autonomous village communities. While culture can be diverse among the elite, even in an imperial order where the dominant culture becomes somewhat cosmopolitan, popular culture is usually far more diverse in its local variations.

Anthropologists and social historians, drawing on comparative studies of agrarian societies, have moved well beyond the problematic old two-tier model of aristocratic culture and folk culture.[5] In most situations there is an interaction between a "little tradition," the "distinctive patterns of belief and behavior. . . valued by the peasantry," and the corresponding "great tradition" of the elite. The popular tradition can absorb influences from the dominant culture, which is often parallel and overlapping, and the "great tradition" can adopt or adapt cultural materials, such as stories of origin, from the people, from among whom the elite themselves may have risen to power. Yet the popular tradition can embody values and express interests sharply different from, even opposed to, the "great tradition." In certain circumstances the "little tradition" can thus become the matrix of "protest and profanation" by popular movements, even of peasant revolts.

The differences and relations between popular culture and dominant culture are particularly salient for investigations into the religious-cultural dimension of people's history. Very recent research on particular aspects of ancient Jewish, Greek, and Roman culture is seriously challenging standard assumptions and generalization in New Testament studies. As a result, we are in a position of having to make educated projections on what the implications may be as we wait for more detailed historical investigations of particular situations and issues.

One marker of the differences between elite and people's culture and religion in the Roman Empire was literacy.[6] It was basically confined to the urban elite and some of those who served them. Most men and some women of the aristocracy could read, although they often had slaves read to them and write letters and other documents for them. Decrees and honorific statements in honor of imperial figures or local magnates were inscribed on monuments in public places to impress the people. But literacy was not used in most social and economic interaction, certainly not among the ordinary people. Even village scribes in Egypt, who were local administrators for the central government, could barely inscribe their name on the shards given as receipts to peasants for taxes paid or on papyri lists sent to district offices.

Literacy was, if anything, more limited in Judea and Galilee than in the rest of the Roman Empire.[7] Writing was confined mainly to scribal circles and the Herodian and high priestly administrations. Oral communication dominated at all levels of the society, completely so in the villages. This makes the old depiction of the ancient Jews as generally literate and a "people of the book" highly dubious. So, too, it also calls into question the frequent assumption that early Christians were also literate and quickly also became a "people of the book." This means, for example, that Judean texts from around the time of Jesus do not provide evidence for what the Jews in general believed and practiced, but only for the literate circles that produced those texts.[8]

We are only beginning to realize that there was no standard and stable text of the Hebrew Bible (still often referred to inappropriately as the "Old Testament" by Christian interpreters). Close examination of the many manuscripts of the books of the Pentateuch (five books of Moses) found among the Dead Sea Scrolls discovered in 1947 indicates that different versions of these books still coexisted among the scribes and literate priests.[9] There was thus no standardized Scripture that operated as *the* authority even in the scribal circles and the priestly circles who controlled the Temple. It is highly unlikely therefore that the Hebrew Scriptures were known to Judean and Galilean peasants. Scrolls, which were extremely expensive and cumbersome, were more or less confined to scribal circles.[10]

The non-literate ordinary people could not have read them anyhow. Galilean and Judean villagers spoke a dialect of Aramaic, so they would hardly have understood Hebrew if it were read to them. The Gospel of Luke is projecting Greek urban practices onto the synagogue in Nazareth in the portrayal of Jesus as opening a scroll of Isaiah and reading from it. Peasants would have known of the existence of the scripture, since it was deposited in the Temple and supposedly read (recited) on ceremonial occasions. And fragmentary knowledge of one or another version of the scripture of the Jerusalem "great tradition" may well have been mediated to villagers through Pharisees and other scribal representatives of the temple-state. Such mediation would have been minimal for Galilean peasants, however, since they had been brought under Jerusalem rule only about a hundred years before Jesus' birth.[11]

While only minimally and indirectly acquainted with the still-developing scriptures of the Jerusalem priestly and scribal elite, however, Judean and Galilean peasants were well-grounded in Israelite tradition—or rather their own popular Israelite tradition. Given the different regional histories of Galilee, Samaria, and

Judea, there must have been local variations in the Israelite "little tradition." Yet many of the most basic aspects of that tradition, such as the foundational legend of the exodus and memories of prophets of renewal such as Elijah, would have been common to all regions. Josephus mentions many incidents that indicate that Galileans were adamantly committed to the basic principles of the Mosaic covenant as the fundamental guide to social-economic life.[12] Josephus' hostile accounts of popular prophetic and messianic movements enable us to see this Israelite popular tradition in action, as it were. The Gospels provide what is perhaps our best access to at least a Galilean version of Israelite popular tradition.

The Problem of Sources

As suggested by the lack of sources for popular culture, investigation of people's history with a view from below faces a serious problem with regard to sources. Investigators of the history of kings and wars, bishops and councils, can easily find written sources in books and archives. Ordinary people in previous eras, however, have seldom left written sources as evidence of their own stories, hopes, and actions. Writers of the literate elite in antiquity, moreover, rarely mention ordinary people, and most modern scholars who interpret ancient sources generally work from a culturally dominant perspective. The people "make the papers" only when they make trouble for their rulers, who then condemn their irrational and unjustifiable "riots" and "banditry." Complaints by writers from the elite thus provide at least some indirect evidence, but we must obviously discount the hostility of such accounts.

Some of the Judean literature produced by the scribal elite of an imperially subjected people took stands against the imperial order. Occasionally some of the various Judean scribal circles who served as retainers of the Herodian and high priestly aristocracy protested when their patrons collaborated too closely with their own imperial patrons. The apocalyptic and hymnic literature they produced (such as the book of Daniel and the *Psalms of Solomon*), however, does not necessarily represent the views and expectations of Judean and Galilean peasants.[13]

With regard to elite written sources, but perhaps particularly with regard to hostile witnesses such as the Judean historian Josephus or the Roman historian Tacitus, it is up to the critical investigator, in effect, to force the issue. Historians must critically pose appropriate questions in order to elicit evidence from such elite sources.[14] Read as a source for an essentialist Judaism subdivided into four sects, Josephus' histories yielded information about the Zealots, along with the Sadducees, Pharisees, and Essenes. Once we recognized the Zealots as a synthetic modern scholarly construct, Josephus suddenly became a source for a variety of popular protests and movements of resistance and renewal that took distinctively Israelite forms.[15] Various birth narratives were just further examples of a vague myth of the birth of a hero until historians asked sufficiently precise questions that led to different social locations of the various stories.[16]

Indeed, sufficient critical source-analysis has been done to provide some useful guidelines for critically cutting through the rhetoric and interests of elite sources, and additional principles will surely emerge. For example, since the authors of written texts, who were almost always male, tended to write women out of history, modern historians must take every clue to discern the presence and often the prominence of women, as feminist scholars have insisted. [17]

The people involved in Christian origins, however, particularly those reflected in the Gospels, are highly unusual, almost unique among ordinary people in antiquity, for having left texts that survive in writing. Insofar as the communities and movements that they represent or address had not yet developed a hierarchy that stood in power over against the membership, most New Testament and related texts, in contrast with Josephus' histories or Pliny's letters, provide more or less direct sources for these people's movements. In the case of the Gospels, the contents are stories and speeches that are not only about peasants but stem from a peasant movement and, in the cases of Mark and Q, even represent a popular viewpoint. As sources from and for popular movements among peoples subject to imperial and local rulers, the Gospel of Mark and Q, and even the Gospels of John and Matthew, appear all the more striking in comparison with literature from the Judean scribal elite, such as the *Psalms of Solomon* or 1 Maccabees. These gospel sources must be used critically, of course. They have distinctive viewpoints and interests. But they are some of those rare historical cases of literature that represents the view from below. We must be more suspicious about the Gospel of Luke. While it includes materials of popular provenance, Luke seems to be addressing later communities in a different cultural ethos from the one in which his gospel materials originate. It is in a mediating position with regard to earlier Jesus-movements.

In addition to literary sources, primarily Gospel texts, we have at least some evidence from very recent archaeology. Archaeologists are finally exploring sites of ordinary people's lives, and not just the monumental sites for which it is easier to obtain funding. An increasing supply of inscriptions from antiquity supply additional evidence. Extreme caution must be used, however, in extrapolating from inscriptions left by the (semi)literate to the views of ordinary people. Crude graffiti, for example, cannot be taken as evidence for literacy.

Leaders and Communities, People and Texts

The relationship between leaders and followers in the communities and movements of the New Testament period is closely related to the question of non-elite sources, since some of the sources were produced by some of those leaders. While leaders of popular movements occasionally come from higher social ranks, they usually emerge from among the people themselves.

Most of the leaders in the movements and communities focused on Jesus, such as the apostles and prophets, emerged from among the ordinary people. As fishermen, Peter and Andrew, James and John, and others of the Twelve were hardly businessmen, but more like sharecroppers who "farmed" the Sea of Galilee (had they lost their ancestral land in Galilean villages?). Diaspora Judeans from various cities of the Roman Empire were prominent in the early leadership. Prisca and Aquila, among those expelled from Rome in the 40s, were poor artisans (were they descendants of slaves or freed slaves?). Leaders such as Mary of Magdala and Phoebe of Cenchreae (Rom 16:1–2), neither of whom is identified by her husband or embedded in a patriarchal family, had apparently become independent women, perhaps by force of difficult circumstances.

Some of the leaders in the communities and movements were also associated with the Gospels. Those texts, moreover, not only constitute our principal or in some case our only sources for communities, but were key factors in their life and development as well. There will thus necessarily be a close relationship, for example, between the Gospel of Matthew and the communities in which it arose and was used. Our purpose is to explore primarily the history of the people involved, not the texts as texts (the principal goal of New Testament studies). It is necessary, therefore, to clarify critically the relation of community leaders and the texts they produced to the communities they addressed.

Agenda, Assumptions, Approaches

In distinction from the standard agenda of New Testament studies, exploration of the people's history of Jesus movements does not focus primarily on interpretation of the Gospels. Those texts provide our principal sources. But we focus rather on communities or movements in Galilee, Judea, and nearby areas, and on basic social forms and factors such as family, village communities, and poverty, and on modes of communication and leadership.

Correspondingly, the investigation will not depend heavily on the standard assumptions, approaches, and interpretive accounts of New Testament studies, which have been heavily determined by Christian theology. Rather, the exploration of new materials and new and different questions addressed to familiar texts will require us to work critically toward the new assumptions and approaches that seem appropriate to the focus on the people, their communities, social forms, and distinctive modes of communication. Insofar as religion is inseparable from the political-economic aspects of ancient life, religious motives and expressions can be understood only in the political-economic context in which they are embedded.

Aware that studies of popular culture in the Reformation and early modern Europe have been criticized for neglecting material conditions,[18] our analysis will include political-economic structures and power-relations. Our main interest here is in the dynamics of those power-relations, however, not in the structures for their own sake. Hence we will move beyond functionalist sociological models applied to biblical texts and history, models which may obscure the fundamental divide between the powerful elite and the mass of ordinary people in Galilee, Judea, and beyond.[19] The rise and expansion of new social movements may be related more to historical shifts and changes in fundamental structures and challenges to basic social forms than to the structures themselves.

Recent research has resulted in more precise information than previously available on local political and economic conditions in Galilee and surrounding areas in which Jesus-movements developed. This enables us to move well beyond older synthetic generalizations about "Judaism" to the distinctive political-economic patterns and cultural features of Galilee, Judea, and Syria.[20] Rarely will it be possible to construct much of a thick description because of the relative lack of evidence from antiquity. Yet with more precise localized information in a few cases it may be possible to investigate indigenous social forms and the particular cultural traditions of communal life in the context of the political-economic-religious pressures impinging on local subsistence communities.

Together with archaeological and historical information and analysis, we are after cultural information for particular areas and communities. To focus on one key example, it is helpful and significant to know that people in Galilee were poor. It is even more useful and significant to know that they are being further impoverished by increasing taxation or rents. To understand the origins and concerns of a new popular movement, however, it would be much more useful and significant to understand the particular cultural meaning and social implications of their impoverishment. To understand and explain the people's movements, stories, and prophecies we are exploring, the key questions might well be the cultural meaning of their desire for dignity and the political-economic-religious mechanisms by which dignity is denied them.[21] Information on that cultural meaning and those mechanisms might also be the clues to why a particular leader, message, or ritual could become an originating catalyst or a continuing cultivator of a movement or community.

The investigation in chapter 2 suggests ways in which the communities of Jesus movements resisted to dominant social-religious as well as political-economic order in Roman Palestine and Syria. Yet the people involved in these communities, as mostly subsistence peasants and artisans, were embedded in that dominant order in various connections. They could not help but adjust and accommodate in various ways. They were communities of resistance, but were still *in*, even if not *of*, the dominant order.

Since our purpose is to explore the development of communities and movements and the key social forms, factors, and modes of communication involved in most of them, we will not emphasize particular methods or models. Our approach will be eclectically multidisciplinary and self-consciously critical when adapting a given method for a particular purpose.

Chapter
Two

Jesus Movements and the Renewal of Israel

═══════════════════════════════

The Middle Eastern peasants who formed the first movements focused on Yeshua bar Yosef eked out a living farming and fishing in a remote region of the Roman Empire. At the outset, their movement was similar in form and circumstances to many others that arose among people of Israelite heritage. Their families and village communities were steadily disintegrating under the increasing pressures of offerings to the Jerusalem Temple, taxes to Herodian kings, and tribute to their Roman conquerors. Large numbers of Galilean, Samaritan, and Judean peasants eagerly responded to the pronouncements of peasant prophets that God was again about to liberate them from their oppressive rulers and restore cooperative community life under the traditional divine principles of justice. The other movements ended abruptly when the Roman governors sent out the military and slaughtered them. The movements that formed around Yeshua bar Yosef, however, survived the Roman crucifixion of their leader as a rebel "king." In fact, his martyrdom became a powerful impetus to the expansion and diversification of his movements.

To understand the earliest Jesus movements in genuinely historical terms requires some serious rethinking of standard assumptions and approaches in conventional New Testament studies. The latter developed as a foundation for Christian theology. Standard interpretation of the Gospels in particular focuses on Jesus as an individual figure or on the Christology of one of the Gospels. It is simply assumed that the Gospels and other scriptural books are religious, and that Jesus and the Gospels were pivotal in the origin of the new, universal, and truly spiritual religion, Christianity, from the old, parochial, and overly political religion, Judaism. In the ancient world in which the Gospels originated, however, religion was not separated from political-economic life. In fact, at the time of Jesus there was yet no such thing as a religion called Judaism, judging from our sources such as the Gospels, the Dead Sea Scrolls, or the contemporary

Judean historian Josephus. Similarly, something that could intelligibly be called Christianity had not developed until late antiquity, well after the time when the books that were later included in the New Testament and related literature were composed by leaders associated with the movements focused on Jesus.

It makes sense to begin from the broader historical conditions of life under the Roman Empire that constituted the historical context of Jesus' mission and to focus first on the many other Judean, Samaritan, and Galilean movements that illuminate the form of the earliest Jesus-movements.

Popular Resistance and Renewal under Roman Imperial Rule

The ancient world was divided fundamentally between rulers and ruled, in culture as well as in political-economic structure. A tiny percentage of wealthy and powerful families lived comfortably in the cities from the tithes, taxes, tribute, and interest that they extracted from the mast majority of people, who lived in villages and worked the land. We must thus first examine the historical dynamics of that fundamental societal division in order to understand the circumstances in which the early Jesus movements formed and expanded.

At the time of Jesus, the people of Israelite heritage who lived in the southeast corner of the Mediterranean world, Judea in the south, Galilee in the north, and Samaria in between, lived under the rule of Rome. A Roman army had conquered the area about sixty years before Jesus' birth. The Romans installed the military strong man Herod as their client king to control the area. He in turn kept in place the Temple and high priesthood. The temple-state and its high priestly aristocracy had been set up by the Persian imperial regime centuries earlier as an instrument of their rule in Judea, the district around the city of Jerusalem. Subsequent imperial regimes retained this political-economic-religious arrangement for the control of the area and collection of revenues. With the decline of Hellenistic imperial power, the Hasmonean high priests extended Jerusalem's rule over Idumea to the south and Samaria and Galilee to the north, little more than a century before the birth of Jesus. After the Roman conquest, however, the high priestly aristocracy at the head of the temple-state in Jerusalem was again dependent on the favor of the imperial regime. Dependent, in turn, on the favor of the high priesthood were the professional scribal groups (such as the Pharisees) that worked for the priestly aristocracy as administrators of the temple-state and custodians of the cultural traditions, traditional laws, and religious rituals in which its legitimacy was articulated.

The old construct of a monolithic Judaism glosses over the fundamental division and multiple conflicts that persisted for centuries in Judean and Galilean history. Conflicts between rival factions in the priestly aristocracy, in their competition for imperial favor, and the corresponding factions among scribal circles came to a head in the Maccabean Revolt of the 160s B.C.E. Further conflict developed as the Maccabean military strongmen consolidated their power as the new high priestly regime. The groups known as the Pharisees, Sadducees, and Essenes, now understood as closely related to the Qumran community that left the Dead Sea Scrolls, cannot be understood in early modern terms as sects of Judaism. They were rather rival scribal factions or parties who competed for influence on the high priestly regimes or, in the case of the Essenes, withdrew into the wilderness when they lost out.[1]

The history of Judea and Galilee in the two centuries preceding and the century immediately after Jesus' mission, however, was driven by the persistent conflict between the peasantry and their local and imperial rulers. In fact, according to our principal sources for these centuries—such as the books of the Maccabees, the *Jewish War* and the *Antiquities of the Jews* by the Judean historian Josephus, and later rabbinic literature—actions by Judean and Galilean peasants drove most of the major historical events. The period of history around the time of Jesus was framed by four major peasant revolts: the Maccabean revolt in the 160s B.C.E., the revolt at the death of Herod in 4 B.C.E., the great revolt against Roman rule from 66–70 C.E., and the Bar Kokhba revolt in 132–5 C.E. In the immediate period of Jesus' mission and the first generation of Jesus movements, furthermore, peasants and ordinary people in Jerusalem mounted numerous protests and formed a number of renewal and resistance movements, most of which the Romans suppressed with brutal military action. Almost all of these revolts, protests, and movements were directed both against the foreign imperial rule of the Romans and against the Herodian or high priestly rulers in Jerusalem.[2]

Such popular revolts are rare in most areas of the world and periods of history. In response to their perpetual subjection to the exploitative practices of the elite, peasants regularly engage in hidden forms of resistance, such as sequestering portions of their crops before the tax collectors arrive. Peasants generally do not mount serious revolts unless their backs are against the wall or they are utterly outraged at their treatment by their rulers. They do, however, organize vocal protests against their conditions and treatment.

We can see the remarkable level of organization and discipline that popular protests were capable of generating in the strike against the emperor Caligula mounted by Galilean peasants a few years after Jesus' mission there (*Ant.* 18.269-84). Gaius Caligula, incensed that diaspora Jews refused to render him divine honors, ordered his statue installed in the Jerusalem Temple by military force. As the military expedition prepared to march through Galilee, large numbers of peasants organized a strike, refusing to plant the crops. The Roman Legate of Syria as well as the Herodian officers in control of Galilee knew well that they faced the prospect of a "harvest of banditry" instead of the crops on which their expropriation of tribute depended. Gaius's timely death prevented an escalation of the conflict. Clearly Galilean and Judean people were capable of mounting serious widespread protests and other movements of resistance.

As the Galilean peasant strike illustrates, most of the widespread peasant revolts, urban protests, and popular renewal-resistance movements, were rooted in and inspired by Israelite tradition. The central social memories of the origin and formation of Israel as an independent people focused on their liberation from foreign rule of the Pharaoh in Egypt and on their Covenant on Sinai with its true, divine King (God), to the exclusion of oppressive human rulers ("no gods other than me," "no images"). Judeans' and Galileans' loyalty to these formative traditions shaped their very identity as a people and led them to oppose both foreign and Jerusalem rulers who conquered them and interfered with their community life directly under the covenantal rule of God.

Perhaps the most vivid example is the Passover celebration of the exodus from foreign oppression in Egypt. Jerusalem rulers had long since centralized this celebration in Jerusalem so that it would associate the formative memory and identity of Israel as a people with the Temple and its priesthood. Celebration of the exodus by pilgrims to Jerusalem, however, became a time of heightened awareness of their own subjection by the Romans and intense yearning to again be independent, in accordance with God's will and previous deliverance. In response to regular outbreaks of protest at festival time, the Roman governors made a habit of posting Roman soldiers on the porticoes of the Temple courtyard to intimidate the Passover crowds. But that merely exacerbated the intensity of popular feeling. At least under the governor Cumanus at mid-first century, the crowds burst into a massive riot, provoked by a lewd gesture by a Roman soldier—and were slaughtered by the troops (*J.W.* 2.223-26; *Ant.* 20.105-12).[3]

Most distinctive and widespread resistance and renewal efforts among the Galilean, Samaritan, and Judean people were the popular messianic movements and the popular prophetic movements. The many movements that took one or the other of these two distinctively Israelite forms are surely most important for understanding why the Galilean and Judean peoples, more than all the others subjected by the Romans, persisted in mounting repeated resistance against Roman rule. These movements are most important for understanding the social forms taken by the Jesus movements. Both the popular prophetic movements and the popular messianic movements were following distinctively Israelite scripts based on memories of God's original acts of deliverance led by the great prophets Moses and Joshua or by the young David as the people's "messiah." Memories of these founding events were still alive in village communities, ready to inform the people's collective action in circumstances of social crisis.[4]

When Herod finally died in 4 B.C.E., after a long and intensely oppressive rule over the people he had conquered with the aid of Roman troops, widespread revolts erupted in nearly every district of his realm (*J.W.* 2.56-75; *Ant.*

17.271-85). In Galilee, Perea across the Jordan River, and Judea itself, these revolts took the form of movements led by figures who were acclaimed king by their followers, according to the Judean historian Josephus. They attacked on the royal fortresses and storehouses, taking back the goods that had been seized and stored there, and they raided Roman baggage trains. In Galilee the movement led by Judas, son of the famous brigand-chief Hezekias, was suppressed within a few months, with great slaughter and destruction in the general area around Nazareth—shortly before Jesus came to live and grow up there. In Judea the movement led by the strapping shepherd Athronges and his brothers managed to maintain the people's independence in the Judean hill-country for three years. Roman troops were finally able to ferret it out, again with much slaughter and the crucifixion of thousands as a means of terrorizing the people into submission.

Again in the middle of the great revolt of 66–70 C.E., Judean peasants acclaimed Simon bar Giora as king (*J.W.* 2.652-53; 4.503-534, 574-78; 7.29-36, 153-55). The Romans having been temporarily driven out, he moved around the countryside in the area of Hebron, where the young David had gotten his start. He liberated slaves, and restored people's property and in general effected justice for the people. Having amassed a peasant army of thousands, he entered Jerusalem, joining other forces from other areas of the countryside that had taken refuge in the fortress-like city to resist the inevitable Roman re-conquest. After being captured in the Roman re-conquest of the city, Simon was taken in chains to Rome. There he was formally executed as the vanquished enemy general (the "king of the Judeans") by the emperor Vespasian and his son Titus in the lavish celebration of their glorious Triumph.

All of these movements appear to have been patterned after the messianic movement led centuries earlier by the young David. As the Philistines continued their attacks against the Israelite peasantry, the people "messiah-ed" David as their king (2 Sam 2:1-4; 5:1-4) to lead them against the oppressive foreign rulers and to reestablish justice among the people. In his accounts of the movements in 4 B.C.E. and 66–70 C.E., Josephus does not use the term *messiah* (anointed), probably because he was writing for a Greek-speaking audience. But if we translate back into the Hebrew-Aramaic culture of Judea and Galilee, these movements must be understood as messianic movements patterned after the liberating revolts led by David and other popularly "messiah-ed" kings in formative Israelite tradition.

That several such messianic movements emerged a generation before and a generation after the time of Jesus' mission is significant when we recognize that literature produced by the Judean scribal elite rarely mentions a messiah. This is in sharp contrast to previous Christian understanding, according to which the Jews were eagerly expecting *the* Messiah to lead them against foreign rule. But as scholars finally began to recognize around forty years ago, there was no such "job description" just waiting for Jesus to fulfill (in his own way). The Judean elite, of course, would not have been interested, since their positions of power and privilege depended on the Romans, who appointed oppressive kings such as Herod. Perhaps it was against just such an illegitimate king set in power by the Romans that the memory of the popularly "messiah-ed" David and other popular kings was revived among the Judean and Galilean peasantry, and came to life in numerous movements for the independence and renewal of Israel right around the time of Jesus.

After the revolt led by Judas son of Hezekias (4 B.C.E.), this Israelite cultural script of a popular messianic movement would certainly have been alive in the area around Nazareth, the very area in which Jesus supposedly grew up. And its brutal suppression by the Romans would have left a collective social trauma of villages pillaged and burned and family members slaughtered and enslaved by the Romans. Such historical events and cultural memories cannot have been without their effect on popular life in Nazareth and other Galilean and Judean villages.

In another distinctively Israelite form, a number of popular movements led by prophets in anticipation of new acts of deliverance by God appeared in mid-first century. According to the ever hostile Josephus,

> Impostors and demagogues, under the guise of divine inspiration, provoked revolutionary actions and impelled the masses to act like madmen. They led them out into the wilderness so that there God would show them signs of imminent liberation (*J.W.* 2.259). For they said that they would display unmistakable signs and wonders done according to God's plan. (*Ant.* 20.168)

The first of these movements led by prophets was among the Samaritans (ca. 36 C.E.). A prophet led a crowd up to Mount Gerizim, the most sacred mountain, promising that they would recover the holy vessels from the tabernacle of the formative exodus-wilderness experience of Israel, buried at the spot where Moses had put them. But the Roman governor, Pontius Pilate, dispatched cavalry as well as infantry, killed some, took many prisoner, and executed the leaders (*Ant.* 18.85-87).

Perhaps the most famous prophetic movement was led about a decade later (ca. 45 C.E.) by Theudas, who:

> persuaded most of the common people to take their possessions and follow him to the Jordan River. He said he was a prophet, and that at his command the river would be divided and allow them an easy crossing. . . . A cavalry unit killed many

in a surprise attack [and] having captured Theudas, cut off his head and carried it up to Jerusalem. (*Ant.* 20.97-98; also mentioned in Acts 5:36)

About another decade later (56 C.E.), just prior to Paul's visit to Jerusalem after his mission in Corinth, Ephesus, and Macedonia, a Jewish prophet from Egypt rallied many thousands in the countryside. He led them up to the Mount of Olives, opposite Jerusalem, declaring that the walls of the city would fall down and the Roman garrison would be overpowered, giving them entry into the city. The Roman governor Felix, with heavily armed cavalry and infantry, killed hundreds of them, before the prophet himself and the others escaped (*Ant.* 20.169-71; *J.W.* 2.261-63).

As with the messianic movements, these prophetic movements were peasant movements clearly patterned after formative events in Israelite tradition. In the general characterization by Josephus (who called them prophets who performed signs of liberation in the wilderness) and in the case of Theudas, who told his followers to take their goods along and expected the waters to be divided, these figures stepped into the role of a new Moses (or Joshua), leading a new exodus (or entry into the land, which had been more or less collapsed with the exodus in popular memory). The "Egyptian" (Jewish) prophet patterned his role and the anticipated divine act of deliverance after Joshua's leadership of Israel taking over their land from oppressive kings in their fortified cities, particularly the battle of Jericho. Judging from the terms used in Josephus' hostile accounts, these prophets and their followers were acting under inspiration.

The most noteworthy aspect of these movements to the ruling elite, of course, was the threat they posed to the imperial order. Josephus says that they were out to make "revolutionary changes." The Israelite traditions they were imitating, the exodus led by Moses and the entry into their own land led by Joshua, moreover, suggest that these movements anticipated a restoration of the people as well as a liberation from alien rule. Given our limited sources, of course, we have no indication of how they imagined the future of an Israel again living in independence of foreign domination. Although Josephus claims that the Samaritans were armed, his accounts of the others suggest that, unarmed, they were acting in anticipation of God's action to deliver them. The Roman governors, however, saw them as serious threats to the imperial order, and sent out the troops to crush them and kill their prophetic leaders.

In all of these protests and movements, the ordinary people of Galilee, Samaria, and Judea were taking bold action, often involving considerable organization and discipline, in making history. The people, facing acute economic distress and a disintegrating political order, took control of their own lives, under the leadership of popular kings (messiahs) like Judas ben Hezekias or popular prophets such as Theudas. These movements of social renewal and political resistance put the Roman and Jerusalem rulers on the defensive. The peasants were challenging the Roman imperial order! In response, the Roman governors, along with the Jerusalem high priesthood in some cases, took brutal, sometimes massive military action, often symbolically decapitating or ceremonially executing the prophetic or messianic leader.

Most striking is how, with the exception of epidemic banditry, these protests and movements took distinctively Israelite social forms. The protests were driven by outrage at the violation of traditional Mosaic covenantal principles. Both the messianic movements and the prophetic movements were decisively informed by (or patterned after) social memories deeply embedded in Israelite tradition. That there were so many of these movements that took one or another of two basic social forms strongly suggests that these distinctive cultural memories, these scripts for movements of renewal and resistance, were very much alive in the village communities of the peoples of Israelite heritage in Palestine around the time of Yeshua bar Yosef.

The Earliest Jesus Movements

It is in precisely this context of persistent conflict between the Judean and Galilean peasantry and their Jerusalem and Roman rulers that we must understand the origins and development of the earliest Jesus movements. Given how prominent the popular prophetic and messianic movements were in the immediate historical context, moreover, we might expect that the earliest movements that formed in response to Jesus' mission would exhibit some similar features and patterns.

Several closely interrelated factors in the traditional Christian theological scheme of Christian origins, however, have worked to isolate Jesus from his historical context, even to keep Jesus from having any direct relation to Jesus movements. First, since he was supposedly a unique person and revealer, Jesus is treated as separate from the social roles and political-economic relationships in which historical figures are usually engaged. Second, rather than being read as complete stories, the Gospels have been taken merely as containers in which to find individual sayings. Jesus' sayings are then understood as artifacts that have meaning in themselves, rather than as genuine communication with other people in historical social contexts. Third, Jesus is viewed as a revealer, separated from the formation of a movement in the context of the village communities in which people lived. It was not Jesus himself but the disciples who supposedly established a community—in Jerusalem after the outpouring of the Holy Spirit at Pentecost—from which they then founded churches in Judea and beyond.

The net effect of these interrelated factors of theologically determined New Testament interpretation is a combination of assumptions and procedures that would be unacceptable in the regular investigation of history. When historians investigate popular movements and their leaders (for example, the civil rights movement and leaders such as Martin Luther King) they consider multiple contextual and relational factors.[5] Since there are no leaders without followers and no movements without leadership, *leader-follower interaction* is central. Leader and movement would not emerge in the first place, moreover, unless there were a *problematic historical situation*. Yet we do not understand why the leader and followers who form a movement find their situation intolerable unless we know something of the previous *historical developments* that led to the problems. And we cannot understand why they found the situation intolerable unless we have a sense of their cultural values. Indeed, we cannot understand how and why the leader's message and program resonate with followers such that they form a movement unless without a sense of the *cultural traditions and values* that provide the media in which they communicate.

To investigate the earliest Jesus movements, including possible similarities with contemporary Galilean and Judean movements, we will follow just such a relational and contextual approach—simply bypassing the problematic assumptions, approaches, and concepts of previous New Testament interpretation. We will focus mainly on what are by consensus the earliest gospel sources, the Gospel of Mark and the sequence of Jesus' speeches that appear in closely parallel versions in Matthew and Luke but not in Mark, and known as Q (for *Quelle*, the German word for *source*).[6]

The Agenda

Both of the earliest gospel texts, Mark and Q, represent Jesus and followers as a prophet-led movement engaged in the renewal of Israel that condemns and is condemned by the Jerusalem (and Roman) rulers.[7]

The people who produced and used the sequence of Jesus' speeches that is called Q understand Jesus as—and themselves as the beneficiaries of—the figure whose activities fulfilled their yearnings for a prophet who would heal and bind up the people and preach good news to the poor (Q/Luke 7:18-35). They even see his exorcisms as manifestation of a new exodus, done "by the finger of God," a clear allusion to Moses' divinely empowered performances in the exodus (Q/Luke 11:14-20; see the Appendix below for Q speeches, which are ordinarily referenced according to their appearance in Luke). In the longest speech of Q (6:20-49), moreover, Jesus speaks as the new Moses enacting a renewal of the covenant as the guiding principles for a renewal of cooperation and solidarity in community relations. Jesus' speech sending envoys out into villages indicates that the movement of renewal of Israel is expanding by sending delegates to more and more village communities. In speeches that take the distinctively Israelite form of prophetic woes and oracles, Jesus pronounces divine condemnation of the Jerusalem rulers and their representatives. He pronounces a series of woes against the scribes and Pharisees and prophetic oracles of lament over the aristocracy who presume on their lineage, the Jerusalem ruling house (Q 11:39-52; 13:28-29, 34-35). The speeches heard by the Q people thus represent Jesus as the latest in the long line of Israelite prophets to be killed by the oppressive rulers.

The people who produced and used Mark's gospel had an even more vivid sense of Jesus, his disciples, and themselves as engaged in a renewal of Israel against, and under attack by, the Jerusalem and Roman rulers. Jesus called and commissioned the Twelve as the representative heads of the twelve tribes of Israel as well as disciples who extend his mission of renewing Israel in village communities. The hearers of Mark's story resonated with the clear allusions to the origins of Israel under Moses and the renewal of Israel led by Elijah in the sequences of sea-crossings, exorcisms, healings, and wilderness feedings in the middle of the gospel (Mark 3:35—8:29). That a renewal of Israel is underway is confirmed by the disciples' vision of Jesus with Moses and Elijah on the mountain. And in a series of dialogues (in Mark 10:2-45) Jesus presents Torah-like instruction to the communities of his followers, teaching that constitutes a renewed Mosaic covenant, indicated by the recitation of the covenantal commandments. After he marched up into Jerusalem with his entourage, he had condemned the Temple itself in a forcible demonstration reminiscent of Jeremiah's famous pronouncement that God would destroy the Temple because of the rulers oppressive practices (Mark 11; Jeremiah 7 and 26). Just before he was arrested, tried, and executed by the Romans, Jesus celebrated the Passover at the "last supper" as a meal that renewed the Mosaic covenant with the Twelve representatives of Israel, announcing that the cup was "my blood of the covenant," an allusion to the original covenant meal (Exodus 24).

Mark and Q are different in overall literary form, the one a complex story in a sequence of episodes, the other a series of speeches on different issues. They appear, moreover, to have been produced and used by different communities or movements. Yet they both represent Jesus as a Moses- and Elijah-like prophet engaged in the renewal of Israel in its village communities and pronouncing prophetic condemnations of the Jerusalem Temple, its high priestly rulers and Pharisaic representatives. That the two earliest gospel sources, so different from one another in form, share this portrayal of Jesus as leader of a movement suggests the same role and relationship with followers at the origin of the respective communities. Within the overall agenda shared by both texts, we will focus our investigation on a few key aspects of both movements: the sending of workers on a mission of building and expanding the movement, covenant renewal, and persecution by hostile authorities.

Before moving to those key aspects, however, we may note some distinctive features of Mark and Q respectively which seem to distinguish their communities from other movements of Jesus followers. Mark appears to be setting its movement's identity off against the Jerusalem community headed by Peter and others of the Twelve. The story portrays the disciples as increasingly misunderstanding Jesus' mission and, in the crisis in Jerusalem, betraying, denying, and abandoning him. Mark represents Jesus as, in a way, patterned after a messianic role in addition to his dominant prophetic role. Yet the narrative qualifies and criticizes the messianic role in decisive ways. Mark also downplays Jesus' resurrection so seriously that it is merely instrumental to calling the hearers of the story back up to Galilee to continue the movement that Jesus had gotten started. The Q speeches indicate no knowledge of a resurrection at all. Jesus' death is understood as the climax of the long line of prophets killed by the rulers. And Q's Jesus demonstrates virtually no messianic traits in his dominantly prophetic agenda.

In these ways and more, Mark's story and the Q speeches appear to address movements that originated in Galilee and spread into the bilingual villages of nearby areas (Aramaic and Greek). They are both different from other communities or movements of Jesus-loyalists, such as the Jerusalem community known from Acts and the assemblies that Paul addresses in his letters. Before exploring these earliest sources and Jesus movements, however, it makes sense to have a more precise sense of the historical conditions in which the Jesus movements developed.

Conditions in Galilee[8]

Galileans were people of Israelite heritage. They shared with their more southerly cousins in Judea and Samaria the formative traditions of Israel. Most basic were stories of the exodus led by the prophet Moses, celebrated annually in the Passover, and Israel's covenant with its divine king mediated through Moses on Sinai. Memories of northern Israelite prophets such as Elijah and Elisha would also presumably have been particularly prominent in Galilee.

Galilee, however, had recently come under Jerusalem rule, about a hundred years before Jesus' birth, after being under separate imperial jurisdiction for hundreds of years. During the lifetime of Jesus, Galilee was again placed under separate imperial jurisdiction, no longer under rule by the Jerusalem temple-state. Galileans thus may well have been ambivalent about Jerusalem rule. On the one hand they were again reunited with others of Israelite heritage, which could well have generated a revival of Israelite traditions. On the other hand, they may not have been overly eager to pay tithes and offerings to the Temple in addition the taxes demanded by king Herod and the tribute taken by Rome.

Moreover, in Galilee more than in Judea there would have been a discrepancy between the Judean-Israelite "great tradition" cultivated by scribal circles in Jerusalem, partly embodied in the scrolls of the Pentateuch, and the "little" or popular Israelite tradition cultivated in village communities.[9] When the

Jerusalem high priesthood took over Galilee, they imposed "the laws of the Judeans" (presumably including the Pentateuch) on the inhabitants. It is difficult to imagine that a century of Jerusalem rule provided sufficient time for Galilean peasants, who lived largely in semi-independent village communities, to assimilate much from the official "laws of the Judeans"—even if they were being pushed on the people by scribal and Pharisaic representatives of the temple-state. The only close contemporary evidence we have, Josephus' accounts of the great revolt in 66–67, indicate that collective actions by Galileans were motivated by their adherence to the basic principles of the Mosaic covenant, and give no evidence for their acquaintance with laws in the Pentateuch.[10]

The Galilean people eagerly asserted their independence of both Jerusalem and Roman rule at every opportunity. After the Romans imposed Herod as "king of the Judeans" in 40 B.C.E., Galileans repeatedly resisted his attempts to control their territory (*J.W.* 1.304-16, 326; *Ant.* 14.415-33, 450). When Herod died in 4 B.C.E., peasants in the area around Nazareth, having acclaimed Judas ben Hezekiah their king, attacked the royal fortress in Sepphoris (*J.W.* 2.56; *Ant.* 17.271). Seventy years later, at the beginning of the great revolt, the peasants quickly asserted their independence of their rulers. In western Galilee they periodically attacked the city of Sepphoris, which remained loyal to the Romans. In eastern Galilee, they repeatedly resisted attempts to bring them under control, whether by the Herodian officers in Tiberias or by Josephus, who had been delegated by the provisional high priestly regime in Jerusalem (Josephus recounts these events in his *Life*).

The Roman imposition of Herod Antipas following the revolt in 4 B.C.E. meant that for first time the ruler of Galilee was located in Galilee itself and not at a considerable distance. The location of the administration within view of nearly every village meant greater efficiency in tax collection. That efficiency and Antipas' need for extraordinary revenues to underwrite the huge expense of building two capital cities, Tiberias as well as Sepphoris, must have exacerbated the economic burden on the peasant producers. Both cities, built in Roman style by a king who had been educated in Rome, must have seemed like alien urban culture set down into the previously Israelite rural landscape remote from the dominant high culture.

With peasant families forced into escalating debt in order to pay taxes and still support themselves, village communities were threatened with disintegration. There is simply no solid evidence to support the romantic notion of the last generation that Jesus attracted primarily the marginalized, such as "sinners" and "prostitutes," or rootless individuals who had abandoned their lands and families. Evidence for economic conditions and land-tenure in Palestine at the time of Jesus suggests that peasants in the hill country of western Judea had indeed been losing their lands to wealthy Herodian landlords. By contrast, that Herodian officers in Galilee had their estates on the east side of the Jordan River suggests that villagers in Galilee were still on their ancestral lands.[11] Mark and Q themselves, moreover, represent Jesus as engaging the poor peasantry in general. The frequent attention to debts and their cancellation point to an audience still on the land but unable to make ends meet, given the demands for taxes and tribute. The people available for hire as day laborers in some of Jesus' parables were previously assumed to be landless laborers. But those looking for work in a society such as Galilee were more likely villagers who needed to supplement the dwindling subsistence living they were still eking out on their land or peasants working off debts. And as studies of peasant revolts have found, it is villagers in just such circumstances who tend to become involved in popular movements and revolts. On the other hand, those who have already lost their land become heavily dependent on wealthy elite families or their agents, hence are less free to join movements.

Mission

Our earliest gospel sources offer a number of indications that a movement developed and expanded in Galilee and areas beyond, catalyzed by and focused on Jesus. These indicators come into focus once we cut through previous assumptions regarding Judaism and Christianity that turn out to be historically unfounded.

In contrast to the portrayal of Paul in Acts as founding a new *ekklēsia* (assembly) as a counterpart to the Jewish *synagōgē* (assembly), in Galilean, Judean, or Syrian villages, it was not necessary to form new communities. As in most agrarian societies, the fundamental form of societal life in Galilee and Syria was the village community, comprised of a larger or smaller number of households. The latter were the basic productive and reproductive unit, while village communities had mechanisms for mutual cooperation and aid to help maintain each household as a viable multigenerational unit in the community.

Both the speeches in Q and Mark's story portray Jesus and his disciples as developing a movement based in village communities. In Q, the covenant renewal discourse (6:20-49), which addresses local social-economic relations, makes sense only in the context of local communities. The Lord's prayer, with its mutual cancellation of debts, and the discourse on anxiety (Q 11:2-4, 9-13; 12:22-31) also presupposes village communities. Mark's story, moreover, has Jesus repeatedly teaching and healing in villages or towns and places. Most significant, surely, is how Mark's story, almost in passing (as if it would be obvious) has Jesus and his envoys carrying out their teaching and healing in the village *assemblies*. The Greek term *synagōgē*, like the Hebrew and Aramaic *knesset* in rabbinic texts, meant *assembly*. In the Gospels and in most references in contemporary Judean texts, it refers to the local village assembly. According to later rabbinic texts, these village assemblies met twice a week (compare with the community fasts mentioned in the *Didache* [The Teaching of the Twelve

Apostles] 8:1—Wednesdays and Fridays, vs. Mondays and Thursdays). As the religious-political form of local cooperation and self-governance of the semi-independent village communities, the assemblies dealt with common concerns such as the water supply as well as held community prayers and discussions.[12]

Independently, Mark (6:6-13) and Q (10:2-16) both have Jesus deliver a speech that commissions workers to assist in the program of extending the movement (of renewing Israel) to other village communities.[13] That these discourses exhibit the same basic structure, with differing wording, suggests that such sending of envoys was a standard practice in the earliest phases of the Jesus movements. In both versions of the commissioning, the workers are sent out in pairs to other villages where they were to stay with, and accept subsistence support from, a household in the community. Given the small houses and crowded conditions known from archaeological excavations (several houses of two rooms roughly six feet by nine feet off central courtyards), they were not working with individual families, but wider village communities. Charged to expand Jesus' own mission of preaching and healing, these workers were apparently also, in effect, carrying out what might now be called "community organizing." The expectation, surely based on experience, was that a whole village might be receptive or hostile. In the former case it apparently became associated with the wider movement. In the latter, curses might be called down upon it for its rejection of the opportunity offered: "Woe to you Chorazin! Woe to you Bethsaida!"[14]

In this connection we should follow up the few clues Mark gives about how the most prominent leaders of the movement, Peter, James, and John may have come from a somewhat different personal and familial situation from the villagers among whom they built the movement. Their fishing enterprise involved the collaborative effort of several men.[15] Herod Antipas, needing to expand his revenues in order to fund his ambitious city-building, developed fishing into an industry. Working through brokers as intermediaries, the king supplied the equipment, especially the costly large (26-foot) boats that required a crew of five or six (the size of boat required in Jesus' sea-crossings in Mark). Collaborative crews evidently contracted to deliver a certain percentage or amount of their catch to the processing depots in return for keeping the rest (somewhat like sharecroppers). The principal processing center for the fish was the burgeoning boomtown of Magdala, "tower of fish" in Aramaic, where people cut loose from their ancestral lands and village communities found work. We might speculate also that the Mary known as "from Magdala," evidently an independent woman (not identified by her attachment to either father or husband), may have been such a destitute person cut loose from her family of origin.

Cross-cultural studies suggest that it is precisely such people with experience beyond a village and contact with outsiders who tend to become leaders in movements or renewal or resistance. Some of the principal leaders of the Jesus movements were apparently "downwardly mobile" people with direct experience of indebtedness to the very power-holders who were oppressing the people with heavy taxation and interest on loans prohibited by Israelite covenantal law. They would have had an unusually poignant sense of how the Israelite ideal of a life of cooperation and justice in semi-independent, self-sustaining communities was disintegrating. Such people would have responded eagerly to a message of God's imminent restoration of Israel. Having already been cut loose from the land, moreover, they would have been free to move about from village to village on speaking, healing, and organizing missions, in contrast to villagers who needed to remain in place in order to work the fields.

The earliest gospel sources both portray the Jesus movements as having developed initially in Galilee. Mark represents Jesus as having his base of operations in Capernaum and a village on the northern shore of the Sea of Galilee—an account which is generally accepted as historically credible. That also fits Peter and Andrew and James and John having been fishermen. In the mission speech in Q, Jesus utters curses on Capernaum and the nearby village of Chorazin, along with Bethsaida, a town across the border in Herod Philip's territory. Such curses presuppose that the mission was active in those communities, but that they later backed away or rejected the mission.

Mark then also has Jesus and his disciples extend their mission beyond Galilee into the villages of Tyre to the northwest, those of Caesarea Philippi to the north, and those of the Decapolis to the east and south of the Sea of Galilee. This may well reflect the movement's extension by the time Mark's story was composed and being performed in the constituent communities a few decades after Jesus own mission. It should not be surprising that movements of local renewal and resistance to rulers among one people would become appealing to others and extend over the frontiers. The episode of the Syro-Phoenician woman in Mark's story indicates that the inclusion of a women specifically known as being from the dominant Hellenic culture was a serious issue for the Jesus movement. Yet the rapid expansion of the Jesus movements beyond the primarily Aramaic-speaking Galilee into Syrian villages, including some Greek-speaking communities, suggests that villagers of previously non-Israelite culture fairly easily identified with Israelite tradition. This is indicated by the very existence of Mark and Q in Greek as texts performed in communities of a movement.

Covenant Renewal

Closely coupled with the exodus, in the formative traditions of Israel, was the covenant with God made on Mount Sinai. The Mosaic covenant and its fundamental principles of political-economic relations (the Ten Commandments) played a crucial role in the people's repeated resistance to oppressive rulers and struggles to restore just social relations. According to Josephus' accounts of the social turmoil of the great revolt, roughly a generation after Jesus' mission in Galilee, violations of covenantal principles by the elite was what mobilized Galilean peasants to collective action. Clearly the covenantal principles still provided the operative foundation for social-economic relations in village communities and for their political-economic relations with their rulers.[16]

Ostensibly, of course, covenantal principles and mechanisms were still observed by the temple-state as well as the peasantry. There was society-wide observance, for example, of the seventh-year rest for fields and the seventh-year cancellation of debts, traditional covenantal mechanisms designed to keep subsistence peasant household viable on their land. Hillel, the distinguished elder of the Pharisees, had promulgated the famous *prosbul* as a by-pass of the sabbatical cancellation of debts, ostensibly to ease credit for already indebted peasants. The covenant was thus clearly still well-known among scribal groups such as the Pharisees, who strove to adapt or vitiate covenantal principles in order to allow the consolidation of power in the Jerusalem temple-state. As we know now from the Dead Sea Scrolls, the dissident scribal and priestly community that withdrew to the wilderness at Qumran used the Mosaic covenant as the basic model for their utopian attempt at the renewal of Israel.

It should not be surprising, therefore, that in both Mark's story and the Q speeches, in which the main theme is the renewal of Israel over against its rulers, covenant renewal should figure prominently. In Mark, the covenant theme runs throughout the narrative, with a covenant discourse and a covenant meal at crucial points in the story. In Q, the longest and must substantive speech is a renewal of the covenant. The prominence of covenant renewal in the earliest gospel sources suggests that it was prominent in the Jesus movements that produced and used them.

The basic components of the Mosaic covenant pattern even provide the structure of the longest speech in Q (6:20-49).[17] In the original pattern, a declaration of God's deliverance (focused on the exodus) as a basis of obligation prefaced the principles of social relations that constituted the core demands of the covenant, which were then sanctioned by blessings and curses. These components can be observed at many conspicuous points in the books of the Hebrew Bible: in covenant making, covenantal laws, and covenantal teachings. They are also prominent in key texts of the Qumran community found among the Dead Sea Scrolls.

Most significant for the covenant speech in Q is how the pattern of components is creatively transformed in the initiation ceremony for those entering the renewed covenantal community found in the Qumran Community Rule (1QS). The covenant speech in Q exhibits a similar adaptation of the basic components. In both the blessings and curses component, what was previously a sanctioning motivation, has been transformed into a new declaration of God's deliverance, only now in the present/future ("Blessed are the poor, for yours in the kingdom of God"). Other materials now provide the sanction (such as the double parable of building houses on the rock or sand). Still central, of course, are the covenantal principles, which allude to and adapt traditional teachings as guidance for community social and economic interaction.

The covenantal discourse in Q, moreover, is couched in performative speech, in other words, speech that makes something happen (such as, "I now pronounce you husband and wife"). The speech enacts a renewal of the Mosaic covenant in the assembled community. The blessings pronounced on the poor, hungry, and mourning announce God's new deliverance happening in the mission of Jesus and the formation and life of the movement, with the corresponding pronouncement of woes on the wealthy. The declaration of covenantal principles (the "love your enemies" set of sayings) give focal instances of ways in which community members are to quit their local quarrels, insults, and conflicts and return to the covenant ideals of cooperation and mutual support. They are to "love your enemies, do good, and lend." The thrust is to restore the mutuality and solidarity of village community life. That presumably would strengthen the village community with regard to the pressures that are contributing to its disintegration, most obviously the heavy taxation resulting in indebtedness to the cursed wealthy, which exacerbates their poverty and hunger.

Closely associated with the covenant commandments in Israelite tradition were the time-honored mechanisms of prohibition of interest on debts and sabbatical cancellation of debts and release of debt-slaves. Debts were the bane of peasant life, and could become a downward spiral from which a family could never recover. That is why Israelites and most other peasantries developed mechanisms of what has been called a "moral economy" (see chapter 10 below), mechanisms that could keep each constituent multigenerational family economically viable.[18] The Lord's Prayer in Q, also performative speech, is thus also a covenantal economic as well as religious prayer. The third petition is a combination of a plea to God for cancellation of debts and the corresponding commitment to cancel whatever debts were owed by fellow villagers. As expressed in the parallel petitions of the prayer, cancellation of debts along with the provision of subsistence food (daily bread) is what the kingdom of God means.

Parallel to the covenantal speech in Q, Mark presents a covenantal discourse in a series of dialogues (Mark 10) that deal successively with marriage, status in the community, economic relations, and leadership. These dialogues feature a number of covenantal law-like pronouncements ("What God has joined together, let no one separate!" 10:9) as well as recitation of the covenant commandments (10:19). Like the original covenant principles, the principles enunciated in this series of dialogues (like the focal instances in Q 6:27-39) govern particular facets of local social-economic relations, such as prohibition of divorce protecting marriage at the core of the family unit (no adultery), sanction against the desire for surplus goods (wealth, no coveting, no stealing of others' goods), and a declaration that leaders must be servants and not aspire to power (one of the purposes of the covenant as a whole).

Besides this covenantal renewal discourse directed to social-economic-political relations within the community of the movement, Mark includes other dialogues with covenantal themes. The most pointed is his charge against the scribes and Pharisees from Jerusalem who urge peasants to "devote" (*korban*) their property to the Temple. He declares that such demands violate the basic covenant commandments. He gives the example of honoring father and mother to illustrate that the goods and produce of peasant families are needed for local subsistence, as in supporting the elders who can no longer labor productively (Mark 7:1-13). This appeal to the original covenantal commandment of God in order to condemn the predatory devices of the representatives of the Temple reinforces peasant families' and village communities' attempts to resist the oppressive demands of their rulers. Similarly, Jesus declares that the scribes based in the Temple "devour widows houses" (household and possessions). He then illustrates how this happens in the widow's donation of the last copper coin of her living to the Temple, again reinforcing the popular resistance to Temple demands. Mark's story thus has Jesus use covenantal references both as principles of community welfare and cooperation and as principles of resistance to the ruling institutions and their representatives.

The covenant renewal discourses and other covenantal teaching in the two earliest gospel sources offer further indications that the Jesus movements that used these texts were based in local communities which they were attempting to restore to the ideals of mutuality and cooperation of Israelite tradition. Other peasant peoples usually had traditional principles and mechanisms that corresponded to Israelite covenantal commandments and sabbatical cancellation of debts. Thus the (renewed) Israelite covenant that forms a central aspect of Jesus movements would have been easily adapted by village communities across the frontier in Syria.

Persecution and Repression

Ancient and medieval rulers seldom kept their peasants under surveillance. The Judean historian Josephus makes it sound highly out of the ordinary even when Herod arranged for informers on the residents of Jerusalem. About the only time that rulers paid any heed to the semi-autonomous village communities over which they ruled was at harvest time when they sent officers to the threshing floors to appropriate taxes. The Roman approach to pacification was to terrorize the populace by brutal slaughter and enslavement of villagers and gruesome public crucifixion of insurgents. As noted above, the Roman governors and their clients in Jerusalem and Galilee seem to have been regularly taken by surprise by protests, prophetic movements, and rebellions. Only after disruptions arose did they send out massive military force to destroy them.

It may be all the more telling, therefore, that there are so many references in Q and Mark to persecution of movement members: the likelihood of being arrested, brought to trial, even crucified (Mark 13:8-9; Q 12:2-3; 14:26). In fact, one of the standard speeches shared, in different versions, by Mark and Q is an exhortation about remaining steadfast when brought to trial and faced with the threat of execution (Mark 8:34-38; Q 12:2-12). The people who heard Q apparently understood themselves as in the long line of prophets who had been persecuted and killed (Q 11:47-51; 13:34-35; see also 6:22-23). All of these references and passages suggest that the movements had come to the attention of the rulers of Galilee and other territories, who periodically took repressive action to check the growth of the movement. This parallels the experience of other movements of Jesus followers: periodic attacks by the high priestly or Herodian rulers on the leaders of the Jerusalem community as portrayed in Acts and Paul's arrest and imprisonment as mentioned in his letters. The gist of the warnings and exhortations about repression in both Mark and Q is that it is only to be expected. The people are not to worry about it, however, but to be ready to face martyrdom, as had Jesus, in the trust that they would receive divine inspiration in the hour of testing and would be vindicated in the divine judgment.

What Happened to These Jesus Movements?

There is no obvious reason to imagine much continuity between any of the early Jesus movements or Christ-believers and what later became established Christianity, since the latter was shaped by later generations of bishops and councils. It was later church councils, for example, that canonized the four Gospels. By the time of those fourth or fifth-century councils, however, Mark was being read differently from the way it was understood in the early communities for which it was produced. The principal way in which Mark and the Q speeches found minimal continuity with later developments was through their absorption and transformation into the Gospels of Matthew and Luke. As the first gospel in the canon, Matthew became the most widely influential in the next several centuries. The initial absorption of Mark and Q into the composition of Matthew's gospel, however, did not dramatically alter the identity and agenda of the movements addressed in Mark and Q. Like its sources, Matthew's gospel and its community still understood themselves as a renewal of Israel, not a new religion.

We simply do not know what the outcome of the Jesus movements in Galilee and southern Syria may have been, how long its influence lasted in the village communities in which it took root. It must be due to the rapid spread and dramatic impact of Jesus' mission in the first generation that we have records of such popular movements in the first place. Peasant movements generally leave no records. Galilean villages in which the movement took root may have been among those decimated in the Roman reconquest in the summer of 67. Villages further north and east in Syria were probably much less affected.

It would be unwarranted to conclude that these movements represented by Mark and Q simply died out and left no trace after a generation or two, and that the diverse branches of later Christianity developed only on the basis of the urban communities established by Paul and others. The letters of Pliny provide evidence that the movements of Jesus followers and Christ believers continued to spread into village communities as well as cities as far away as northern Asia Minor and on into the second century. It is tempting to imagine that the teachings included in the movement manual or handbook known as "The Teaching of the Twelve Apostles" (*Didache*) may have been directed to Greek-speaking village communities of a movement in Syria similar to the one addressed in the Q speeches. The issues addressed and the teachings given appear as a likely later stage in the development of a movement parallel to the one addressed in the Q speeches. For example, the covenant discourse that opens the "Teaching" is expanded with traditional Israelite covenantal teachings, but lacks the performative power involved in the Q speech's transformation of the covenantal components. And the workers (prophets) sent out in the mission discourses in Q and Mark have now become a problematic drain on the economic resources of subsistence communities when they want to prolong their prophetic mission. The communities to which the Didache is addressed do not appear to be the same as those addressed in Q or Mark. The instructions for the Eucharist assume that Jesus stands in continuity with "the Holy Vine of David," that is, the popular messianic tradition, not the popular prophetic tradition of Moses and Elijah, and baptism is done with a full-blown trinitarian formula. These communities addressed in the Didache, however, are a network of village and small town assemblies that parallel those addressed in Q and Mark.

The Renewal of Israel

The earliest Jesus movements, known from the earliest gospel sources Mark and Q, did not comprise a new religion. They were rather movements whose agenda was the renewal of Israel in resistance to the imperial rulers of the people. These movements did not form new communities, but set about renewing the social-economic relations of already existing Galilean village communities according to the basic principles of the Mosaic covenant. They quickly spread to villages across the frontier under the jurisdiction of other Roman client rulers. But they continued to cultivate the Israelite tradition and covenantal principles, as adapted and transformed in Jesus' teaching and practice. And they continued their distinctively Israelite identity even after they took root in Greek-speaking communities and performed the story and speeches of Jesus in Greek.

In their origins the earliest Jesus movements are part of the history of the Galileans, Judeans, and Samaritans under the rule or continuing authority of the high priestly rulers in Jerusalem. Jesus and the movements that formed in response to his mission are closely parallel in basic ways to other popular movements at the time among the Judeans and Samaritans as well as the Galileans. All of these popular movements formed in resistance to the Jerusalem as well as the Roman rulers, consistent with the general division in ancient societies between rulers and ruled. In social form, these Jesus movements parallel the popular prophetic movements insofar as both Mark and Q, with numerous allusions to Israelite tradition, represent Jesus as a Moses- and Elijah-like prophet leading a renewal of Israel. Mark complicates this somewhat with some messianic motifs, yet cautiously and critically so.

Whereas the other popular prophets called their followers away from their village communities into the wilderness, the Jesus movements focused on renewal of village communities themselves. And that may explain why the rulers of Galilee and nearby areas did not destroy the Jesus movements in the same way the Roman governors simply eliminated the Samaritan and Judean prophetic movements. The imperial authorities, however, after executing Jesus as a rebel leader, did carry out periodic repression of his movements. In so doing, they perhaps sensed that these movements aimed to strengthen village independence, mutual support, and solidarity in resistance to the imperial order and its disintegrative effects on the subject peoples.

Part II: Oral Performance

==========

Chapter
Three

Oral Performance and Tradition in "Q"

==========

Some student friends recently commented to me, after reading one of the most widely marketed books on the historical Jesus, that modern Gospel scholarship appears to be laboring under a double disability. Gospel scholars and Jesus interpreters, they said, seem to have an extremely limited attention span, often focusing on no more than a single verse at a time. This limited attention span then becomes a contributing factor in the second disability. In addition they focus only on the printed text, without considering how gospel materials or a complete gospel story might have come alive in oral recitation. I attempted to explain how biblical studies arose from a tradition of reading the Bible verse by verse, often as proof-texts for theological and ethical doctrine, from the King James Bible, where it was all codified by chapter and verse for easy referencing. One of the students, a performing musician, responded by drawing an analogy from music. It seemed to her like Gospel scholars tend to focus on one or two measures of a score at a time, but never realize that the notes on that score are merely symbols for parts of larger melodies, fugues, and movements or of whole choruses and arias, cantatas, and operas. They have not yet discovered the work as a whole, much less considered what it would be like in performance.

In the last few decades many interpreters of the Gospels have been overcoming the first disability: they have begun to break with the long established habits of reading the Gospels in fragments, verse by verse, pericope by pericope, lesson by lesson. Matthew, Mark, Luke, and John have all been recognized as sustained stories with clear narrative structure. Most of this literary criticism has been anachronistic, applying analysis developed on modern fiction. But it has given an opening for those with greater sensitivity to ancient narrative patterns.

There are also promising signs that at least American interpreters are beginning to recognize the broader structure and coherence of a collection of Jesus' teachings known as Q, short for the German term *Quelle* (source). Q is a hypothetical text known only from the speeches of Jesus that appear parallel and often verbatim in Matthew and Luke, but not in Mark. Despite the recognition by a key early analyst[1] that this material constitutes clusters of sayings in the same order in Matthew and Luke, Q has been viewed predominantly as a collection of individual sayings. The discovery of the *Gospel of Thomas*, which took the form of single or double sayings or parables, strongly reinforced the dominant view of Q. In a highly sophisticated compositional analysis, John Kloppenborg revived the earlier perception that Q materials took the form of clusters of sayings, short discourses.[2] Most interpreters still interpret Q materials individual saying by individual saying. But there appears to be an emerging consensus that the literary structure of Q is a sequence of speeches by Jesus on various topics or issues such as mission or prayer or woes against the Pharisees (Q 10:2-16; 11:2-4; 11:39-52; Q is usually referenced according to its appearance in Luke).[3] The implications for interpretation are clear. As in any verbal communication, the function and meaning of any particular component saying of a speech in Q depends on its literary context, both in that speech and in the sequence of speeches as a whole. The speeches and not the individual sayings were the units of communication, intelligibility, and meaning. And the communication and meaning of each speech depends further on its place in the overall sequence of speeches that constitute Q.[4]

Limited Literacy in an Oral Communication Environment

The second disability my student friends noticed is far more deeply entrenched in an established academic field of study. Biblical studies developed as a field devoted to the interpretation of Scripture, that is, the sacred *written* texts of Judaism and Christianity. Just as Judaism had in ancient times been a "people of the book," so also Christianity quickly produced its own written texts. Biblical scholarship has simply proceeded on the assumption of general literacy and availability of written texts. It was even assumed that Jesus, who presumably spoke Aramaic, was fully literate (in Hebrew) and that he, like everyone else, had access to written texts of the Scripture. After all, according to Luke, when he entered the synagogue in Nazareth he was handed "the scroll of the prophet Isaiah," which he unrolled and "found the place where it was written. . ."(Luke 4:16-21). Similarly, it was assumed that the written text of Scripture was stable and that nascent Christian literature featured literate interpretation of "the Law and the Prophets."

In recent decades, however, an ever-widening stream of recent scholarship has been challenging such assumptions. During the 1980s, scholarly investigations clearly demonstrated that literacy in the Roman Empire was limited to a small percentage of the population even in the cities, and was rare in the countryside. Written scrolls were extremely cumbersome to handle and read as well as extremely costly to possess. Scrolls were rare in Judea, confined mainly to the Temple and to scribal communities such as that at Qumran. Communication, including most transmission of culture, was predominantly oral, with literacy simply being unnecessary for most people.[5] Pioneering biblical scholars explored the features of Jesus-tradition, including Q materials, as oral performance[6] and detected traits of oral performance in the Gospel of Mark.[7]

Previous estimates of the extremely limited presence and function of literacy, documents, and scribes in Galilee (and Judea) based on broader studies of the Roman empire generally[8] have recently been confirmed by far more extensive and detailed investigations, particularly of evidence in rabbinic literature.[9] In contrast with Egypt, precious few documents survive from ancient Palestine. The rabbis do make references to both documents and scribes. But it is clear that documents were optional and scribes were few and late, particularly in Galilean villages.

In cases of marriage contracts, testaments, and deathbed donations, only those with considerable property bothered with written documents.[10] The writing of marriage contracts was not the norm in the second century C.E.[11] Written marriage settlements may have been the invention of the rabbinic period;[12] a number of the rabbis were themselves possessed of considerable property. The Babatha letters found in the Judean wilderness attest the concerns of a local affluent and "materialistic, litigious coterie"[13] whose use of Greek reflected the attitudes of the local Jewish aristocracy.[14] Transactions among ordinary villagers (the vast majority of people) concerning matters such as land, moveable property, loans, marriage, on the other hand, were apparently conducted mainly by oral declaration or ceremonial action involving oaths and witnesses, judging from references in both the Mishnah and the Talmud Yerushalmi.[15] Ordinary people could not afford to hire scribes. Like everyone in antiquity, they placed more trust in the personal presence of living witnesses than in documents that could easily be forged, changed, destroyed, or lost.[16] Moreover, since writing was often used by the wealthy as an instrument of power over them, in records of loans drawn up by the rich creditors, marginal peasants and artisans were understandably suspicious of written documents. One of the first acts of the Jerusalem crowd in the summer of 66 C.E. was to burn the archives, "to destroy the money-lenders bonds and prevent the recovery of debts" (Josephus, *J.W.* 2.426-27).

In her search through the evidence, Hezser finds a general lack of scribes in small towns and villages.[17] Tannaitic literature lacks references to scribes outside of Jerusalem. She concludes that they were rare in rural areas until the third century. Talmud Yerushalmi refers to what are apparently town-based scribes in the formulaic "X the scribe of Y" (such as in Magdala).[18] The indications are, however, that they were trained only in the techniques of preparing writing materials and the formats and formulaic language of documents, and not the general education that might have prepared them for literary composition.[19] The rare scribe who lived in a Galilean village in late antiquity could apparently copy but not compose.

The resulting picture of the limited function of literacy, documents, and local scribes in Galilee corresponds to what Harris and others found in the Roman empire generally, what Thomas found earlier in Greece, and what Clanchy and others found later in medieval Europe.[20] By the first century B.C.E., the Roman aristocracy had written contracts drawn up, particularly for large-scale loans and other transactions. Peasants and artisans, however, had little use for writing, conducting most of their dealings orally, face to face.[21] Little in Roman times had changed since classical Greece, where even most legal practice was conducted orally. While the wealthy had contracts written for large-scale loans and leases, sales and contacts among ordinary people were confirmed by live witnesses. Even receipts were still unknown.[22] Similarly in the middle ages, whereas the higher and lower nobility used documented transactions in writing, among the peasantry and artisans transactions were conducted by the transfer of symbolic objects and by oral agreements and personal statements, confirmed by oaths and witnesses.[23] As Greg Woolf concludes in his recent survey of literacy in the Roman empire, "Where writing was used in the countryside. . . it was the product of the power of the classical city and of the Roman empire over the rural hinterland. No separate rural writing practices can be attested for the early Roman empire and writing always remained a component of either the urban or the military versions of Roman civilization."[24]

The Oral Performance of Texts

Recent studies in the limited extent and functions of literacy in Palestine and the Roman empire generally, however, lead to far more serious questioning of the assumptions and procedures of modern biblical studies on texts such as Q. Werner Kelber has been perhaps the most persistent voice insisting that biblical studies examine its basis in and commitments to the assumptions of typographic culture.

> Print is the medium in which modern biblical scholarship was born and raised, and from which it has acquired its formative methodological habits. . . . It is eminently reasonable. . . to conduct the search for the historical Jesus, itself a product of logic's intellectual history, in keeping with the laws of logical consistency and by application of a logically-devised classificatory apparatus. . . . It makes sense in typographic culture to visualize texts as palimpsests, with layer superimposed upon layer, and stratum superseding stratum, building up to layered edifices. . . .[25]

Many scholarly studies of Q—and not just the hypothesis of strata—illustrate Kelber's observations even better perhaps than the closely related approach to sources for the historical Jesus by Crossan and others in the Jesus Seminar.

> Ordering, the methodical arrangement of items, is a favorite child of logic. Confronted with a multiplicity and multiformity of phenomena, logic administers the implementation of organizing principles. Words are sequestered and regrouped by virtue of resemblances or successiveness. In order to be arranged systematically, items need first to be indexed. Words must, therefore, be categorized so as to be apportioned to divisions of classification. Stratification is one form of classification.[26]

The fundamental question, however, says Kelber, is "whether Jesus and the early tradition that delivered him unto writing have played by our rules. . . . Were they committed, as we are, to the ethos of pure formality, compartmentalization of language, [and] stratigraphic causality?"[27] And once we recognize that communication of all kinds was predominantly oral in antiquity, it seems clear by contrast that the way biblical studies reconstructs and construes texts "runs counter to speech, to interpersonal communication."[28] This has obvious implications for working on the further assumption at home in modern typographic culture of written composition of literature by individual intellectual authors.[29]

Since in the ancient biblical world texts, both oral and written, operated in a context of communication which was predominantly oral, it makes sense to examine the practices of "reading." To dramatize the stark contrast between ancient and medieval reading practices and the private silent reading assumed in modern western (typographic) culture, Daniel Boyarin focuses attention on key biblical passages using the term *qr'* which is usually misleadingly translated "read."

> And he took the Book of the Covenant, and he *qr'* [proclaimed] it in the ears of the people, and they said, "All that the Lord has spoken, we will do and we will obey." (Exod 24:7)

> When all of Israel come to appear before the Lord . . ., *qr'* [recite/ proclaim] this Torah in the presence of all of Israel, in their ears . . . in order that they hear and . . . that they learn and they fear the Lord . . . and perform all of the words of this Torah. (Deut 31:11)

> And you shall come and *qr'* [recite/proclaim] the scroll [of the prophetic oracles of Jeremiah] which you have written in accord with my dictation. (Jer 36:3)

In every example the usage of *qr'* indicates "an act of the speaking that is virtually identical to that when there is no written text present," says Boyarin.[30] Moreover, "all of these acts of speaking (*qr'*) are immediately followed by the desired or actual result of the performance of the speech act in the performance of the listener." Such recitation or proclamation, as that of the Torah, functions as the speech-act whose intended perlocutionary effect is obedience—as opposed, for example, to an illocutionary act of exhortation whose intended effect would be persuasion.[31] As indicated further on in the story of Baruch, moreover, the term *qr'* can cover what we would call dictation from memory or a process of oral-performative re-composition as well as an act of proclaiming unrelated to any written text.

Furthermore, as Baruch explains to his audience, "He (Jeremiah) called-out" all of the words, and I wrote them on this scroll" (Jer 36:16-18).[32] What Baruch proclaimed (*qara'*) before the king and his court was what Jeremiah had dictated (*qara'*) from memory for him to write down on the scroll. As Boyarin suggests, it is not that much of a jump from the communication between Jeremiah and Baruch and the royal audience in Jerusalem to later rabbinic and synagogue "reading" of the text of the Torah, in which a clear distinction was made between "the written" and "the read."[33] As William Scott Green explains, "The writing of the *sefer Torah* was mute. . . . Scripture" was conceived by rabbinic culture as "a holy object, a thing to be venerated . . . with its holy and allegedly unchanged and changeless writing. . . . Because it had no vowels, and hence contained no discourse, in another way the Torah-writing was also meaning-less—evocative but profoundly inarticulate. . . . To transform that script into a text, to make it readable, necessarily meant imposing a determinate discourse on it."[34] The tradition of *qere'* ("what is read"), including the essential vowels, accents, stresses, and pauses, along with euphemisms and the customary melody in which the text was chanted, which were not properties of the script, was different from *ketiv* ("what is written"; b. Berakhot 62a; Megillah 32a). In rabbinic circles "reading the *sefer Torah* was less a matter of deciphering an inscription than of reciting a previously known discourse and applying it to the writing."[35]

Martin Jaffee has generalized from such oral recitation of Torah in rabbinic circles and synagogues to the relation of written texts and oral performance generally. Fully aware of how cumbersome and costly scrolls were in antiquity, as emphasized by studies of ancient literacy, he points out that "a scroll was virtually useless as a handy source of information." But that was no obstacle since the text that was inscribed on the scroll "was as much a fact of their memory as it was a physical object. . . . 'Reading' was the activity of declaiming a text before an audience in a social performance approaching the gravity of ceremonial ritual."[36] The text was accessed through memory, not by consulting a written copy.[37] A telling illustration of his point is the procedure for a meeting of ten recorded in the "Community Rule" handbook from Qumran:

> And the congregation shall watch in community for a third
> of every night of the year, to recite the book (*sepher*) and to
> search the ruling (*mishpat*) and to bless in common. (1QS
> 6:6-8, my own translation)

Assuming that "the book" refers to (one of the books of) the Torah and "the ruling" to the community's own ordinances, the Qumranites were regularly engaging in ritual oral recitation of both Scripture and their own legal rulings that were also inscribed on scrolls possessed by the community (as in 1QS itself). (The standard translations of "read the book" and "study the law" are potentially misleading, insofar as those terms have distinctive connotations in modern typographic culture, particularly in academic circles.) Thus it was standard practice even in literate scribal circles that possessed written scrolls for texts to be recited orally from memory.

Approaching Q as Oral Performance

Recent studies of the media of communication in the ancient Mediterranean world have thus made unavoidably clear that gospel materials and the complete Gospels as texts were produced in a predominantly oral communication environment. Even if a text such as Q existed in writing, it was recited orally in a group setting. So we interpreters of Gospels and gospel materials need help. Having been focused so heavily on analysis of written texts and so deeply immersed in the assumptions of print culture, we are left singularly unprepared to appreciate oral communication and performance. Other academic fields with somewhat similar materials and issues, fortunately, have gained new perspectives and explored new approaches that may be helpful for gospel materials. Ethnographers, folklorists, medievalists, and classics scholars have been carrying out ever more innovative and sophisticated analyses of oral performances and of written texts that derived from originating oral performances.

Of particular importance for Gospel studies, John Miles Foley, the leading theorist of "verbal art," has brought together insights from oral-formulaic theory and other studies of oral-derived classical and medieval literature, on the one side, and sociolinguistics, ethnopoetics, and the ethnography of performance, on the other, into highly suggestive theorizing of "immanent art" and oral performance.[38] It is that interplay and combination of historical investigation, ethnography, experimentation, comparative reflection, and theory that Jonathan Draper and I attempted to adapt for exploration of the speeches in Q as oral performance.[39]

The following exploration represents an attempt to further adapt this developing mix of comparative studies and theory in application to Q speeches. The focus is not on the issue of whether Q was originally composed in writing or orally. We know of Q, of course, only because parallel speech materials of Jesus were transmitted in writing in the Gospels of Matthew and Luke. Gospel texts such as Q speeches or Markan narrative continued to be recited orally, however widely distributed they may have become in written manuscripts. This is increasingly evident to text critics, who explain the extensive variation is the written manuscripts of the Gospels as a function of continuing interaction between manuscripts, memory, and oral recitation that lasted into late antiquity.[40] The speech material parallel in Matthew and Luke that is called Q exhibits many marks of oral performance (see further below). The Jesus speeches in Q that can be reconstructed from the parallels in the written manuscripts of Matthew and Luke thus offer an unusual opportunity to appreciate how they may have worked in oral performance.

Outline of an Approach

In approaching Q as oral performance we can no longer ask what individual sayings in themselves mean. That might be appropriate for the separate sayings of the *Gospel of Thomas* as object of reflection or contemplation. But individual sayings are and were not the basic units of communication. To find units of communication, we must focus rather on the speeches or discourses constituted by the clusters of sayings still evident in the parallel materials in Matthew and Luke (see the Q speeches blocked in verse in the Appendix below). Since Q consisted not of individual sayings but of shorter or longer speeches that were performed orally before a community, we should ask rather how the speeches communicated to their listeners. For the speeches in Q, as in any act of communication, it is necessary to consider the interaction between speaker and hearers as they live out of their cultural tradition in a particular context. That in Q we are dealing with what Foley would call a "voice from the past" means that to hear this historical oral communication appropriately we must listen, insofar as possible, in a historical cultural and social context.[41] To simplify our analysis to four interrelated aspects, to hear Q discourses as oral performance, we must determine the contours of the "*text*," attend to the performance *context* in which the speaker addresses the hearers, sense the *register* of the speech appropriate to that context, and cultivate knowledge of the cultural *tradition* out of which the speech resonates with the hearers.[42]

This approach to Q speeches as communication moves beyond the standard approach developed in Gospel studies and complicates the theory of "verbal art" developed by Foley in a number of respects. Two respects in particular require special critical attention, in connection with *context* and *tradition*.

"Text" and Context

The first step is to figure out what the *text* or message communicated is and was. For an orally-derived text for which we are dependent on a "transcript" of the performance, we have little more than the "libretto" before us in manuscript or printed form. Given the previous habit of treating Q as a collection of separate sayings, it will be particularly important to listen for what may be the complete units of communication. Individual sayings or verses were not intelligible units of communication, but merely fragments thereof. To work from analogies with other performances, we want to consider not just a few isolated lines but whole arias or speeches in the larger context of the complete libretto of an opera or the complete script of a play. In Q the intelligible units of communication would presumably be particular speeches or discourses focused on particular issues.[43] It would also help to hear those as components of the complete sequence of speeches that constituted Q.

In order to understand a message or communication properly, it is further necessary to hear it in the appropriate *context*: wedding, funeral, political rally, intimate embrace. Context determines the expectation and the appropriate hearing of the message. We would not expect to hear the aria by the Queen of the Night from Mozart's *Zauberflöte* at the Grand Ol' Opry. Often to tune into a message we adjust to particular contexts within a general context of communication. In the general context of a Christian church service, for example, we shift from one particular context to another, from adoration and praise to prayer to scripture reading to sermon to offering.

Attempting to appreciate Q speeches as messages communicated by a speaker to a collective audience thus requires the interpreter to combine critical attention to the context with critical attention to the text. Text cannot be considered apart from context. The grandfathers of form-criticism (Bultmann and Dibelius) said something similar: that form could not be considered apart from social function—which the next generation of Gospel interpreters tended to forget in their focus on form abstracted from social function. Similarly, some recent interpreters of Q assumed that they could establish the meaning of sayings considered separate from consideration of the context (and cultural tradition), and then on that basis deduce the social context. Texts in performance, however, like any messages in communication, are always already in a relational context. Just as the performance context of the liturgy of the mass is presumably a congregation gathered for worship, so the performance context of Q speeches was presumably a community gathering of participants in a Jesus movement.[44]

Consideration of the context of Q speeches in recitation, however, is more complicated than that of other types of oral poems and the performance of epic poems such as the Iliad or Beowulf, key texts on which the theory of verbal art has been developed. The performance context of the Q speeches was not one standardized over many generations of repeated performances. It was rather a gathering of community in a newly developed movement apparently among the peasantry in Galilee and beyond. If we are to attempt to hear Q speeches in the concrete historical context of their more narrowly considered performance context, therefore, the historical context must be considered with as much precision as possible. Recent research has made accessible the multiple political-economic-religious conflicts that characterized Roman Palestine at the time of the early Jesus movements. Modern essentialist constructs such as Judaism and apocalypticism and other anachronistic concepts block rather than facilitate access to historical context.

Register

The message must then match, or be in the appropriate *register* for the context. A funeral dirge would not go over very well at a wedding, or the Hallelujah chorus at a rock concert. The appropriate register depends on three factors: the subject matter being communicated, who is participating in the communication, and the mode of communication. The language-of-love would thus be the appropriate register for the expression of love between partners whispering sweet nothings into each others' ears. Often a certain discourse, including body language and paralinguistic gestures, is dedicated to a certain communication context, as in the case of weddings or funerals or the introduction of distinguished professors to deliver endowed lectures at an august institution of higher learning. A certain register of language is often activated by sounds or phrases that set up expectations in the listeners, signaling the communication context and the register of discourse about to be heard. If we are in the right context and clued into the register for a regularly repeated performance, we already know what is being communicated. "Dearly beloved, We are gathered here together. . . ." "The Lord be with you. . . ." One Q speech offers an example of the failure to appreciate the register and context of Jesus' and John's prophetic performances in their program of renewal of Israel:

> We played the flute for you, and you did not dance;
> We wailed, and you did not weep. (Q 7:32)

Often the performer is assuming a certain role appropriate to the communication. Funerals are usually conducted by clergy. In political rallies candidates and other speakers address followers or concerned citizens. In ancient scribal circles, instruction involved a teacher addressing his students: "Oh my children, . . ." (Sirach 2:1; 3:1; 4:1; 6:18; etc.). At the popular level, a prophet, such as Yeshua ben Hananiah, repeatedly pronounced a lament over the imminent fate of the ruling city Jerusalem (Josephus, *J.W.* 6.300-309), a message in a prophetic register heard by crowds and overheard by an anxious aristocracy. The clues or cues to the register (and context) of the message being communicated is often indicated in the way it references the cultural tradition shared by speaker and listeners—which makes knowledge of the tradition all the more important for us modern interpreters.

Tradition and Metonymic Referencing

When the audience hears the message in the register appropriate to the communication context, they then resonate to the message out of the cultural *tradition* in which they and the performer are grounded. In every one of the communication contexts and registers offered as illustrations above, there is a cultural tradition out of which the hearers resonate with the message, whether at weddings, political rallies, or the Grand Ol' Opry. The cultural tradition, however, is far more important for communication through oral performance of texts in a traditional society where oral communication is far more dominant than in a highly literate modern society or postmodern multimedia society. It is particularly important for biblical scholars still striving to cut through the assumptions of print culture in which we are so deeply embedded to recognize this. And since recent literary analysis of biblical narrative, while helpful in many ways, may have perpetuated those assumptions, it may be appropriate to illustrate from the difference between a modern novelist's communication with a silent reader and an ancient performance of the Iliad or Beowulf or the Gospel of Mark.[45]

A modern novelist individually manipulates inherited or idiosyncratic materials in a new direction or from a new perspective, thus *conferring* meaning on her fresh new literary creation (that is then read privately by a silent reader). The traditional oral performer, on the other hand, depending on standard strategies long familiar to his collective audience, summons conventional connotations of conventional structures evoking a meaning that is *inherent*. Communication through a performance or recitation, therefore, depends much more heavily on extratextual factors as meaning is evoked *metonymically* from the tradition with which the listeners are familiar. In contrast to the originality of conferred meaning in modern literary texts, traditional oral performance cannot depart from, because it depends upon, traditional references of symbols, phrases, and formulas. Each performance causes what is immanent to come to life in the present; it recreates the networks of inherent meaning. The what and how of communication in the performance of a text such as the Iliad or the Gospel of Mark depends on a whole range of cultural memory in which the social identity and self-image of a people or community is embedded. In emphasizing the crucial importance of cultural tradition or memory for the communication happening in gospel materials such as Mark and Q, Kelber has compared it to a biosphere in which a people's whole life is encompassed and nurtured.[46]

While cultural tradition is far less significant for us post-moderns, we also experience how metonymic referencing works in experiences that may enable us better to appreciate how it worked in oral performance of texts in societies more embedded in their cultural traditions. Whenever I hear on the radio, say around mid-January, the voice of Martin Luther King saying "I have a dream . . . ," then simply that brief phrase spoken in King's inimitable cadence resonates deeply within my memory in metonymic referencing that evokes a whole movement, a whole period of my life and the life of American society. It evokes intense feelings of eager hopes, vivid experiences, outrage, and deep sorrow. When that happens, moreover, I cannot help but renew my own personal commitment to certain values and causes.

As interpreters who stand at a considerable distance from the original historical context of a text such as Q, we are unusually dependent on the cultural tradition in our attempts to hear the message appropriately. Our only clues as to the performance context and the register in which the message should be heard may come from our acquaintance with the tradition that it references.

The Special Importance of Israelite Tradition
for Hearing Q as Oral Performance

It is thus particularly important for us as "eavesdroppers" or "overhearers" of Q speeches who stand at a distance from the original historical situation to become as thoroughly acquainted as possible with the tradition out of which the performer spoke and the hearers resonated. It seems fairly clear that the Q speeches are rooted in Israelite tradition. Despite the recently fashionable interpretation of individual Q sayings on the basis of perceived parallels to counter-cultural Cynic philosophical materials, there is a great deal of agreement among interpreters that Q exhibits numerous allusions to Israelite figures and motifs.[47] Recent research into the cultural life of ancient Judean and Galilean society, however, has seriously complicated how ancient Israelite cultural tradition operated and requires us to move well beyond the standard conceptual apparatus of Gospel studies.

The first problem that should be faced seriously is that Israelite tradition was not unitary and existed on different social levels. A consensus seems to have emerged, at least among American interpreters of Q, that Q materials originated in a Jesus movement based in Galilee (keying on the place-names Bethsaida, Capernaum, and Chorazin, and on the agrarian imagery), but not in elite literate circles in the newly built cities of Sepphoris and Tiberias. Four factors that have become clear from recent research on various aspects of life in first century Galilee, however, make it highly unlikely that Galileans would have known Israelite tradition in the form previously imagined in New Testament studies on the assumption of a widely-known standard version of the Hebrew Bible. First, no standardized version of "the Law and the Prophets" existed, perhaps until well after second-temple times.[48] Second, scrolls of the books of the Torah and the Prophets would have been extremely costly and unwieldy; the limited number that existed belonged in the Temple and in scribal circles.[49] Third, it appears that few Galileans would have been literate, able to read a scroll in Hebrew.[50] Moreover and fourth, Galileans had come under the rule of the Jerusalem high priestly regime and "the laws of the Judeans" only about a century before the birth of Jesus, and the scribal and Pharisaic representatives of the Jerusalem regime would hardly have been able to "re-socialize" the people in the Jerusalem-based protobiblical version of Israelite cultural tradition during that time. They certainly had no basis in the synagogues of Galilee, which in the first century were not (yet) Jewish religious buildings (archaeologists have not yet found such), but Galilean village assemblies which met to discuss community affairs as well as to hold prayers.[51]

Insofar as Q speeches are rooted in Israelite tradition based in Galilee, therefore, it must have been what anthropologists would call the Israelite "little tradition."[52] That is, assuming that Galileans, the vast majority of whom lived in village communities, were descendants of ancient Israelites or of Israelite heritage, they cultivated popular Israelite tradition orally in those village communities. Galilean Israelite popular tradition may well have come into some interaction with the Jerusalem-based "great" tradition during the first century B.C.E., but would hardly have been identical with the version we know from the Jerusalemite great tradition that formed the basis of the later canonized Hebrew Bible. For interpreters of Q, however, the difference between the Galilean Israelite popular tradition and the Jerusalem-based "great tradition" means obvious problems of sources for the former. What scholars know as the Hebrew Bible, derived from one of the versions of the Jerusalemite great tradition,[53] does not provide a direct source for the Galilean Israelite little tradition. At best it provides an indirect source. A modern scholar can only extrapolate from it, fully aware that it has been shaped and edited by Jerusalem scribal circles working for and articulating the perspective and interests of the ruling Jerusalem priestly aristocracy. Among the effects of recent researches into the fluid condition and variety in Israelite cultural tradition is to lead scholarly interpreters of texts to recognize that we are not working with the kind of control over written textual sources that we may have assumed previously.

The second problem is closely related to the first. The Israelite popular tradition in Galilee would almost certainly have been cultivated orally in the dominant language among Galileans, Aramaic. But Q was in Greek. There might be two possible explanations of the relationship of Q speeches in Greek to the Israelite tradition in which they were deeply rooted, each one based in a theory about how the Jesus movement that produced and used Q spread. One is that the movement had expanded into the Galilean cities of Sepphoris or Tiberias, where more Greek was spoken than in villages, taking nascent Jesus traditions with them. The other is that the movement had expanded into villages and towns of the surrounding countries, such as those subject to Tyre, Sidon, Caesarea Philippi, the Decapolis, and so forth, in which the villagers and townspeople presumably spoke more Greek than in Galilean villages.[54] The second possibility at least appears to have a potential parallel in the Gospel of Mark, in which Jesus is portrayed as having worked in the villages or regions of Tyre, Caesarea Philippi, and the Decapolis (perhaps grounding the later expansion of a Jesus movement in the ministry of Jesus himself). In this second scenario, the participants in the movement who performed or heard the Q speeches need not have been descendants of Israelites, but could have been people who identified with Israelite tradition as the basis of the developing and expanding movement. People who had only recently and secondarily learned and identified with Israelite tradition would have been less deeply yet intensely attached to it.

The third problem is that culture involves more than particular items such as names, place names, and motifs, but broader patterns, connections, and discourses, as well. The very concept of *register* implies such cultural realities as discourses devoted to certain memories and other cultural patterns. Just as the very sound of M. L. King's voice evokes the memory of a whole period of American history for people of my generation, so a reference to Moses would evoke a whole set of associations of exodus, wilderness wanderings, and covenant making. Culture also involves distinctive patterns that persist over many generations. I stumbled on some of these in gathering and examining Josephus' accounts of several movements in 4 B.C.E., and again from 66–70 C.E., led by popularly acclaimed kings and several other movements in mid-first century led by popular prophets. The distinctively Israelite similarities exhibited by these two types of popular movements, despite their differences in particulars, can only be explained by particular patterns embedded in cultural memory of earlier movements led by the young David and others (a popular messianic script) and earlier movements led by Moses and Joshua (a popular prophetic script). The discovery of the Dead Sea Scrolls, and the Community Rule and the Damascus Rule in particular, enabled us to realize that Mosaic covenant patterns had persisted into late second-temple times, at least among scribal-priestly circles. As long as study of Q and other gospel materials focused mainly on individual sayings, broader cultural patterns remained unseen partly because they were not sought. Once we recognize their persistence, however, we must be open to the possibility that Q speeches and the Markan narrative may be metonymically referencing whole cultural patterns.

Awareness of these complicating aspects of Israelite tradition should better enable interpreters to appreciate how performance of Q speeches may have referenced that tradition metonymically, in order to better detect the context and register of the speeches and to appreciate how the speeches resonated with the hearers by such referencing. In contrast with previously standard procedure based on assumptions of print culture, in which scholars looked for "quotations of scripture" (even if only words or phrases), we can attend more sensitively and subtly to images, motifs, and patterns of cultural memory.

There is yet another aspect of the cultural tradition that Q speeches reference as they resonate with hearers. Insofar as communities of Jesus adherents who comprised the audience of the Q speeches were part of a popular movement that had built upon a rich Israelite cultural tradition, the tradition out of which the Q speeches resonated was a double one. In addition to and building on the broader and deeper Israelite tradition, a more focused and recent tradition of Jesus-lore had developed. The broader and deeper Israelite tradition featured a long line of prophets, some of whom had pronounced God's judgment against oppressive rulers and some of whom had led the formation or renewal of the people. In the developing Jesus tradition, Jesus was apparently understood as the fulfillment of that line of prophets. He had both pronounced God's condemnation of current rulers and led a (new) renewal of Israel. The broader and deeper Israelite tradition included an increasing longing for "the kingdom of God," when God would finally take action against oppressive human rulers to heal their suffering, relieve their indebtedness, and restore just social-economic relations. In the developing Jesus tradition, Jesus had proclaimed, manifested, and restored practice of the kingdom of God. The Jesus tradition was the exciting and inspiring fulfillment of the old. This can be seen in several of the speeches. Q 6:20-49 is performative speech in which Jesus renews the Mosaic covenant (explored below). Q 7:18-35 proclaims that Jesus had been manifesting the kingdom of God in healings, exorcisms, and preaching. In Q 9:57—10:16 Jesus commissioned envoys to help heal, preach and organize people in the village communities.[55]

Prior to closer examination of the Q covenant speech in particular, we can note a few examples of how we may be able to detect the performance context and register of some Q speeches by closer attention to Israelite popular tradition. The speech in 7:18-35 that identifies Jesus as the coming one who is already accomplishing the prophetically articulated longings of Israel for the blind to see, the deaf to hear, and the poor to have good news preached suggests the sense of fulfillment in the prophetic mission carried out by Jesus. This further suggests that the performance context of the speech is a popular movement of renewal of Israel and the register one of fulfillment of prophetic expectations. The allusions to Elijah's commissioning of Elisha that preface the mission speech in 9:57—10:16 suggests that, by analogy, Jesus' envoys are also sent on a prophetic mission to renew Israel. Again the allusions suggest that the performance context is a popular movement of renewal and the register that of commissioning for mission. In this case the use of what appear to be a popular cycle of Elijah-Elisha stories by the Deuteronomistic History in the Jerusalemite "great tradition," combined with the occurrence of (other) popular prophetic movements right around the time of Jesus, provide fairly strong indications that such a register continued in the popular memory, along with periodic prophetic movements of renewal.

The series of woes against the Pharisees in Q 11:39-52 take the same (oral-performative or oral-literary) form as the series of woes that appear in the books of Amos, Isaiah, and Habakkuk, and has parallels in the Epistle of Enoch. This indicates fairly clearly that Q is using standard prophetic forms still alive in the popular tradition. The performance context is, again, a prophet-led renewal or resistance movement, and the register is that of prophetic woes against rulers and their representatives for their treatment of the people. Similarly, the prophetic lament against the Jerusalem ruling house resembles earlier Israelite prophetic laments and has a striking parallel in the near contemporary prophetic lament by the peasant prophet Yeshua ben Hananiah mentioned by Josephus. Clearly the Q speeches not only refer significantly to key memories in Israelite culture, but utilize basic Israelite cultural forms, particularly prophetic forms, that were still very much alive in popular circles. And such references aid us in detecting the performance contexts and registers of the Q speeches.

Hearing Q 6 in Oral Performance

As suggested in the theory of oral performance outlined above, the first step is to ascertain the text or message that was recited before a Jesus-movement community. For modern interpreters relatively unfamiliar with the cultural tradition of the speaker and audience, the next step is to become more familiar with the Israelite tradition out of which it resonated with the hearers. That will enable us better to appreciate the way the speech worked as it resonated with the audience by referencing that cultural tradition.

Q 6:20-49 as a Coherent Speech

Attempting to ascertain the complete text or message being communicated is a departure from standard studies of Q, for which the text is an unproblematic given (once the wording of particular sayings is reconstructed from the parallels in Matthew and Luke). Assuming that Q was a collection of sayings, standard studies focus attention on sayings as separate entities. Since they are based on the presuppositions of print culture, standard approaches to Q and other Gospel materials are uninterested in communication (which would be difficult, if not impossible, in separate individual sayings). Rather they treat gospel materials as discrete (written) textual artifacts to be examined and interpreted as if they contained some inherent meaning in themselves.

Representative of what has been the standard approach to Q as a collection of separate individual sayings, Tuckett[56] treats sayings as separate abstract entities that possess meaning in themselves. Like previous Q scholars, he attends to the sequence of the sayings in Matthew and Luke, in order to establish the existence of Q. But interest in the order of Q does not carry over into consideration of possible patterns formed, for example, by the sequence of sayings in Luke 6:20-49 (which is usually judged to be closer to Q), in contrast with that in Matthew 5–7, and the issues that such combinations of sayings might be addressing. Rather, separate sayings (or short combinations such as Q/Luke 6:22-23) are discussed largely according to the Christian theological issues to which they appear relevant. In his earlier compositional analysis, Kloppenborg[57] did attend to the pattern of Q/Luke 6:20-49. He argued that this cluster followed the pattern found in sapiential discourses such as Proverbs 1 and 3:13-35. In his later study of the social context of Q and substantive issues addressed by Q, however, he did not discuss Q 6:20-49, or any of the other discourses he identified in his compositional analysis, as a complete discourse. He rather followed the standard practice of discussing individual sayings according to the historical or, more commonly, the Christian theological issues they seem to match. Analysis of Q 6:20-49 as a complete discourse in oral performance, however, like Kloppenborg's and Kirk's compositional analysis, suggests that it displays a coherent structure as a speech.[58]

Insofar as we have been trained, on the assumptions of print culture, to read texts silently from the print on a page, it is difficult for us even to imagine how a given text would sound. In trying to appreciate Q speeches in oral performance, I have found helpful Dell Hymes' suggestion that oral-derived texts often take the form of lines (clause), verses, stanzas, and scenes or acts. When we attend to language patterns in Q, its speeches sound like poetry, with parallel lines usually of three or four words or phrases each. The parallel lines then seem to form verses and stanzas. Since Q as a whole is not a story or epic poem, the overall structure cannot be heard as a sequence of scenes and acts. It is rather a sequence of short speeches on various concerns of the audience.

Given our habituation to print, it may be helpful to see the text of Q 6:20-49 blocked in measured verse in order to begin to imagine how it might have sounded in oral performance (see pages 76-83). This is presented in transliteration to enable those without Greek to appreciate the Greek sounds. The English translation may not only help to render the sense but also to facilitate an indirect appreciation of the repetition of words and verb-forms in parallel lines and across stanzas. While usually following the wording agreed upon by the International Q Project, I have at points been led to an alternative by poetic considerations of oral performance. Further reflection on the text-in-performance has resulted in some changes in the reconstruction of the text transliterated and translated in my previous work with Jonathan Draper.[59] Perhaps it is well to keep in mind that the text below is based on a reconstruction (by the International Q Project) that is also based on reconstructions (of the critical texts of Matthew and Luke) from comparison of ancient manuscripts that text critics are now recognizing involved a certain interaction with continuing influence of memory and oral performance.

Some of the key markers of oral-derived texts are repetition of words, sounds, and verbal forms, and parallel lines and sets of lines. The speech in Q 6:20-49 is remarkably rich in this regard. As a careful overview and reading aloud of the transliteration or the translation blocked in poetic lines will indicate, the stanzas of this speech consist largely of parallel lines, even four or five, which repeat the same or similar words in the same verbal forms. Even where the form moves away from parallel poetic lines into dual prose parables, the latter are closely parallel formulations. Where the lines are not precisely parallel (about trees and fruit, good and wicked men), they feature different combinations of the same words. Even beyond the parallel lines and other formulations, there is much repetition of sounds between lines and stanzas.[60] Among other features typical in oral performance, figurative language comes to the fore in the later stanzas.[61]

Even short of a fuller awareness of Mosaic covenantal tradition we can discern the language patterns within the stanzas and steps, and the connections and cohesion of the various steps in the speech. In a series of parallel lines, the two stanzas in step I deliver well-balanced blessings and woes on people at the opposite ends of the economic divide.

The teaching section in step II has a well-defined argumentative structure. The first stanza gives commands in (two or more likely four) parallel lines, the first being the more general category of "loving enemies," the rest being more specific about local conflictual economic relations. In another four parallel lines, the second stanza moves the commands into mainly economic relations in the local community, focusing on borrowing and lending. The third stanza applies "the golden rule" to these relationships as both explanation and motivation. Then in three parallel lines of rhetorical questions and reply, the fourth stanza calls the hearers to a standard of economic relations higher than that displayed by outsiders and (other) categories of people who are known for having lesser standards. This section of the speech is then summarized by a recapitulation of the commands, moving from the more general to the more specifically economic, and sanctioned by a promise of great reward and a call to imitate God's generous treatment of even unkind and wicked people, presumably referring back to the enemies and those who abuse.

In the third step of the speech, the commands shift focus to conflictual social relations in the local community. In an argumentative pattern less elaborate than the previous section, the first stanza gives a general command and principle, the second offers two (negative) illustrations, and the third, in an elaborate play on words and three rhetorical variations on the same theme, exhorts the listeners to

Q 6:20-49 Blocked in Measured Verse for Hearing

Step I.

1. *Makarioi*   *hoi ptōchoi,*   *hoti hymetera estin*   *hē basileia tou theou.*

2. *Makarioi*   *hoi peinōntes,*   *hoti chortasthēsesthe.*

3. *Makarioi*   *hoi penthountes,*   *hoti paraklēthēsesthe.*

4. *Makarioi*   *este hotan*   *oneidisōsin*   *hymas*

     kai diōxōsin

     kai eipōsin poneron   *kath' hymōn*

     heneka   *tou huiou tou anthropou.*

5. *Chairete*   *kai agalliasthe,*   *hoti ho misthos hymōn*   *polys en tō ouranō.*

6. *Houtos gar*   *ediōxan/epoioun*   *tous prophētas*   *tous pro hymōn.*

1. *Ouai*   *hoi plousioi*   *hoti apechete*   *tēn paraklēsin hymōn.*

2. *Ouai*   *hoi empeplēsmenoi*   *hoti peinasete.*

3. *Ouai*   *hoi gelōntes*   *hoti penthēsete* [or: *klausete*].

4. *Ouai*   *hotan hymas*   *kalōs eipōsin*   *pantes*

5. *Houtōs gar*   *ediōxan / epoioun*   *tous pseudoprophētas.*

Step II.

1. *Agapate*   *tous echthrous*   *hymōn,*

2. *kalōs poieite*   *tois misousin*   *hymas.*

3. *Eulogeite*   *tous katarōmenous*   *hymas,*

4. *proseuchesthe*   *peri tōn epēreazontōn*   *hymas.*

Q 6:20-49 Translation in Measured Verse Blocked for Hearing

Step I.

1. Blessed are	the poor	for yours is	the kingdom of God.
2. Blessed are	those who hunger,	for you shall be filled.	
3. Blessed are	those who mourn,	for you shall laugh.	
4. Blessed are	you when	they reproach	you
		and speak evil	against you
		on account of	the son of man.
5. Rejoice and	[be glad]		
for your reward	is great	in heaven	
6. For so	they did	to the prophets	[before you].
1. Woe	to those who are rich,	for you have received	your consolation.
2. Woe	to those who are full,	for you shall go hungry.	
3. Woe	to those who laugh,	for you shall mourn.	
4. Woe	when all people	speak well	of you.
5. For so	they did	to the false prophets.	

Step II.

1. Love	the enemies	of you(rs),
2. {Do good	to those who hate	you.
3. Bless	those who curse	you,}
4. Pray	for those who abuse	you.

1. *Hostis rapizei se*	*eis tēn siagona,*	*strepson*	*auto kai allēn.*
2. *kai* [ ]	*sou to himation*	*aphes auto*	*kai ton chitōna.*
3. *Tō aitounti*	*se*	*dos,*	
4. *kai apo tou danizomenou*	*ta sa*	*mē apaitei.*	
1. *Kai kathōs thelete*	*hina poiōsin*	*hymin*	*hoi anthrōpoi,*
houtōs	*poieite*	*autois.*	
1. *Ei agapate*	*tous agapōntas*	*hymas,*	*tina misthon echete;*
Ouchi kai telōnai	*to auto*	*poiousin;*	
2. *Kai ean agathopoiēte*	*tous agathapoiountas*	*hymas,*	*tina misthon echete;*
Ouchi kai hoi [hamartōl]oi	*to auto*	*poiousin;*	
3. *Kai ean danisēte*	*par' hōn elpizete*	*labein,*	*tina misthon echete;*
ouchi kai hoi [ethnik]oi	*[to auto]*	*[poiousin]*	
1. *Plēn agapate*	*tous echthrous*	*hymōn*	
kai agathopoiete	*kai danizete.*		
Kai estai [polys]	*ho misthos*	*hymōn*	*[polys].*
2. *Hopōs genesthe*	*huioi tou patros*	*hymōn,*	
hoti ton hēlion autou	*anatellei*	*epi ponerous*	*kai agathous . . .*
[??] Ginesthe	*oiktirmones*	*hōs ho patēr hymōn*	*oiktirmōn estin.*

Step III.

1. *Mē krinete*		*[hina] mē krithēte.*	
[En hō gar krimati	*krinete*	*krithēsesthe.]*	
2. *Hō gar en metro*	*metreite*	*metrēthēsetai hymin.*	

1. To the one who strikes you	on the cheek	turn	also the other.
2. And [from the one who takes]	your coat	[offer]	also the tunic.
3. To the one who asks from you		give,	
4. And from the one who borrows		do not ask back.	
1. And as you wish	that people	would do	to you,
2. thus		do	to them.
1. And if you love	those who love	you,	what credit is that to you?
For even the toll-collectors	do the same.		
2. And if you do good to	those who do good to	you,	what credit is that to you?
For even the [other] peoples	do the same.		
3.{and if you lend to those from	whom you hope to receive,	what credit is that to you?	
Even...	lend to...}		
1. But love	your enemies,	and do good,	and lend,
and your reward	will be	great.	
2. And you will become	sons	of your Father,	
for he is	kind	to the ungrateful	and the evil.
3. Be	merciful,	as your Father	is merciful.

Step III.

1. And do not judge		and you will not be judged
[for with the judgment	you judge	you will be judged,]
2. for with the measure	you measure	it will be measured to you.

1. *Meti dynatai*	*typhlos*	*typhlon*	*hodēgein?*
Ouchi	*amphoteroi*	*eis bothunon*	*pesountai?*
2. *ouk estin mathētēs*		*hyper ton didaskalon*	
arketon tō mathētē	*hina genētai*	*hōs ho didaskalos autou.*	
1. *Ti de blepeis*	*to karphos*	*to en tō ophthalmō*	*tou adelphou*
	tēn de en dokon	*tēn en tō [idiō] ophthalmō*	*ou katanoeis?*
2. *pōs [dynasai*	*legein]*	*tō adelphō sou:*	
aphes ekbalō	*to karphos*	*ek tou ophthalmou sou,*	
kai idou	*hē dokos*	*en tō ophthalmō sou?*	
3. *Hypokrita.*			
Ekbale prōton	*tēn dokon*	*ek tou ophthalmou sou,*	
Kai tote diablepseis			
ekbalein	*to karphos*	*ek tou ophthalmou*	*tou adelphou sou.*

Step IV.

1. *Ouk estin*	*dendron kalon*	*poioun*	*karpon sapron*
oude palin	*dendron sapron*	*poioun*	*karpon kalon.*
2. *Ek gar tou karpou*	*to dendron*	*ginōsketai.*	
mēti syllegousin	*apo akanthōn*	*staphylas.*	
ē	*ek tribolōn*	*syka.*	
1. *Ho agathos anthrōpos*	*ek tou agathou thēsaurou*	*ekballei agatha*	
kai ho poneros anthrōpos	*ek tou ponerou thēsaurou*	*ekballei ponera.*	
2. *Ek gar perisseumatos*	*kardias*	*lalei*	*to stōma.*

1. Can a blind person	guide	a blind person?	
Will not both	fall	into a pit?	
2. A disciple	is not above	his teacher.	
but everyone trained	will be like	his teacher.	
1. Why do you see	the speck	in the eye	of your brother,
but	the log	in your own eye	you do not notice?
2. How [can	you say]	to your brother:	
"Let me remove	the speck	from your eye,"	
and behold,	there is a log	in your own eye?	
3. Hypocrite!			
Remove first	the log	from your own eye,	
and then you will see (clearly)			
to cast out	the speck	from the eye	of your brother.

Step IV.

1. There is no	sound tree	which bears	bad fruit,
nor again	a bad tree	which bears	sound fruit.
2. For from the fruit	a tree	is known:	
they do not gather	figs	from thorns,	
or	grapes	from a bramble bush	
1. The good man	from the good treasure	brings forth	good (things).
The evil man	from the evil treasure	brings forth	evil (things).
2. For from an overflow	of the heart	speaks	the mouth.

Step V.

1. *Ti*   *me kaleite*   *kyrie, kyrie,*

kai   *ou poieite*   *ha legō?*

1. *Pas ho akouōn*   *mou tous logous*   *kai poiōn autous*

2. *Homoios estin anthrōpō,*

hos okodomēsen   *autou tēn oikian* *epi tēn petran.*

3. *Kai . . . kai . . .*   *hoi potamoi . . .*   *prosepesan . . .*   *tē oikia ekeinē,*

kai ouk epesen   *tethemeliōto gar*   *epi tēn petran.*

1. *Kai pas ho akouōn*   *kai me poiōn*
                       mou tous logous   *autous*

2. *Homoios estin*   *anthrōpō,*

hos oikodomēsen   *authou tēn oikian* *epi tēn ammon.*

3. *Kai . . . kai . . .*   *hoi potamoi . . .*   *prosekopsan*   *tē oikia ekeinē,*

kai epesen   *kai ēn hē ptōsis autēs*   *megalē.*

Step V.

1. Why	do you call me,	"lord, lord,"	
And	not do	what I tell you?	
1. Every one	who hears my words,	and does	them
2. is like	a man		
who built	{his} house	upon the rock.	
3. And the rain came down	and the river beat upon	that house,	
and it did not fall,	for it had been founded	upon the rock.	
1. And everyone	who hears my words,	and does not do them,	
2. is like	a man		
who built	{his] house	upon the sand.	
3. And the rain came down	and the river beat upon	that house,	
and it fell	and its [fall] was	great.	

tend first to the beam that is obscuring their own vision, before lashing out against their neighbors.

The final two steps in the speech focus on motivation and sanction for the commands and exhortations given in the previous two steps. The first stanza of step four, with more word play in parallel lines, picks up on the economic theme of the first and second steps with the image of bearing fruit. The second stanza then addresses motives of speaking good and wicked things, picking up on the commands in the third step of the speech. The final step gives a sanction on all the commands given in steps two and three with a double parable. Thus not only is there coherence within the different steps of the speech, but there is a clear cohesion across the sections that enable us to discern a clear rhetorical structure in the speech as a whole. The text, the word that we are trying to hear through the words in the lines and stanzas and sections, is the overall speech of Q 6:20-49.

Even before we move more fully into the covenantal tradition that this speech references, we can detect at least a few clues as to its performance context and register. Insofar as the content of the commands given in steps two and three pertains to economic and social relations of people in regular interaction with each other, borrowing and lending, insulting and criticizing one another, the context and the register of the discourse must have some connection with local community relations.[62] Further investigation and awareness of the Israelite covenantal tradition, however, will enable us to become far more precise about the key aspects of this speech in oral performance.

Israelite Covenant Tradition

Since the Mosaic covenant was central to Israelite tradition generally, it may not be surprising that we have several sources from the scriptural great tradition, and the scribal communities that cultivated it, that help us project likely cultivation of a parallel little tradition in the villages of Galilee in connection with which Q materials originated.[63]

The Mosaic covenant given to Israel on Sinai (Exodus 20:2-17) exhibits a distinctive structure. It opens with a brief statement of God's deliverance of the people from bondage in Egypt, then presents ten fundamental principles of social policy, four demanding exclusive loyalty to God and six concerning key aspects of social-economic relations among Israelites. Inserted into the second and perhaps the fifth principle are blessing-and-curse-like sanctions on keeping the principles (20:5b-6, 12b). The covenant proper is then followed by a covenantal law code or ordinances (Exod 21-23) that apply the basic principles of social policy to social-economic life. The whole is framed by covenant ceremonies (Exod 19 and 24).

The covenant renewal recounted in Joshua 24 exhibits the same structural components. Following the lengthy recitation of what Yahweh has done for

Israel (24:2-13) comes a call and commitment to·exclusive service to Yahweh (24:14-28) that involves obligation to observe "statues and ordinances" (24:24-26), with the people witnessing against themselves (24:22), the setting up of a large stone as a witness (24:26-27), and the threat of punishment for violation of the ordinances (24:19-20). The book of Deuteronomy is structured according to these same components: a recitation of God's deliverance of the people, a sustained body of covenantal laws and ordinances interspersed with covenantal exhortation, followed by a long list of blessings and curses. The book concludes with another recitation of the Mosaic covenant, with emphasis and reminder of God's deliverance and remembering the blessings and curses.

The fundamental structure in all of these covenantal materials is three-fold: a pronouncement of God's deliverance, presentation of covenantal principles, laws, and teachings, and a promise of reward (blessing) for keeping and of punishment (curses) for not keeping those principles, laws, and teachings.

The Mosaic covenant was also simplified and continued in other forms. Already in Deuteronomy covenantal materials were couched in terms of two ways, the way of life and the way of death (30:15-20), in which the blessings and curses became the rewards or punishments that would result from the choice of way. Also as scribal circles began to cultivate mosaic covenantal materials, they identified the wisdom they had traditionally cultivated with the Torah (Prov 1–9; Sir 24). Sayings that might be formally classified as "sapiential," therefore might well be sapientially shaped covenantal teaching. For example, Sirach 29:1 ("The merciful lend to their neighbors; by holding out a helping hand they keep the commandments") perpetuates the central Mosaic covenantal theme stated in Exodus 22:25 of mercy manifested in local economic relations.

Because of the importance of the economic basis of life in an agrarian society, Israelite tradition included in the covenantal statues and ordinances and other covenantal teachings elaborate provisions for maintaining the economic viability of each family in the village community that constituted the fundamental social unit of Israel. Israelites were to give or lend to unfortunate neighbors, and they were to lend without interest (Exod 22:25-27; Deut 15:7-11; Lev 25:35-38). For more serious difficulties of spiraling indebtedness and enslavement for debt, Israel developed the principles of cancellation of debts and release of debt-slaves every seven years (Exod 21:2-6; Deut 15:1-5, 9, 12-18; Lev 24:39-43).

Some traditional covenantal teachings go well beyond case laws for concrete occurrences of violence and injury to address the social tensions and conflicts that fester in social relations and that might lead to violence. For example, the covenantal teaching in Leviticus 19 includes admonitions against holding grudges, harboring resentment, and allowing hate to simmer (19:17-18).

The discovery of texts from the Qumran community has provided a remarkable window onto the continuation of Israelite covenantal tradition, including the remarkable tenacity of the fundamental structure of the covenant.[64] While heavily adapted to suit the apocalyptic perspective and rigorous discipline of the community, the Community Rule from Qumran (1QS and parallels from 4Q) not only includes basic Mosaic covenantal material, but is a renewed Mosaic covenant in form. It even includes instructions for the ceremony of covenant renewal. Remarkably, the document both follows the basic structure of the Mosaic covenant and also adapts that traditional structure in ways that are highly suggestive for our hearing of the longest speech in Q. The key section that runs from 1QS 3:13—4:26 follows the basic three-step structure of the Mosaic covenant. But that whole section also constitutes an overview of the declaration of God's eventual deliverance as a prologue to the remainder of the rule that lays down covenantal rules for the community, its council, and its master (1QS 5:1—11:24).

Moreover, the Damascus Rule also found at Qumran follows the same broad covenantal structure. After the opening prologue reviewing Israel's history under its God (1:1—6:11) come covenantal rulings for the community (6:11—7:4) followed by declarations of long life and salvation for those who keep the covenant and retribution for those who do not (7:4-6, 8-10; and in recension B, 2:28-36). The laws and instructions for community life in the rest of the document appear to flesh out the basic principles of community life, somewhat parallel to the way the covenantal law code in Exodus 21–23 does in the original Mosaic covenant.

Even more significant for our hearing of the speech in Q 6:20-49 are the adaptations made to the covenant components at Qumran. First, in the opening section of instructions for covenant renewal ceremonies, the blessings-and-curses component has shifted function. While still effectively keeping the covenant laws, the blessings and curses now reassure the members of the community of their own redemption by God. In the longer covenantal instruction that follows, the blessings and curses no longer function as closing sanctions, but have been taken up into the declaration of God's deliverance. Thus a declaration of God's deliverance in the present or the future complements or replaces that of God's deliverance in the past as the basis of the people's obligation and motivation to keep the covenantal laws and teachings.

Second, the Scrolls retain the sanction component. The Damascus Rule declares salvation for covenant keepers and destruction for covenant violators, only now without the explicit language of blessings and curses (see further the parallel in Barnabas 21:1).

Third, the Community Rule indicates clearly that renewal of the Mosaic covenant was ceremonially enacted (1QS 5:6-11; 6:14-16). The master or priests and Levites delivered covenantal instruction to the covenantal community. They were literally "blessing the men of the lot of God" and pronouncing "curses on all the men of the lot of Belial." The renewal of the covenant was an annual performance (1QS 2:19-22). Members of the Qumran community, which was literate, wrote this down (with serious variations from manuscript to manuscript). But the written form of covenant renewal was incidental or merely instrumental to oral performance or enactment of covenantal renewal.

Fourth, a number of themes and particular features of covenantal teaching at Qumran may be significant windows onto what other communities might also be doing. The prologue proclaims "an end of injustice" (1QS 4:18-24; cf. Q 6:20-21). The community that holds fast to the renewed covenant "shall practice . . . justice and uprightness and charity and modesty, . . . [and] no stubbornness of heart" (1QS 5:4-6), and the community members "shall love each man his brother as himself; they shall succor the poor, the needy, and the stranger" (CD 6:20-21; cf. Q 6:27-39). No one is to "address a companion with anger or ill-temper . . ." or "hate him, . . . but [is to] rebuke him . . . [and] admonish him in the presence of witnesses (1QS 5:25—6:1; paralleled in CD 7:2-3; 9:2-5; cf. Q 6:37-38; and the closely related Q 17:1-4).

Hearing Q 6:20-49 as a Covenantal Renewal Speech

Once we have refreshed our own cultural memory of what were the likely contents of ancient Israelite tradition, the number of allusions that the speech in Q 6:20-49 makes to Israelite covenantal laws and teaching is striking. Insofar as the Israelite tradition in which Q speeches were grounded was unwritten popular tradition, it is inappropriate to look for "scriptural quotations." Yet insofar as Israelite popular tradition was paralleled in the Jerusalem-based great tradition, one version of which lies behind what we know as the Hebrew Bible, we can catch many of the allusions to Mosaic covenantal tradition from our familiarity with written texts such as Exodus 20–23, Deuteronomy, and Leviticus 19 and 25. "Be merciful, just as your Father is merciful" clearly alludes to or even recites a covenantal principle, such as the one found in Leviticus 19:2. The set of commands and exhortations in Q 6:27-36 remind us of traditional covenantal teaching such as seen in Leviticus 19:17-18, which concludes with the injunction to "love your neighbor." To love your enemy is reminiscent of traditional covenantal teaching such as found in Exodus 23:4-5 and Deuteronomy 22:1-4. The reference to the cloak in the Q commands is clearly an allusion to the garment taken in pledge, dealt with in Exodus 22:25-26 and Deuteronomy 24:10-13 (cf. Amos 2:8). Jesus' command to lend freely is surely a reference to the covenantal command to lend freely, as in Exodus 22:25 and 25:35-38.

These multiple references in the exhortations of Q 6:27-36 to covenantal commands, laws, and ordinances should be sufficient to lead us to listen for other covenantal components in the speech. Matthew's expansion and reshaping of this Q speech, "the Sermon on the Mount," has long been recognized as a covenantal discourse. What about the Q speech Matthew used? In fact, if we simply attend to the structuring elements in Matthew 5–7, which he apparently derived directly from Q, we can recognize the fundamental covenantal components as the structuring elements in Q as well.

To take the more obvious ending of the speech first, "hearing my words and (not) acting upon them" (Q 6:47-49) performs the same function in the Q speech as did the blessings and curses in the early versions of Mosaic covenant (as evident in Deut 27–28). Heard in isolation, the double parable of the houses built on the rock and the sand sounds simply like just another piece of wisdom. In this speech, however, it is framed as a simile to "keeping my words," a term used traditionally for the basic covenantal commands, and it is located structurally as the concluding sanction on covenantal teaching (in the tradition of Exod 21–23; Deut 15; Lev 19). The Damascus Rule and the Epistle of Barnabas (and Deut 30:15-20) provide other examples of the sanction component pronouncing salvation and punishment without the explicit language of blessings and curses.

Blessings and curses, of course, are prominently present in the Q covenant speech. But what formed the closing sanctioning component in the early Mosaic covenantal texts has been transformed in the Q speech into the opening declaration of new deliverance. Even Q interpreters who are convinced that Q 6 is comprised almost exclusively of wisdom instruction admit that the beatitudes are not typical blessings in wisdom materials. And the Community Rule from Qumran provides a clear example of how the blessings and curses component of the covenant could be relocated and transformed into (part of) the prologue as a declaration of God's deliverance expected in the imminent future.

Even from this brief survey it is possible to recognize that the speech in Q 6:20-49 not only makes numerous references to covenantal teaching, but that structurally and substantively the speech constitutes a covenantal discourse standing in a long tradition of covenantal teaching. This also enables us to catch certain indications of the text, context, and register of the speech. The text being performed is the whole speech, not the separate sayings or sections. "Blessed are you who. . ." signals God's new action of deliverance on which the renewal of covenant commands and commitment can be based. And the covenant renewal is not complete until the closing sanctions are delivered in the double parable motivating the hearers to "keep my words." While the speech seems to have five steps or sections, when analyzed somewhat as Hymes blocks out stories in scenes, the overall structure of this covenantal speech has three parts:

> declaration of God's deliverance: "blessed are the poor; woe to the rich," Q 6:20-26

covenantal teaching and admonitions: "love your enemies; do not judge," Q 6:27-36, 37-42

motivation and sanction: "from the fruit a tree is known; houses built," Q 6:43-45, 46-49

Matthew's Sermon on the Mount has the same three-part overall structure: blessings (5:3-16); covenant law and teaching (5:17—7:12); and sanctions (7:13-27).

Within the more general context of the assembly of a movement or community, the particular performance context of this speech is the community's celebration of covenant renewal. In a new movement it is conceivable that this might have been on a weekly basis. The speech, moreover, is clearly in the covenant register. This is evident both in the structural framing components, the blessings and the "keep my words," and in the many covenantal commands and exhortations that allude to traditional covenantal teachings.

What makes the whole speech work is that it references the Israelite covenantal tradition in multiple ways, one after another, on basic economic issues and on troublesome social conflicts that would have been dividing and weakening the village communities. Hearing pronouncement of God's new act of deliverance gives the hearers a new lease on life, renewed hope that their lives will indeed be blessed. And that enables them to then hear the admonitions to get their act together on the basis of the deeply-rooted traditional Israelite covenantal values of mutual sharing and solidarity over against the difficult political-economic circumstances they all have to deal with. It is also important to recognize that the referencing of Israelite covenantal tradition lies not only in all the particular allusions to familiar customary covenantal laws and teachings such as that about a garment taken in pledge, but in the structural components and the very action that is taking place in the performance of the speech. The hearers are invited to resonate with the whole tradition of covenant making and covenant renewal in their culture, from Moses and Joshua to John the Baptist's preaching that preceded Jesus' own. To play with our analytical categories, the communication context and register both reference the tradition and thereby resonate with the hearers in the community that identifies with and lives in and on the basis of that tradition.

In considering the ways in which the hearers would likely have resonated with this speech as it metonymically referenced the popular Israelite covenantal tradition, we may focus on possibilities not evident from other modes of appropriating Q materials. The opening declaration of blessings and woes, for example, would have resonated with people who believed their situation hopeless because they were suffering under the implementation precisely of the covenantal curses. To those who believed themselves unworthy and perhaps even cursed, the speaker proclaimed "yours is the kingdom of God" and then, correspondingly declared that it is the rich who stood under the curses for having violated the covenant.

A major factor in the way that the covenantal speech in Q resonated with its hearers as it referenced covenantal tradition would have been its relevance to their concrete life situation. As noted above, the exhortative content of the speech pertained to local economic and social interaction, evidently in circumstances of poverty, hunger, debt, and multiple social conflicts that were found in village communities. Villagers, who comprised the vast majority of any traditional agrarian society, such as in ancient Palestine and Syria, are always marginal economically, under pressure to render up their produce to multiple layers of rulers, and left with insufficient resources for family and community life. That scarcity—hunger and debt ("Our Father, . . . give us bread. . . and cancel our debts")—leads to internal social tensions and conflicts. The covenantal speech in Q begins with the assurance of God's action in addressing precisely such economic and social distress. The covenantal teachings that reference covenantal tradition through focal instances, such as the garment taken in pledge and generous lending, then challenge and empower the people to renew their own commitments to the communal sharing and mutual support that stood at the basis of traditional Israelite community life. But that tradition and references to it would also have resonated with other, non-Israelite villagers as well. As we can explore in chap 10, comparative studies of other peasantries make clear that the Israelite covenant tradition addressed some of the most fundamental issues faced by villagers nearly anywhere, regardless of their particular cultural-ethnic heritage and language. The covenantal speech in Q and the Mosaic covenantal tradition in which it was rooted and which it referenced would have been easy to identify with and to appropriate by other ancient peoples. And that enables us to understand also how a movement sustained by repeated performance of speeches such as Q 6:20-49 could easily spread from Aramaic-speaking Galilean villages to Greek-speaking villages in southern Syria and beyond.

Chapter
Four

Understanding Mark as Oral Performance

O ne of the exciting innovations in New Testament studies in the last generation has been literary criticism of the Gospel of Mark. Various approaches borrowed from literary studies were applied to the gospel with highly suggestive results for interpretation. Biblical scholars even generated their own distinctive brand of narrative criticism. And reader response criticism made an important contribution of new insights into Mark.

But what if the supposed first "readers" of Mark could not read? What if virtually no one involved in the Jesus movement from which the gospel originated could read or write? In fact, what if almost no text of literature in antiquity was actually read? Interpretation of the Gospel of Mark, like the field of New Testament studies generally, will soon have to come to grips with the fact that oral communication was dominant in antiquity and that texts were inscribed on memories as much as on papyri and that texts were usually performed rather than read.

Limited Literacy

Virtually no one in antiquity could read and write, except for a few aristocrats and scribes. In classical Athens, where the leisure of the elite was underwritten by slave labor, the rate of literacy may have risen to between five and ten percent of the overall population.[1] In the Roman Empire, the rate was probably under ten percent. The best evidence comes from papyri preserved in the sands of Egypt. The vast number of papyri, written largely by professional scribes, indicate that the vast majority of male and almost all female artisans and farmers were illiterate, in their indigenous language as well as in Greek. Even the village scribes, evidently unique to Egypt as the lowest level of an elaborate government bureaucracy, did not have to be literate. The village clerk of Ptolemais Hormou named Petaus, for example, apparently never learned even to sign his name without using a model.[2]

Literacy corresponded to social location in classical Greece and in the Roman Empire generally. The wealthy and powerful Roman patricians used writing to control the inheritance of property, with records of large loans, wills, and marriage contracts. Aristocrats with social ambition patronized literary culture. The urban elite of the Roman Empire, while generally literate, often had specially trained slaves handle heir correspondence and read aloud to them rather than read and write themselves.[3] For the vast majority of people, writing was simply unnecessary, whether in everyday life or for special occasions such as weddings and funerals. Most transactions, including buying and selling, were conducted orally in face-to-face interaction.[4]

Oral communication was no less dominant and literacy no less limited in ancient Judean and Galilean society. Scholars in biblical studies and related fields, dedicated to the study of Hebrew and Christian Scriptures, while often acknowledging the limits of literacy in ancient Greece and Rome, continue to trust old generalizations about high rates of literacy and use of written texts among ancient Jews.[5] "According to Josephus, in first-century Judaism it was a duty, indeed a religious commandment, that Jewish children be taught to read. . . . [R]abbinic sources suggest. . . there is little question that by the first century C.E. Judaism had developed a strong interest in basic literacy and that even small communities had elementary schools."[6] The passages from Josephus that supposedly attest Jewish children being taught to read, however, indicate rather that the teaching and learning of the laws was carried out by public oral recitation (at sabbath assemblies). Those passages thus also indicate both that Jewish communities were largely non-literate and that communication of the most important matters was oral. Writing in these passages, moreover, is conceived to operate in an almost magical way: by hearing the sacred laws taught aloud, the laws would become "engraved on their souls . . . and guarded in heir memory" (*Ant.* 4.210; 16:43; *Ag. Ap.* 2.175, 178, 204; cf. Philo, *Embassy* 115, 210). "To learn *grammata*" in *Ag. Ap.* 2.204, in the context of the study of the law, suggests not learning to read, but learning Scripture, which is done through public oral teaching, as indicated earlier at *Ag. Ap.* 2.175. Rabbinic passages previously cited to attest general literacy and the ubiquity of schools refer, in fact, only to the tiny circles of the rabbis themselves, and rabbinic texts that supposedly attested people reading refer instead to reciting certain psalms and prayers from memory.[7]

In Judea and Galilee, as in the rest of the Roman Empire, writing was used primarily by the political and cultural elite. Officials in the Herodian administrations in Jerusalem and the two cities of Galilee were presumably literate in Greek. Scribes and Pharisees, retainers of the Temple administration in Jerusalem, were literate in Hebrew and presumably Aramaic as well. But the vast majority of Judeans and Galileans would not have been literate in any language.[8]

The Relation of Writing to Oral Communication

If the vast majority of people in antiquity were nonliterate, then interpreters of texts need to rethink the relationship between a text, such as the Gospel of Mark, and its audience. Modern assumptions about literacy and books are inappropriate to the gospel or any other ancient text. The appropriate focus is the relationship between the text and its audience, who must have been listeners in a predominantly oral communication environment.

Nearly all literature in Greek and Roman antiquity would have been performed or recited orally, not read, at least not read privately, as is the modern practice in book culture. All types of ancient poetry were sung or chanted. The words comprised only a part of the overall performance, which included accompaniment on a musical instrument, such as a lyre or flute, and perhaps dance as well. Greek and Latin plays were performed publicly in theatres. Both poetry and plays were performed on special occasions for which they were customary: hymns at public religious festivals, victory odes at games, elegies at private symposia, dirges at funerals.[9]

Some of these texts may have been written down, but not necessarily for reading. The writing down of texts must be understood in the broader context of continuing oral performance and aural hearing, with a fluid relationship between composition, performance, and written text. Aristophanes' description of poets in the process of composition makes no mention of pen and papyrus (Acharnians 383-479; Thesmophoriazusae 95-265).[10] Apparently the poet composed in his head prior to or during the process of rehearsal for performance. A written copy was probably made afterwards, and recorded only one aspect of the performance, which involved music and dance as well as words. Even ancient philosophy, which seems to us moderns such dense discourse, was orally cultivated, the later written texts being an echo of oral give and take, often dialogue, perhaps a teacher's summary or a student's notes.[11]

Many texts were indeed written down. But in a time long before the invention of the printing press, there were no publishers and no mass production. Papyrus or parchment rolls were extremely expensive and very cumbersome, and copying by hand time consuming. Since no spaces were left between words, it was difficult to follow texts with the eyes and especially to locate specific passages.[12] To read aloud from an ancient scroll would have required considerable familiarity with the content. Even if the contents of ancient drama or poetry was in some cases transmitted with the aid of written texts, traditional performance continued for centuries, with each successive generation learning from the older one. The availability of written texts did nothing to disrupt the continuity of oral performance. Even narrative history continued in public performance.[13] "There was no such thing as 'popular literature' in the Roman Empire, . . . Greek romances [being] the light reading of a limited public possessing a degree or education."[14] This suggests that the Gospel of Mark cannot be explained as a kind of popular writing.[15] Ordinary people had no need for literacy in order to experience literature. They had plenty of opportunities, at public places, especially at festivals and games, to hear storytellers relating Aesop's fables, poets singing poems, and historians recounting their histories. In antiquity literature was regularly heard rather than read by its audience.

The relationship between written text and oral-aural cultivation of texts was only somewhat different in Judea and Galilee. The development of sacred writing on scrolls in Judea played an important role, especially among the literate elite, in the cultivation of cultural tradition. But the cultivation remained predominantly oral-aural.

The ancient Athenians inscribed new laws on stones erected as public memorials of the legislation, along with curses sanctioning their authority. Somewhat analogously, the ranking priests and scribes in the Jerusalem Temple state wrote laws and narrative legitimating the temple-state on parchment scrolls that were then laid up in the Temple, thus shrouded in mystery, hidden from the people. In its periodic ceremonial presentation and reading, the scroll of the teaching of Moses commanded authority as a numinous sacred object of veneration almost iconic in function (for example, Nehemiah 8). The reading was oral, and because it was in a strange archaic language (Hebrew), it required interpretation by the Levites. Such sacred scrolls may have become more familiar to Judeans through regular presentation and recitation, although we have precious little evidence for such. Scrolls of "the laws of Moses" existed in at least some first-century Judean and Galilean towns. Josephus mentions such a scroll burned by Roman soldiers in a Judean village, and tells of a heckler in the Galilean town of Tarichaeae holding up a copy of "the laws of Moses" (*J.W.* 2.229; *Life* 134-35). Because they were so costly and cumbersome, however, it is highly unlikely that many villages had such a scroll or an assembly building in which to house it (nearly all synagogue buildings dug up by archaeologists date from centuries later).

Israelite culture, including texts of Torah, prophets, and psalms, continued to be cultivated in memory and oral communication. Even the literate elite, such as the Essenes at Qumran, the Pharisees, and the later rabbis, cultivated Israelite cultural traditions primarily in oral recitation, as Judean texts themselves indicate. The Qumran community left many scrolls (the Dead Sea Scrolls), including scrolls of their own compositions. The latter, however, attest the intense oral-aural life of the community, from ceremonies of covenantal induction to recitation of texts of Torah. Community members composed and recited hymns and blessings at communal meals and meetings (1QSa 2:21-23; 1QH; 1QSb=1Q28b; 4Q408; 4Q503; 4Q507–509). They delivered sapiential exhortation and they rehearsed holy war (4QS184–185; 1QM). Many of scrolls they produced are written copies of (often regular) oral performances and rituals. Insofar as the leaders of the community were performing the ceremonies and presenting the teachings written down in the Community Rule on a regular basis, they would hardly have needed to consult a written text.[16]

The Pharisees, who were presumably literate, were known for their cultivation of "regulations (*nomima*) from the teachings of the fathers which were not recorded in the laws of Moses," regulations that were included in the official laws of the Jerusalem temple-state (Josephus, *Ant.* 13.297, 408-09). Such oral cultivation of cultural contents, including Torah, continued into later rabbinic circles. While written texts were preserved, their use in instruction was discouraged. "Rather, the exposition of Sages' teachings took place in a highly ritualized setting designed to recreate and represent an original imparting or oral tradition from Moses to his disciples. . . . Within such a milieu, written texts enjoyed an essentially oral cultural life. . . ."[17]

Oral Cultivation of Israelite Cultural Tradition as Evident in the Gospel of Mark

If the cultivation of Israelite cultural traditions was predominantly oral even among the literate groups such as the scribes and Pharisees, then cultivation of the popular Israelite traditions was most certainly oral in village communities and popular movements. The standard assumptions and generalizations in biblical studies about the presence and function of written texts in the context of Jesus' ministry and the composition of the Gospels are simply anachronistic. Since scrolls were so costly and cumbersome and since villagers were generally not literate, for example, it is highly unlikely that the source of Jesus' "knowledge of Scripture" was hearing "Scripture read aloud."[18] The usual proof text for Jesus' supposed literacy, "The Spirit of the Lord is upon me. . ." to "read. . ." in Luke 4:16-20 is Luke's projection of literacy onto Jesus.

While villagers such as Jesus and his followers were almost certainly not literate, they were well acquainted with Israelite cultural traditions.[19] Evidence for this is scarce, of course, since non-literate peasants rarely left any textual remains. The Gospels are some of the only cases in history of popular movements having produced texts that survived in written form. But popular movements do leave indirect evidence. Such evidence, from outside the Gospels, survives in Josephus' accounts of the popular messianic and prophetic movements, whose forms were informed, respectively, by popular cultural memories and traditions of David as anointed ("messiah-ed") by the people to lead them against the Philistines and Moses and Joshua leading the exodus through the water and entry into the land.[20] Josephus also provides evidence from the revolt in 66–67 C.E. that the Galilean peasants were adamant about observance of the covenantal commandments.[21] What the Galilean villagers cultivated is what anthropologists would refer to as the Israelite "little tradition," as distinct from the Judean "great tradition." While parallel and sharing much in common, these would have been cultivated at different social-political levels of Judean and Galilean society for centuries. Insofar as the high priests and their representatives attempted to induce or force the peasants to observe many provisions of the official tradition (what Josephus calls "the laws of the Judeans," which they forced the Galileans to obey after their takeover of Galilee in 104 B.C.E.), there would have been at least some interaction between the popular and the elite versions of Israelite tradition.

As we attempt to come to grips with the origins of the Gospel of Mark in popular culture, informed by Galilean Israelite popular tradition, we can fruitfully probe the text for evidence of the oral cultivation of Israelite tradition. Mark's Gospel makes many references to Israelite tradition, and many of them have been taken as quotations of or allusions to Scripture (that is, authoritative written texts). Many of these, however, should never even have been considered quotations. Jesus' entry into Jerusalem riding on a colt alludes to an Israelite tradition about a king coming to the people riding on an ass, but that does not imply access to and consultation of a scroll of Zechariah. Jesus' reference to David and his men eating bread from the altar is at serious variance with the story known from the best manuscripts of 2 Samuel. The numerous allusions in Mark's passion narrative are to well-known psalms and prophecies, not to written scrolls. Other references are to what a character said, and not to written texts (such as Mark 10:4; 11:9-10; 12:36). And some references are to the most basic principles that would have been widely known among Judeans and Galileans (Mark 7:9-10; 10:19). Even in some cases that are presented explicitly as citations, the words clearly come from memory, not written texts. Mark 1:2-3, for example, ostensibly quotes Isaiah. But the "quote" begins with lines that resemble Exodus 23:20 and Malachi 3:1, and not anything in Isaiah. Now that we are aware of the operation of popular tradition, the likely explanation is that such a composite recitation comes from popular cultivation of Israelite popular tradition rather than consultation of a written scroll.

It is understandable that, in the field of biblical studies so deeply embedded in the assumptions of print culture, the passages in Mark's narrative introduced with the formulaic "it is written" or "Scripture" (*gegraptai* and *graphe*), have been taken as quotations of written texts. This must now obviously be considered in the light of the function of sacred writing in Judea as well as the predominantly oral cultivation of Israelite tradition. In ancient Greece the laws and decrees passed by the city-state assembly were inscribed on public monuments. The purpose was to embody the authority of the laws, not to make them available for public reading or reference. Professional "rememberers" were consulted when accurate references to the laws were required.[22] The corresponding representation of the authority of the laws in Judean society was the inscription of texts of Torah on scrolls that were then laid up in the Temple. The account of Ezra presenting and reciting from the "document of the laws of Moses" in Nehemiah 8 provides a paradigmatic case of the aura of authority that adhered to the written law of the temple-state. The Scriptures, that is, authoritative written texts of the Torah or one of the books of the prophets were symbolic of the *authority* of the text in writing (and housed in the Temple). It seems highly likely that many of the references to "it is written" or "Scripture" in Judean texts and early "Christian" texts are to the *authority* and not to the wording of such a written text. To take an example from the earliest text of Jesus materials, when Jesus, in discussing John the Baptist in Q and Luke 7:27 says "it is written," he must be referring to the authority of the text, since it is quite unclear what particular lines in what text he is citing. Similarly in the temptation story in Q and Luke 4:1-13, "as it is written" must be a reference to the authority of the Scripture rather than a quotation formula or a reference to a particular passage in a written scroll. Furthermore, in cases where a text is being cited in Mark or in Q, it is being cited from (popular) memory.[23]

Some of the ostensible citations of Scripture in Mark invite us to go a step further. Once we are aware of the parallel but variant popular and elite versions of Israelite tradition, we must ask whose authority is being referenced in the ostensible citations. If we look closely at some of the episodes in which Jesus cites Scripture ("it is written"), it is evident that he is polemically throwing it back in the face of the scribes and Pharisees, the guardians and expert interpreters of the written texts. This is what is happening when he cites Isaiah against the Pharisees' "traditions of the elders," and a "Jeremiah" prophecy and a festival psalm against the priestly rulers of the Temple. Jesus, representative of the popular oral tradition, throws at the rulers and their representatives the very authoritative texts that they claim as legitimation for their power. In Mark 9:12-13, he appeals to the authority of Scripture in general against the scribal authorities on Scripture; in Mark 10:3-5, Jesus throws a reference to Moses' laws back at the Pharisees; and in 12:18-27, he refers to the written text of Moses against the Sadducees, who accepted only the written Torah. It begins to appear that, in most of the explicit references to Scripture in Mark, Jesus is citing the elite who claim it as authorization for their power over the people. The latter was precisely one of the main uses of writing in ancient Judea and the Roman Empire generally, according to the extensive recent studies mentioned at the outset. In village communities and in popular movements, on the other hand, Israelite tradition was cultivated (remembered and recited) orally. This is precisely what was happening in Mark's gospel. If Scripture was being cited orally, from memory, in Mark, however, is there any reason to believe that Mark itself was written and being read?

Recognition of Orality in the Synoptic Tradition and Mark

The pioneers of form criticism, Rudolf Bultmann and Martin Dibelius, differentiated the synoptic gospel tradition from *belle lettres*. Influenced by the Romantic tradition of the Brothers Grimm, as mediated through the work of Hermann Gunkel on oral tradition behind the Old Testament, they viewed the synoptic gospel tradition rather as *Kleinliteratur* that had arisen from the anonymous matrix of the people. They viewed synoptic materials as communally shaped and shared folk traditions, arising out of typical situations in the life of a religious community. Unlike Gunkel, however, Bultmann did not engage in a study of folk traditions in order to derive a model for analysis of the synoptic gospel tradition. Rather he derived the tendencies supposedly followed by the oral gospel tradition from the way that Matthew and Luke handled Mark and Q. Ironically, Bultmann thus used the model of how literary authors handled their already written sources as a model for the tendencies of supposedly oral tradition.[24] Even perceptive critics of Bultmann considered the distinction between the oral and the written irrelevant: "the tendencies of the one are presumably the tendencies of the other."[25] Form criticism thus in effect worked on a model of literary editing and composition based on free-floating Jesus sayings. Form critics never really considered how genuinely oral cultivation worked in a traditional oral communication environment.

Werner Kelber almost single-handedly pioneered the effort to break through the print-oriented hermeneutic in our study of the Bible.[26] In a highly innovative work, he sounded a long overdue wake-up call for Gospel studies to take oral communication seriously. In countering the prevailing tendency to perceive the written gospel in continuity with oral tradition conceived on a literary model, Kelber adapted the theory of orality versus literacy developed by Walter Ong and others.[27] Most important, he replaced form criticism's literary model for the oral transmission of Jesus traditions with an illuminating analysis of orality as a distinctive mode of communication. In opposition to the notion of a passive transmission of Jesus sayings, he insisted that social context was an essential factor—thus expanding on an insight of early form criticism that had subsequently been forgotten by its later practitioners. Most remarkable, perhaps, is that Kelber accomplished his pioneering breakthrough without the benefit of recent investigations of the low degree of literacy and the predominantly oral medium of communication in antiquity. With the advantage of hindsight, and subsequent studies of the relations between writing and oral communication, it is possible to recognize how certain assumptions of New Testament studies have simply blocked the extension to Mark of some of the insights Kelber developed.

Others picked up on the innovative investigation that Kelber had started. Appreciating how residual oral communication was in antiquity, Joanna Dewey applied Eric Havelock's and Walter Ong's analysis of orality to the Gospel of

Mark itself. She suggested not only that Mark used oral materials but that Mark composed for a listening audience using techniques of oral composition.[28] Picking up Ong's and Havelock's observations about particular features of oral narratives,[29] Dewey emphasized the additive content and aggregative structure of Mark, its agonistic tone, and especially its participatory character.[30] Mark displays the very characteristics that Plato attacked as the mere *doxa* (opinion) of the poets' mimesis: "happenings" (in which teaching is embedded, not explicit), "the visible," and "the many" (the additive "one thing after another").[31] Typical of the chaining style of oral narrative are the many prospective and retrospective references in Mark that "interweave and integrate disparate and episodic" materials. Dewey's portrayal of the oral features of Mark's narrative suggests that questions pursued in recent literary criticism of Mark, which still works on the assumptions of print culture, are not appropriate if the gospel is to be understood in its historical context, where oral communication was dominant.[32]

While Dewey gave attention to participation of hearers, dependence on Ong's and Havelock's studies of orality led to a focus mainly on the features and techniques of oral composition, with relatively little attention to meaning in context. Dewey also seemed to downplay the political conflict and struggle in the political-social context of composition. The sharp conflict between Jesus and the Jerusalem rulers and their Pharisaic and scribal representatives that dominates Mark cannot be explained as simply part of the agonistic tone of an oral narrative. It must also be at least partly a reflection of the historical situation, judging from the conflict between other prophetic and messianic leaders and the Jerusalem and Roman rulers, as represented in extra-gospel sources such as Josephus' histories. Contrary to the typical modern Christian discipleship reading of Mark, moreover, Mark portrays a criticism of the disciples that cannot be ascribed simply to agonistic oral-narrative style or the hearers placing themselves in the roles of all the participants.[33] If, as Dewey argues, oral composition was done for hearing not by an individual but by a group in a particular historical context, then Jesus' conflict with the disciples, particularly Peter, James, and John, portrayed in Mark more likely reflects a historical conflict between the Markan audience and the disciples.

While Kelber thought that the asymmetrical oral utterances of Jesus sayings were implicitly analogous to the performances of the singers of tales studied by Parry and Lord, he insisted that the latters' oral-formulaic theory could not be directly applied "in contemplating the feasibility of an oral gospel."[34] The oral-formulaic theory, with its focus on formulas and themes used in oral performance, had been used, often in rather wooden fashion, to test literatures from a variety of cultures for their oral features. Kelber thus appropriately rejected the search for "direct correspondences" between metrical oral epic poetry and the prose-narrative gospels. Pieter Botha then explored the indirect applicability of oral-formulaic theory to Mark. "The true impact of the theory does not lie in testing for orality."[35] It can be used to illuminate the distinctive features of Mark as composed and recited 'oral literature.'[36] Botha looked not for the formulas ("fixed verbal and metrical combinations") and themes ("repeated incidents and descriptive passages") that directly match those in the Iliad, but for those distinctive to Mark's narrative.[37] As he notes, some of the formulas in Mark do not so much "contain meaning in themselves" as "signal knowledge that is already shared" with the hearers.[38] Certain words, images, and references are used to draw on a whole range of experience shared with the hearers, who thus resonate with the message or story delivered by the performer.

The explorations of Kelber, Dewey, and Botha are foundational and suggestive for further work on Mark as oral performance. The contrast between oral tradition and written redaction or composition as quite separate stages and processes previously elaborated in Gospel studies has been too sharply drawn.[39] The features of oral communication that Kelber discerned in pre-Markan and Q materials are also evident in Mark. As an oral-derived text or an oral composition, Mark stands in continuity with the oral cultivation of Jesus stories and Jesus teachings, only not in the linear print model followed by the form critics. The evangelists (teachers or prophets) who regularly recited or performed the Jesus stories and Jesus teachings had no need to memorize them. They were not simply the carriers or bearers of the synoptic gospel tradition, they were organically part of it. As regular performers, they were composing on the basis of what was already familiar.

Accordingly, exploration of gospel materials and Mark as oral performance and oral-derived texts will expand the scope of inquiry into the Gospels and synoptic gospel tradition significantly. Previous study of the oral tradition of Jesus materials has focused narrowly on transmission and preservation, and recent study of the Gospels has focused on the redactors' theologies and the particular evangelists' composition. Recently revived rhetorical criticism has sensitized us to the rhetorical situation of texts. The realization that Mark may have been orally composed drives us further into social and historical contexts and the corresponding political and relational circumstances. Texts such as Mark were performed or read aloud in communities, which entailed particular cultural background and were involved in particular political contingencies. As Kelber has recently insisted, "gospel composition is unthinkable without the notion of cultural memory, which serves ultimately not the preservation of remembrances per se but the preservation of the group, its social identity, and self-image. Mark avails himself of rich cultural memory. . . ."[40] In an oral communication environment, such cultural memory can be maintained only in and through performance. The focus of inquiry into the synoptic gospel tradition and Mark's narrative must be broadened far beyond mere transmission of Jesus' sayings, for the latter is only an accident of the cultivation of cultural memory that takes place in repeated performance.

Approaching the Gospel of Mark as Oral Performance

Embedded as it is in the assumptions and approaches of print culture, biblical studies leaves us unprepared to appreciate Mark or any other text as oral performance. Scholars in related fields such as the Greek classics, medieval European epic poems, and Native American storytelling, however, have developed approaches that may be helpful to us. The leading theorist of oral poetry, John Miles Foley, drawing upon recent studies in several fields, along with reflections in social linguistics, presents reflections that are particularly suggestive for dealing with oral-derived texts such as Mark's gospel.[41]

Considering that Mark's story was performed before communities in a particular historical context, the key questions to ask may be not what is meant by words and verses and pericopes, but how the performed text resonated with the audience. Our approach must hold together all aspects of performance (or communication): the text performed, the audience, and the context (broadly understood), since the text did not mean something in itself, but only as an act of communication. Perhaps Foley's distinctive and most important observation is that the performed text or message resonates with the audience on the basis of their situation and experience, including their cultural tradition. This is in contrast to modern literature written in print culture, where the author as individual writer manipulates inherited or idiosyncratic materials from an original perspective, conferring meaning on a fresh new literary creation. An oral performer, on the other hand, performing an already familiar story, summons conventional connotations of cultural traditions, evoking in the hearers a meaning that is inherent. Such inherent meaning, moreover, cannot be stated by modern interpreters in so many words because it is relational to the hearers in the context, requiring situational appreciation rather than interpretation.

The key to how a performed text resonates with the hearers is that certain images or phrases or statements evoke a whole range of connotations. In such metonymic referencing, the part evokes or stands for the whole in and from the cultural tradition shared by performer and audience. For example, for many Americans hearing the phrase "We hold these truths to be self-evident" summons up the values they hold dear as well as the foundational events of the Declaration of Independence, the Revolutionary War, and the Constitution of the United States. For the hearers of the Gospel of Mark, the episodes of the sea crossings and wilderness feedings would presumably have evoked memory of the exodus and wilderness journey to the promised land, the formative events of the people of Israel. Or hearing that the name of the demon that had caused extreme violence to its host and his community was named "Legion" would have evoked the experience of being conquered and controlled by the Roman army. The key to how the orally performed text resonates with the audience is thus its metonymic referencing of their cultural tradition. Taking a leaf from the notebook of sociolinguistics about how communication happens, three other aspects are closely interrelated with the metonymic referencing of cultural tradition: the *text*, or what the performer performs, the *context*, or the situation in which the performance occurs, and the *register*, or the kind of communication appropriate to the particular type of communication context. We will focus mainly on the *text* of Mark below. But since the *context* and *register* of communication are so important, a brief discussion of each may help us understand the text of Mark as oral performance.

Context

We all take our cues for how we receive a message from the context. The context gives us certain expectations. At a funeral, we expect to hear words about the deceased and to feel sympathy for the family. At the ballpark, we do not expect to hear a Mozart symphony. During the performance of a play, changes of scene determine how we hear the dialogue. Similarly a church worship service moves from one communication subcontext to another, signaled by key phrases or even cues from the organ. Form criticism focused on too narrow a context (*Sitz-im-Leben*)—and too fragmented a text—for the cultivation of Jesus traditions. The Greek terms *ekklēsia* and *synagōgē* both referred to a village or town assembly that dealt with all manner of community self-governance as well as religious ceremonies. Meetings of such assemblies, in which the Gospel was likely performed, would thus have been more like meetings in the civil rights or labor movement than the modern church service. Assembly meetings would thus have dealt with more than just worship. In addition to discussion of how to respond to political repression by the rulers, delegation of representatives to expand the movement to other villages, and keeping the movement egalitarian, they surely celebrated the Lord's Supper. But of course the Gospel of Mark deals with all of those and more (see especially Mark 8:34-38 and 13:9-13; 6:7-13 and 10:10; 10:35-45; and 14:22-25). Thus the subcontexts of hearing the Gospel performed evoked, touched upon, and overlapped other subcontexts in community meetings of the Jesus movement. The implication for the modern readers who want to appreciate Mark as oral performance is that they become as familiar as possible with the historical situation of the hearers of Mark so that they can attend a performance of the gospel in the appropriate context.

Register

This is the term that some sociolinguists use for the particular styles or configurations of speech associated with the particular types of communication contexts. We are familiar with distinctive registers of speech or music for weddings, funerals, or political rallies. Sociolinguists find three aspects of such speech linked to particular contexts important: what is being transacted, the relations among the participants, and the mode of communication (oral or written). Especially for oral communication, the register of communication, which is concrete, is far more important than a determination of literary genre, which is abstract. Even if we had consensus about Mark's genre (biography, history, and so forth), we would still need to have some sense of the particular registers in which Mark's Jesus speaks and acts. When the focus is on the Temple, Jesus speaks and acts in a prophetic register of indictment and condemnation. In its prolonged narrative Mark has adapted standard traditional registers familiar from Israelite tradition—which modern readers would need to know far better in order to be clued into what is happening in the story.

The Gospel of Mark as Oral Performance: The Text

Like nearly all texts in antiquity, the Gospel of Mark must have been performed before a group. And since it was impossible for someone to follow undivided words on a parchment scroll or papyrus roll without already being familiar with the text, the gospel must have been performed from memory, not read aloud from a written text. Comparative studies of oral performance have shown that each performance of a text is somewhat different from others, yet the overall structure of the poem or narrative and most of the wording remains the same. If we are interested in appreciating Mark as oral performance, then it makes sense to focus broadly on the overall story, not on the meaning of particular words and pericopes, as we have been trained to do in biblical studies. The details, critically considered, will become important only in the sequence of episodes that make up the whole gospel.

While the original composition of Mark is not in focus here, it may help to imagine, on the basis of earlier studies, how the overall gospel story emerged. Werner Kelber has provided a most illuminating investigation of the oral storytelling behind Mark.[42] The gospel can no longer be thought of as a bunch of independently circulating stories strung together end to end. It is too complexly plotted for that. Yet from what we know of composition of texts in antiquity, it seems highly unlikely that some single author, following a generic model of biography or history in an unprecedented act of creativity, composed the gospel *de novo*. The overall narrative of Mark would appear, rather, to have developed out of earlier collections or narratives comprised of shorter component stories. Certain sections of Mark's overall narrative appear to incorporate or to adapt already existing oral texts such as a collection of parables, chains of stories of acts of power (behind 4:35—8:26), a sequence of healing and pronouncement stories (2:1—3:6), and a prophetic discourse (behind chapter 13). Whether

Mark adapted an already performed account of Jesus' arrest, trial, crucifixion, and resurrection is still hotly debated.

In attempting to hear the gospel as an oral performance, we must still work from the written text before us in koine Greek or in various translations. On the analogy of music, however, we can learn to look at the written text of Mark as the mere libretto of the performance, and then use our educated imagination to appreciate the possible extra-textual aspects of performance such as gestures, facial expressions, varying volume, emphases, pauses, pace, and so on. Whitney Shiner has presented a well-researched exploration of how to imagine Mark having been performed, judging from what we know of performance of texts in antiquity.[43] It would help immensely to view a recorded performance of the gospel, such as a performance by David Rhoads.[44] Better yet, witness a live performance of Mark, now more and more frequently available, perhaps by a member of the Network of Biblical Story Tellers.[45]

Cross-cultural studies of performance are especially helpful in appreciating the dramatic flow and patterning of the gospel narrative. Traditional Serbian and Bosnian singers of epic poems told Parry and Lord that the "word" they sang was, alternatively, a set of lines, a speech, a scene, or even a whole epic. The lines they sang were of ten syllables, not a single word, as in the printed texts we are accustomed to reading.[46] Recent analysis of Native American storytelling is particularly suggestive for imagining a performed text of Mark. In performance or in written transcripts, such stories have sequential patterns that we might call, on the basis of traditional poetry and plays, lines, verses, stanzas, scenes, and acts.[47] In Mark the episodes of healing, exorcism, or controversies with the Pharisees are the fundamental narrative components that correspond to the stanzas or scenes of the Native American storytellers or the ancient Greek or Serbian epic singers. The episodes include proverbs, sayings, dialogues, or citations of Scripture. But those are intelligible only as components of the episodes as the fundamental units of narrative communication.

Cross-cultural comparisons also enable us to appreciate that these episodes do not stand on their own as independent units of communication, but are components of a much longer narrative which is plotted in a particular sequence to tell an overall story. That complex story of Mark's gospel, moreover, flows in a sequence of acts as the drama unfolds. As elementary steps in appreciating the text of Mark as oral performance, we will first consider some of the striking (and often strange) features of the oral narrative style of Mark. Then, most important, we will consider the overall flow and coherence of the gospel story in a sequence of acts interspersed with speeches. Then we can examine some of the patterns within the acts of the drama.

"Just One Thing after Another"

When assigned to read Mark all the way through in one sitting, my students—like other modern readers—would observe that the story seemed like "just one thing after another," with no evident connection between the episodes. Living in print culture they were accustomed to reading modern authors who set up causative, temporal, and other relations between clauses. Traditional oral narrators, however, simply told one episode after another and, within episodes, spoke one clause after another, with no explicit indications of interrelationship. Plato complained that Greek poetry consisted merely of multiple "happenings," many things with no cause and effect.[48] Oral narrative is additive, or paratactic, with simple "ands" linking line to line and episode to episode. Most episodes in Mark begin with *kai* ("and"), and many lines within episodes also begin with *kai*. Mark's narrative is also full of stereotypical connective devices such as *archesthai* with infinitive verbs ("began to"; 1:45; 2:23; etc.), adverbial *euthys* and *kai euthys* ("(and) immediately"; 1:29; 3:6; etc.), the iterative *palin* and *kai palin* ("(and) again"; 2:1; 7:31; etc.), and the formulas *kai ginetai* and *kai egeneto* ("and it happened"; 1:9; 2:15; etc.).[49] The full effect of the additive or paratactic style of Mark has been moderated in most English translations by paraphrasing with subordinate (temporal or causative) clauses in order to render a more familiar English style. To appreciate the full effect, therefore, one must use the Greek text.

Perhaps the most salient feature of oral performance of all kinds is the repetition of words and sounds, even phrases, from line to line, verse to verse. Again this is often missed in translation. Such repetition aids the memorial storytelling and the listening audience. Thought intertwined with patterns of memory also typically comes to expression in "repetitions or antitheses, in alliterations and assonances, in epithetic and other formulary expressions, in standard thematic settings (the assemblies, the meal, etc.), in proverbs which come to mind readily. . . ."[50] Such oral features as the paratactic *kai* and the repetition of sounds in Mark can be illustrated from an early episode (Mark 1:21-28) printed in transliteration (with the *kai*'s and some of the repeated words and sounds italicized), so that those who cannot read Greek script can read it aloud, listening to their own voice (and looking at the italicized "sounds") to appreciate these features.

*kai eis*poreuontai *eis* Kapharnaoum
kai euthys tois sabbasin *eis*ēlthon *eis tēn synagōgēn edidask*en.
kai exeplēssonto epi tē *didachē autou*
en gar *didask*ōn autous *hōs exousian* echōn
kai ouch *hōs* hoi grammateis.
kai euthys en *tē synagōgē* autōn anthrōpos en pneumati akathartō

kai anekraxen legōn:

ti hēmin kai soi, *Iēsou* Nazarēne?

Ēlthes apolesai hēmas?

Oida se tis ei, ho hagios *tou* the*ou*.

kai epetimēsen *autō* ho *Iēsous*:

phimōthēti kai *exelthe ex autou*.

Kai sparaxan *auton* to *pneuma* to *akatharton*

*kai phōnē*san *phōnē* megalē *exēlthen ex autou*.

kai ethambēthēsan hapantes

Hōste syzētein *autous* legontas:

ti estin touto?

Didachē kainē kat' *exousian*?

Kai tois *pneumasi tois akathartois* epitassei

Kai hypakouousin autō.

Kai exēlthen hē akoē autou *euthys* pantachou

Eis holēn tēn perichōron tēs Galileias.

Narrative Steps and Coherence of the Overall Story

While it does not have a suspenseful plot like many modern novels, Mark does present an escalating conflict that moves toward a climax in a series of major steps. The story unfolds in five major steps, with speeches in between the first and second and the fourth and fifth. After a brief prologue that introduces Jesus as a fulfillment of prophecy (Mark 1:1-13) and his announcement that the kingdom of God is at hand (the theme of the whole story, 1:14-15), he launches a series of exorcisms, healings, and debates with scribes and Pharisees in Galilee (1:14—3:35). The action then pauses for a speech in parables explaining or calling for recognition of mystery of the kingdom (4:1-34). Action expands from Galilee into the regions of Tyre, Caesarea Philippi, and the Decapolis in sea crossings, more exorcisms and healings, wilderness feedings, and disputes with the Pharisees (4:35—8:26). In the third major step of the narrative Jesus announces three times that he must be killed (and rise again) and delivers important teaching to his disciples in response to their escalating misunderstanding, as he moves into Judea, toward Jerusalem (8:22—10:52). After he rides up into Jerusalem, Jesus prophetically confronts the chief priests and scribes in the Temple, where they are based (11:1—13:2). Jesus then delivers a second speech, about the future. In the climactic final act of the drama, as Jesus declares at the Passover meal with his disciples, he is betrayed, arrested, abandoned, tried, and crucified (14–15). The story then has an open ending, or non-ending, with the empty tomb and the direction of the disciples—and the hearers of the gospel—back to Galilee where Jesus will meet them (16:1-8).

These five main acts in the drama are linked by overlapping episodes and repetition of types of episodes and main themes. Somewhat as in Greek drama and poetry, Markan narrative seems to "operate on the acoustic principle of the echo,"[51] that works both by anticipation and recollection in the course of the story. "The narrative turns back on itself, as it were, assisting the memory to reach the end by having it anticipated somehow in the beginning."[52] Earlier episodes forecast later ones, which in turn recall the earlier ones, while bringing the story further and adding to the drama and, often, conflict. Numerous connections resonate back and forth through the overall narrative even as they resonate with the audience by referencing the cultural tradition.

One of the most obvious examples of anticipation and repetition, the episode of Rock's (Peter's) declaration that Jesus is "the Messiah" (8:27-30), is introduced in the same way as the story of John the Baptist's execution by Herod Antipas in the previous narrative step (6:14-29), by reciting popular views of Jesus. It is then followed immediately by Jesus' first announcement of his own execution and his rebuke of Rock's objection (8:31-33). The episode of John's beheading anticipates Jesus' announcements of his impending execution and the longer narrative of his arrest, trial, and crucifixion. Jesus' announcements of his own execution echoes John's death, and anticipates his prolonged passion. Complicating both the anticipation and the echoes are Rock's misunderstanding and later denial.

Mark's narrative establishes several other links across the sequence of acts that add coherence to the story. Jesus' announcement that the kingdom of God is at hand not only opens the first narrative step but also sounds the theme of the whole gospel story. The summarizing episode toward the end of the first act (3:7-12) also looks forward to subsequent exorcisms and healings and offers a general statement of all the other cases that are not included in the story. The episodes of healing blind men that frame the third act that focuses partly on the failure of the disciples to see what is happening also link it with the preceding and succeeding narrative steps. The first healing of the blind man completes the second act while beginning the third. And the healing of Bartimaeus anticipates the confrontation in Jerusalem by introducing Jesus as "son of David." With these and other connecting links, Mark's narrative is far more than "just one thing after another." It is a dramatic story in which the dominant conflict between Jesus and the rulers is interwoven with subplots of the conflicts between Jesus and the disciples and Jesus and the demons. The dominant plot and the subplots all come to a climax in the confrontation in Jerusalem.

Patterns in the Narrative

In addition to the links between the steps of the narrative, certain patterns within the narrative steps aid the memory of the performer and the hearing of the audience. In somewhat of an *inclusio*, Jesus calls disciples in the first episode, then appoints the Twelve in one of the last episodes of the first act (1:16-20; 3:13-19). A sequence of episodes begins with an exorcism in which Jesus, who speaks with authority, is contrasted with the scribes, who do not, and closes with a healing set pointedly against the Temple and high priests that the scribes represent (1:22-28; 1:40-45). The second narrative step (4:35—8:26) is structured by two sequences of five acts of power (sea-crossing, exorcism, healing, wilderness feeding) into which other episodes are inserted (between the healings and the feeding in the first sequence and between the sea-crossing and the exorcism in the second). The third narrative step (8:22—10:52) is structured around three announcements of the trial, killing, and rising of Jesus, followed by the disciples' blindness to what is happening, and framed by healings of blind people.

Other techniques of oral presentation also facilitate the memory of performers and the hearing of audiences of the narrative steps. It has long been recognized that Mark's story deploys a sandwich-like insertion of one episode into another, which then narratively frames it. In most cases the less ominous episode frames the more ominous episode. Best known perhaps are the framing of Jesus' trial by Rock's denial (15:52-72) and the cursing of a fig tree framing Jesus' prophetic demonstration against the Temple (11:12-25). Earlier in the story, Jesus' family's concern that he is possessed frames the scribes' accusation that Jesus is working in the power of Beelzebul (3:20-35) and the healing of the twelve-year-old woman frames the healing of the older woman who has been hemorrhaging for twelve years (both symbolic of Israel being renewed; 5:21-43).

Mark's narrative also frequently employs ring or chiastic arrangements, another typical technique of oral performance. In Mark these sometimes help performers remember and hearers discern significant relations between several episodes and sometimes mark the beginning and end of individual episodes. Joanna Dewey explored carefully the remarkable A-B-C-B-A chiastic pattern of the fine episodes in 2:1—3:6.[53] This sequence is also a prime example of how the parallel stories are patterned in similar or parallel fashion. The first and the fifth stories (2:1-12; 3:1-6) display similar subjects and parallel internal structure: healing—dispute—healing. The characters are the same or similar: Jesus, a man with a paralyzed leg or withered hand, and the scribes and Pharisees. In both the dispute is touched off by Jesus' direct address to the healed man. In both Jesus discerns the objection which is unspoken. The reactions correspond to one another and significantly are diametrically opposed: the people are amazed and glorify God, the authority figures (who lack authority) seek to destroy Jesus. The second and fourth episodes, both controversies (2:13-17, 23-28), display parallel structure, similar subjects, eating, and the same set of characters, Jesus, the disciples, and the Pharisees. And the episodes both conclude with parallel proverbs followed by parallel "I"/"son of man" sayings. The central episode, finally, focuses on the opposite of eating, that is, fasting. And this issue leads to the real question of the episode and the sequence: what time is it? What is happening in Jesus' actions? Something new that breaks through the standard old social-religious forms that the scribes and Pharisees are defending. The whole sequence, moreover, in anticipation of the main plot (dominant conflict) of the whole story, dramatizes the sayings in which Jesus challenges, and threatens, the established order headed by the high priests and defended by the scribes and Pharisees.

Performance and Participation—and Investigation

The experience of the earliest hearers of the Gospel of Mark would have been quite different from that of a modern individual silent reader. Modern readers read variously to be entertained, to be stimulated, or to gather information. The earliest hearers of Mark would have listened as members of a community of a new movement, people who had recently come to common commitments in a common life situation. As hearers they would have participated in the performance of the story. As Walter Ong pointed out, "public verbal performance in an oral culture is participatory and essentially integrative. Speaker and audience and subject matter are raveled together."[54] The early hearers of Mark resonated with the narrative in their life situation.

The standard Christian theological reading of Mark as a paradigmatic story of discipleship might also claim that modern individual silent readers also identify with the story. This would be similar to the individual cathartic identification that Aristotle thought happened in Greek plays, in which the spectator was induced to identify with the suffering of the tragic hero and underwent inner catharsis through a tragic emotional upheaval or a comic release. Today, individual hearers may indeed still experience cathartic identification with the suffering Jesus in performances of passion plays and of "the Seven Last Words of Christ" or the stations of the cross, which are based on the climactic section of Mark's and other gospels' narrative.

The Gospel of Mark, however, is about far more than (a negative model of) discipleship or the suffering of Christ. Oral performance of and group resonance with the story of Mark are always "both/and. . . ." "The kingdom of God is at hand." New life-giving and empowering forces are at work in Jesus, who is launching a renewal of Israel. Oppressive rulers and institutions stand under

God's judgment. The crucifixion is not the end of the story. When the narrator finishes speaking the story continues. Besides announcing his upcoming arrest, condemnation, suffering, and death three times, Jesus also announces his rising. In his farewell covenantal meal, which has a future, he also announces that "after I am raised up, I will go before you into Galilee" (14:28). Then at the empty tomb, the white-robed youth says that Jesus "is going ahead of you to Galilee," where he had inaugurated the movement and where it was continuing when the gospel was being originally performed. The hearers who were resonating with the story were invited to continue it, and the movement it informed. The gospel thus continued to be performed, repeatedly, and its story continued in the hearers following every performance. The gospel story (and history) continued in the on-going movement, which in turn was motivated by the continuing performance of the gospel.

But what about today's would be hearers? These would appear to be moved by one or the other or both of two sorts of motivation: those motivated to keep the faith with the story as performed and heard in the original context of performance, and those motivated to appreciate Mark in performance as historians interested in Mark in performance or as a historical source for Jesus and Jesus movements. For people in the developed world (North America, Europe, and elsewhere) who want to keep the faith with the gospel, who live in such different circumstances from the ancient Galileans and Syrians who first listened to performances of Mark, it would be extremely difficult to re-locate into more analogous circumstances. So they may be in the same position as the historians, only with different reasons for attempting to appreciate the original historical performance context of Mark (that is, to then move to the implications for their faithfulness in different modern historical circumstances).

To appreciate Mark as performance in its own historical context as it resonated with the original hearers by referencing their cultural tradition requires us to become as knowledgeable as possible about that historical context and about that cultural tradition. Such knowledge is essential for us to even begin to share the common meanings and nuances of images, cultural conventions, historical experiences, and historical worldview that are different from our own in ways we cannot even begin to imagine. Appreciating Mark as oral performance in context, moreover, will require relinquishing or even intentionally cutting through some of the most fundamental assumptions and approaches of the field of biblical studies in which we are trained. It will mean trading modern individualistic orientation for a more collective community orientation, and trading in theological interests and concepts for political interests and appreciation of storytelling, innuendo, and body language. And it will mean trading standard modern Christian issues for ancient peasant issues.

Part III: Social Memory

Chapter

Five

Social Memory and Gospel Traditions

The ancient Athenians knew that Mnemosyne, mother of the Muses, was the wellspring of civilization. Modern biblical studies, however, has little use for Memory, even as a midwife. While studies of social or cultural memory have been burgeoning in most other fields of the humanities and social sciences, biblical scholars have been relatively oblivious to all the excitement. Thanks to the pioneering scholarship of Werner Kelber[1] and to the initiatives of Alan Kirk and Tom Thatcher,[2] we now have the opportunity to discover just how important a critical understanding of memory may be for the study of New Testament texts and history. More particularly—as standard study of the gospel tradition seems to have ended up in a cul-de-sac of inappropriate assumptions, approaches, and interpretive concepts—recent studies of social memory can help us discern how the standard way of thinking about gospel tradition is seriously problematic and how we can think about it more appropriately.

Our learning from social memory studies, however, will be different from the recent importation of various types of criticism in two important respects. First, it will not be yet another case of borrowing an already delineated theory from literary studies or a ready-made model from sociology and applying it to biblical texts. Since social memory studies are being carried out across the disciplinary boundaries of many fields, the enterprise is "non-paradigmatic, transdisciplinary, and centerless."[3] Social memory should not be reified as something in itself. It is rather a sensitizing concept that leads us to recognize social and cultural relations that we might otherwise miss or misunderstand.

Second, our learning from social memory studies will not be a matter of applying a new perspective or type of criticism while not questioning the standard assumptions, conceptual apparatus, and generalization of biblical studies.

Social-scientific models and methods are often applied without taking advantage of more sophisticated literary analysis of the texts from which data is derived. And literary criticism often proceeds as if more precise recent historical reconstruction and ideological criticism had not challenged the standard old essentialist theological constructs. Social memory studies will conspire with recent researches on other, related fronts, such as orality-literacy and social history, which are challenging some of the standard assumptions of biblical studies. Social memory studies can be combined with insights from these other researches to generate more appropriate ways of thinking about New Testament texts in historical context.

Rather than bring a synthetic scheme of social memory to bear on gospel texts, therefore, I would like to note how standard study of the gospel tradition is deeply problematic, suggest a different approach, and then note how study of social memory may lead to more adequate assumptions and approaches, in tandem with new research in related areas.

Deconstruction

Standard Assumptions and Approaches Inappropriate to Ancient Realities

The assumptions and approaches of standard study of the Gospels and gospel traditions about Jesus have been determined by Christian theology and print culture. Recent studies on a number of interrelated fronts are now exposing these as inappropriate to the ancient realities they were designed to study.

Standard study of the gospel tradition assumed that the gospel tradition was all about the development of a new religion breaking away from an old religion. But religion was inseparable from political-economic life in the ancient world. The Lord's Prayer and the Beatitudes, for example, deal with economic life, having enough to eat and cancellation of debts. The gospel tradition portrays Jesus as executed not by stoning as a blasphemer, per order of a high priestly court, but by crucifixion as a provincial insurrectionary against the Roman imperial order, per order of the Roman governor.

Standard study of the gospel tradition assumed that the gospel tradition was making a break from "Judaism." But "Judaism" is an essentialist modern concept, a largely European Christian scholarly construct, like Orientalism.[4] It is not clear that "Judaism" has any historical referent, at least not until late antiquity at the earliest. Research of the last two or three decades has demonstrated that the concrete historical context in which the gospel tradition began was ancient Galilean and Judean society. That society consisted largely of agrarian village communities controlled and taxed by client rulers of the Romans, Herodian kings in Galilee and the Jerusalem priestly aristocracy in Judea, assisted by scribal retainers such as the Pharisees. Our sources indicate that the principal divide, manifested in repeated conflicts, protests, popular resistance movements, and widespread revolts, lay not between Judaism and Hellenism but between the Galilean and Judean peasantry, on the one hand, and their Roman and Herodian and high priestly rulers, on the other.

Standard study of the gospel tradition assumed that its sources were stable written texts, or at least that text-criticism could establish stable original texts, on the model of modern printed documents in archives. Recent research is now demonstrating, on the basis of parchment scrolls and papyri, that neither the books of the Hebrew Bible nor the Gospels existed in stable written textual form until late antiquity at the earliest. Into the first century C.E., two or three different textual traditions of the books that were later included in the Hebrew Bible competed, and all were still developing.[5] As for the Gospels, the earliest papyri indicate multiple versions that were still developing. In both cases, it is becoming evident that the "original text" is a modern projection of print culture.

Standard study of the gospel tradition treated the Gospels as box-like containers of individual traditions of or about Jesus. Mark was understood as a "string of beads," each of which could be detached for analysis and interpretation. In the last generation, literary criticism of the Gospels has enabled appreciation of the Gospels as sustained narratives, stories in which the multiple episodes are components. Abstracting the episodic components from the overall narrative does violence to the Gospels' literary integrity.

Standard study of the Gospels assumed that the original units of the Jesus tradition were individual sayings of Jesus or stories about him that must be isolated from their literary context in the Gospels, which was secondary or tertiary, for analysis and interpretation as separate artifacts. But this ignores that text fragments have no meaning apart from context and ignores the only indication we might have of what that meaning context might have been.

Standard study of the Gospels also assumed that in oral tradition the sayings of Jesus behaved like written statements, and underwent changes on the model of how one written source adapted another, for example, how Matthew revised Mark or Q.[6] Recent research on orality and literacy have recognized that communication was predominantly oral in antiquity, with literacy limited mainly to the cultural elite.[7] With regard to the Gospels, even after texts had been written down, they were still read or rather recited orally to a group or community.[8] Many texts were composed and continued to develop in repeated performance. Even among literate groups, such as the rabbis and their scribal predecessors, texts were inscribed on the memory as well as on scrolls, which played a role in the continuing instability and development of texts.[9] To understand this we must hyphenate what has previously been distinguished, that is, texts were oral-written or written-oral in composition and cultivation. It might be said, therefore, that instead of Jesus sayings behaving like written statements in print culture, written texts operated like oral tradition in repeated composition-and-performance.

Standard study of the gospel tradition, finally, assumed that its text fragments were artifacts, objects in themselves whose meaning was to be probed and interpreted. In their historical situation, however, the Gospels and pre-gospel materials were means of communication. They were irreducibly relational and contextual, with a reader-reciter-performer delivering a message to a community of hearers in a particular context in a register appropriate to the context. And the way communication happened was that the text or message resonated with the hearers as it referenced the cultural tradition shared by performer and audience.[10]

All of the above aspects of what we are coming to recognize (versus the problematic assumptions of standard study of the gospel tradition) come together in texts as *communication*. Communication is a matter not of what a text means but of what work it does in being performed before a community of people embedded in a particular historical context.

Problematic Aspects of the Standard "History of the Synoptic Tradition" and Form-Criticism

The standard "history of the synoptic gospel tradition," as constructed by Bultmann, Dibelius, and classical form criticism, had three stages. First, simply assumed and not critically argued, in the beginning were individual sayings of Jesus remembered by individual disciples. Second, these sayings were supplemented by sayings from the exalted Lord and became overlaid by tradition in the early church. Third, Jesus sayings and tradition were then interpreted and develop in linear fashion into the Gospels.

This construction, which forms the working assumption of the Jesus Seminar and has been enshrined in magisterial Jesus books by Crossan, Funk, and others is deeply problematic. Even before the discovery of memory studies, we had begun to recognize some of the reasons why.

First, it is determined by the standard three-stage Christian theological scheme of the origins of early Christianity. (a) Jesus, the unique, *sui generis* revealer (prophet, teacher or, recently prominent, "sage"), unencumbered by social relationships, taught sayings to individual disciples (who were not yet formed into a community), who remembered them with varying degrees of realiability. (b) After the trauma of the crucifixion, the resurrection led the disciples to form the first community in Jerusalem and to suddenly begin remembering and repeating the sayings of Jesus and telling stories about Jesus. (c) After the Roman destruction of Jerusalem, Jesus traditions came together into the Gospels. But this is all a (modern) Christian theological scheme, heavily dependent on the book of Acts, and is historically indefensible as well as theologically problematic. No human being is so unencumbered with social relations. Jesus is thus denied genuine historical communicative interaction, as well as genuine humanity. Many gospel materials, moreover, give clear indications of being addressed to groups of people in agrarian settings, even in local communities. As I pointed out twenty years ago, the social *context* is often evident in the *content* of the sets of sayings.[11] Furthermore, the contexts indicated by much gospel material would have existed before and after the crucifixion of Jesus and regardless of a possible resurrection faith. Gospel materials themselves do not attest the scheme of Christian origins on which their three-stage development is based. In short, the gospel tradition must have begun with communicative interaction during the mission of Jesus.

Second, the standard view of the gospel tradition assumes that the Gospels were mere containers of Jesus sayings and traditions. The Gospel of Mark, for example, was characterized as "a string of beads," from which individual beads of Jesus tradition could be easily detached for analysis and interpretation. More sophisticated literary criticism, however, has led to the recognition of the Gospels as plotted stories, sustained narratives built up from multiple episodes which are all components of a whole story.

Third, individual Jesus sayings and stories purposely isolated from the supposedly later interpretive overlay of the gospel are treated as separate artifacts to be analyzed and interpreted for meaning in itself. But meaning depends on meaning context, to which our only guide is the sustained gospel narrative.

Memory studies leads to recognition of additional problems with the standard construction of the gospel tradition and powerfully reinforces criticism from recent initiatives on other fronts such as orality-literacy. As Werner Kelber pointed out over twenty years ago, form criticism depends on the assumptions of modern print culture.[12] The model for how the disciples' memory handled Jesus' sayings was how Matthew and Luke, understood as modern writers, handled what they found in the written texts of Mark and Q. This is close to the modern individualistic copy-and-save model of memory. Recent studies of memory, however, have shown that memory simply does not work in that way.

The most basic recognition of memory-studies, beginning with Maurice Halbwachs, is that memory is irreducibly social. Even contemporary psychologists are clear about this. "Memory is produced by an individual, but it is always produced in relation to the larger interpersonal and cultural world in which that individual lives. Memory is *embedded*. . . the rememberer remembers in a contemporary world, peopled by others who collectively contribute to the construction of memory and help determine the importance that the past holds for an individual in the present."[13] Memory involves communication in communities of people.[14] What is remembered is remembered because and insofar as it has significance for the rememberers and others they communicate with.[15] Memory is thus closely related to and tied up with group needs and interests. Memory involves a distillation and transmutation of experience and not simply a reflection and much less a copy of it.[16] This powerfully reinforces the point about individual sayings and other fragments having no meaning isolated from a meaning context. The three stages assumed by form criticism should simply be collapsed. From the outset, including interaction with Jesus himself, the development of the gospel tradition was a product of the social memory of groups, communities of Jesus followers. That memory is fundamentally social, moreover, pushes us strongly toward understanding the gospel tradition in terms of communication in group formation rather than mere transmission from one individual to another.

Reconstruction

Step One: The Gospels as Plotted Narratives (Q as a Series of Speeches)

Since the standard construction of the development of the gospel tradition by form criticism is so problematic, we must start again, informed by memory studies and related researches. And since they are our primary, often our only sources, the obvious starting point would appear to be the Gospels, each in its own literary integrity.

Even this, however, is problematic, since we can no longer assume that there was a single original version that can be established by text criticism.[17] We must apparently assume, rather, that a given gospel functioned in multiple versions in repeated performance, as communication in a particular historical context. The story or the sequence of speeches or the combination in a given gospel was presumably already familiar to the performer and hearers. Their memory was thus also involved in the communication event of the recitation-and-hearing of the gospel. Since there were variations of emphasis, tone, and even wording from performance to performance, the particular wording of a given gospel matters far less than the overall story and the thrust of a component speech. Yet, rather than ignore or eliminate the textual variations by positing a scholarly construct as the "original" text, we must take the ancient textual multiformity into consideration as a significant indicator of how the gospel texts were functioning. To simplify matters, I will focus on the Gospel of Mark and the parallel Jesus speeches in Matthew and Luke, commonly called Q.

Partly as a result of a generation of sophisticated literary criticism that has become ever more sensitive to the difference between ancient and modern narrative, we are able to understand the Gospel of Mark as a sustained story, a narrative with plot and subplots, not a mere string of beads. The main plot presents Jesus leading a movement for the renewal of Israel against the Roman rulers and their clients, the priestly aristocracy in Jerusalem and Antipas in Galilee. At the end of the open-ended story, Jesus directs the hearers back to Galilee to continue the movement. In the subplot of Jesus' conflict with Peter and the twelve disciples, the story seems to reflect a conflict between the Markan hearers, who are to get back to basics as Jesus exemplified, and the Jesus-appointed heads of the renewed Israel who are apparently now heads of the movement in Jerusalem. The remembered episodes of Jesus' call of disciples, healings and exorcisms, debates with the Pharisees, teaching in parables and dialogues, all together constitute a founding story for the movement. But they also all constitute inspiration and instruction for the communities of the movement. The stories of healing and exorcism continue the healing effects of Jesus' mission in assuring the people that God's healing power has restored them to wholeness. In the debates with the Pharisees, Mark's Jesus defends the (Galilean) people's covenantal practices versus the Jerusalem elite's attempt to control or exploit. And the teaching dialogues are renewed covenantal teaching that guide community life.

Just as Mark was not a mere string of beads, so the Jesus speech material paralleled in Matthew and Luke was not a mere collection of sayings. If we examine its sequence and ordering in Matthew and Luke, it was a series of speeches that ostensibly continued Jesus' own prophetic teaching. The speeches addressed particular concerns of the movement and community life. The covenant renewal speech in Q/Luke 6:20-49 was both an enactment of community renewal and a guide for people's social-economic interaction in the communities of the movement. The mission speech gave instructions for continuing the mission started by Jesus. The Lord's Prayer taught the foundational prayer for the Kingdom to come in economic sufficiency and mutual cooperation. The exhortation to bold confession urged commitment and solidarity in the face of persecution. The prophetic condemnations of the Jerusalem rulers and their Pharisaic representatives reassured the hearers that God stands in judgment of their injustice and exploitation. That is, the speech, the prophetic teaching of Jesus that was remembered and performed anew in this series of speeches was what was pertinent to and usable by the communities that heard the speeches performed.

Clearly a rich mix of episodic materials and speech materials had been cultivated in the social memory of Jesus movements from which the Markan story and the Q series of speeches could be composed. In Mark and Q social memory took distinctive literary and textual forms in plotted narrative and sequential speeches, respectively. The distinguished theorist of cultural memory, Jan Assmann, makes a distinction between "formative" texts, narrative genres of constitutive histories and myths, on the one hand, and "normative" texts, instructional genres calibrated to inculcate the cognate norms.[18] Yet these may not be quite applicable to Mark and Q, respectively. As noted just above, many of the constituent episodes in Mark's foundational history of Jesus' renewal of Israel, especially the debates with the Pharisees and the dialogues with the disciples in chapters 8–10, also serve to instill the norms and discipline of the movement and community by precept and example. And some of the same speeches in Q, particularly the longest speech which enacts a covenant renewal, the mission speech, and the prayer, have a foundational function as well as an instructional role. Both texts carry both functions.

Step Two: Between Jesus and the Gospels

Once we gain a more satisfactory sense of the Gospels in their own (albeit multiform) literary integrity, the next step would be to examine them as sources for possible forms of communication in or behind them. Again, for manageability I focus only on Mark and Q. For reasons sketched above the principal criterion is probable function as a unit of communication in a community.

Perhaps the most obvious clue comes from the several parallel discourses in Mark and Q. The ones usually recognized include the mission speeches (Q 10:1-16 and Mark 6:6-13) and the Beelzebul controversy (Q 11:14-20; Mark 3:22-28). To those I would add the parallel covenantal speeches (Q 6:20-49; Mark 10:2-45) and the exhortations to bold confession (Q 12:2-12; Mark 8:34—9:1). One reason we can imagine these as, on occasion, separate units of communication is that they would each have had a social function as speeches in contexts other than that of the performance of the whole series of Q speeches or the whole story of Mark. The Q covenant speech in Q 6 could well have been spoken as performative speech in a periodic covenant renewal ceremony in communities of Jesus followers. The expanded covenantal speech in Matthew's Sermon on Mount, the parallel covenantal section at the opening of the *Didache*, and the covenant renewal ceremony described in the Community Rule from Qumran all reinforce our sense that covenant renewal speeches were a standard form of communication independent of, as well as within gospels. Various versions of a mission discourse could well have been used on occasions of commissioning and sending out envoys to build the movement in other villages. Speeches of exhortation to bold confession in various versions would have been used on appropriate occasions to encourage movement members who were hauled before the rulers (as is suggested at various points in gospel materials). Those speeches might then serve as examples against which to measure other speeches in Q that may have functioned separately from whole series of Q.

If we are scrupulously critical about what constituted a unit of communication in a social context, we will want to be cautious about jumping to conclusions about separate healing stories or parables or debates with the Pharisees. For example, a parable seems to communicate little in isolation. Parables demand an occasion, a situation to which they might provide an instructive or illuminating analogy. Parables might well, at an early stage in the history of Jesus movements, have addressed a conflictual political-religious relation between retainers of the

temple-state and Judean or even Galilean peasant communities. But it is difficult to imagine the precise situation of communication in which they might
have functioned separately or in sets. That several seemingly parallel parables are
grouped into a speech in Mark and then expanded into a larger one in Matthew
suggests that sets of parables might have functioned as semi-separate units of
communication in an appropriate setting. Intriguing are the two parallel chains
of sea-crossing, exorcism, healing, and wilderness feeding stories in Mark that
may have somewhat of a parallel in the Gospel of John. They have a clear principle of coherence, telling of Jesus as the Moses-and-Elijah-like agent who is
leading a renewal of Israel in a series of episodes that parallel and resemble those
of the great heroes of the foundation and renewal of Israel.

Step Three: Relationship between Pre-Markan Forms of Communication and the Gospels

With the recognition of the predominantly oral communication environment
in antiquity and the integral relation of orality and written texts, two important
conclusions have been drawn that only seem to be opposed to one another. On
the one hand, although Mark and the other Gospels are not particularly long for
oral composition, we think of writing having been involved in their composition. And we are fairly certain that Mark's story existed in written copies. On
the other hand, we recognize that even after a text had been written, it was still
recited orally in a group setting, and that Mark's story (or Matthew's or John's)
displays features of oral composition and performance. These conclusions may
stand in a certain tension, but they are not at all mutually contradictory. There
was simply no great divide between orality and literacy in the ongoing communication situation of Jesus movements. Perhaps we should not make too much
of a supposed shift from orality to literacy in the emergence of Mark or Q or
John from the pre-gospel forms of communication such as covenantal speeches
or chains of wonder stories.

   This might make us cautious about applying too directly the distinction that
Jan Assmann makes between "communicative memory" and "cultural memory"
and the shift from the first to the second. He offered this distinction, not with
reference to particular local movements, such as communities of Jesus followers,
but with reference to the emergence of a whole corpus of (written) literature in
the great civilizations of Egypt, Israel, and Greece as a major way in which social
memory was stabilized, secured, and controlled. The distinction surely applies
to the development of Christianity and its emergent Scripture in the broad
sense, but perhaps not to the communities that produced and used Mark or Q.

   We may question whether, in the first eighty or 100 years (four generations)
of such popular movements, in which writing was not common and scrolls not

readily available, writing was really a more efficient means of securing and stabilizing the groups' memory. Texts, which continued to be performed orally, continued to develop, as attested by the multiple textual traditions of Mark now being recognized from early papyri.[19] Mark and Q were further "developed," according to the two-source hypothesis, by Matthew and Luke, Q perhaps thus having been "developed" right out of existence, whether or not it existed in written form. Both before and after the crisis of the destruction of Jerusalem, several somewhat separate movements of Jesus believers coexisted, mainly in different areas, and several different gospels were produced and written down. They took several different forms, from a composite such as Matthew to a passion narrative such as Peter, to a collection of sayings such as Thomas. And it is not clear whether the latter secured social memory as much as focused individual believers' spiritual meditation. Later, in the second and third centuries, Christians hauled before the courts, when asked what was in their bags, answered, "the Gospels and the books." But we should ask whether those scrolls or perhaps codices were used for actual reading or functioned more as symbols signifying that their sacred stories had the status and authority of being written.

Key Aspects of Social Memory in the Gospel Tradition

Both in the Gospels themselves and in the discernible pre-gospel forms of communication involved in the gospel tradition, we can observe several major features that recent studies of social memory in other fields can help us appreciate and understand.

Social Memory of Jesus Embedded in Israelite Social Memory

In the gospel tradition and the Gospels, the social memory of Jesus is embedded in and is a continuation of Israelite social memory. Directly and pointedly contrary to previous Christian theological assumptions and constructs, the Q speeches, the Gospel of Mark, and even the Gospel of Matthew present Jesus as leading a renewal of Israel. For example, contrary to common claims in recent interpretation of Q as a sayings collection, Q speeches do not reject "all Israel." Rather, some of the speeches pronounce only God's condemnation of the Jerusalem rulers and their scribal Pharisaic representatives—in the form of prophetic laments and woes derived from Israelite prophetic tradition. The Gospels, including many non-canonical gospels, display numerous references and allusions to events, figures, and forms from Israelite history and culture. Particularly striking are the Israelite figures and forms already mentioned in connection with the pre-gospel forms of communication. These include, most notably, the speeches that take the form of renewal of the Mosaic covenant, with additional adaptations of traditional covenantal teaching, the mission discourse with allusions to Elisha as protégé of Elijah, and the chain of wonder stories of Jesus as the new Moses and new Elijah performing sea crossings, healings, and wilderness feedings as manifestations of his program for the renewal of Israel, and the debates with the Pharisees in which Jesus defends fundamental covenantal principles as the commandment of God. The recent literature on memory, particularly by historians, contains much about figures in various societies who became heroes of societal renewal in various ways similar to how Jesus figures in the gospel tradition.

Social Memory Shaped in Broader Cultural Patterns

The gospel tradition was structured not in tiny individual units of sayings or little vignettes about Jesus, but in terms of broader and more complex cultural patterns, patterns derived and adapted from Israelite tradition. We can identify these because they appear in more than one gospel and in Judean literature such as books later included in the Hebrew Bible, some of the Dead Sea Scrolls, and Judean texts closer to the time of Jesus such as *Psalms of Solomon*, and even in other popular movements contemporary with the Jesus movements. The principal reason we have not previously discerned such broader Israelite cultural patterns in gospel materials is that we were focused narrowly on Jesus sayings and brief vignettes of Jesus. To use an old metaphor, we were focused so narrowly on the twigs of trees that we simply could not see the glades and glens that make up the overall contour of the forest. Again, studies of how social memory works in other societies offers numerous examples of broad cultural patterns that will help us understand what to look for in materials of the gospel tradition in the context of broader Israelite cultural memory.

Perhaps the pattern most evident in these texts is that of the Mosaic covenant. A generation ago, Hebrew Bible scholars discerned the pattern explicit in such Mosaic covenantal texts as Exodus 20 (the giving of the covenant on Sinai) and Joshua 24 (the covenant renewal ceremony) by comparison with ancient Near Eastern treaties. The basic structure of the six principal components consisted of

(1) declaration of deliverance (brought you out of bondage in Egypt)
(2) principles of social-economic policy and interaction (no killing, no stealing)
(3) motivating sanctions (periodic reading, witnesses, and especially blessings and curses)

The same basic three-component structure was prescribed for covenant renewal ceremonies in the Community Rule at Qumran (1QS 1–4). But the structural components have been adapted to address a new situation under the imperial rule of the Kittim (the Romans) and the local rule of the Wicked Priesthood in Jerusalem, with the blessings and curses having been transformed into part of the elaborate new declaration of deliverance, and new sanctions substituted for the blessings and curses.

This same structure is then evident in the speech in Q/Luke 6:20-49—if no longer focusing on individual sayings separately, we have "ears to hear" the overall pattern of the speech. The basic components are evident in the sequence of blessing and woes at the outset (as in the Qumran Community Rule) and the covenantal teaching that makes many allusions to traditional Israelite covenantal teaching (as known from Exodus 21–23; Leviticus 18–19, 25; and parts of Deuteronomy). The double parable at the end functions as a new motivating sanction. The transformation of the blessings and curses into a new declaration of (imminent) deliverance is even parallel to that in the Community Rule (see further chapter 3 above).

Less obvious and more implicit structurally is the sequence of dialogues in Mark 10:1-45, two of which explicitly recite covenantal commandments and all of which deal with the fundamental concerns of the Mosaic covenant for law-like principles that guide community social, economic, and political life.[20] We can also see the covenant theme at key points earlier and later in the Markan narrative, especially in the Last Supper, which is explicitly a ceremonial meal of covenant renewal, as indicated in the word over the cup. And the same broad Israelite cultural pattern appears again structurally and substantively in Matthew's Sermon on the Mount and in the first long section of the *Didache* (chapters 1–6) both of which include different versions of the covenantal teaching in the Q speech ("love your enemies. . ." Q 6:27-36).

From several other less obvious cultural patterns that we can discern in gospel materials, we can focus on one that requires us to loosen up our habitual, microscopic focus on sayings and pericopes. In a series of articles and in *Bandits, Prophets, and Messiahs*, I argued that the several popular prophetic movements that emerged in Judea around the time of Jesus were informed by the same Israelite tradition of Moses and Joshua as prophets leading movements of deliverance from the Egyptian Pharaoh or other foreign rulers.[21] Once we examine the Gospel of Mark as a whole story and the series of speeches in Q, we notice that Jesus is represented as doing Moses-like (or Joshua-like) actions again and again. Often these are combined with Elijah-like actions. Most obvious in Mark are the Moses-like sea crossings and the wilderness feedings that frame Elijah-like healings, followed by Jesus' appearance with both Moses and Elijah on the mountain.

Studies of social memory offer us great encouragement to think along these lines, with some basic observations and numerous comparative examples from other societies about how memory is organized and focused in groups. As Yael Zerubavel and Alan Kirk explain:

> A community *marks* certain elements of its past as being of constitutive significance. . . . Memories of the community's origins and other landmark events. . . . These memories are shaped into a community's "master commemorative narrative" . . . then as it moves forward through its history, it aligns its fresh experiences with this master narrative, as well as vice versa.[22]

The social memory of Jesus' disciples and the movements they led would not have been a matter of the mere transmission of pithy aphorisms and distinctive vignettes about Jesus. Social memory seeks and expresses the significance and coherence of past experience through conceptualization and schematization in focused expressive forms of shared discourse. Even psychologists and phenomenologists recognize that memory "acts to organize what might otherwise be a mere assemblage of contingently connected events."[23] And historians can explain how "commemoration lifts from an ordinary historical sequence those extraordinary events which embody our deepest and most fundamental values."[24] Heroes of those extraordinary events become symbolic figures to whom whole configurations of memory are attached. Just as Washington and Lincoln and, more recently Martin Luther King "have become national symbols which embody the values, virtues, and ideals of American democracy,"[25] so Moses and Elijah, and later Jesus, became symbols embodying the liberation-and-renewal of Israel.

Social memory thus generates certain distinctive frameworks or patterns of cognition, organization, and interpretation. The salient past thus becomes immanent in particular narrative patterns in which it has become ingrained in social memory. And it is through those narrative and other patterns that a group or community orients itself and has its "being in the world."[26]

These basic observations about social memory apply directly to and help illuminate the development of the Jesus tradition and Jesus movements on the basis of Israelite social memory in Galilean and Judean society. Master commemorative narratives and other forms that have achieved secure status in social memory are not inert, museum-piece representations of the past, not like the Jesus sayings that form criticism treated as objectified artifacts to be examined. Rather they vitally shape perception and organization of reality. They are cognitive schemata, nuclear scripts for interpreting and processing streams of experience.[27] As Barry Schwartz explains what he calls a "frame image of collective memory," it "is a shorthand reference to the way invocations of the past confer meaning on present experience."[28] Social memory makes sense of the present through keying present experiences and predicaments to prototypical images and narrative representations of the commemorated past. "Frame images are in this sense pictorial counterparts of 'emplotment,' defining the meaning of problematic events by depicting them as episodes in a narrative that precedes and transcends them."[29]

That is an illuminating description of what I see as having happened in the formation and development of gospel tradition about Jesus as it can be discerned in the Gospel of Mark and even before. This can be seen in the chains of Moses-and-Elijah-like episodes, or in the recruitment and commissioning of Elisha-like protégés by an Elijah-like Jesus in both Markan narrative and Markan and Q mission speeches. Moses and Elijah had long since become the central symbolic heroes of Israelite social memory around whom whole schemes of significance revolved. They had led the foundational events of the formation and renewal of Israel against oppressive rule. The frame images and prototypical narratives centered on Moses and Elijah then provided ready-made scripts through which Judean popular movements led by prophets as a new Moses went out into the wilderness to experience a new deliverance from foreign rule. And they provided the scripts through which Jesus and his followers and developing Jesus movements understood their recent experiences and continued to interpret them.

Studies of social memory provide numerous examples from other societies of just this sort of scripting of a new movement in schemes of memory that then continue in the movement's own memory of its formative events. In many cases memory of a highly significant event is so formative for the group that subsequent experience appears to be a virtual replay of and is shaped in terms of the paradigmatic memory. For many years in my Hebrew Bible course, when we covered Abraham's binding of Isaac I used the work of Solomon Ash on how medieval Jewish fathers would be forced by the attacks of Christian mobs to kill their family members as well as themselves, lest they be killed by the mobs.[30] Fentress and Wickham[31] recount two examples of such highly significant events at considerable length. For coal miners in Durham and South Wales, the General Strike of 1926 was so formative that in the later strikes of 1972, 1974, and 1984–85 they were simply replaying the same drama with the same cast of characters: the mine owners, the police, and the miners themselves in their communities. In the other case, the Cevenol peasants experienced later struggles against local attacks and official persecution as replays of the Camisards's revolt in 1702–04 (Cevennes is a mountainous region in central France). In a very recent example, the particular patterns, which significantly, are not widely known in the Orientalist West, the Iranian revolution against the Shah that came to a head in 1979 took the form of a sequence of funeral processions. In those processions each new martyr was commemorated as having recapitulated the martyrdom of Husayn, Muhammad's grandson, at Karbala at the hand of Yazid, the evil Umayyid caliph.[32] The latter two cases, particularly that of the Cevenol peasants and the Camisards, are strikingly parallel to the gospel tradition, the social memory of Jesus movements.[33]

Popular Anti-Hegemonic Memory versus Elite Hegemonic Memory

Third, one of the most important observations about social memory, for our purposes, is that the past is often used to legitimize and advance political goals. Most evident is how powerful ruling groups or institutions who control the cultural means of production shape public memory for their own purposes.[34] In perhaps the most suggestive work on modern nationalism, *Imagined Communities*, Benedict Anderson lays out how, first in western Europe and then elsewhere, the elite that controlled the state and media of communication appropriated history and cultural artifacts selectively to construct nationalist ideologies that mobilized people in support of nation-states.[35] Leading historians associated with the journal *Past and Present*, in a now historic conference, laid out several cases studies of how political-cultural elites invented tradition to legitimize, for example, British imperial rule in India.[36] In the United States, families gather annually to celebrate Thanksgiving, an invented tradition that holds together the highly disparate people of the United States. And with Thanksgiving begins the most elaborate invented tradition in history, the "Holidays." The "old timey" Christmas on display in malls and departments stores for weeks on end was tradition invented by the Victorians.[37] These are all examples of what Assmann would call "hegemonic memory."

   We may be less aware that Herod the Great and, before him, the Hasmoneans ware grand masters of the exploitation of Israelite memory to legitimize their very illegitimate regimes. The Hasmoneans had 1 Maccabees composed to cloak their father and founder Mattathias in the aura of ancient heroes such as Phinehas and to have a grand assembly acclaim his grandson, Simon, "leader and high priest" when he and his father had actually become high priest because they had a strong army and had been appointed by the Seleucid imperial regime. Herod, made king of the Judeans by the Roman Senate, not only reconstructed the Temple on a massive scale, but further surrounded his regime with monumental tombs commemorating the great heroes of Israel's origins, such as Abraham and David. Very likely it was under Herod that the elite began constructing "the tombs of the prophets," mainly in Jerusalem itself.

   While political-economic and cultural elites usually have the power to shape and control the dominant social memory in public discourse, subordinated groups are quite capable of cultivating their own alternative or anti-hegemonic memory and of actively resisting the hegemonic forms of commemoration.[38]

Anti-hegemonic memory should perhaps be understood along a spectrum from a contested, popular version of past events and figures shared with or parallel to the hegemonic memory to an alternative memory that may even have been suppressed by the dominant forces. A prime example of the latter is the Cevenol peasants, whose struggles against persecution are virtual replays of their vivid memory of the Camisards revolts of 1702–04, which usually do not make the official French history books. The Welsh miner's vivid memory of their grandfathers' bitter strikes fall somewhere in the middle of the spectrum.

The gospel tradition is anti-hegemonic memory. It is deeply rooted in Israelite tradition, but the popular version of Israelite tradition. The Gospel of Mark and Q speeches are full of references and allusions to what is clearly contested Israelite memory. The main plot of Mark's story has Jesus spearheading a renewal of Israel against the Jerusalem rulers based in the Temple. Most explicit are Jesus' pointed attacks on the Pharisees and their traditions of the elders that he declares are undermining the basic commandment of God. When Mark's Jesus refers to what is written in the scriptural scrolls deposited in the Temple, under the custody of the scribes and Pharisees, he uses it against them. In the Q speeches, John and Jesus both mock the elite's zeal for their genealogy, as descendants of Abraham ("God can raise up children of Abraham from these stones"). Jesus vehemently denounces the elite's building of monuments to the prophets at the climax of his sequence of woes against the Pharisees and scribes, accusing the Jerusalem ruling house of having murdered God's messengers. (Q 11:39-52; 13:34-35).

What studies of social memory refer to as popular or anti-hegemonic memory is more or less the same as or part of what anthropologists have for some time been analyzing in terms of the "little tradition" parallel to yet opposed to the "great tradition." The "little" or popular tradition is "the distinctive pattern of belief and behavior valued by the peasantry," while the "great' or official tradition is the corresponding pattern among the society's elite, sometimes embodied in written documents.[39] The popular messianic and prophetic movements in Judea and Galilee, like Jesus' mission and prophetic teachings, were rooted in and manifestations of Israelite popular tradition.[40]

Anti-hegemonic memory is also similar to or can be understood as central to what James C. Scott has more recently called "the hidden transcript" as opposed to "the public transcript."[41] The latter is the dominant discourse of a society, controlled by the elite, in which the dominant and subordinate interact in public, and in which the latter must hold back what they may really be thinking and feeling. But both the dominant and the subordinate have their own hidden discourse in which they communicate with one another when off stage and now being overheard. Scott explains how groups of subordinated people can sustain an alternative view of their life situation in this off-stage communication and how popular movements are rooted in and nurtured from it. Key to the emergence of rare resistance movements is for a popular spokesperson to catalyze popular resentment by braving a public declaration of the popular "hidden transcript." We are just beginning to explore how Jesus traditions can be understood as rooted in a Galilean Israelite "hidden transcript."[42] Analysis in terms of both of these sets of concepts and the corresponding rich supply of comparative material can supplement our use of cases from recent studies of social memory in exploring how the gospel tradition is both rooted in and adapts Israelite popular memory. And such comparative studies and overlapping concepts are all the more important insofar as we have virtually no direct sources for the Israelite popular tradition other than gospel literature itself and the accounts of Josephus, who castigates popular movements for causing trouble. Otherwise we must surmise by extrapolation from sources for the great tradition, such as books of the Hebrew Bible. Analysis in terms of both of these sets of concepts and the corresponding rich supply of comparative material can supplement our use of cases from recent studies of social memory in exploring how the Gospel tradition is both rooted in and adapts Israelite popular memory.

Chapter
Six

Patterns in the Social Memory of Jesus and Friends

═══════════════════════════════

> All beginnings contain an element of recollection. This is particu-
> larly so when a social group makes a concerted effort to begin with
> a wholly new start. There is a measure of complete arbitrariness in
> the very nature of any such attempted beginning.... But the abso-
> lutely new is inconceivable.... In all modes of experience we always
> base our particular experiences on a prior context in order to ensure
> that they are intelligible at all; prior to any single experience, our
> mind is already predisposed with a framework of outlines.... [1]

Jesus had little or no memory. At least that is the impression one receives
from presentations of prominent members of the Jesus Seminar. More conservative interpreters leave Jesus' memory seemingly intact. There appears to be
an irony in the way Jesus scholarship has developed in the last decade or so. Some
of the liberal leaders of the Jesus Seminar who further honed the critical methods developed earlier in the twentieth century produce a Jesus who is seemingly
detached from his culture. Israelite tradition does not play a prominent role in
their construction of Jesus. More conservative interpreters, on the other hand,
who give less attention to critical methods, view Jesus as still connected (negatively
or positively) with Jewish tradition, at least as constructed by Christian theological scholarship. Both, of course, are under pressures, whether those of Christian
doctrine or those of presenting a Jesus compelling to contemporary readers, to
come up with a distinctively different if not an utterly unique figure.

Research into various concerns of biblical studies and related fields, meanwhile, has problematicized a number of the basic assumptions and concepts
of standard scholarship on Jesus and the Gospels. Recent exploration of new
approaches to and previously unrecognized aspects of the (canonical and non-
canonical) Gospels and other texts that provide the principal sources for interpretation of Jesus, moreover, bring new light to old problems and solutions.
Scholars in other fields have called attention to "social memory" or "cultural

memory" as a historical force that has far more influence on people's lives than the ideas and literature of cultural elites. Werner Kelber has pioneered exploration of cultural memory as an important factor in the development of gospel materials in connection with the interface of orality and literacy.[2] Gospel scholars Alan Kirk and Tom Thatcher are calling the wider field of New Testament studies to attend critically to the importance of social memory.[3] Recent studies of social memory happen to overlap compellingly with, and to deepen the insights of, other new approaches to Jesus and the Gospels. Critical attention to social memory and how we can get at it might well enable us to discern that Jesus indeed had a memory. Interspersed with discussions of the implications of new research and approaches, I will examine how the highly sophisticated method developed by leaders of the Jesus Seminar tends to detach Jesus from Israelite cultural tradition, and then explore how recent studies of social memory can enable us to see Jesus and the early Jesus movement as firmly rooted in Israelite social memory.

New Research and Fresh Approaches

During the last three or four decades a combination of new questions, fresh perspectives, borrowed methods, and expanding research has dramatically changed the way we approach and interpret biblical texts. The standard assumptions, concepts, and approaches of the New Testament field in general and of Gospel and Jesus studies in particular have been challenged and undermined and, to a considerable degree, replaced. The landscape of the historical context of the Gospels has undergone the most extensive change. The way we read texts has also broadened. Most recently extensive new research is undermining standard old assumptions about the cultural context of New Testament texts. Now the introduction of the approach and comparative materials of studies in social memory (or cultural memory) will strongly reinforce some of the most significant challenges to older assumptions and approaches, confirm some of the new approaches, and induce distinctive new insights.

An early and elementary historical opening came with the recognition of the considerable social and cultural diversity in ancient Judea.[4] This recognition gradually cut through the theologically constructed scheme of Christianity, developing from and succeeding Judaism that had previously effectively blocked the recognition of that diversity. Standard essentialist concepts, such as Judaism, normative Judaism, and Christianity, turn out to have no historical referents. What could be called Judaism or Christianity had not yet emerged in late second temple times. The Sadducees, Pharisees, and Essenes together comprised only a tiny fraction of the Jewish people. From soon after his crucifixion, followers of Jesus formed differing groups. While some scholars resist acknowledging the diversity, still projecting a monolithic Judaism (Sanders), and many still write of (early) Judaism and (early) Christianity, others at least take such half-way measures as speaking about Judaisms or formative Judaism.

Such timid scholarly moves, however, still operate on the anachronistic assumption that religion was separate from political-economic structures and institutions. When we deal with the Jerusalem Temple and high priesthood, for example, we are dealing unavoidably also with the political-economic institutions that headed the temple-state maintained in Judea by imperial regimes as an instrument of their political domination and economic extraction. The high priestly aristocracy was responsible for collection of the tribute to Caesar as well as sacrifices on behalf of Rome and the emperor. The Passover festival celebrated the people's political-economic as well as religious deliverance from bondage to Pharaoh, under the watchful eyes of the soldiers that the Roman governor had posted on the porticoes of the Temple.

The dominant reality in the political-economic-religious structure was the fundamentally conflictual divide between the imperial rulers and their Herodian and high priestly clients whose wealth and power derived from the tribute, taxes, and tithes they extracted, on the one hand, and the village producers they ruled and taxed, on the other. Nearly all the sources portray this clearly (Sirach, 1–2 Maccabees, *1 Enoch*, Josephus' histories, Mark, and others). Perhaps the most dramatic illustration of the fundamental political-economic-religious conflict is that the period of the mission and movements of Jesus were framed historically by five major widespread popular revolts against the imperial and Jerusalem rulers: the Maccabean Revolt in the 160s B.C.E., the prolonged resistance to Herod's takeover from 40–37 B.C.E., the revolts in Galilee, Judea, and Perea after Herod's death in 4 B.C.E., the great revolt of 66–70 C.E., and the Bar Kokhba Revolt in 132–35 C.E. The sources also feature division and conflicts between scribal groups and the Jerusalem high priestly rulers and their imperial sponsors (such as in the *Psalms of Solomon*, Dead Sea Scrolls, and Josephus).

Compounding the conflictual divide between rulers and ruled were the historical regional differences between Galilee (and Samaria) and Judea and Jerusalem.[5] Galileans, many of whom were presumably descendants and heirs of earlier Israelite people, were not brought under Jerusalem rule until a hundred years before Jesus. Interpreters of Jesus, Jesus movements, and the Gospels have barely begun to deal with the implications of these differences.

Simultaneous with these changes in the landscape of the historical context of Jesus, Jesus movements, and the development of the Gospels, some interpreters were learning how to read New Testament literature (Gospels, Acts, Epistles) as more than the text fragments of isolated sayings and decontextualized pericopes. Especially significant was the recognition that Mark and other Gospels are complexly narrated stories, with plot, subplots, multiple conflicts, and their own narrative styles and agenda.[6] More recently some also recognized, for example, that while the *Gospel of Thomas* presents a collection of sayings and parables, the hypothesized document Q is evidently a sequence of speeches rather than a mere collection of sayings.[7]

Recent research has also decisively undermined some major standard assumptions about the culture of ancient Judea and Galilee, particularly assumptions about literacy and the Hebrew Scriptures. Not only are some scholars now suggesting that the composition of the Torah and prophetic books should be dated relatively later than previously thought, perhaps even in Hellenistic times, but those who have closely examined the multiple scrolls of books of the Torah found at Qumran are also concluding that the text of the books of the Torah was not yet uniform or stable.[8] Different textual traditions still existed in the same scribal community (and presumably in Jerusalem as well), each of which was still undergoing development. The Dead Sea Scrolls also supply further examples of alternative Torah (4QMMT; the *Temple Scroll*) and alternative versions of Israelite history and tradition (not rewritten Bible; *Jubilees*; Pseudo-Philo, *Biblical Antiquities*) that coexisted and competed, at least among scribal circles.

Compounding the implications of such research is the mounting evidence and recognition that literacy was at least as limited in Judea and Galilee as in the rest of the Roman Empire.[9] Oral communication dominated. Indeed, even scribal circles such as the Qumranites apparently recited their texts aloud.[10] Besides being extremely expensive and therefore rare, scrolls were cumbersome and virtually unreadable to anyone who did not already have the text memorized.

The recent research in these areas thus gives powerful confirmation to hypotheses that only a few interpreters were previously ready to entertain and willing to argue. First, Israelite culture was as diverse as were the groups and communities that comprised Judean, Galilean, and Samaritan society. Different versions of Israelite tradition coexisted and competed. The well-known differences between the Sadducees and the Pharisees can be multiplied.

Second, since they were expensive as well as cumbersome, and few could read them, scrolls of different textual traditions of the Torah and alternative Torah would have existed even in Jerusalem, much less in the villages of Judea and Galilee. That most people were non-literate, however, does not mean that they did not know and cultivate Israelite tradition. It simply gives powerful reinforcement of the hypothesis that, as in other agrarian societies, popular Israelite traditions paralleled and competed with versions of Israelite tradition maintained in scribal circles and in the Temple—for which anthropologists use the terminology "little tradition" and "great tradition."[11] It may well be that the Hasmonean insistence that the Galileans accept "the laws of the Judeans" when they took over the area (Josephus, *Ant.* 13.318-19) meant that they assigned the Pharisees and other scribal retainers to press their own "traditions of the elders" and other officially recognized temple-state law on the populace. But "the laws of the Judeans" would hardly have replaced the local customs, covenantal teachings, Elijah and Elisha stories, and other Israelite traditions cultivated in Galilean village communities.

Third, whether written copies existed, texts were recited or performed aloud to groups of people, not read silently by individuals. From Judean texts themselves (for example, 1QS 6:6-8) it is clear that texts were recited to groups, almost certainly from the text that existed in memory, not from a written copy.[12] Thus, even in scribal circles, texts existed more in the memory than written on scrolls, and were learned as well as heard communally by recitation. How much more, therefore, in village communities that lacked both scrolls and literacy were traditional Israelite materials such as stories of heroes, covenantal laws and teachings, and victory songs, performed and cultivated orally.

Fourth, in a social-cultural context dominated by oral communication, where even when written scrolls existed, the texts were recited from memory, composition was usually carried out not only for but also in performance. Greek and Latin writers describe how they composed texts in their heads, relying on memory for certain materials, and only later dictated their composed text to a scribe who wrote it down.[13] The same seems the likely procedure among Judean scribal circles (such as for *Psalms of Solomon, 1 Enoch,* and Daniel). If it was the rule among literate circles, then composition in performance is all the more likely for popular literature such as the Gospel of Mark and Q in communities where literacy would have been even more limited than among the elite.

Recognition that gospel texts, even if they existed in written form, were performed in groups of people changes dramatically the way they must be understood to have worked and therefore the way they should be approached. In standard older biblical studies, the theological interpreter was trying to reconstruct the meaning of a text fragment such as an individual saying or pericope. The text fragment, abstracted from its fuller literary and historical context, was assumed to possess meaning-in-itself.

If the text is rather taken as a complete unit of communication performed (regularly) to groups of people in a particular historical situation, then interpreters must try to understand how the story or speech did its work in resonating with the group to whom it was performed. Standard New Testament studies has left us ill-equipped to carry out such a challenging task.

Yet help is now available from other fields that are also just discovering oral-derived texts that can, to a degree, be understood in performance. Recent work in social linguistics, ethnography of performance, ethnopoetics, and recent theory of verbal art all draw attention to the special importance of two aspects in particular: the group context in which an oral-derived text was performed, and the cultural tradition that the text referenced metonymically in order to resonate with the community of hearers.[14] As Werner Kelber[15] has recognized, studies of social memory promise to be especially helpful in approaching the relationship of oral-derived texts and the tradition they reference, the cultural biosphere in which they do their work.

Social Memory versus Assumptions of Jesus-Questers

There are already some fundamental reasons why the standard procedure used by the Jesus Seminar and, before it, by form criticism (in which many of us were trained) to identify data for reconstruction of the teaching of Jesus is seriously problematic as a method of historical investigation. The Gospels are assumed to be mere containers of data. The data, however, must be removed from the containers for critical evaluation. Modern rational ("scientific") criteria determine what is potentially good data. While tending to dismiss narratives as too mythic and corrupted by miraculous elements, liberal Jesus-scholars in particular tend to focus heavily on sayings. The determinative criteria derive from the dominant modern western literate definition of real knowledge as being stated in propositional terms. In contrast to subjective feelings and values, only the sayings material from the Gospels sufficiently resembles this propositional knowledge that it can be relied upon as historical data for Jesus. Accordingly, rigorously critical Jesus scholars carefully isolate sayings from their literary contexts that are flawed by faith perspectives in order to evaluate their potential as data.

This procedure is seriously problematic. It is difficult, in the first place, to imagine that anyone could communicate effectively by uttering isolated individual sayings. Purposely isolating sayings from their contexts in the ancient texts, moreover, effectively discards the primary guide we might have as historians to determine both how a given saying functioned as a component in a genuine unit of communication (a speech or a narrative) and in its possible meaning contexts for ancient speaker and hearers. With no ancient guide for its meaning context, then, interpretation is determined only, and almost completely, by the modern scholar, who constructs a new meaning context on the basis of other such radically decontextualized sayings.

Recent studies of social memory not only confirm those observations, but explain further why and how the standard procedure of form criticism and some members of the Jesus Seminar is fundamentally flawed as historical method. A major problem is that these Jesus scholars, along with many others in the New Testament field, are working with a modern misunderstanding of memory rooted in the modern western understanding of knowledge. Studies of social memory can help us identify several interrelated aspects of this fundamental misunderstanding. Much of the following discussion engages the work of John Dominic Crossan because his *Historical Jesus*[16] has been highly influential and because, recognizing memory as a problem, he has seriously grappled with understanding how it works in another methodologically sophisticated and magisterial treatise.[17] But the discussion is also an attempt to grapple critically with what have been standard assumptions and operating procedures in the field of Gospel and Jesus studies that now seem problematic.

The "Textual Model" of Memory

Form critics and their more recent heirs assume that the route that Jesus sayings took from Jesus himself to the literary containers in which they can now be found was oral tradition, that is, the memories of Jesus' followers. As Kelber[18] pointed out twenty-five years ago, form criticism depends on the assumptions of modern print culture. The model for how the followers' memory handled Jesus' sayings was how Matthew and Luke handled what they found in Mark and the reconstructed, hypothetical Q, in other words, texts that the modern scholars understood in term of print culture. That is, not only were the sayings understood as texts, for which Jesus scholars strove to establish the original wording (*ipsissima verba*, or at least *ipsissima structura*), but the scholars worked with a textual model of memory.

Students of social memory have explained that this textual model of memory is also an expression of a modern literate definition of knowledge, propositional knowledge that can be separated out as "objective" from the "subjective" aspect of memory.[19] Not only is each piece of knowledge like a text, but the part of memory that carries those pieces is like a text. Thus for the form critics and their successors in the Jesus Seminar, the memory of the Jesus followers was a container for Jesus sayings, just like the Gospels into which they fed the sayings.

The textual model of memory, however, rests on a fundamental misunderstanding of memory. The reason propositional knowledge in memory seems objective is merely that "we can communicate it in words more easily" than we can the memory of subjective feelings. "But that has nothing to do with the structure of memory. It is a social fact. What emerges at the point of articulation is not the objective part of memory but its social aspect."[20] Drawing on Durkheim's insight about the social character of collectively held ideas, Halbwachs recognized that memory is social and the result of social and historical forces.[21] With regard to the Gospels and gospel tradition as sources for the historical Jesus, the memory involved in oral tradition was not a text-like container but a social process. Moreover, insofar as the Gospels themselves as written texts were almost certainly transcripts of particular performances of the texts, they also were products of social memory. Use of the Gospels as historical sources requires the understanding of social memory.

The "Copy-and-Save" Concept of Memory

Closely related to their textual model of memory, form critics and many Jesus scholars also have a "copy-and-save" conception of memory. In the tradition form-ing process, some disciples were able to remember and repeat Jesus sayings. As indicated by the voting by members of the Jesus Seminar, in some cases the copy-and-save mechanism of memory worked well (red and pink), whereas other sayings involved a considerable degree of creativity (gray and black). While assuming the operation of this mechanism, Crossan is skeptical about how accurately it works. He concludes that in many cases the copying reproduces the "gist" of sayings, but not the precise wording of the "text." This modern intellectual misunderstanding of memory (copy-and-save) is illustrated both by Frederic Bartlett's well-known experiments among his Cambridge colleagues and friends in the 1930s and by Crossan's selective use of the results to show how undependable memory is for reliable reproductions.[22] As Fentress and Wickham see, Bartlett set up the experi-ment to prove what he suspected about memory in modern intellectual society. Bartlett had his friends read (twice) a story from the Chinook people recorded by the anthropologist Franz Boas and then repeat it soon thereafter and again years later, with mixed and unimpressive results. Crossan takes some of the results of the experiment as applicable to ancient Mediterranean peoples.[23]

Both, however, turn out to be comparing apples and oranges, or rather an apple tree and an orange. As Fentress and Wickham note, Bartlett presented to his friends a story taken completely out of its own cultural context and quite unintelligible to his friends and utterly alien to their own culture. If he had presented them a clever new limerick similar to those commonly shared in Oxbridge culture, the results would have been dramatically different. An appropriate use of the Chinook tale for testing memory, which is social, would have been within Chinook culture. An appropriate illustration of how memory worked among early Jesus communities would have to come from the culture of those communities. It is Crossan's very appropriate distrust of copy-and-save memory that leads him to depend so heavily on written, textual containers of sayings as sources for Jesus sayings. But as Fentress and Wickham point out, "The ability of society to transmit its social memory in logical and articulate form is not dependent on the possession of writing."[24]

Memory as Individual

Like Bartlett, Crossan (and perhaps most interpreters) apparently assumes that memory is an individual operation. Given the orientation of modern Western culture, particularly in the United States, to the individual, many of us conceive of Jesus' sayings as teachings to individuals, remembered and transmitted by indi-viduals. It is true that memory operates through individual consciousness. But the main point that Halbwachs and his successors have been explaining is that memory is thoroughly social, the product of social forces operating through communities, movements, and societies.[25] Leading historians such as Marc Bloch and Peter Burke have been clear in recognizing this fundamental reality.[26]

Jesus Sayings as Cultural Artifacts with Meaning in Themselves

In accordance with the modern theory of knowledge on which they are operating, Jesus scholars and others assume that the Jesus sayings transmitted by individual memory have meaning in themselves. That they were operating on this assumption may explain why Crossan and others in the Jesus Seminar were concerned merely to date the documents they took as containers of Jesus sayings. They did not give careful attention to the different meaning contexts and implicit hermeneutics of those different sources. Students of social memory point out that this assumption—that a statement has meaning in itself—is quite unwarranted. In social memory and social knowledge, a particular statement or tale operates in a larger meaning context. When the context changes, the same statement or tale takes on a more or less altered meaning appropriate to the new context.[27]

Jesus Sayings as "Unconventional" or "Countercultural"

The assumption that Jesus' sayings were text-like propositional statements carried in container-like memory underlies another prominent aspect of Jesus research. Under the old theological imperative to find Jesus distinctively different from Judaism, an earlier generation of Jesus-questers established the criterion of dissimilarity (from his Jewish cultural context as well as from the early church) as one of the principal measures for the authentic sayings of Jesus. While the Jesus Seminar and other scholars have seriously qualified that criterion in the direction of some continuity, some leading members of the Jesus Seminar perpetuate the notion in finding Jesus' sayings to be "unconventional" or "counter-cultural."[28]

As historians, of course, we could immediately ask how Jesus could have become a significant historical player if he had been uttering sayings that were so dissimilar to anything in his cultural context, how anything he said would have been remembered if it had not resonated with followers embedded in a particular culture. Recent theory of performance places great emphasis on how speech works by referencing the hearers' cultural tradition and memory. Studies of social memory strongly reinforce such reactions to the "dissimilarity" criterion and the "unconventional" interpretation. Especially in a new movement, as Connerton emphasizes in the first paragraph of his analysis of social memory, "the absolutely new is inconceivable." The followers of Jesus who remembered his teaching and action were responding from "an organized body of expectations based on recollection."[29] Their experience of Jesus would have been embedded in past experience. Memory represents the past and the present as connected to each other.[30] This closely parallels the recognition of oral performance analysis: tradition is key to the communication taking place.[31] More particularly, the images held in social memory are a mixture of pictorial images, slogans, quips, and snatches of discourse. A figure such as Jesus could not have communicated without tapping into those images in ancient Galileans' and others' social memory. Further, the images he used would have communicated effectively only by being "conventionalized and simplified: conventionalized, because the image has to be meaningful for an entire group; simplified, because in order to be generally meaningful and capable of transmission, the complexity of the image must be reduced as far as possible."[32] Of course, while Jesus' teaching had to be conventionalized for effective communication with his followers, who were embedded in the Israelite "little tradition" of the peasantry (including fishers and the marginalized), it was indeed most likely "counter" to the culture of the elite in Jerusalem and Tiberias. That Jesus' teaching may well have been counter to the elite culture of Jerusalem and scribal circles, who produced the Judean literature that constitute many of our written sources for late second temple times, should not be mistaken for Jesus' teaching having been counter to Israelite culture generally. It is necessary to be more critically attentive to the differences between the elite and the popular versions of Israelite culture.

The fundamental insight of Halbwachs and his successors that memory is social is simple but profound in its implications for academic endeavors such as studies of Jesus and the Gospels. In order to use the Gospels appropriately as historical sources for Jesus and early Jesus movements, therefore, we have to abandon several interrelated aspects of the modern western misunderstanding of memory: the textual model, the copy-and-save conception, individualization, the notion that Jesus sayings have meaning in themselves, and the presumption that Jesus sayings could have been somehow distinctively different from his cultural context.

Why and How Study of Social Memory Is Useful as an Approach to Jesus and Jesus Movements

The prominent historian Peter Burke noted some time ago that historians have two principal interests in memory. "In the first place, they need to study memory as a historical *source*, to produce a critique of the reliability of reminiscence on the lines of the traditional critique of historical documents."[33] Against the stiff resistance of their more traditional colleagues, some younger historians of the recent past moved to include oral history in their research. Yet historians of earlier periods also need to understand social memory, in order to deal with "the oral testimonies and traditions embedded in many written records." Secondly, historians should be concerned with "memory as a historical phenomenon," including the principles of selection, variations by location, and changes over time.[34] Given the character of the orally derived texts that they study, biblical historians also have a keen interest in social memory in both of these respects.

It is curious, however, that a social historian of Burke's stature did not mention a third reason for understanding the workings of social memory—for which the two interests he identified would be ancillary. Historians, especially social historians, would presumably have an interest in social movements, particularly popular movements, and more broadly people's history in general. Social memory is often the most important source for such movements. Indeed, for those popular movements that did not become prominent and gain wide notice, social memory may be virtually the only historical source. More significantly, for movements of mainly non-literate people, their social memory would have been one of the principal forces driving their collective actions. Burke makes a passing comment that unofficial memories may differ sharply from official memories and "are sometimes historical forces in their own right," offering the examples of the German Peasant War of 1525 and the "Norman Yoke" in the English Revolution.[35] Although he does not pursue the implications himself, his passing comment that "unofficial memories" become historical forces themselves leads us to consider how popular Israelite social memory may have played a creative and formative role in the movement resulting from the interaction of Jesus and his followers.

In the academic division of labor, the subject matter that we New Testament scholars deal with provides prime examples of popular leaders and movements that became historical forces that local and imperial officials had to reckon with. As suggested above, moreover, given the oral derivation of the Gospels and gospel materials, the literature we interpret was apparently the product of those movements' social memory. Gospel materials, moreover, mediated both through literature (the Scriptures) and through continuing orally cultivated social memory, comprised an important component of the social memory that motivated both the German Peasant War, the English Revolution, as well as the earlier Hussites, Lollards, and many other popular movements. Interpreters of Jesus and the Gospels have compelling reasons to understand social memory.

One of the most important possibilities that social memory studies help open up for an appropriate approach to Jesus and the Gospels is a critical focus on the diversity and conflict of memories. Students of social memory have long since moved beyond the limitations of Halbwachs' teacher Durkheim, with his emphasis on societal cohesion, to the avoidance of social dissent and conflict.[36] They are as aware as any that the role of professional scholars, like that of school teaching and the media, is to reinforce official or established memory more than to critically investigate dissenting memories.[37] They are aware that the struggle of peoples against hegemonic memory is often the struggle of their memory against enforced forgetting, against the elimination of alternative memory.[38]

The study of Jesus, Jesus movements, and the Gospels can learn from them. Interpreters of Jesus and the Gospels focus on literature and movements that express opposition to the local and imperial rulers. The latter attempted to suppress those movements and their memory, through the crucifixion of Jesus and subsequent repressive action against his followers. In some cases the rulers succeeded, except that the memory of Jesus survived in the oral-derived texts of the Jesus movements. Ironically, established biblical studies has sometimes effectively suppressed the subversive memory carried in the Gospels that the Roman rulers could not stamp out. This has been done by treating the texts as merely religious and by reducing the focus to Jesus as a teacher or to individual discipleship, while virtually ignoring the collective activity and solidarity of a popular movement. Recent studies of social memory can help interpreters of Jesus and the Gospels to appreciate how the adversarial gospel tradition and literature are rooted not only in the subversive popular memory not only of Jesus and his movement, but also in the memory of earlier Israelite leaders and movements. Such studies of social memory can help New Testament scholars rediscover the memory of social movements whose voice has been silenced by established scholarship. This means that, like the gospel literature itself, study of social memory in Jesus movements will be subversive of long established scholarship—challenging standard assumptions, concepts, and approaches in order to discern oppositional memories and the conflicts they engage.

Crossan declares confidently that what has been discovered about how Balkan bards, their texts, and their audiences are rooted in centuries-old tradition "has nothing whatsoever to do with the memories of illiterate peasants operating within the Jesus tradition," because of the latter's "total newness."[39] Indeed, judging from the "data-base" listed in the Overture of his *Historical Jesus*,[40] the Cynic-like sage he presents is almost completely memoryless. Only one name (Adam) from Israelite tradition remains in the aphorisms and parables that Crossan has declared admissible as evidence. When he comes to presentation and analysis, he does admit to a few other allusions. But we are left wondering what the basis is for concluding that Jesus was a *Jewish* and not just a generic Mediterranean peasant.

Suspicious of the authenticity of most of Jesus' prophetic sayings, he thus eliminates from his data base references to Abraham, Isaac, Jacob, Solomon and the Queen of the South, and Jonah, as well as the traditional Israelite prophetic forms of some of those sayings. Following standard critical criteria in extracting sayings from narrative context, he ignores the prominent references and allusions in Mark and elsewhere to Moses, Elijah, the exodus, the twelve tribes of

Israel, and the covenant meal. Because, in standard procedure, he focuses on individual sayings, he does not even notice Jesus' use of traditional Israelite forms and patterns, such as components of Mosaic covenantal patterns and allusions to covenantal teaching.

Although Crossan's procedure tends to eliminate references to Israelite tradition, the data-base of the Jesus tradition in which he finds "total newness," if we attend to it closely and sensitively, does indeed make numerous references or allusions to Israelite tradition. "Finger of God" refers to the exodus. The issues of adultery and of giving tribute to Caesar are rooted in the Mosaic covenant. Blessings and woes are components of the Mosaic covenant and woes crop up prominently in the prophets. The clever saying about giving one's shirt as well as one's cloak refers to Mosaic covenantal law. "Go bury my father" alludes to the story of Elijah's commissioning of Elisha. The parable of the tenants in the vineyard resonates deeply with the song of the vineyard in Isaiah's prophecies. The image of a division of families was used by the prophet Micah. The prophetic action and prophecies against the Temple are reminiscent of Jeremiah's prophecies and prophetic actions. Moreover, other images (swearing by Jerusalem) and figures (the Samaritan, the Levite, and the priest) in Jesus' teaching refer directly to more recent Israelite institutions and history. The "newness" of Crossan's Jesus tradition is in fact not "total." His followers' memory, even when its copy-and-save mechanism is judged dysfunctional, cannot help but carry memory of and allusion to Israelite tradition, including many references to central aspects of that tradition, such as exodus and covenant, Moses and Elijah, prophetic oracle and covenantal teaching.

If we broadened our purview beyond Crossan's critically restricted "data-base" to include the prophetic materials in Q and the narrative in Mark, then the Jesus tradition (however it be judged for "authenticity") is simply permeated with social memory of Israelite tradition. The obvious implication: the Jesus tradition is far from "totally new." It cannot possibly be understood except as rooted in Israelite social memory. That holds even if Mark were located in its composition and performance in Syria or even in Rome. Even if the (pre-canonical) Gospel of Mark belonged to communities of Gentiles, they apparently identify with and understand the text in terms of its resonance with Israelite tradition. In seeking help from studies of social memory to understand Jesus and the Gospels, therefore, we must focus not only on the Jesus tradition itself but also on its grounding in and continuity with Israelite tradition. That is, we are dealing not only with social memory in the development toward and formation of the oral-derived texts of the Gospels themselves but also with the social memory of Israelite tradition that those texts referenced in order to resonate with their hearers.[41]

How Do We Gain Access to the Social Memory of Jesus People?

The obvious next question then is how we can gain access to the social memory of the earliest and subsequent followers of Jesus, the bearers of the social memory of Jesus' mission and message who were also embedded in Israelite social memory. Students of social memory seek access through various kinds of sources, including oral traditions, memoirs and written records (memory transformed through writing), public monuments and other sources of images, places and landscape images, and rituals and other actions. Students of social memory of Jesus tradition and Israelite tradition have only some of these available as sources. How we might be able to use those sources, moreover, requires some critical analysis, given recent research on late second temple Israelite society and culture.

For social memory of Jesus tradition itself, we largely lack monuments and landscape images and have minimal access to rituals (the Lord's Supper and baptism). Recent recognition of the predominantly oral communication environment and the likelihood that texts were orally composed and performed prior to and subsequent to being written down has problematized the use of the Gospels as sources. We must still figure out, and almost certainly will be debating among ourselves for some time, the degree to which the Gospels represent transcripts of oral-derived and performed texts or written records representing memory transformed by written composition.

For social memory of Israelite tradition, it can no longer be a matter of consulting the Hebrew Bible passages listed in the apparatus of our copy of the Greek New Testament. As recent research has shown, few manuscripts existed in ancient Judea and Galilee, and those mainly in scribal circles where texts were nevertheless recited from memory.[42] As noted above, moreover, different versions of the Torah and Prophets coexisted even in literate elite circles. The people who responded to Jesus, who participated in Jesus movements, were largely ordinary people who would have had little or no direct contact with written texts, perhaps not even indirect contact. They would have known Israelite tradition through oral communication mainly in their village communities, with perhaps some indirect influence from scribal retainers (such as Pharisees) who represented Jerusalem interests in occasional interaction with villagers. We therefore cannot use biblical and other Judean literature as direct sources for the Judean and Galilean "little tradition." Because it was apparently parallel to and in some regular interaction with the "great tradition" represented by the developing texts of the Torah, Prophets, and other versions of Jerusalem-based tradition, however, we can use written biblical and other Judean texts as indirect sources for the Israelite popular tradition. We also have other indirect sources.

Often we can discern from Josephus' portrayal of popular movements and protests that such actions are informed by Israelite tradition.[43] This seems fairly clear, for example, from his accounts of the popular movements led by prophets and popularly acclaimed kings and by protests in the Temple at Passover. Finally, the Gospels themselves, insofar as they are products of popular circles, provide evidence for Israelite social memory among Galilean and Judean popular tradition, both of traditional figures and traditional cultural forms.

The net effect of these critical complications regarding our sources only serves to indicate the historical importance of Israelite social memory for understanding Jesus, Jesus movements, and their literature. Another effect, of course, is to make all the more important and exciting (in anticipation) the help that studies of social memory can provide us, particularly as it appears to dovetail with and supplement the results of recent research that has undermined standard older assumptions, concepts, and approaches in the field of Gospel studies.

The Social Memory of Jesus Built on Israelite Social Memory

Finally, the way social memory analysis might contribute to a more defensible approach to the historical Jesus can be illustrated in focusing briefly on two particular complexes of material in Mark and Q that resonate with those same complexes in Israelite social memory: renewal of Mosaic covenant and renewal of Israel by a new Moses and Elijah. Given the usual orientation in New Testament studies to culture divorced from concrete historical political-economic life, it is important to emphasize that Mark and Q to reflect and respond to the violent domination of the Roman imperial rulers and their client rulers over subject peoples and the continuing struggle of the latter to resist. That struggle, moreover, had intensified in the time of Jesus and his mission, which is so vividly framed by the widespread revolts of Judeans and Galileans in 4–2 B.C.E. and 66–70 C.E. Many recent treatments of social memory may be all the more helpful for investigation of Jesus and the Gospels because they give special attention to subordinate groups and peoples.

In this connection, we can perhaps work analogously from Connerton's critique of the approach followed by some oral historians when we focus on gospel materials and Jesus followers. In both cases the aim is to open channels for the hearing of voices that are otherwise silenced by scholarly concepts and procedures. Like recent Jesus interpreters (note Crossan's subtitle "*The Life of a Mediterranean Jewish Peasant*"), however, oral historians approached their sources with the concept of a life history, as if their subjects thought like educated modern "men of affairs." This approach, however, may actually impede the aim of the historians.

> The oral history of subordinate groups will produce another type of history: one in which not only will most of the details be different, but in which the very construction of meaningful shapes will obey a different principle. Different details will emerge because they are inserted, as it were, into a different kind of narrative home. . . . In [the] culture of subordinate groups, . . . the life histories of its members have a different rhythm. . . not patterned by the individual's intervention in the working of dominant institutions.[44]

Analogously, seeking out what Jesus actually said or did, much less his individual life, will only block access to a Jesus who was historically significant as a catalyst of movements who remembered him. Not only was their memory social, but Jesus became significant for his interaction with them in action and speech taken in his and their fundamentally conflictual historical situation. As suggested by this analogy from Connerton, as by all the above discussion, an approach to the historical Jesus and the Gospels must be relational and contextual.

In a complex multi-faceted approach, I have recently attempted to understand how we can appreciate certain broad (Israelite) cultural patterns that are discernible in the speeches of Q and in the story of Mark.[45] By focusing on individual sayings and narrative episodes extracted from the speeches and overall narrative that formed the units of communication, we render them unintelligible, because we decontextualize them. In their own historical communication context, however, what our standard scholarly analytical practices render into unintelligible text fragments were held together intelligibly by cultural patterns or scripts derived from Israelite tradition, which provide the tacit infrastructure as well as the cultural meaning context of the speeches or the broader narrative of which they were integral components. Ancient Judean and other texts may well provide our only sources for and access to these patterns and scripts. Yet their operation in Mark and Q was probably not derived from written texts, but rather from their continuing presence in popular Judean and Galilean tradition. Central among these were the social memory of Mosaic covenant and of popular prophetic and messianic movements. Combined with the recent research and new approaches outlined at the outset above, recent studies of social memory can help open the way to discerning how such popular Israelite social memory was operating in the interaction of Jesus and his followers as represented in Mark and Q.

Alan Kirk (drawing on several studies of social memory) explains that the past—itself constellated by the work of memory—provides the *frameworks* for cognition, organization, and interpretation of the experiences of the present. "The salient past, immanent in the narrative patterns in which it has become engrained in social memory, provides the very cognitive and linguistic habits by which a group perceives, orients itself, has its 'being in the world.' . . . It is precisely because of this framework's orienting, stabilizing effect that free, innovative action in the present becomes possible."[46]

One of the *frameworks* for cognition, organization, and interpretation of political-economic-religious life in ancient Israel, perhaps the principal framework, was the Mosaic covenant. The six-component structure discerned by comparison with second-millenium B.C.E. Hittite suzerainty treaties by Mendenhall and others can be discerned in Exodus 20 and Joshua 24. From fragments of prophetic oracles such as Micah 6:1-7 and Isaiah 1:2-3; 3:13-15, it is clear that this deeply rooted framework (that still included the appeal to witnesses) continued to inform prophetic protests (literally in the name of God) against the rulers' oppression of the people. Readers of the Community Rule and Damascus Rule from Qumran can recognize that the framework—in the somewhat simplified three-part form of God's deliverance, commandments to the people, and pronouncement of blessings and curses as sanction on those commandments—continued to inform the organization of dissident movements into late second temple times.[47] Those Qumran texts also demonstrate that the form could be transformed so that the blessings and curses became the new declaration of divine deliverance, with other devices marshaled to serve as sanctions.

This same covenant framework turns out to be prominent in the earliest gospel texts. As I have argued in larger treatments of the speech in Q/Luke 6:20-49, all those sayings that have been classified into the essentialist category of "sapiential" (wisdom) can be more intelligibly understood as components of a performative speech of covenant renewal.[48] After declaring God's current or imminent action of deliverance and judgment in the blessings and woes, Q's Jesus pronounces renewed covenantal teachings which make numerous allusions to traditional covenantal principles and exhortations, followed by the double parable of houses built on rock and sand, which serve as sanction on keeping his word. Similarly, argued in a larger treatment of Mark as a complete story,[49] the series of dialogues in Mark 10 which explicitly recite the covenantal commandments, can also be discerned to be a coherent renewal of Mosaic covenant at a crucial point in the narrative sequence, following the announcement and demonstration that the kingdom of God is now at hand. As is particularly clear in Q/Luke 6:20-49, moreover, the covenantal pattern is not simply the framework for organization of sayings and dialogues in the texts of Q and Mark, but the framework of organization of the communities of the movement among whom the speeches and gospel story were being performed. That means also that the traditional covenantal pattern was also the framework of orientation, aiding discernment of what was wrong (people were divided among themselves, not observing the fundamental covenantal principles), and the framework of stabilizing innovation (creatively updating the covenantal form and teaching to effect renewal of mutual cooperation, sharing, and solidarity).

In Mark, especially, the Mosaic covenant pattern extends beyond the covenant renewal dialogues into other episodes.[50] Most prominently, Jesus insists on the basis of the covenantal commandments of God ("honor your father and mother") that local economic needs must take priority, rejecting the pressure on the people to devote resources to the Temple, as advocated by the Pharisaic representatives of the Temple in their "traditions of the elders" (Mark 7:1-13). Jesus' final Passover meal with the Twelve, and presumably the regular celebration of the Lord's Supper among the Markan communities, was a meal of covenant renewal, as indicated in the allusion that the blood of the covenant makes to Israel's covenantal meal with God on Sinai (Mark 14:17-25; Exod 24). Less explicitly, Jesus' prophetic demonstration against the Temple, in reciting part of Jeremiah's oracle against the Temple, alludes also to the covenantal basis on which God is condemning it. Studies of social memory thus confirm and further illuminate how the traditional Israelite cultural pattern of the Mosaic covenant, alive and well in the social memory of Jesus' contemporaries, provided a fundamental framework of organization and interpretation in Mark and Q and the movements they addressed.

Kirk also points out that "Social memory makes available the moral and symbolic resources for making sense of the present. It does this by aligning, or better, 'keying' present experiences and predicaments to images and models in the past that have particular saliency for a community."[51] As Fentress and Wickham explain, in popular culture, "stories do more than represent particular events: they connect, clarify, and interpret events in a general fashion. Stories provide us with a set of stock explanations which underlie our predispositions to interpret reality in the ways that we do."[52] The same process happens in the assimilation and interpretation of historical events. What Barry Schwartz calls "frame images" work as "pictorial counterparts of 'emplotment,'" defining the meaning of events by depicting them "as episodes in a narrative that precedes and transcends them."[53]

Another broad cultural pattern that operates in Mark's story of Jesus is evident in the double sequence of "acts of power": sea crossing, exorcism, healing, wilderness feeding. The same broad cultural pattern also appears in Mark's overall story as the "script" of a popular prophet and movement, a script also evident in the many prophets and their movements that Josephus mentions. The sequence of miracle stories in Mark, of course, may have been semi-separable from the broader script of a popular prophetic movement. It is difficult to tell whether the similar sequence of "signs" in the Gospel of John is part of such a larger script that can be clearly identified in the rest of the story. In the main plot of the renewal of Israel in Mark's overall story, the double sequence of miracle stories has been interwoven and overlaid with subplots of Jesus' conflict with the disciples and of the women's role in the renewal of Israel. The underlying pattern of "miracle chain," however, remains unmistakable in the duplicated sequence of episodes.[54]

Analysis of these episodes in terms of social memory readily confirms and deepens the sense that they are shaped by numerous allusions to the formative events of Israel led by Moses and the renewal of Israel led by Elijah. This is clinched, in Mark, by the ensuing episode of the appearance of Jesus with both on the mountain before the three disciples. The crossings of the stormy sea are reminiscent of Israel's crossing of the Red Sea led by Moses. Jesus' feedings of the thousands in the wilderness allude to Moses' feeding of the people in the wilderness. By implication, in resonance with the audience's Israelite social memory, Jesus is thus leading a new exodus, a new or re-formation of Israel. Jesus' exorcisms and healings in the middle of the sequence (including a raising of the [almost] dead, and perhaps also the multiplication of food) are reminiscent of Elijah's (and Elisha's) healings in renewal of a disintegrating Israel under the despotic foreign rule of Ahab and Jezebel. The stories to which these episodes in Mark are alluding were basic elements of Israelite popular tradition long before they were taken up into the Judean great tradition, some textual traditions of which developed into the Septuagint and the Masoretic text.

While the allusions these stories make to scriptural events have long been recognized, however, standard New Testament scholarship tended not to look for broader patterns of culture. Yet sequences of several incidents in the formative Israelite exodus wilderness story, such as the sea crossing and the wilderness feeding, appear in any number of Psalms and other passages in Judean literature. The wondrous deeds of Elijah and his disciple Elisha, moreover, were recited in texts as divergent as the popular stories taken up into the Deuteronomistic History (1 Kings 17–21; 2 Kings 1–9) and a section of Ben Sira's hymnic "Praise of Famous Ancestors." These sequences appearing in written texts are sufficiently different to suggest not common prototypes but general patterns in Israelite culture, versions of which could be deployed as appropriate in given circumstances. Werner Kelber[55] demonstrated how individual healing or exorcism stories could be understood as orally composed and performed from a standard repertoire of motifs according to a basic three-part narrative pattern. Given evidence of broader patterns of Mosaic or Elijah-Elisha stories, we might build on Kelber's insight to hypothesize that Israelite social memory included a broader repertoire of distinctively Israelite stories and story motifs. Included in that repertoire were several stories organized in sequences. Precisely such resources from Israelite social memory provided the *frameworks* and *frame images* used in emploting and defining the meaning of Jesus' exorcisms, healings, feedings, and other actions, "depicting them as episodes in a narrative that precede[d] and transcende[d] them."[56]

It was long since recognized, according to Enlightenment criteria of reliable historical accounts, that there is no point asking whether and how individual miracle stories adequately or authentically represent an incident of healing or exorcism. Studies of social memory confirm that social memory of events is not stable as accurate historical information. Social memory, however, "is stable at the level of shared meanings and remembered images."[57] If we focus not on individual stories but on the two parallel sequences of stories, then it is clear that in Mark's story (and prior to and independently of Mark) Jesus' followers understand his exorcisms, healings, and so forth, as a renewal of Israel, drawing on and resonating with a deeply rooted pattern of the social memory of Moses and Elijah.

Discerning how Mark and Q are informed by, draw upon, and adapt broader cultural patterns of Israelite social memory, of course, does not constitute direct evidence for Jesus in mission. Since we are just beginning to explore the implications of the important insight that memory is social, it would be premature to attempt to draw conclusions about how Israelite social memory functioned in the interaction between Jesus and his immediate followers. Combined with the recent research and it implications sketched at the outset above, however, studies of social memory enable us to begin constructing a far more defensible set of assumptions and approaches than those of form criticism and the Jesus Seminar. Crossan, critical leader of the Jesus Seminar, presents a Jesus whose teaching exhibits little or no Israelite memory that is acknowledged in discussion. In effect, we are asked to believe that, historically, Jesus did not operate in Israelite culture in Galilee.[58]

The Gospel of Mark, whether composed in Syria or even as far away as Rome no later than the 70s, presents Jesus' action and teaching as deeply rooted in Israelite tradition in nearly every episode. Similarly the speeches of Q exhibit multiple Israelite figures, motifs, and cultural forms. This may not be a problem for standard New Testament studies. On the assumptions of academic print culture, Mark can be pictured as "composed at a desk in a scholar's study lined with texts."[59] Recent research, however, has simply "pulled the rug out from under" such anachronistic assumptions and the resulting procedures. The combination of the recent research cited above and studies of social memory lead to the conclusion that there was considerable continuity between Jesus (in interaction with his immediate followers) and emergent texts such the Q speeches and Mark's gospel. That continuity is provided by the social memory of Jesus-in-mission, which is a continuation in key ways of Israelite social memory, including broad cultural patterns such as those of Mosaic covenant and Moses and Elijah led renewal of Israel. The social memory of Jesus-in-mission accessible in Q speeches and Markan story does not give us access to exactly what Jesus said or did, but it does enable us to discern the shared meanings of his typical preaching and practice in the broader cultural patterns operative in the historical situation in which he worked.

Chapter
Seven

Popular Memory and Cultural Patterns in Mark

═══════════════════════

The way we understand the Gospel of Mark has been changing dramatically in the last thirty years. Once we recognize that the gospel is a sustained narrative, indeed a complete story with a main plot and several subplots, we can no longer treat individual episodes in isolation, the way we were trained in graduate school. Once we recognize that, in the predominantly oral communication environment of antiquity, stories such as Mark were performed before communities of people, even after they were written down, we can no longer project the assumptions and typical approaches of literary study that assumes a writer at a desk and an individual reader. And once we recognize that only a tiny literate elite possessed written copies of texts, we can no longer assume that our sources for the reconstruction of ancient history can be treated as if they were documents in modern archives. The composition-performance and the appropriation of the Gospel of Mark were embedded in a broader cultural memory in which written scrolls were one among many media of communication.

Werner Kelber was one of the first to explore Mark's Gospel as a dramatic story. He then pioneered the recognition of the difference and relation of orality and literacy and the implications for Mark and other New Testament literature. More recently he has discerned the importance of studies of cultural memory in other fields and how understanding memory will further change the way we approach the composition and use of Mark and other gospels.[1] I would like to pursue some of the implications of Kelber's insights into the importance of cultural memory for fuller appreciation of the Gospel of Mark.

Formulating a Complex Approach to the Complexities of Israelite Cultural Memory

Since memory is always social-cultural, it is necessary to focus both on the particular social-cultural memory involved in Mark and on the way in which memory works in the composition and performance of the Gospel in its historical social context. Insofar as the contents of the Gospel are inseparable from its form, it is clear that the overall story and most of its component episodes were embedded, not merely in the memory of Jesus and the synoptic tradition, but more deeply in Israelite cultural memory. The principal settings, Galilee, Judea, Jerusalem, the Temple, are sites laden with and bearers of Israelite cultural memory, and the principal characters come into conflict over customs, rituals, festivals, and religious and economic practices central to Israelite memory. Jesus is represented as acting out roles reminiscent of some of the prime heroes in Israel's history. The past that the Gospels are appropriating for present community concerns is that of Israel as well as Jesus' ministry. The latter is embedded in the former and cannot be separated from it.

Insofar as Mark (however widely available in written form) was being orally performed, moreover, its reception and its hermeneutics were oral-aural. While established Gospel studies in particular and New Testament studies in general are ill equipped to understand orally performed narratives, help is readily available from related fields that have given considerable thought to the practice and theory of oral performance in relation to and comparison with written texts. In striving to appreciate Mark's story as oral performance I have found most compelling the work of John Miles Foley, which in turn draws on ethnography of speaking, ethnopoetics, and sociolinguistics in developing his own theory of immanent art. Key for my explorations of Mark and other orally derived texts are the interrelated components of the *text* itself, the performance *context*, and the way the text *metonymically references* the cultural *tradition*.[2] Kelber, who interacts closely with Foley, stated the importance of extra-textual *tradition* in both the production and reception of a text in comprehensively strong terms as a circumambient context or "biosphere in which speaker and hearers live, . . . an invisible nexus of references and identities from which people draw sustenance, . . . and in relation to which they make sense of their lives."[3] In attempting to appreciate a gospel in oral performance, we are thus no longer searching for the meaning of the text, but attending to *the work that a text does in a community of people*. We are focused squarely on the historical social context in attempting to understand the work done by an orally performed text *as it metonymically references the tradition*. The cultural tradition of a community is the key to appreciating how a text in performance did its work.

But we are now faced with serious problems as we attempt to investigate the Israelite cultural memory and tradition in which Jesus' ministry and pre-Markan Gospel materials were embedded and the way that tradition was metonymically referenced by the performed text. In the field of New Testament studies in which we are trained, it has simply been assumed that Israelite tradition and cultural memory were virtually identical with and known through the medium of the Hebrew Bible, the "Law and the Prophets." It has also simply been assumed that ancient Judeans and Galileans dealt with the cultural memory that they presumably knew via the biblical text mainly in fragmentary units of a verse, a proverb, a law, a motif, or even a phrase. Recent research, however, has demonstrated that these assumptions of standard Gospel studies, which are deeply rooted in print culture, are quite unwarranted and simply anachronistic. We can focus on three interrelated areas of this recent research.

First, literacy in Judea and Galilee was limited mainly to circles of scribes and priests concentrated in Jerusalem and the Herodian administrations. As noted at the outset, moreover, scrolls were both cumbersome and expensive. Thus about the only people who had direct knowledge of the nascent Hebrew scriptures were scribes and priests connected with the Temple in Jerusalem or the dissident scribal-priestly community at Qumran, who left the Dead Sea Scrolls. It seems highly unlikely, on the other hand, that Judean and Galilean villagers, the vast majority of the populace, who could neither afford expensive cumbersome scrolls nor read them, would have had direct knowledge of the nascent Hebrew scriptures. Villagers and townspeople presumably knew of the existence of the writing (scripture) kept mainly in the Temple in Jerusalem. They shared with scribal circles a reverence for the aura and authority that surrounded the written word on those huge, heavy scrolls. Josephus tells of two incidents in which a Torah scroll not only is found in a small town in Judea and a large town in Galilee, but carries a special symbolic significance for ordinary people. The burning of a scroll by a Roman soldier in a Judean town touches off a widespread protest (*J.W.* 2.229-30). And an outspoken fellow in Taricheae during the great revolt in 66–67 accuses the duplicitous aristocratic priest Josephus of preparing to betray "the laws of Moses" symbolized by the scroll on which they are written (*Life* 134-35). Yet it seems highly unlikely that the non-literate Galilean villagers, among whom memories of Jesus' mission were originally cultivated in the context of Israelite cultural memory, would have had direct contact with scarce and cumbersome scrolls of "the Law and the Prophets." The distinctive account in Luke 4:16-21 that portrays Jesus reading from a scroll of Isaiah has been shaped by Luke from knowledge of practices in assemblies (*synagōgai*) of the Jewish diaspora.

It has simply been assumed that references in the Gospel of Mark to "the writing" or "it is written" (often accompanied by an ostensible citation of or allusion to a particular passage) indicate that a biblical or scriptural text is being quoted.[4] Closer examination suggests that the references in Mark to "it is written" do not mean that a literate author was consulting a written text.[5] Rather "it is written" refers to the existence, up there somewhere, of written scrolls with supposed authority to which Jesus' opponents, the scribes and Pharisees, have access and supposedly know only too well. Most, but not all, of these references are polemical, throwing the authority of the writing or the written version back in the face of scribal groups. The Gospel of Mark knows of the existence of the writing, but it is not at all clear that the gospel is quoting from direct knowledge of a written scroll.

Second, the written text of "the Law and the Prophets" was not standardized among scribal-intellectual circles who possessed written scrolls until well into the second century C.E. or later. Scholars who have spent a lifetime poring over the scrolls of books that were later included in the Hebrew Bible found among the Dead Sea Scrolls are concluding that two or three different textual traditions coexisted in the same scribal community at Qumran.[6] Those different textual traditions, moreover, were still unstable, still undergoing development in the form of continuing interpretation-composition in the process of being recopied. In addition to the different textual traditions of the books of the Pentateuch and prophetic books, moreover, there were alternative versions of Israel's history, the Torah, and prophetic lore (and *not* "rewritten Bible") in books that were not later included in the Hebrew Bible, such as the *Biblical Antiquities* of Pseudo-Philo, *Jubilees*, the *Temple Scroll*, 4QMMT, the different sections of the book of *1 Enoch*. Thus even in scribal circles different versions of Israelite cultural tradition competed for authority. If there were different, competing versions of Israelite tradition among scribal circles who possessed written scrolls, how much more in popular circles who did not. We should not conclude that the peasantry was ignorant of Israelite tradition. They simply cultivated their own versions that would have been influenced only indirectly by the written versions of the scribal elite.

In the Gospel of Mark, most of the references and allusions to Israelite tradition do not make an explicit connection with a particular passage in a nascent scriptural text. Jesus does a number of Moses-like or Elijah-like acts, but with no reference to particular passages in Exodus or Numbers or 1–2 Kings. Jesus commandeers a colt for his ride into Jerusalem, but with no explicit reference to Zechariah 9:9. Where reference is made to "it is written," moreover, the references turn out, for example, to be combinations of sayings by different prophets (Mark 1:2-3; 11:17). It is difficult, if not impossible, moreover, to determine that a particular version of the nascent scripture is being quoted from, for example, the Septuagint, Masoretic, or another textual tradition. Given the existence at the time, even in scribal circles, of different versions of Israelite tradition, even of books long since written on scrolls, therefore, it seems far more likely to imagine that the Gospel of Mark drew on multiple forms and versions of Israelite tradition. The reference to the story of David and his companions eating "the bread of the presence," which names Abiathar rather than Ahimelech as high priest at the time (Mark 2:23-28), evidently did not depend directly on either the Septuagint or the proto-Masoretic version, but on yet another of multiple versions of the tradition of David's career. The dispute between Jesus and the scribes and Pharisees in Mark 7:1-13, moreover, is not between the "written Torah" and the "oral Torah," as earlier Protestant interpreters supposed. It was rather explicitly between the Pharisees' "tradition of the elders" and the fundamental covenantal "commandment of God," which would have been widely known and recited orally in Israel for generations.

Third, even the literate elite, the scholars of scribal circles, such as the Pharisees and Qumranites, depended as much or more on oral cultivation and memory than they did on their precious, but cumbersome scrolls. Modern biblical scholars, working on the assumptions of print culture, project pictures of the ancient scribes, Pharisees, and rabbis in their own image as eagerly engaged in study and interpretation of sacred written (biblical) texts. That picture does not fit with evidence from our sources. Ironically, we have been aware for some time that the Pharisees cultivated oral "traditions of the elders" (Mark 7) that were not written, yet that they claimed derived from Sinai every bit as much as had the laws written in the books of Moses. The scribal-priestly community at Qumran that left the Dead Sea Scrolls also had extensive rules and regulations, "laws and ordinances," that are couched in language similar to that in legal material of the Pentateuch, yet are not quotations of or explicit interpretations of the latter. In later rabbinic circles, the Torah was learned by recitation rather than by pouring over the lettering on scrolls. The text was thus available in rabbis' memory.

As Martin Jaffee has pointed out, if we look closely at the self-descriptions of how the Qumran community proceeded in common meetings, it is clear the members recited their scriptures orally. According to their regulations for a gathering of ten (or more),

> The congregation shall watch in community for a third of every night of the year, to *recite* the scroll (*sepher*) and to *search* the ordinance (*mishpat*) and to bless together. (1QS 6.6-8)

To translate the Hebrew with "to read" and "to study" conforms their procedure anachronistically to modern print culture, especial biblical study. Their practice was clearly oral recitation of some text committed to memory (some version of Deuteronomy?), a performance of some collection of regulations (some version of ordinances like those transcribed in the Community Rule [1QS] or the Damascus Rule?), along with oral delivery of communal blessings. As Jaffee points out, the scriptural text was inscribed in their memory, as much as it was on their scrolls.[7] Even scribal-priestly circles, the literate elite, thus cultivated their cultural tradition in oral forms that were not explicit interpretations of scripture. And while some parts of their cultural tradition had been written on scrolls and perhaps thus somewhat stabilized, their cultivation of even those parts depended on memory and oral recitation. Among the non-literate villagers, of course, Israelite cultural tradition would have depended almost completely on oral communication, on social memory cultivated orally, without writing.

In the Gospel of Mark, most of those numerous references and allusions to figures and incidents in Israelite tradition can most easily have derived from oral cultivation of Israel's cultural memory. Stories of Moses, Elijah, David, and other heroes would have been widely known and cultivated and not confined to the scriptural and other texts produced and used by the scribal-priestly elite. Covenantal principles or psalms and probably many prophetic sayings would have been widely known and cultivated in ways not confined to written texts.

Research in these three interrelated areas has thus undermined the previous assumptions of Gospel studies. What were previously imagined as "people of the book" did not have their knowledge of Israelite tradition primarily from the Hebrew Bible. The work of Kelber and others has fostered a much fuller appreciation of the importance of Israelite cultural memory for the development, composition, and use of the Gospel of Mark. But especially for the ordinary people among whom the gospel developed and was recited, the written scrolls of books that were later included in the (Hebrew) Bible, which modern scholars had assumed were *the* medium through which Jesus followers knew Israelite tradition, played a relatively peripheral role in their cultural memory. Their cultural memory depended rather on extra-textual media, or variant versions of stories, songs, rituals, and customs that were cultivated orally.

Israelite cultural memory was far more complex than it appeared previously from concentration on scriptural books. That, in turn, suggests that our approach to Israelite cultural memory and the central importance it played in the emergence and use of the Gospels will need to be correspondingly complex. In the limited context of this chapter we can briefly explore only two main theses: that Israelite cultural memory was contested in a struggle between official and popular tradition, hegemonic and anti-hegemonic memory; and that Israelite cultural memory operated in certain prominent patterns, at least at the popular level at which Mark was produced and performed.

Popular versus Official Tradition—Anti-Hegemonic versus Hegemonic Memory

The difference between the literate scribal circles in possession of written texts and the non-literate villagers who did not points to a deeper division in Israelite cultural memory. It has been standard in Gospel studies to posit Judaism as the context in which Jesus and his followers were involved and out of which the gospel tradition developed. Essentialist constructs such as Judaism, however, simply obscure historical differences exposed by recent research. The source for what constituted Judaism has been the Hebrew Bible. Since it is highly unlikely that the vast majority of Judean and Galilean villagers had direct knowledge of the books that became the Hebrew Bible, we cannot use them as sources for their cultural memory and social identity. Nor can we assume that the oral versions of Israelite tradition cultivated orally by villagers existed merely at an innocuous cultural level without political-economic import and implications. We cannot posit a unitary ancient Jewish cultural memory as if the same social identity were expressed and attested somehow by all the various versions. Ancient Israelite cultural memory was more complex. The difference between elite versions of Israelite tradition and popular versions corresponded to and expressed a fundamental political-economic division in ancient society.

The emphasis that memory is social and closely related to group identity in recent studies of cultural memory focuses attention on the historical social context of Mark and the community that shaped and used it. Attending to the story as a whole, moreover, rather than individual verses and pericopes in isolation, exposes the fundamental political conflict central to the dominant plot of the gospel's narrative: Jesus and his followers, in carrying out a renewal of Israel, stand opposed to and opposed by the Jerusalem high priestly rulers; their representatives, the Pharisees; and their patron, the Roman governor. This fundamental conflict parallels the division noted in recent research on orality and literacy.

The political-economic-religious conflict between Jerusalem rulers and their scribal representatives and the Galilean villagers corresponds to the cultural difference between those who command literacy and written texts and the non-literate. These divisions, moreover, are not merely literary artifice, but were fundamental historical divisions in the society. They are indicated also in documents produced by the literate elite, such as the histories of Josephus. These other Judean documents from the time portray the same fundamental divide and persistent conflict between the wealthy and powerful rulers, with their intellectual-scribal retainers, on the one side, and the subsistence villagers from whom they expropriated taxes, tithes, and tribute, on the other. This makes it all the more likely that in the story of Jesus and his followers the community whose identity was being reinforced by the cultural and social memory that both shaped the story and was referenced by it also was embedded in sharp conflict with powerful rulers and their literate representatives. The cultural dimension, the social memory, corresponded to and was embedded in a historical political-economic-religious conflict, a conflict that had existed for centuries during which different cultural memories and social identities had developed.

The Temple in Jerusalem headed by the high priesthood had been set in place and maintained by imperial regimes as an instrument of their rule and taking of tribute. Judging from the limited sources we have for the second temple period (such as Ezra, Nehemiah, and Sirach), the wealthy and powerful aristocracy oppressed the peasants of Judea, despite the efforts of imperial governors such as Nehemiah or scribal sages such as Ben Sira to mitigate the worst effects. The imperial attempt to suppress increasing resistance in the 170s and 160s B.C.E. only served to evoke the Maccabean Revolt against the Hellenistic Empire as well as the high priestly aristocracy. Galilean villagers did not come under the Jerusalem high priestly regime's control until about a hundred years before Jesus' birth, at which point they were required by the Jerusalem high priesthood to submit to "the laws of the Judeans."

The Romans only intensified the fundamental divide between rulers and ruled when they imposed the military strongman Herod as king and then his heirs as rulers in various districts of his realm. Herod then created a new set of high priestly families loyal to his own regime and the Romans. Our principal sources for Judean and Galilean history in Roman-Herodian times indicate that the period was framed by widespread popular revolts: a three-year struggle against Herod's conquest of his Rome-bestowed realm, revolts at his death in every district of his kingdom, and the great revolt of 66–70 C.E. The period was further punctuated, moreover, by persistent protests by both scribal circles and Jerusalem crowds and by distinctive Israelite movements among the peasantry.

Given the fundamental political-economic-religious conflict in Judea and Galilee it is difficult to discern what if any forces or factors of cohesion might have provided some sort of social cohesion between Judeans and their Jerusalem rulers. Even less does there appear to have been a common cultural memory shared between the Jerusalem rulers and Galilean villagers, who during Jesus' lifetime and the following generation were no longer under the jurisdiction of the temple-state and its laws, after only a century of Jerusalem rule. It seems likely, in fact, that cultural memory worked as much as a source of division and conflict as it did as a source of cohesion.

How this continuing conflict between rulers and ruled, between the Jerusalem highly priestly families, on the one hand, and the Judean and Galilean peasants, on the other, worked itself out in terms of cultural memory can be seen, for example, in celebration of the foundational memory of the exodus in the annual Passover festival. The ritual reliving of the exodus in the Passover celebration was originally celebrated in households. Starting presumably under king Josiah in the late seventh century B.C.E. (1 Kings 23), celebration of the Passover was centralized in Jerusalem as a pilgrimage festival (2 Kings 23:21-23; Deut 16:1-8). The centralization of the celebration in the Temple was a way of associating the memory of the people's formative event of liberation from oppressive foreign rule with Jerusalem, as well as a source of revenue for the high priesthood and the Jerusalem economy. At least in late second temple times, however, the thousands of Judean peasants and the handful of Galileans who came to Jerusalem as pilgrims for the Passover festival were still celebrating the people's liberation from foreign rule. Josephus provides abundant evidence of how the Passover was the occasion for popular protests against Herod's oppression of the people, partly by his control and manipulation of the high priesthood. The people also knew very well that, after Herod's death, the high priests were appointed by and collaborated with the Roman governors during the first century. Not surprisingly, the pilgrims' celebration of the Passover had potential as a time of protest against Roman and high priestly rule. Recognizing the threat, the Roman governors habitually brought troops into the city and posted them on the porticoes of the Temple complex as a show of force, further exacerbating the structural conflict. Cumanus even unleashed the troops against Passover demonstrators (Josephus, *Jewish Antiquities* 20.105-12).[8]

The memory of exodus, as perpetuated primarily in the Passover festival, was thus hardly the constitutive memory for the identity of all Judeans and Galileans as a unified people. Because of our paucity of sources, we have little idea of how the priestly aristocracy thought of the exodus, presumably the focus of the festival over which they presided in the Temple. Certainly Moses and his leadership of the exodus is dwarfed by the extensive praise of Aaron and God's eternal covenant with the Zadokite and Aaronid priesthood in Ben Sira's hymn to the great ancestral heroes and officers (Sirach 44–50). For the villagers who came as pilgrims to the festival in Jerusalem, the Passover was a way of expressing their resentment of and struggle against their rulers—that is, what this constitutive memory was about in the first place. It is surely significant that the one point we know of where memory of the exodus plays a central role among scribal groups is the Qumranites' opposition to and withdrawal from Jerusalem high priestly rule, as articulated in their Community Rule.

It is just such discrepancies between the ways in which Israelite tradition was understood, interpreted, and acted upon by popular groups and movements, on the one hand, and in scribal literature and rulers' behavior, on the other, that has led me to adapt the anthropological distinction between the "great tradition" and the "little tradition." In other agrarian societies anthropologists have noticed the difference between the ways the ruling elite and the peasants understand and use the cultural tradition that they share in various degrees. In the work of James C. Scott that is most helpful, I believe, for study of ancient Judean history and the Gospels, the "little tradition" refers to "the distinctive patterns of belief and behavior which are valued by the peasantry." The "great tradition" refers to the corresponding patterns among the aristocracy and their intellectual-scribal retainers, sometimes to a degree embodied in written documents.[9] Depending on the historical development of the tradition, there is considerable parallel and a degree of interaction among them. Despite their overlaps and interaction, however, Scott insists that each of these parallel traditions "represents a *distinct* pattern of belief and practice."[10] The differences would vary with such factors as residence, income, consumption, language, education, juridical status, and ethnicity. On such factors, the differences between the official Jerusalem tradition and the Israelite popular tradition would have been considerable. Insofar as Galilee had been subject to Jerusalem rule for only a hundred years prior to the lifetime of Jesus and followers, the Israelite popular tradition in Galilee would have diverged even more from the Jerusalem based "great tradition."

The overlap and interaction between the official and popular traditions in Judea and Galilee can be illustrated again from the exodus and Passover. Stories of Israel's constitutive exodus from bondage under foreign rule into an independent people under the direct rule of its God originated among the early Israelite peasantry. In the broad narratives sponsored by the monarchy and temple-state, such as the Yahwist and the Priestly narratives, the exodus was inserted into or framed by the promises to Abraham and its presumed fulfillment in the Davidic monarchy, Solomonic Temple, and Aaronid high priesthood. Stories of prophetic leaders such as Moses, Joshua, and Elijah and of popularly acclaimed kings such as Saul and the young David originated among people struggling for independence of oppressive rulers. They were then later inserted into—and their explosive potential blunted by—broader narratives that served to legitimate royal or priestly regimes in Jerusalem. Thereafter, the exodus, and its celebration in the Passover festival, represented something very different in the "great tradition" of Jerusalem elite and the "little tradition" of the Judean and Galilean peasantry.

In the Gospel of Mark itself, the Passover festival celebrating the exodus is the occasion for Jesus' forceful prophetic condemnation of the Temple and high priesthood (Mark 11:15-17; 12:1-9; and so on) and the Jerusalem rulers' and their Roman patron's actions to destroy (Mark 14:2) the threat to their position by the representative of the popular tradition. Elsewhere, Mark's story portrays repeated conflicts between the official and the popular traditions. This come out explicitly in Jesus' debates with the Pharisees, for example, when the Pharisees' "traditions of the elders" provide for the economic support of the Temple through the device of the dedication of peasant property and produce to the Temple, to which Jesus responds with the basic commandment of God that insists that local produce be retained for local needs ("honor father and mother," Mark 7:1-13).

Studies of cultural and social memory discern an important difference in collective memory that corresponds to a considerable extent to the difference between "great" and "little" traditions found by anthropologists in complex agrarian societies. Classic work on collective memory tended to focus on the social identity and cohesion of large-scale social systems, given the Durkheimian roots of Maurice Halbwachs and his pioneering reflections. More recent analysis of social memory, however, includes attention to "anti-hegemonic" memory as well as "hegemonic" memory.[11] In a large-scale society peasants, industrial laborers, women, and minority groups usually have distinctive social memory of their own that usually differs considerably from the "official" memory of the dominant culture. In fact, what purports to be the official memory of a society is often the hegemonic culture of the dominant group that controls the media of cultural production. But underneath the officially propagated cultural memory are vernacular and folk memory (among others) that enable subordinated groups to maintain a degree of social identity not completely controlled by the dominant culture.[12]

Critical studies of popular memory also recognize that, like the "great" and "little" traditions, official and popular memories are engaged in an ongoing process of interaction. Or, more to the point, anti-hegemonic memory is engaged in a persistent process of contestation and resistance with hegemonic memory. To focus on popular culture as something in itself, as if it had sole claim on authenticity, would only essentialize it, just as the dominant culture has previously been essentialized as *the* culture of a nation or people. That would only obscure the ongoing struggle between dominant and subordinate groups over memory that is more often than not sharply contested.[13]

The differences and ongoing struggle between official and popular traditions or between hegemonic and anti-hegemonic cultural memory discerned in other societies at other times can provide considerable illumination of the Gospel of Mark. Throughout the story, in episode after episode, Israelite memory is contested. In Mark's story, which emerged from and in regular performance articulated the identity of a Jesus movement, Jesus repeatedly engages in actions that resonate with the people's memory of Moses and Elijah and in declarations that oppose the Pharisees' attempt to control local life according to their own official memory of what constitutes proper observance of Sabbath and offerings to the Temple. Most obvious and dramatic of all, perhaps, is Jesus' confrontation with the high priest and elders in Jerusalem at the climax of the story. In a series of disputes, he recites prophetic sayings and traditional images from their own scriptures against them to insist repeatedly that they stand condemned by God for persistent oppression of the people (Mark 11:12—12:40).

Prominent Patterns in Israelite Cultural Memory That Inform Mark's Gospel

In Gospel studies we have been trained to focus on and to seek the meaning of text fragments, of particular pericopes or individual verses. We then look, among other things, for possible references or allusions to particular verses, laws, motifs, and so forth, in the Hebrew Bible and other Judean literature.

Our research tools are even codified by chapter and verse. We then tend to assume that the producers and users of Mark or other gospels did the same, that is, that they appropriated Hebrew biblical literature mainly in fragmentary units such as verses, sayings, laws, and motifs.

There are several reasons why this assumption and this procedure are inappropriate. One is that, as Kelber and others have explained, the Gospel of Mark itself was almost certainly composed and read or performed aloud as a whole story rather than in fragmentary units, one or two at a time. As explained above, moreover, recent research on orality and literacy in the ancient world and on the development of variant textual traditions in Judea at the time indicates that the producers and users of Mark's gospel probably did not have direct contact with the books of the Hebrew Bible. And, as suggested by the previous point, scrolls of scriptural books written in Hebrew were almost certainly not the primary means by which Judean and Galilean villagers and Greek-speaking Syrian villagers who joined Jesus movements knew and cultivated Israelite cultural tradition.

It is necessary to seek an approach to the importance of cultural memory in Mark more appropriate to the Gospel understood as a whole story produced and used in a predominantly oral communication environment. Hebrew biblical books and other Judean literature are indeed our primary sources for Israelite tradition at that time, especially for the "great tradition" concentrated in Jerusalem. And modern scholarly reference works, often now available electronically, codified by chapter and verse are still invaluable research tools. But we have no good basis for believing that ancient Galileans, Judeans, and Syrians knew and cultivated their Israelite cultural memory primarily in fragments such as individual sayings, lines of poetry or song, or other biblical verses. Fragments such as proverbs, laws, customs, poetic lines, and prophetic sayings communicated nothing without a broader meaning context. There are good reasons for looking for broader patterns of communication and meaning in cultural memory as well as attending to the fragments that may lead us to them. Indeed, in attempting to appreciate the Gospel of Mark as a whole story I have become convinced that we can discern some broader patterns of Israelite cultural memory operative across the narrative.

It has long been seen, for example, that the several dialogues in Mark 10:1-45 have a certain coherence. They all include a formulaic statement, previously called "sentences of holy law." And they may all go together as aspects of instruction and discipline for the communities Mark addresses. Two of the four dialogues, however, make unavoidably explicit references to Israelite tradition. Are we to imagine that a sequence of dialogues in Mark's story have a coherence but that no such coherence existed in the Israelite tradition that it references? Although we can no longer assume that Israelite tradition and memory was confined to the Hebrew biblical literature and parallel Judean texts, as argued above, this literature does provide many of our principal sources for it. And if we but look in Hebrew biblical literature and other Judean texts, we can find a coherent pattern that parallels and illuminates the perceived coherence between the dialogues in Mark 10. Over a generation ago, Hebrew Bible scholars discerned a previously unrecognized pattern in the covenant given on Sinai in Exodus 20 and Joshua's covenant renewal speech in Joshua 24 by comparisons with ancient Hittite suzerainty treaties.[14] The same basic pattern was then recognized in and behind the covenant renewal texts from Qumran (The Community Rule and the Damascus Rule).[15] Recognizing this pattern in the Mosaic covenant then enables us to discern the same pattern of covenant renewal in the longest speech of Jesus in the series of speeches paralleled in the Gospels of Matthew and Luke (Q/Luke 6), in the first long discourse in Matthew (Matthew 5–7), and to a degree in *Didache* 1–6.[16]

As suggested by the explicit citation of the covenantal principles in the dialogue in Mark 10:17-31 and the focus on one of those principles in Mark 10:2-12, the same covenantal pattern underlies and informs the whole series of dialogues in Mark 10.[17] It seems that there were relatively stable patterns in the Israelite cultural tradition to which Mark's narrative makes reference. Indeed, the Mosaic covenantal pattern provides further continuity in Mark's story as it did in Israelite tradition. The recitation of "honor your father and mother" as a paradigmatic basic commandment of God in Mark 7:1-13, referencing again the Ten Commandments, and Jesus' offering and sharing of the cup of "my blood of the covenant" in the last supper, referencing the covenant ceremony on Sinai in Mark 14:22-25, locate Jesus' mission directly in the deep-running covenantal tradition of Israel. Drawing attention to particular chapters and verses in the Hebrew biblical text helps us, but the whole of the covenantal pattern and covenantal tradition is far greater than the sum of its proof text parts. And the appearance of the same covenantal pattern in the Qumran "Rules" and the discourses in Q, Matthew, and the *Didache*, without explicit citations of covenantal passages in nascent scriptural texts, suggests that the pattern was operative in the social memory cultivated in scribal circles and village communities.

In seeking to discern broader cultural patterns operative in Judean and Galilean society around the time of Jesus, however, caution should be exercised not to combine motifs and images from a variety of sources into a synthetic scheme or concept of our own making. That is what happened, for example, in the standard Christian scholarly construct of Jewish messianic expectations. The synthetic Christian scholarly projection of expectations of "the Messiah" began to break down when closer investigations indicated that different texts spoke of different figures as agents of future deliverance, whether a prophet, a messiah, a "son of man," or even God's direct intervention. Only later had Christian texts fused images of these separate figures in various ways as doctrines of Christology began to emerge. Then in the 1960s and 1970s, scholars were surprised to discover that ancient late second temple Judean literature in fact attested very little concerning expectations of a messiah and displayed virtually no expectation of an "eschatological prophet" or a "prophet like Moses." Essentialist constructs such as "Judaism" had been blocking scholarly recognition that the cultural elite that produced Judean literature were not particularly interested in such figures remembered for their actions against foreign and domestic rulers.

The non-literate peasantry in Judea, Galilee, and Perea, however, produced numerous concrete movements led by a charismatic leaders acclaimed as king. Although he avoids the term "messiah," it is clear from Josephus' accounts that these movements were modeled on the Israelite resistance to Philistine occupation led by the young David. In the Deuteronomistic History accounts, David's followers from the tribe of Judah and then all the Israelites anointed ("messiah-ed") him "king" (2 Sam 2:4; 5:2). Since, in the imperial Israelite monarchy attested by the royal Psalms, the anointing was done in a formal ceremony with pomp and circumstance (see especially Psalms 2 and 110), those accounts may well reflect older popular tradition. The Judean, Galilean, and Perean peasants who formed the movements led by kings against Roman rule, however, do not appear to be dependent on the texts of the Jerusalem great tradition. That there were so many such movements led by popularly acclaimed kings in various areas of Israelite heritage and over so many generations, from 4 B.C.E. to the great revolt in 66–70 C.E. to the Bar Kokhba Revolt in 132–135, suggests that these movements were informed by persistent and distinctive popular Israelite memory. They had their own versions of Israelite tradition that provided a ready made script for active resistance to Roman rule and the Herodian kings and high priests that the Roman set in power over them.[18]

The Gospel of Mark seems to be informed by this popular Israelite memory, but is sharply critical of it. Jesus is declared "son of God" or "messiah" at the beginning, middle, and end of the story. But when Peter declares the Jesus is the messiah, and then immediately rebukes him for having to go up to Jerusalem to be killed, Jesus rebukes Peter right back: "get behind me, Satan." And at the end of the story he is labeled "king of the Judeans" by Pilate and the Roman soldiers and "king of Israel" by the high priests, that is, by the rulers who, threatened by his mission, are desperate to destroy him. Particularly in Jesus' rebuke of Peter and in his admonition to James and John who ask for positions of power when Jesus comes into his kingdom, one senses that the Gospel of Mark may be reacting against the script of messianic movements of insurrection that were deeply embedded in popular Israelite cultural memory of the time. Perhaps that very script had come to play a role in branches of the Jesus movement.

More central to the main plot of the gospel, however, is memory of Moses as the prophet of Israel's formation and memory of Elijah as the prophet of Israel's renewal. The memory of Moses' and Elijah's work in the founding and renewal of Israel is instrumental to the main plot of Mark's story, which has Jesus spearheading renewal of Israel over against its rulers and their Roman sponsors. Most obvious are the two sequences of miracle stories in which Jesus performs sea crossings and wilderness feedings, exorcisms and healings, like Moses and Elijah, respectively (Mark 4:35—8:26). Shortly thereafter, Jesus appears on the mountain with both Moses and Elijah (9:2-8). Like both Moses and Elijah, Jesus spends a time of preparation in the wilderness before launching his mission (1:9-20). Just as Elijah commissioned Elisha to continue his mission of renewal of Israel (the twelve tribes explicitly symbolized in the twelve stones of the altar, etc.) in opposition to oppressive domestic and foreign rulers, so Jesus calls and commissions disciples to help implement his similar mission (3:13-19; 6:6-13; again with much explicit symbolization by twelve disciples, baskets of leftovers, years of hemorrhage, and so on). Finally, as noted in connection with the broader covenant pattern in Mark, as if a new Moses, Jesus delivers a covenant renewal discourse and presides over a renewed covenant meal in his final meal with the disciples (10:1-45; 14:22-25).

Mark's narrative, however, gives no indication that any of the particular episodes involved in this new Moses and new Elijah pattern correspond with or make explicit allusions to particular passages involving Moses in Exodus or Numbers or Elijah in 1–2 Kings. They are not quotations of or allusions to protoscriptural books. It now seems unlikely that they were explicit references to texts anyhow, given what we are learning about the fluid state of those books in the first century C.E. The books that were later included in the Hebrew Bible and the books of the Septuagint, moreover, were not the only, and probably not the principal, source of Israelite cultural memory.

One medium of the cultural memory of Israelite prophets was monuments constructed evidently by the high priestly or Herodian rulers and tended by the scribes and Pharisees, as suggested by Jesus' woes against the latter in Q/Luke 11:47-51. The many recitations in a wide range of biblical literature (including in many Psalms) of various sequences of Moses' wondrous acts of deliverance, including his command of the Red Sea waters and the water from the rock and manna in the wilderness, suggest widespread oral recitations in Israelite society, some of which were preserved once they were written down in the Psalter (see also 1 Cor 10:1-13). Among scribal-priestly circles, cultural memory of Moses was carried both in oral tradition and in texts that were later not included in the Hebrew Bible. Some of these are now know from the Dead Sea Scrolls. At the popular level memory of key figures such as Moses, the prophetic liberator and founder of Israel, and Elijah, the great hero of the people's renewal, would have been cultivated orally in village communities. For example, that the stories of Elijah's and Elisha's healings and other wondrous actions in 1–2 Kings appear in style so different from the rest of the Deuteronomistic History has suggested to some that they reflect popular narratives. If such narratives continued to be cultivated in village communities, particularly in the northern Israelite territories where those prophets were so prominent, it would help explain how the portrayals of Jesus' healings are so reminiscent of stories of Elijah's and Elisha's healings without any indication that they are closely patterned on the literary accounts in 1–2 Kings.

As attestations of a pattern in popular Israelite culture that lies behind and emerges in Mark's story of a peasant prophet who is spearheading the renewal of Israel, the several concrete cases of prophets active in Judea and Samaria right around the time of Jesus' mission are striking.[18] Each of these prophets led followers in anticipation of a new divine act of deliverance. Like a new Moses, a Samaritan prophet led people up Mount Gerizim where, he declared, they would find the precious remains of the tabernacle from Mount Sinai. Like a new Moses or Joshua, Theudas led his people out to the Jordan River to cross into (or from) the wilderness. The prophet who returned to Judea "from Egypt," stepping into a role like that of Joshua at Jericho, led his followers up to the Mount of Olives from which they would witness the collapse of the walls of Jerusalem and the disappearance of the Roman garrison. The fact that, according to Josephus, there were many such movements, all clearly patterned after the formative actions of deliverance led by Moses or Joshua offers clear evidence of a general and widespread popular memory of these heroic Israelite prophets of old and the people's liberation and entry into land that they spearheaded. These multiple movements led by prophets like Moses and Joshua right around the time of Jesus suggest the active presence of a distinctively Israelite cultural pattern that provides the script followed in Mark's story of Jesus engaged in a renewal of Israel over against the rulers.[20]

That Judean and Galilean villagers' cultural memory was focused on the figures of Moses, Joshua, and Elijah and their leadership of Israel in times of crisis fits a common pattern found among other people by students of cultural and social memory. These studies find that a group or people invests only certain events with extraordinary significance. In their ongoing social life, a process of selection, emphasis, condensation, and reconfiguration continues to refine and redefine such key events and figures. These constitutive memories ("what must not be forgotten")[21] then leave lasting marks on communities, defining their identities and normative values.[22] Focal or constitutive memories can become, or can become linked into, a master narrative that is all the more effective in shaping social identity. This is apparently one of the key effects of Israelite cultural memory in the Gospel of Mark as well as in the other popular prophetic movements at the time.

An Analogy: Cultural Patterns in the Cevenols' Memory of the Camisards

As biblical interpreters trained in the assumptions of print culture, it is difficult for us to understand how memory works in a predominantly oral society. As members of the intellectual elite who have received training in the dominant culture, it is difficult to appreciate anti-hegemonic memory in which resistance to the dominant culture is rooted. Perhaps an analogy from a different society and different time might be helpful in understanding Mark's story and the movement in which it was produced and used. The case of the Cevenol peasants in mountainous central France studied by social historians can provide a sense or how anti-hegemonic social memory works among peasant societies in circumstances somewhat similar to those of the ancient Galileans and Syrians who used Mark.

While conducting research in the mountains of Cevennes, the French historian Philippe Joutard discovered from conversations with contemporary peasants in the area that their group identity and their periodic active resistance to the state was intensely focused on and shaped by their memory of the Camisard revolts of 1702–4.[23] When local enforcement of the Revocation of the Edict of Nantes (thus outlawing Protestants) began in Cevennes, preachers provoked violent resistance led by local leaders (for example, Jean Cavalier, Pierre Laporte, and Henri Castanet). Mainly by guerrilla action, they held off the armies of Louis XIV for two years. After establishment historians and even the Protestant elite had condemned them as religiously fanatical bandits and rebels, nineteenth century Romantic Protestant historians produced glowing accounts of the Camisard uprising and its leaders. Joutard and his team of oral historians discovered, however, that contemporary Cevenol peasants' memory of the Camisards had roots far deeper and more integral to their identity than the accounts of the Protestant historians. While their memory had been shaped to a degree by having read such histories, Cevenol peasants' accounts of the Camisard heroes and uprising focused on local skirmishes and episodes, including the experiences of family ancestors.

> These accounts are essentially structured by village and family memory, even though it is clear that all informants see the wars as being experienced by the Protestant community as a whole; they are in this respect independent of nineteenth century historiography, and many of them seem indeed to derive directly from eighteenth-century experience, which had remained underground, commemorated in oral culture.[24]

Joutard and his students learned that stories of Camisard exploits had been told to children much as folk tales were told in other areas of Europe. Many of these children's stories, far from being mere legends, it turns out, are verifiable from eighteenth-century documents with regard to the historical information about persons and events that they carry. Others are unverifiable, and probably contain little reliable historical memory. That so many are verifiable suggests that information from such stories can supplement what is known from written documents regarding the Camisard uprising.

More important for my purposes here is the role or effect of the popular memory of the Camisards, what some theorists of cultural memory have called anti-hegemonic memory. These stories strongly informed the Cevenol Protestants' identity as a community of resistance to attacks and interference in its affairs by the French state and other outsiders. Memory of the Camisard resistance fed further resistance, which continued into the late twentieth century. Subsequent actions and movements of resistance in which Cevenol Protestants became involved, whether the French Revolution, the Republic, the Resistance during World War II, and support of the Left, were understood in terms of their memory or reliving of the Camisard uprising and leadership.

Cevenol Protestants' memory, moreover, differed significantly from the dominant French national memory in terms of relative importance ascribed to events. As with other peasant villagers, even though they had supported the Revolution, memory of revolutionary events in Paris were far less important for them than memory of their lords' oppressive practices during the *ancient regime*. Napoleon and World War I were hardly even blips on the screen of their memory, even though these were peasants who had been through the state-sponsored schools where they read the standard history books. What university historians, Paris journalists, and French national school curricula deemed to be the important great events of history, however, were simply not accepted as important and were not assimilated into the Cevenol peasantry's memory. On the contrary, the Protestant mountain villagers understood themselves as communities of resistance to the dominant order, their own identity formed by their memory of the Camisard prophets and their sustained uprising.

Although the Cevenol peasants interviewed by Joutard and his associates were literate, living as they were in a highly literate dominant society and having themselves attended school, their collective memory was clearly dependent more on orality than on writing. Their patterned memory and the collective identity it provided was shared and sustained mainly in orally narrated stories, many focused on the exploits and episodes of the Camisard resistance that had taken place in the mountain areas where their ancestors had lived. Particular memories and reminders of the Camisard lore, moreover, were carried and cultivated in the course of local and relatively fluid conversational discourse that would be virtually impossible to document (short of ethnographers living in a village as participant observers).

Comparisons and Further Reflections

This brief survey of the social memory of the Camisards among the Cevenol peasants provides a comparative example of how Gospel scholars can imagine Galileans and Judeans working from Israelite memory. Three points seem particularly pertinent.

First, the way in which popular memory of the Camisards worked among the Cevenol peasants can enable students of Jesus and the Gospels to imagine how popular memory of Moses, Joshua, and Elijah worked among ancient Galileans and Judeans. Although the Protestant peasants of the Cevennes were literate and had even read written accounts of the Camisards, their own memory of their heroes of resistance depended on local oral communication. Ancient Galileans and Judeans, however, were non-literate and did not even have access to written documents. Their cultural memory was thus far more dependent on oral cultivation of Israelite tradition in their village communities. Even if they did have contact with the scribal and Pharisaic representatives of the Temple and high priesthood, their cultural memory was probably not heavily influenced by it, if we judge from the Cevenol analogy. Their memory of Israel's formative events under Moses and Joshua was independent and surely differed in significant ways from the great tradition in Jerusalem. What the book of *Jubilees* or Josephus regarded as great events may not have mattered much to them, except in their general deleterious effects in military devastation and increased taxation. Even if the media of the Galilean and Judean peasants were children's stories and narratives with legendary embellishments, such stories carried the gist of serious historical memory, if, again we go by what Joutard and his colleagues found in the Cevennes.

Second, just as stories of the Camisard resistance had become basic for the social identity of Protestant villages in the Cevennes, so apparently had memory of the actions of Moses, Joshua, and Elijah become basic for the social identity of ancient Galileans and Judeans, and Israelites before them. The Cevenols understood themselves as a separate people defending their communities against attacks by hostile outside rulers, as had their Camisard heroes. Similarly, Galilean, Judean, and Samaritan peasants understood themselves as a distinctive people properly independent of foreign rule under the sole kingship of God, as established under the leadership of Moses and Joshua and reestablished through the prophetic movement led by Elijah and Elisha. Memory of Moses and Joshua, perhaps also of Elijah and Elisha, may have been so fundamental as to be constitutive of Galilean and Judean villagers' social identity and then for the Markan community that derived from the origins of the Jesus movement in Galilee.

Third, out of their identity as communities of resistance to outside rule grounded in memory of the Camisards, in every new situation of attack and resistance the Cevenols understood themselves to be repeating or reenacting the Camisards' resistance. Similarly, the ancient Galileans and Judeans understood their own resistance to the oppressive rule of the Romans and their high priestly or Herodian clients as repetitions of the formative actions taken by Moses, Joshua, and Elijah. Indeed, their memory of Elijah was shaped somewhat to the memory of Moses in key respects, such as the time of preparation in the wilderness for leading the liberation or renewal of Israel against oppressive rulers.

A couple of observations that Fentress and Wickham make in their general discussion of "Class and Group Memories" may open up further insights for interpreters of the Gospels. First, "events can be remembered more easily if they fit into the forms of narrative that the social group already has at its disposal."[25] Analogously, Jesus' healings were more easily remembered insofar as they fit the pattern familiar in stories of Elijah's healings, and Jesus' Last Supper fit the pattern familiar from the covenant ratification ceremony presided over by Moses on Sinai. Secondly, "memories can be analysed as narratives; but they also have functions, and can be analysed . . . as guides to social identity."[26] Similarly, both the Israelite memories of Moses, Joshua, and Elijah and those of Jesus take the form of narratives. What the narrative is about, however, is more than just a literary pattern, but a memory that may figure in the very identity of a group, such as the Galilean or Judean peasantry generally, or a Jesus movement in particular. This insight meshes with what emerges in analysis of oral performance of Mark's story. Studies of cultural/ social memory also suggest that the performance of stories is integrally linked with the group identity of performer and audience in historical social context.

Fentress and Wickham's generalizations, however, are as significant for what they fail to maintain as much as for what they do discern about class memories. First, they do not take into account the persistent pattern of power relations. Why do the Cevenol Protestants continue to focus their memory on the Camisards, from which they derive their identity as a community of resistance? Among other reasons, because the structure of their life vis-à-vis the political economy and culture of the larger society has not changed. Likewise the recurrence or persistence of oppressive domestic and foreign rule similar to what was remembered in stories of Moses, Joshua, and Elijah set up a continuing or recurring context in which those paradigmatic figures and events of resistance or revolt were again directly applicable. Precisely because of this recurrent or persistent structure of power relations, memory of Moses and Elijah were compelling.

Second, it is not enough to say that new events are more easily remembered if they fit into central or key narratives in the group's shared memory. It must also be taken into account that new events cannot help but be experienced according to those central or key stories and prominent patterns of a people's memory. The memory of key events informs and shapes experience of events that produce new memory. It would seem that this would be a key insight from study of social memory. The Cevenols experienced the German occupation and local resistance to it as a recurrence of earlier royal repression of their Protestant ways and their resistance.

Similarly, Galilean and Judean peasants experienced Roman, Herodian, and high priestly oppression and repression as a recurrence of Pharaoh, the Canaanite city-state kings, Solomon, and Ahab and Jezebel. Their own resistance was experienced as a recurrence of the exodus and the popular resistance to Ahab and others by the "sons of the prophets" (*bene-nabi'im*). Jesus' immediate followers can thus easily have experienced his mission of renewal of Israel, in such episodes as feedings and covenant teachings, in terms of Moses' leadership of the exodus and wilderness journey, and his healings and exorcism in terms of Elijah's remarkable acts of healing in his restoration of Israel. That is, studies of social memory such as that of the Cevenols suggest that what was remembered of Jesus's actions and teachings had, to begin with, something to do with the Israelite social memory of his first followers, which was focused on the prophets of Israel's origins and renewal. In terms perhaps strange to Gospel scholars but familiar among students of social memory, memory of the movements led by Moses, Joshua, and Elijah provided the fundamental framework for cognition, organization, and understanding of what was happening in Galileans' interaction with Jesus. Stories of their actions, narrative patterns deeply ingrained in social memory, constituted the very "cognitive habits" by which Jesus' first followers experienced and understood what was happening in his teaching and action.[27]

Third, memory does not function simply as a guide to social identity. As Fentress and Wickham point out, central to the memory of many peasantries are ways of recounting resistance or even revolt against the state. More than identity is involved in these memories. They are a reservoir of motivation and strength to persist in the struggle to maintain their special way of life over against an often hostile, repressive state. Sometimes the dominant order has the power simply to impose its view of things or even simply destroy the subjected community. But subject people can often generate sufficient power to resist by cultivating their own stories and tradition and view of reality. For peasants, such as Galileans and Judeans at the time of Jesus, subject to conquest, invasion, and economic pressures that cause disintegration of village communities, their identity is under attack. Maintaining their identity, which is sustained by their cultural memory, is a matter of constant struggle against the invasive dominant order. No wonder such people identify themselves as communities of resistance. Remembering the great heroes of resistance in the past is a powerful means of maintaining not just an identity of resistance but of maintaining resistance. We can easily imagine that for Judean pilgrims the annual celebration of the Passover under the watchful eyes of the Roman military posted on the Temple porticoes helped reconstitute their identity of resistance, but it also constituted an act of resistance, at least in ritual form. Similarly, the very action of celebrating the Lord's Supper in commemoration of the renewal of the Mosaic covenant would have constituted an act of resistance by a community of resistance.

It is thus possible, fourth, that cultural and social memory can have a mobilizing effect on a people,[28] enabling them to reestablish the cooperation and solidarity necessary to resist and perhaps even rebel against the impact and invasion of those who wield power. The active regeneration of cultural memory would thus serve not simply to maintain and reinforce social identity, but to restore bonds that may have disintegrated. In the case of new movements, revival of cultural memory can create and secure new bonds among the members. When a people evokes memory of an ideal past of freedom, it can easily inspire resistance to oppression in the present. A people's memory can even supply a kind of program or paradigm according to which they can form a new movement in similar circumstances. Like the Cevenols remembering the Camisards, the Galilean, Samaritan, and Judean memory of Moses and Joshua inspired them to form movements of resistance and renewal in mid-first century C.E. The same pattern of social memory of Moses, Joshua, and Elijah seems likely to been the inspiration of the Jesus movement. And this can have happened already in the interaction of Jesus and his immediate followers as well as among those who subsequently joined Jesus movements such as the one that produced Mark's gospel.

Fifth, and closely related to the previous points, there is an ongoing dialectic between the dominant culture and subordinate memory. Fentress and Wickham offer a good illustration in how standard establishment history books provided at least some of the content of the Cevenol Protestant villagers' memory of the Camisards, most of which was distinctively different in emphasis and focus from "great events" history. A similar relationship seems to have existed in ancient Galilee and Judea in the interaction of the "great" and "little" traditions. Galileans and Judeans may well have gleaned some of their prophetic tradition through interaction with scribal and Pharisaic representatives of Jerusalem based "great tradition." As indicated in the Gospel of Mark, insofar as he refers to it polemically, the Galilean prophet Jesus knows of the existence of "the writing." But Mark's Jesus rejects much of its content, such as "the traditions of the elders" and the Deuteronomistic code about divorce and remarriage, as oppressive or problematic for Galilean peasant families. And he does this on the basis of the (basic) commandment of God (for example, in Mark 7:1-13; 10:2-9).

Pulling together all of these interrelated aspects of the role of memory among peasants and popular movements of resistance and renewal, we can return to one of our two basic theses: the recognition that memory of Moses and Elijah or of Jesus' mission and message did not operate in fragments such as aphorisms and discrete stories of healing or wilderness feeding. All memory is social, relational, belonging to groups in certain historical contexts. Particular memories belong to broader patterns of memory. And the latter tend to be centered on and organized around focal memories, that are constitutive of group identity and, among peasant groups, resistance. There are abundant indications in our sources that memories of Moses, Joshua, Elijah, and other Israelite prophetic leaders were focal, constitutive of Galileans' and Judeans' social identity and struggle to resist the pressures of the Roman imperial order. These foundational memories provided the broader cultural patterns of popular Israelite memory in which the first and subsequent followers of Jesus could have made sense of what was happening. Jesus' actions and teachings made sense and took their place in a broader narrative that preceded and transcended them. For those who formulated, performed, and heard Mark's narrative, Jesus' actions and teachings were understandable as episodes in a longer story of the renewal of Israel led by a figure whose mission was reminiscent of and fit the pattern of the prototypes Moses and Elijah in popular Israelite cultural memory.

Part IV: Moral Economy and the Arts of Resistance

Chapter

Eight

"Hidden Transcripts" and the "Arts of Resistance"

Biblical studies focuses heavily on the religious and cultural dimension to the neglect of other aspects of life that are also abundantly evident in biblical texts. This is understandable for a field devoted to illumination of the Jewish and Christian Scriptures. As the product mainly of Protestant theology and North Atlantic societies that operate with a separation between church and state, biblical studies focuses on "the things of God," as opposed to "the things of Caesar." James C. Scott's work offers a rich range of knowledge and theory that help biblical studies broaden and deepen approaches to texts in contexts. Trained as a political scientist, Scott is an expert in "the things of Caesar." Yet he insists throughout his scholarship that politics cannot be understood apart from culture and religion. His work can help biblical scholars understand the relation between the often separated dimensions of texts and history.

Biblical studies, devoted to understanding the sacred writings that played an instrumental role in Western European colonial rule over other peoples of the world, have tended to ignore power relations in both texts and history. Yet all civilizations, including Western civilization in which the Bible has been central, have been based on the domination and exploitation of the vast majority of people by an elite ruling class. Scott is unusual among political scientists not only in acknowledging the power relations that constitute civilizations, but also in repeatedly coming up with sophisticated, original ways of understanding domination and resistance that can be helpful to biblical scholars, who are only recently discovering such issues.

Biblical studies, because of the Herculean tasks involved in learning ancient languages and sophisticated methods of criticisms, tend to be focused intensively but narrowly on the particular languages and cultures of ancient Israel and early Jewish and Christian groups in the ancient eastern Mediterranean world. In his rich and varied scholarly work, James Scott has drawn upon a wide-ranging knowledge of a wide range of people and periods (medieval European, modern English and Russian, modern Chinese and Indian, modern American, as well as contemporary Southeast Asian) and several academic disciplines (social and political history, sociology, and especially anthropology, as well as political science). His work can therefore be highly instructive to biblical scholars who are struggling to become more comparative and interdisciplinary.

Biblical scholars have assumed responsibility, in the academic division of labor, for significant ancient texts and their historical contexts in periods and places for which only limited and fragmentary evidence is available. It is impossible, of course, for them to observe and question the people who produced the texts they study. Scott, by contrast, has done fieldwork in Malasian villages, during which he had sustained opportunities to observe the concrete situations and circumstances in which people subject to domination and exploitative political-economic relations live and work. This gives his observations on and theorizing about subjugated peoples a down-to-earth sense lacking in many studies, and one that seems particularly appropriate to certain biblical materials that deal with similar situations and lore of common people's lives.

It should not be surprising, therefore, that in the last decade or so several biblical scholars have found Scott's work stimulating and have used it to advantage, especially in examining domination and resistance. Clearly one of the principal reasons that Scott's analysis and theory are attractive to biblical scholars is its usefulness in aiding their own interest in liberative readings of the biblical text, in contrast with readings that authorize cultural and political forms of domination. The anthropological distinction between the "great tradition" and the "little tradition" was a key concept in the delineation of Judean and Galilean popular movements in late second temple times, and Scott's illuminating cross-cultural discussion of its importance in peasant movements in "Protest and Profanation: Agrarian Revolt and the Little Tradition,"[1] has played an important role in subsequent studies of Jesus and gospel materials.[2] Similarly his books on the roots of peasant revolt and hidden forms of resistance, *The Moral Economy of the Peasant*[3] and *Weapons of the Weak*,[4] began to inform treatments of Jesus and Jesus movements.[5] The book that has proven stimulating to New Testament scholars on a wider range of issues is the more recent and theoretically oriented *Domination and the Arts of Resistance*[6] (to which the pages in the text below refer).

A More Comprehensive Approach to Domination

In dealing with patterns of domination and subordination that have structured many historical and contemporary societies, Scott not only insists that religion and culture operate in close interrelationship with politics and economics, but presents subtle and sophisticated ways of dealing with that interrelationship. In many academic fields, particularly the humanities, an understandable reaction against a reductionist focus on the cultural dimension to the exclusion of the political and economic led to what may have been an overemphasis on the material and social-structural dimensions. While holding the material dimension of domination and subjugation in focus, Scott shows how domination operates in the interrelated area of human feelings and passions through cultural forms of interaction in ways that make material domination possible and effective. Not only can Scott help biblical studies avoid reductionism, he also demonstrates how to enrich investigations of the domination and resistance evident in or just under the surface of many biblical texts. Scott's analysis focuses on heavily dominated peoples, such as African American slaves and European serfs, and draws on many studies of peasant movements. It is not difficult to sort out the observations and generalizations applicable to the Palestinian peasantry among whom Jesus operated from those more specific to master-slave and patron-client relations in the cities where Paul carried out his mission.

Scott devised the concept of *public transcript* to deal with the most obvious aspects of domination. This is "a shorthand way of describing the open inter-action between subordinates and those who dominate" (2). "Given the usual power of dominant elites to compel performances from others, however, the public transcript is "highly partisan," controlled by the powerful. "It is designed to be impressive, to affirm and naturalize the power of dominant elites, and to conceal or euphemize the dirty linen of their rule" (18). The public transcript consists of mechanisms of "public mastery and subordination (for example, rituals of hierarchy, deference, speech, punishment, and humiliation)" and "ideological justification for inequalities (for example, the public religious and political world view of the dominant elite)" in order to manage the "material appropriation (for example, of labor, grain, taxes)," which is "largely the purpose of domination." Whereas materialist analysis "privileges the appropriation of surplus value as the social site of exploitation and resistance, our analysis here privileges the social experience of indignities, control, submission, humiliation, forced deference, and punishment" (111).

Insofar as "appropriation is, after all, largely the purpose of domination" (111), "these forms of domination are institutionalized means of extracting labor, goods, and services from a subject population. They embody formal assumptions about superiority and inferiority, often in elaborate ideological form, and a fair degree of ritual and 'etiquette' regulates public conduct within them. In principle at least, status in these systems of domination is ascribed by birth, mobility is virtually nil, and subordinate groups are granted few if any political or civil rights" (21). These generalizations apply to both the Herodian and high priestly rulers who controlled Palestine for the Romans and the magnates who dominated the Greek cities of the East where Paul worked. The arbitrary personal rule that operated through mechanisms such as sexual violation and other forms of personal terror were characteristic of master-slave relations in the Greco-Roman world, but less of the Jerusalem temple-state or Herodian rule.

Scott's analysis of rituals of "public mastery" and "ideological justification for inequalities" suggests ways of interpreting the Jerusalem Temple and high priestly practices that differ dramatically from standard presentations of Judaism (such as by Sanders). It also provides illuminating complements to recent analysis of the increasing conflict between the high priesthood and the Judean and Galilean people in the first century c.e.[7] The rituals and ideology of the Jerusalem Temple and high priesthood, suggests Scott's analysis, would have been an elaborate "respectable performance," for the benefit both of the Judean people and of the priestly aristocracy, although in almost opposite ways.

To the extent that the high priestly performance was aimed at the people, its purpose was "not to gain the agreement of subordinates but rather to awe and intimidate them into a durable and expedient compliance" (67). The ideology of the Temple and high priesthood, both being institutions of venerable antiquity, aimed to symbolize that these institutions ruled on behalf of the people, ensuring God's favor and blessings. By performing rituals and symbolic ideology as grand ceremony in the awesomely constructed sacred space at the center and height of the capital city, ceremony that only they were qualified to conduct, the priestly aristocracy (in collaboration with Herodian and Roman rulers) controlled public discourse (50–54). Anything else was defined as dangerous riot by the urban rabble or pilgrim mob (as Josephus' accounts repeatedly illustrate).

Much of the public performance by the elite, however, in this case the priestly aristocracy in the Temple, was done for its own consumption, according to Scott. Rituals performed in such an awesome setting exclusively by those set apart by hereditary rank and special codes of purity were performed to bolster the priestly aristocracy's own self-image as powerful and justified in their positions of dominance. They served to create the appearance of unity among themselves and of consent among the ordinary Jerusalemites who served the hierocratic apparatus and its operation in one capacity or another, as well as among the Judean peasants who supported the whole with their tithes and offerings (45–55). Sacrifices and service at the altar and in the holy of holies vividly illustrate Scott's comment that at points "the show is all actors and no audience" (59). The priests were literally "consumers of their own performance," including, at the material as well as symbolic level, the choicest portions of the animals sacrificed on the altar (49).

The purpose of all the ceremony, suggests Scott, would have been primarily for the priestly aristocracy "to buck up their courage, improve their cohesion, display their power, and convince themselves anew of their high moral purpose," or in this case their divinely instituted role in channeling blessings to the people and land (67). The paean of praise lavished on the Oniad High Priest Simon II and his Aaronid brothers in Sirach 50 suggests that such performances were convincing to circles of scribes who assisted the high priests in running the temple-state.

From Josephus' accounts, however, it is clear that neither the Jerusalem mob nor the Judean and Galilean peasantry were effectively impressed and intimidated. And the distinctive literature produced by the Qumran community indicates that dissident Judean scribal-priestly circles were so severely alienated from the incumbent high priesthood that they remained in their wilderness exile for several generations. Nevertheless, even if such rituals and symbols of power do not gain the consent of the subordinated people, they are an impressive "means of demonstrating that, like it or not, a given system of domination is stable, effective, and here to stay" (66).

Scott includes yet another sort of ritual performance of domination (and subordination) that pertains directly and centrally to the historical Jesus, an action whose ceremonial dimension is not usually noted in New Testament studies. In the already "civilized" areas of the Empire like the Greek cities, ceremony and festival generally sufficed to maintain order and elicit obedience from the laboring populace—or at least from the freeborn population. In the more recently subjugated areas like Palestine, the Romans simply terrorized the conquered people with slaughter and enslavement. Then subordination and especially rebellion were handled with further terror, only ritualized, in public execution by torturous crucifixion.[8] As Paul reminds the Galatians, Christ "was publicly exhibited as crucified" (Gal 3:1). The public defiance involved in "the traditional crime of lese-majeste . . . requires a public reply" (57). The Roman reply to rebels was the public ritual of crucifixion, in which the rebels were beaten and publicly displayed, being tortured to death on a cross in order to further intimidate the rest of the populace.

Motives of Resistance and Revolt

Wherever there is domination by the powerful, however, there is almost invariably resistance by the subordinated. Scott's analysis of resistance is not only innovative and insightful, but opens to view aspects of resistance that previously went unnoticed in academic investigation. In many academic fields, it is common to think of social-political order and disorder in terms of simple alternatives. Either people accept and acquiesce in the established order or they protest and rebel. In the absence of rebellion, then, people are assumed to have been relatively content (the "happy slave"). This is the way that New Testament scholarship has tended to treat the life and times of Jesus. While it is sometimes recognized that Judeans and Galileans repeatedly mounted movements of active resistance and wider revolts against Roman rule, Jesus is portrayed as a politically quiescent religious teacher.

Scott discerns that discontent and resistance are far more prevalent, widespread, and complex in their motives and methods than these simple alternatives allow. Subordinated people, says Scott, have developed a whole range of different forms of resistance that should be discerned as part and parcel of more complex political processes, forms of resistance in which the rare outbursts of rebellion and revolution are rooted and nurtured. It is in this connection that his work has greatest potential for our understanding of Jesus with wide ranging implications for what our texts represent and for how we use them as historical evidence. To state the possibilities bluntly: Just because Jesus does not lead an armed assault on the Temple and the Roman garrison in Jerusalem does not mean that he was not engaged in a message and program of revolutionary change.

Most significantly, perhaps, Scott can help biblical scholars expand the spectrum of social reality that they deal with. To derive meaning from texts, biblical studies focuses heavily on cognitive and symbolic dimensions of words and stories. Dissatisfied with confinement to the cultural plane, some biblical scholars have recently dealt also with the material interests of biblical stories and the characters in them. The political scientist reminds biblical scholars that what mediates between meaning and material circumstances are human feelings and desires, that people have a desire for dignity yet are deprived of it by the circumstances of their lives. As noted above, domination and its purpose, appropriation, unavoidably entail subordination that imposes indignities of one kind or another on the weak (111). And it is these indignities of submission, humiliation, forced deference, and punishment that generate the anger, indignation, and frustration that fuels resistance with passion, energy, and cunning.

Reminded of the importance of dignity, biblical scholars can immediately discern frustration and anger in text after text. The deep resentment of early Israelite peasants erupts in the mocking of Sisera's fatal submission to the cunning of Yael and of his aristocratic mother's soliloquy from her palace, in the Song of Deborah (Judges 5). Jesus gives voice to Galilean peasants' sense of humiliation in many passages of Mark and Q. Domination evokes resentment and resentment evokes resistance. Awareness of these dynamics should enable New Testament scholars to appreciate more fully the deep motives underlying the Jesus movements in Palestine.

Seldom, however, does popular resentment fuel resistance that escalates into peasant revolts or popular movements with cadres of prophets, envoys, and community organizers. In earlier path breaking work (*Weapons of the Weak*) that led toward the insights of *Domination*, Scott opened to others' eyes the remarkable range of "hidden forms of resistance" as far more prevalent, more widespread, and more effective over the long haul than revolt, given the repressive power of the dominant. In effect, he discovered the fuller range of subversive popular politics that standard political science and other fields had been unaware of. In *Domination and the Arts of Resistance*, Scott offered a critical theory of that previously unnoticed fuller range of political life involved in domination and resistance that results from the interaction between the "public transcript" controlled by the dominant and the "hidden transcript" of subordinated people that is cultivated off-stage, beyond the control of the dominant. It is this hidden transcript, he suggests, that provides the seedbed of more extensive and organized popular resistance—such as the widespread Judean and Galilean revolts in 4 B.C.E. and 66–70 C.E., the popular prophetic movements in mid-first century Judea and Samaria, and the Jesus movements in Galilee and beyond.

Varieties of Popular Politics

If the public transcript involves performance by the dominant elite, then it requires performance by the subjugated even more. What appears to be acceptance of the dominant order may be only a mask of acquiescence. Neither the slave nor the serf nor the sharecropper dare speak truth to power. Living constantly under the repressive power and sometimes the regular surveillance of the dominant, the subordinate learn to wear masks of obedience. Unable to say what they are really thinking or to act on their feelings, they learn, rather, to act the part they are given in life while on the public stage.

When they are offstage, however, the subordinate do say what they think and vent their feelings to each other. Domination and exploitation typically generate insults to human dignity that in turn foster a hidden transcript of indignation (7). Slaves or serfs or other peasants, subject to subordination, have a common interest in together creating "a discourse of dignity, of negation, and of justice" (114). In addition to its continuing cultivation as a shared *discourse*, the hidden transcript encompasses a whole range of *practices* such as, among peasantries, poaching, pilfering, and clandestine tax-evasion. But it definitely has an ideological dimension. "Inasmuch as the major historical forms of domination have presented themselves in the form of a metaphysics, a religion, a worldview, they have provoked the development of more or less equally elaborate replies in the hidden transcript" (115). Since subordinate groups live under elaborate ideologies that justify inequality, bondage, and exploitation, resistance requires a counter-ideology that justifies resistant practices invented in self-defense by any subordinate group (118).

Perhaps one of the most important potential gains in recognizing the reality of the hidden transcript is the enlargement of the field of vision to include the emotional-cultural dimension of subordinated people's lives. The extraction of labor or grain from a subordinate population has something of a generic quality to it. Personal domination, however, is likely to be far more culturally specific and particular (112). It is illuminating to Jesus' teachings to know that many Galilean villagers were poor and hungry. We know far more about the cultural meaning of their poverty if we know that they were in despair because they could not afford to feed guests at a child's wedding or bury their parents properly. Learning the cultural meaning of their poverty is to know the shape of their indignity and thus to gauge the content of their anger. These experienced indignities are what form the bridge between their condition and their consciousness (113). Awareness of such indignities enables interpreters to understand what motivates a popular movement and to explain and interpret its origins and politics.

In explaining how a hidden transcript develops and works, Scott makes two interrelated moves that have great potential importance for New Testament studies, a field dominated by methodological individualism. He points out that the articulation of anger requires language (an unarticulated feeling of anger is strictly hypothetical!) and that resistance is social (the individual resisting subject is "an abstract fiction"). The articulation of indignation and an indigenous discourse of dignity require social space for their cultivation. The expression of anger in language, moreover, imposes a disciplined form on it. As "raw" anger becomes "cooked" indignation, the most resonant expressions rise to the sub-cultural surface. If a particular expression of indignation and dignity is to become shared by the subordinates in a particular situation, it must carry effective meaning for them and reflect the cultural meanings and distribution of power among them. Furthermore, in contrast to much previous treatment of Jesus' sayings, "the hidden transcript has no reality as pure thought; it exists only to the extent it is practiced, articulated, enacted, and disseminated" (118–119).

Two requirements are therefore necessary for the cultivation of a hidden transcript. One is a "social space insulated from control, surveillance, and repression from above." (120–23) It is especially difficult for slaves to create and defend such sequestered spaces. But many peasantries already have relatively autonomous social spaces. The dominant do not interfere with their village communities except to collect taxes or to further humiliate and subordinate those who fail to pay up. Elites, of course, may deploy loyal retainers to keep the sites of the hidden transcript under surveillance, and subordinate groups may have to defend their sites which are often won only through resistant struggles (124–133). Second, particularly if subject people's indignity is to be transformed from "raw" to "cooked," is the role of active human agents who cultivate and disseminate the discourse (123–24). Such carriers of the hidden transcript are often people who have become displaced and marginalized, which has perhaps made them unusually sensitive to fluctuations in the fortunes of the subordinated and less vulnerable to the power that the dominant still wield over ordinary peasants or slaves.

If the hidden transcript is to give birth to a movement beyond local venting of indignation, moreover, a third component emerges in the discipline and internal politics that develops between leaders and participants. The sequestered sites in which the hidden transcript becomes more "cooked" are little centers of localized power in their own right, and "serve to discipline as well as to formulate patterns of resistance." Thus "the hidden transcript is a social product and hence a result of power relations among subordinates" as they struggle to win and defend a relative autonomy "in the teeth of power" (118–19).

The political dynamics of the conflictual relations between the dominant and the subordinated then develop in the interaction between the public and hidden transcripts. Here, finally, is the pay-off, as Scott's reflections enable us to discern that the dynamics of political conflict is far more complex than social stability, on the one hand, and violent rebellion, on the other. Scott delineates four varieties of political discourse among subordinate groups (18–19). First, the safest and most public form takes as its basis the flattering self-image of the elites. Owing to the rhetorical concessions that this self-image contains, it offers a surprisingly large arena for political conflict that exploits the elite's ideological justification that they rule for the benefit of the people in certain ways. A second mode of popular political discourse is the hidden transcript itself. This, moreover, is the nurturing matrix of bolder forms of resistance. Third, in the area between the first two, "is a politics of disguise and anonymity that takes place in public view but is designed to have a double meaning or to shield the identity of the actors." "Finally, the most explosive realm of politics is the rupture of the political *cordon sanitaire* between the hidden and the public transcript." Some brave subordinate who can't take it anymore speaks truth to power. Such "moments of challenge and open defiance typically provoke either a swift stroke of repression or, if unanswered, often lead to further words and acts of daring." In an unusually favorable conjunction of circumstances, such moments may also lead to a wider popular movement, even one that might pursue a revolutionary vision of ending domination and establishing a just social order. Scott thus opens up for New Testament interpreters a whole range of popular political dynamics that often lie hidden (underneath or between the lines of our sources) between passive acquiescence and active revolt.

Implications for New Testament Studies

Scott's exposé of the deeper dimensions of the politics of domination and resistance has some serious implications for New Testament studies as a field, as well as for the texts and history we interpret. For some of the subordinated peoples Scott examines, the Bible provided much of the central content of the official transcript of Western culture that legitimated various forms of domination, for example of medieval European peasants and African American slaves. Indeed, insofar as the Bible was integral to Western European colonization of much of the rest of the world, and biblical studies, like other academic fields, developed during the heyday of Western imperialism, the assumptions, concepts, perspectives, and approaches of the field may well be implicated as part of the grand official transcript of academic and wider public interaction.

Yet subordinate peoples also found in biblical traditions materials they could use in resistance. Medieval English peasants asked, "When Adam delved and Eve span, who was then the gentleman?" Africans enslaved in the United States identified with Israel's slavery in and liberation from Egypt. German peasants' sense of God's justice was informed by stories they had heard of Jesus' declarations about the kingdom of God. And it was not lost on women listening to Bible lessons that some of the leaders of the ostensibly Pauline communities were women, such as Prisca and Phoebe. Thus perhaps the first implication of Scott's work is the question whether the books, stories, laws, songs, and speeches in the Bible provide and can be appropriated as something more than simply part of the official transcript of Western culture. I conclude that it does, despite the ambivalence of some biblical material and the clear subordinationist message of much biblical material. Whatever the Gospels became in established Christianity, their materials, in their historical origins, represent hidden transcripts, the politics of disguise, and even more public forms of resistance by subordinated people.

The obvious starting point for examination of those materials would then appear to be a reconsideration of how we evaluate the sources and their relation to historical events, processes, and movements. Since only a tiny elite in antiquity could write, most extant written sources not only represent the interests of the dominant, but are representations of the public transcript. Yet, as Scott points out, "the public transcript is not the whole story" (3). In fact, it may even be positively misleading (2). Not surprisingly, taken by itself, the public transcript provides "convincing evidence for the hegemony of dominant values [and] discourse. Any analysis based exclusively on the public transcript is likely to conclude that subordinate groups endorse the terms of their subordination" (4). Behavior that results from inequalities of power is taken as evidence of ideological hegemony in the sense of active consent (66). In the most perverse cases, academic generalizations even come to resemble the racist, sexist, or classist views of dominant groups who assume that the deferential behavior of slaves or women or peasants or colonized people is normal and natural, an inborn characteristic of a whole category of people (28, 35–36).

Thus standard works in the New Testament field, based squarely on extant sources for the public transcript, present generalizations about standard beliefs and practices of Judaism shared by "all Jews" or the "ordinary people,"[9] about Galileans as loyal to Temple and Torah.[10] Completely missing from studies based primarily on sources from the public transcript is any sense of the effect of domination on the views of both the dominant and, especially, the subjugated, who comprised the vast majority in Palestine, and certainly those involved in Jesus' movement. Scholarship that fails to distinguish public and hidden transcripts in the context of domination and resistance in effect perpetuates the pretense of unanimity in the past and how that pretense may contribute to the perpetuation of domination in the present.

Gospel and Jesus scholars can broaden their historical competence and balance their treatment by borrowing a few leaves from Scott's notebook. The first step would be to discern whether their sources provide a record of the public transcript (nearly all public inscriptions, coins, and most extant documents) or a record of the hidden transcript of the subordinated (such as Mark's Gospel) or a record of the hidden transcript of the dominant (for example, Josephus's *Life*?). Key would be a comparison between the public transcript and the hidden transcripts—or in the absence of the latter, a critical suspicion about the former—in order to discern the effects of domination on popular views and actions and the rich variety of modes of popular political resistance delineated in Scott's four types (15). A little subtlety and sophistication with regard to language and gestures in grasping the difference between appearance and reality would help. "What we confront in the public transcript is a strange kind of ideological debate about justice and dignity in which one party has a severe speech impediment induced by power relations. If we wish to hear this side of the dialogue, we shall have to learn its dialect and codes. Above all, recovering this discourse requires an appreciation of the arts of political disguise" (138).

The Earliest Gospels as "Well-Cooked" Hidden Transcripts

Investigations into most places and periods are handicapped by the unavailability of sources for the hidden transcript of the subjugated. Peasants, serfs, slaves, and untouchables generally did not write. They left no records other than what archaeologists might dig up. Of course, sources from the literate elite do complain bitterly when uppity underlings dare to disrupt the public order. One of the most instructive aspects of Scott's work is how he is able to utilize extremely limited sources for or from a variety of subordinated groups, such as novels and slave narratives, in order to overhear the off-stage discourse. In contrast to most other academic fields, Gospel and Jesus studies are in an enviable position with regard to sources for the hidden transcript. According to scholarly consensus, the Gospel of Mark and the speeches of Jesus paralleled in Matthew and Luke (Q) arose from and addressed communities of Jesus followers who were opposed to and opposed by the rulers. Luke-Acts still address communities of subordinate people, but seems they have acquiesced in various ways to the dominant order.

Thus at least Mark and Q, from the synoptic gospel tradition (and perhaps other gospel materials), can be seen to stem from and represent the hidden transcript of what started as peasant movements. Once we recognize the pre-dominantly oral communication environment in antiquity, it is evident that the Gospel of Mark, even if it existed in writing, was performed or read aloud in communities of ordinary people. Similarly Q (which was not a collection of sayings but a sequence of speeches on issues of importance to a movement), even if it existed in written form, was performed aloud, apparently in Galilean or nearby village communities. Mark and Q were not addressed to outsiders—certainly not the Herodian or high priestly rulers in Palestine—and neither source figured in open discourse on the public stage of Tiberias or Jerusalem, even though Mark portrays events in which Jesus publicly confronted the rulers in Jerusalem.

Much scholarly investigation of the synoptic gospel tradition since the early days of *Formgeschichte* (form criticism) has paid little attention to social context. In his own monumental analysis, *The History of the Synoptic Tradi-tions*, Rudolf Bultmann emphasized the importance of the social context that another key formulator of form criticism, Martin Dibelius, was exploring more fully.[11] Bultmann's and Dibelius' successors, however, failed to follow through with more precise investigations of the folklore that helped inspire form criti-cism in the first place. And neither the developers of form criticism nor their successors who study gospel materials have paid much attention to the fun-damental social forms that provided the social context in which Jesus sayings originated and developed (that is, households and village communities). The limitations of these investigations, of course, are rooted in certain theological assumptions, notably that many of those Jesus sayings were divine revelations through early Christian prophets, and that not Jesus but the disciples and apos-tles founded the churches, making the social forms involved in Jesus' mission virtually irrelevant to the investigation.

Scott's analysis of comparative material can help New Testament scholars appre-ciate the importance of the fundamental social form (the village community) that provided the sequestered sites of Jesus' mission and of the early development of the synoptic gospel tradition. Recent work on Mark and Q finds internal indications that these texts emerge from and address the concerns and situations of Galilean and other village communities. They repeatedly portray Jesus as active in villages of Galilee and nearby territories, hostile to the ruling cities and rulers, and drawing upon and adapting Israelite tradition in a version that Scott and others would call the "little tradition" of the peasantry.[12] Jesus and his movement worked on the basis of an already existing Galilean Israelite hidden transcript, and creatively developed it, for example, in new exodus and new Elijah miracles (Mark 5–8), covenantal teaching (Mark 10; Q/Luke 6:20-49), and prophetic pronouncements against the Jerusalem rulers (Q/Luke 13:34-35; Mark 11–12). It seems fairly clear therefore that, in Scott's terms (120), the hidden transcript in Mark and Q was voiced in the sequestered sites of village communities beyond the effective control of the rulers and their representatives and among communities composed of people who shared similar experiences of domination. One might even conclude that Jesus himself was a socially marginal figure insofar as his family must have lost its family inheritance at some point and had to make a living as artisans.

The earliest gospel texts, however, were highly unusual records of hidden transcripts. Most of the contents of Q and much of Mark seem parallel to the hidden transcripts cultivated by other peoples in secure off-stage locations. These components of the synoptic gospel tradition build upon and further develop Israelite popular traditions of a Moses or Elijah-like prophet renewing covenantal teaching, wilderness feedings, and healings of a people suffering under oppressive, unjust rulers. Understanding the Q speeches of Jesus as parts of a popular hidden transcript enables us to move well beyond abstract categorization of Jesus sayings, say, as "wisdom" and into deeper appreciation of how they resonated with Galileans' emotional-cultural sense of dignity and indignation. "Blessed are the poor, . . . but woe to the rich . . ." restores a sense of dignity. "Love your enemies, do good, and lend" appeals to and revitalizes the traditional "moral economy" (see chapter 10 below) of the Galilean Israelite "little tradition" that the peasants were having difficulty maintaining because of the escalated economic pressures on household subsistence. Both Mark and Q also, at points, address problems of surveillance and repression and the people's resistance. Mark's extensive representation of the Pharisees' close surveillance on Jesus' and his disciples' every move is highly schematic (and surely questionable historically). Mark and Q both include repeated references to persecution of members of their respective movements or their prophetic predecessors. And both include an episode in which Jesus admonishes his followers to boldly confess their solidarity with the movement if and when they were apprehended and brought to trial (Mark 8:34—9:1; Q/Luke 12:2-12).

Similarly familiar from the hidden transcripts of other peoples are anticipations of political-economic reversal and divine condemnation of the dominant oppressors (199): the prayer for the kingdom, the beatitudes on the poor and woes on the rich, the baptism of fire, the promise of the kingdom coming with power in judgment on their persecutors, and the demonic (Roman) "Legion" being driven back into the sea and destroyed (Q/Luke 11:2-4; Q/Luke 6:20-26; Q/Luke 3:7-9, 16-17; Mark 8:34—9:1; Mark 5:1-20, respectively).

Yet other Q and Markan materials portray Jesus as having moved into what Scott calls "the arts of political disguise" and anonymity. At certain points in the Q speeches, Jesus pronounces prophetic condemnation of the Jerusalem ruling families in sufficiently ambiguous language that modern scholars who do not share the cultural knowledge of the Judean and Galilean peasants' Israelite "little tradition" (or hidden transcript) tend not to "get it" (Q/Luke 13:28-29, where the "sons of the kingdom" who presume on their lineage from Abraham think they are secure in God's promise, as suggested already in John's speech in Q/Luke 3:7-9, 16-17!). Mark is full of Jesus' politics of ambiguity, anonymity, and disguise. Jesus chooses the anonymity of a large festival crowd for the semi-anonymous demonstration of his entry into Jerusalem as a popular messiah riding on a donkey (peasant mode of transportation; Mark 11:2-11; compare with Zech 9:9). And in that connection he chooses the occasion of the Passover festival, when the elite not only allowed but sponsored (in an attempt to control) the people's celebration of Israel's liberation from oppressive foreign rule, as the occasion for mounting his prophetic condemnation of the Temple and confrontation with the Jerusalem rulers. He articulates his condemnation of the high priestly rulers in the ambiguous language of the parable of the tenants, which resonates with Isaiah's prophetic love song of the vineyard that indicted the Jerusalem rulers of old (Mark 12:1-9; Isa 5:1-13). He couches his declaration that the people did not owe Caesar a thing in a classic ambiguity that enabled him to wriggle out of the trap set by the Pharisees and Herodians even though anyone familiar with Israelite covenantal tradition understood his meaning (Mark 12:13-17).

In Q and especially in Mark, however, Jesus even goes beyond the politics of disguise and boldly declares the hidden transcript of the Galilean and Judean villagers against the rulers on the public stage. Jesus' pronouncement of a prophetic lament over the Jerusalem ruling house as already condemned to destruction by God in Q/Luke 13:34-35 is hardly ambiguous, since the traditional Israelite form was as familiar to the elite as it was deeply resonant with peasants rooted in Israelite prophetic traditions. Similarly, Jesus' woes against the Pharisees and scribes in Q/Luke 11:39-52 are public condemnations addressed (ostensibly) directly to the representatives of the Jerusalem rulers. Even bolder is Jesus' action in Mark 11–12. Although he appears almost like the standard trickster figure in his cunning counters to the Pharisees' challenges earlier in Mark's story, his obstructive demonstration against the Temple constituted an unmistakable prophetic condemnation of the whole system of domination at the center of the public stage in Jerusalem, the Temple courtyard. Despite the disguised message of the parable of the tenants and his declaration about the tribute to Caesar, moreover, everyone knew full well that this was a public condemnation of the Temple-state and its incumbents. And in Mark explicitly and Q implicitly (insofar as he is the successor of all the prophets that the Jerusalem rulers killed), Jesus' challenge and open defiance provokes a swift stroke of repression in the arrest, trial, and crucifixion of the leader who boldly spoke truth to power.

Mark and Q are thus no longer just hidden transcripts proper, according to Scott's definition. They incorporate all four varieties of political discourse used in popular resistance, not just the hidden transcript itself. Or better, the new hidden transcripts that developed into the sequence of speeches in Q and the Gospel of Mark, performed in secure sites of communities of Jesus movements, included portrayals of Jesus engaged in all of those forms of resistance, including boldly speaking truth to power in public space. Those portrayals, moreover, are not purely the inventions of those communities. Jesus had apparently taken prophetic actions and delivered prophetic pronouncements. That is the most likely reason why he was apprehended and executed—by crucifixion—as a rebel against the Roman imperial order. And those bold prophetic actions and declarations, because they resonated among the people, were remembered and (re-) performed. He was apparently one of those rare cases among popular leaders whose irrevocable declaration of the hidden transcript in condemnation of the dominant order constituted a political breakthrough that escalated into a broader movement.

The texts of Mark and Q are thus hidden transcripts that are the result of open political resistance that is highly unusual in peasant politics. Yet they are nevertheless still hidden transcripts in the sense that they are still cultivated and performed off-stage, still communication among peasants (or communities of urban poor) in sequestered sites in village synagogues (assemblies). The new hidden transcript of the Jesus movements, however, now includes and cultivates those bolder forms of popular political resistance, and shifts the balance of power insofar as Jesus' breakthrough encourages participants in these movements to stand in solidarity against the dominant order that stands condemned under the rule of God proclaimed by Jesus. Scott, taking a leaf from the notebook of Levi-Strauss, speaks of a developed hidden transcript as "cooked," as opposed to "raw." Mark and Q are very well-cooked hidden transcripts that portray to their hearers a prophet who was spearheading bold, determined, and persistent popular resistance against their domination by Romans and their client rulers.

Jesus and the Arts of Resistance

Established biblical studies tends to reduce Jesus and the Gospels to their religious dimension. This is rooted in Western separation of church from state, and of religion from politics and economics. Biblical studies, of course, is not alone. As Indian historians involved in the subaltern studies project point out, Western colonialist and Marxist historians alike tended to dismiss Indian peasant movements as merely religious, with no relevance for politics.[13] The Iranian revolution of 1979 may have been a wake-up call. In a context where the American-backed Shah had blocked all forms of ordinary political participation, traditional mourning rites for martyrs in the Shiite Muslim tradition became the occasions and form for the massive demonstrations that toppled the secular regime. These events caught American scholars in various fields totally off guard, baffled that it defied all of their disciplinary models that did not take the people's grounding in traditional culture and religion seriously.[14] Previous attempts to overcome the religious reductionism in New Testament studies have tended to overemphasize the material dimension in popular discontent, as if poverty by itself could explain the origin of the popular movement touched of by Jesus. Now we can understand how the material and political dimensions are interconnected with the emotional and religious dimensions.

The key to understanding the dynamics of power relations is the recognition that political resistance by the subjected is rooted in the off-stage hidden transcript. "So long as we confine our conception of *the political* to activity that is openly declared we are driven to conclude that subordinate groups essentially lack a political life or that what political life they do have is restricted to those exceptional moments of popular explosion. To do so is to miss the immense political terrain that lies between quiescence and revolt and that, for better or worse, is the political environment of subject classes" (199). Like other subjected peoples, Jesus and his followers were denied participation in official politics, which were controlled at the center by the dominant. Much of their behavior, which seems to have acquiesced in or even supported the dominant order was coerced by the prevailing patterns of power.

Jesus, like other peasant leaders, however, further developed the people's hidden transcript in village communities in catalyzing a movement based in those sequestered sites. Scott argues that "we can view the social side of the hidden transcript as a political domain striving to enforce, against great odds, certain forms of conduct and resistance in relations with the dominant. *It would be more accurate to think of the hidden transcript as a condition of practical resistance rather than a substitute for it*" (191). In the case of Jesus and his movement, we can perhaps go even further. Renewing those village communities in their covenantal cooperation and solidarity with one another (their traditional Israelite "moral economy"; Q/Luke 6:20-49; Mark 10:1-45) was already a significant form of political resistance to the Roman client rule of Herod Antipas and the Jerusalem temple-state, whose control was enhanced precisely by the disintegration in families and village communities caused by their economic exploitation. Then this renewed discourse of dignity grounded in covenantal renewal formed the basis for Jesus' bolder expression of the now well-cooked articulation of Galilean peasants' indignation in parables and prophecies that condemned the rulers for their oppression of the people. Finally, Jesus apparently dared to con-

front the Jerusalem rulers directly in a bold declaration of the people's indignation in the courtyard of the Temple itself. Jesus, as represented in Mark and Q,
engages in all of the varieties of popular political resistance that Scott outlines.
Scott's illumination of these previously unrecognized forms of popular resistance makes possible a whole new understanding of Jesus as fully and actively
engaged in the politics of Roman Palestine, but in the area between quiescence
and active peasant revolt.

The swift act of repression by the rulers made him into a martyr, whom
his followers believed had been vindicated by God, confirming his now well-
cooked discourse of indignation, and further motivating organized long-range
resistance by a wider movement of Israelite peoples that expanded into Judea
and Samaria and to diaspora Jewish communities, as well as among villagers
in nearby areas. As Scott emphasizes, "It is only when this hidden transcript is
openly declared that subordinates can fully recognize the full extent to which
their claims, their dreams, their anger is shared by other subordinates with
whom they have not been in direct touch" (223). It was in the Jesus movements
in and beyond Galilee, apparently, that what became the elaborate hidden transcripts of those movements developed into regularly performed texts such as the
Gospel of Mark and Q. They portray Jesus boldly declaring popular indignation
in direct confrontation with the dominant in prime public space. Yet they are
still hidden transcripts *and* they constitute political resistance in the wide area
between acquiescence and active insurrection.

Chapter
Nine

Jesus and the Arts of Resistance

It is difficult to imagine that American historians would construct the life of "the historical Abraham Lincoln" or "the historical Martin Luther King" by focusing on their sayings removed from the contexts of their speeches. Indeed, in approaching a figure such as Lincoln or King, historians consider far more than their speeches. They rather analyze and bring together several interrelated facets of (1) their subjects' relations with the particular historical crisis in which they operated and its historical roots, (2) the cultural ideals and tradition out of which they operated, (3) the particular offices they held or roles they played, (4) the ways they interacted with and affected their contemporaries, particularly their immediate associates and followers, and (5) the impact and historical significance of their actions.[1] Critical historians' approach to a figure of historical significance is usually relational and contextual.

The purposeful isolation of Jesus sayings from their literary contexts (in order to ascertain their "original form" and "authenticity") so basic to the standard approach to the historical Jesus has become severely limiting to historical understanding in at least three interrelated ways. First, the isolation of Jesus' sayings from their literary contexts blocks access to Jesus' historical impact and the historical significance of his speech and action. The only sources for the latter are the texts derived from communities of Jesus' followers, mainly the Gospels (non-canonical as well as canonical). Second, a separate and individual saying has no meaning in itself, since meaning depends on context.[2] But the only sources which can guide us toward the ancient historical meaning-context of those sayings are the Gospels. Third, no one communicates in isolated sayings, which are not intelligible units of communication. Isolated individual Jesus sayings are merely like artifacts displayed in museum cases. Jesus emerged as a catalyst or leader of a significant historical movement by interacting and communicating effectively with other people who became motivated into action in the problematic historical circumstances of their lives. Jesus and his followers, moreover, were rooted in and acted out of the Israelite cultural tradition, perhaps even by adapting certain "scripts" deeply ingrained in those cultural traditions.[3]

For a defensible historical inquiry, therefore, we must not dispense with but work from the only sources that provide indications, from close to the historical situation, of the significance and meaning context of Jesus' speech and action. Since individual sayings are meaningless outside of a meaning context, the only viable historical approach appears to be backing up, as it were, to the earliest gospel sources, that is, the Gospel of Mark as a complete story and the whole series of Jesus' speeches in Q. At the very least, we must work from the infrastructural components of Mark and Q, such as the parallel chains of miracles in Mark and John or the parallel discourses in Mark and Q, which also provide indications of meaning context. Mark's story and the Q series of Jesus' speeches constituted basic units of communication about Jesus. And these fundamental units of communication also provide clear ancient indicators of meaning context and historical significance. We can first discern the respective representations of Jesus in context in the earliest gospels sources and then triangulate back to the leader in a movement in context.

Many previous constructions of the historical Jesus have concluded that since Jesus' "authentic" sayings, as isolated from literary contexts, do not indicate that he was engaged in any direct, active revolt against the rulers, he was therefore relatively innocuous politically, quiescent and perhaps even an advocate of non-resistance. If, instead of focusing on isolated Jesus sayings, we attend to the literary forms that constituted the means of communication, such as Q speeches and Mark's narrative, which portray Jesus engaged in political conflict, we are forced to deal with the concrete historical context, which was also rife with political-religious conflict. For an adequate historical approach, we must attend not only to Jesus' context in a movement of followers, but also to the cultural tradition in which they are embedded, as well as the historical conditions of and for his work and the movement he catalyzed.[4]

The work of James C. Scott, particularly *Domination and the Arts of Resistance*[5] (to which the pages in the text refer), can help us move toward a more adequate approach to the historical Jesus. Scott's work can help us contextualize Jesus' speech and action in historical social-political relations, and can help us better understand how the movements that developed indicate Jesus' historical significance. Scott opens for fruitful investigation the usually unrecognized emotional and cultural dimension of people's subordination to power that mediates between political-economic conditions and people's consciousness.

Jesus scholars generally have reached an impasse on Jesus and politics, partly because, reflecting the views of their own culture, they view politics as separate from religion, and partly because they understand politics in the relatively narrow terms of public affairs on the public stage. If Jesus had engaged in political activity, as this view sees it, it would have been in the form of revolt. Since gospel sources give little or no indication of Jesus as leading or advocating a revolt, then he must have been engaged in religious activity, with little or no implications for political-economic power relations.

Scott's work can help us move past this impasse by discerning an ordinarily unrecognized area of political activity and forms of popular resistance to power present in many historical circumstances (as discussed in chapter 8). In Scott's terms, Jesus operated in this area between quiescence and revolt, (1) by cultivating the "hidden transcript" of Galilean and other villagers, (2) by spearheading peasant politics of anonymity and disguise, and (3) by bold declaration of the "hidden transcript" in the face of power—that is by exercising three of the four types of the politics that Scott suggests are available to subjected people (18–19).

Jesus' Teachings as a Hidden Transcript of Popular Indignation and Dignity

Scott devises the concept of "hidden transcript" for the "discourse of dignity" developed by subordinated peoples in sequestered sites off the public stage to counter the regular indignities of domination. The public actions and behavior of slaves, serfs, and peasants are coerced by the forces of domination arrayed against them. Evidence from a wide variety of historical situations, however, indicates that domination and exploitation generate a set of counter-values. Regular experience of degradation and insult generates a hidden transcript of indignation among groups of slaves or peasants determined to preserve their own dignity, resist the worst effects of domination, and insist on justice (114). Beside and behind the many hidden and disguised forms of resistance stands a popular ideology that comprises an alternative to the values and views articulated in the official public transcript controlled by the dominant. Insofar as the major historical forms of domination have authorized themselves in a religion or a worldview, they have provoked the development of more or less equally elaborate ideologies that justify inequality, oppression, and even bondage. Resistance has required a counter-ideology for the resistant practices invented in self-defense by the subordinate (118).

Scott's analysis highlights several interrelated features of the hidden transcript. It is cultivated beyond the effective reach of the eyes and ears of power in sequestered sites such as slave barracks, ale houses, and village communities. As resentment and anger are articulated in language, they acquire disciplined forms, indeed can even acquire relatively "cooked" articulation in sophisticated and stable cultural forms. Insofar as humiliation and fantasies of justice are always experienced within a cultural tradition and social framework, a discourse of dignity that becomes the property of a whole category of subordinates must develop and resonate with that cultural tradition as it responds to developing dynamics of power. And the hidden transcript, like folk culture, has no reality as pure thought, but continues effectively as it is regularly articulated, disseminated, and enacted in the secure off-stage sites (119).

When examined with fresh eyes, Jesus' teaching exhibits all of the features of what Scott discusses as a hidden transcript. Not only do the earliest gospel sources, Mark and Q, portray Jesus as delivering most of his teaching as a hidden transcript, but the gospel texts themselves can only be understood as hidden transcripts, albeit very well-cooked ones. Although in later centuries Mark became part of the official scripture of the established church, hence part of the official transcript, in its origins the gospel derived from and was addressed to communities that were off-stage. Far from being a public document addressed also to the high priests, Pharisees, Herodians, and Romans, Mark and Q were produced by and performed in small communities of popular movements meeting apparently in houses and villages.

To start with, as represented in Mark and Q, Jesus delivers his teaching in sequestered sites. His teaching assumes relatively elaborate and sophisticated cultural forms. The substance of his teaching combines sharp declarations of God's judgment against the forms and practices of domination and hopeful declarations of the sufficiency and justice possible under the direct rule of God. His speech resonates vibrantly with Israelite popular tradition.[6] Far from being pure thought or theology, Jesus teaching displays features of regular performance in community settings, even in some cases of performative speech.

When Jesus scholars purposely isolate the sayings of Jesus from their literary contexts in the Gospels, they wind up with no social location and no historical meaning context for the communication that was presumably happening in Jesus' speech. But those literary contexts in the Gospels provide the only possible indications from close to the time of Jesus of the communication and meaning context needed to investigate Jesus' speech.[7] If we proceed, instead, by beginning with the literary contexts, they give indications aplenty of the social location and historical circumstances of Jesus' speech. The Gospel of Mark, by consensus the earliest gospel, portrays Jesus and his disciples as teaching and healing in village communities, particularly in the synagogues, which were local village assemblies, not religious buildings. Once we inquire into the basic form of society in Galilee and surrounding rural areas where Jesus operated, Mark's historical verisimilitude is obvious, for the fundamental societal form was the village community.[8] The only episodes in Mark that lack this historical verisimilitude are the disputes with the Pharisees (mainly in Mark 2:1—3:5), for rulers of agrarian societies do not generally delegate their retainers to maintain such close surveillance of village affairs. The non-Markan Jesus speeches that can be identified through the parallel speech material in the Gospels of Matthew and Luke, moreover, are clearly addressed to agrarian people who are poor, hungry, and heavily in debt, that is, peasants living in village communities. The context of Jesus' teaching is consistently the local village community. And that is precisely where he sends his envoys to heal and teach, in the parallel mission speeches in Mark 6:6-13 and Q/Luke 9:57—10:16.

Correspondingly the substance of Jesus' teaching fits what Scott calls a "discourse of dignity," the hidden transcript that is cultivated precisely in "sequestered sites" of the village communities where Jesus taught. The elaborate and sophisticated forms of a well-cooked discourse of dignity combining judgment and justice, and resonating with the forms and contents of Israelite popular tradition, can be discerned in any number of Jesus' speeches and debates.

It is now increasingly being recognized that the speeches of Jesus paralleled in Matthew and Luke took the form not of a collection of separate sayings (like the *Gospel of Thomas*) but of a sequence of speeches on various issues of concern to communities of a Jesus movement.[9] Some of these speeches focus only on encouragement of the people, such as assurance that if they focus single-mindedly on pursuit of the kingdom of God subsistence food and shelter will somehow materialize (Q/Luke 12:22-31). Many of them, however, combine blunt statements of God's judgment against the wealthy, unjust, and arrogant rulers with statements of deliverance and justice for the people. God's prophet is at hand with baptism of both Spirit (renewal of social life) and fire (judgment; Q/Luke 3:7-9, 16-17). Indeed Jesus is that prophet, who brings personal and social healing with good news for the poor, set over against those who wear "soft raiment" in their luxurious palaces, and in a contested struggle entailing the advent of God's kingdom (Q/Luke 7:18-35). The rhetoric of divine judgment heats up in speeches such as the prophetic woes that Jesus declares against the Pharisaic retainers of the Jerusalem rulers for their scribal practices that exacerbate the exploitation and suffering of the people through tithing and other mechanisms. That Jesus is articulating long-standing grievances and anger at the rulers and their retainers is vividly articulated in the next to last woe and declaration of punishment: because earlier generation of Jerusalem rulers had consistently killed the prophets God sent to pronounce judgment, "the blood of all the prophets, shed from the foundation of the world, will be required of this generation!" (Q/Luke 11:47-51). Similarly, God, like a mother hen solicitous for the welfare of the people, is about to destroy the Jerusalem ruling house because of its violence against the prophets sent to warn them. And while Israel is finally gathered together in the feast of the kingdom, those who presumed so much on their illustrious ancestry will be weeping and gnashing their teeth in outer darkness (Q/Luke 13:28-29, 34-35)!

These prophetic declarations of fulfillment (Q 7:18-35) and judgment (Q 11:47-51; 13:28-29, 34-35) not only perpetuate and resonate with the strong Israelite tradition of prophecy, but they also assume distinctive prophetic forms familiar from that cultural tradition. Beyond the earlier Israelite prophets known from the canon of the Hebrew Bible, sources are scarce in the extreme. Yet the fragmentary sources for the oracular prophets John the Baptist and Jesus son of Hananiah, as well as for the prophetic leaders of popular movements such as Theudas and the Egyptian Jewish prophet, indicate that prophetic figures were still periodically emerging from and renewing the hidden transcript of the Galilean and Judean peasantry.[10] The appearance of other such prophetic figures contemporary with Jesus of Nazareth lends further credence to our discernment that the latter was rooted in and creatively generating a discourse of dignity in Galilean villages.

Most striking of all the Jesus speeches in Q, in terms of its creative adaptation of traditional Israelite cultural forms and its resonance with Israelite tradition, is the renewal of the Mosaic covenant that Jesus enacts in performative speech in Q/Luke 6:20-49. Because of the standard focus on individual sayings, interpreters have not often considered this speech as a whole, much less recognized that it follows and adapts the standard formal components of the Mosaic covenant at the core of Israelite cultural tradition. The parallel adaptation of the same covenantal components and overall form in the Community Rule (and the Damascus Rule, to a degree) from the scribal-priestly community at Qumran now confirms that covenant forms and covenant renewal were still alive in late second-temple Palestine.[11] As in the covenant renewal ceremony at Qumran (1QS 1–2), so also Jesus transforms the blessings and woes that originally functioned as sanctions on covenant keeping (but had come to be instruments of self-blame for the people's historical suffering) into new declarations of deliverance, only now in the present or imminent future rather than the distant past. The effect of the declaration, "Blessed are you poor, for yours is the kingdom of God. . . . [but] Woe to the rich, for they have received their consolation!" (Q 6:20-26), was to restate the dignity of the peasantry, over against the injustices emanating from the wealthy and powerful. The ensuing restatement of covenantal principles, deeply rooted in traditional Israelite covenantal teaching, then provided guidelines for the restoration of covenantal justice in the village community. Bolstered by an opening declaration that God was again responding to their distressed conditions with new deliverance, the people could now regain the spirit of mutual sharing, cooperation, and solidarity traditional in their covenantal "moral economy," (see further chapter 10 below) as they cancelled each others' debts, again lent freely, and broke the cycle of petty local quarreling and disputes (Q 6:27-38).[12]

Similarly in the Gospel of Mark, Jesus' teaching, often in dispute with the Pharisees or dialogue with the disciples, comes alive as a discourse of dignity that resonates deeply with Israelite popular tradition, over against the behavior of the wealthy elite and the exploitative practices of the ruling institutions. In Mark 2:2-12, in the context of a healing, Jesus declares that "humanity" has the authority to forgive sins, over against the sacrificial apparatus of the Jerusalem Temple, for which the people paid dearly. In Mark 7:1-13, set up by a mocking dispute with the Pharisees and their Temple-based purity codes, Jesus declares that the demand for peasant support of the Temple apparatus (*korban* = dedicated produce or property) was a violation of the basic Mosaic "commandment of God" to "honor your father and mother." That is, against the temple-state's retainers' attempts to secure support for the Temple, Jesus insists that the people reject the efforts of the Pharisees and retain locally, in their own households, the scarce economic resources they needed to support their families.

In Mark 10:16-31, using as a foil a wealthy man who claims to be keeping the Mosaic covenantal principles while all the time gaining his wealth by defrauding the peasants (presumably through forbidden interest on loans)—and declaring it impossible that the rich could get into the kingdom of God—Jesus insists upon the Mosaic covenantal "moral economy" as the principles that should guide local social-economic life. And in the next dialogue with the disciples (Mark 10:32-45) he similarly insists upon egalitarian political leadership, in pointed contrast with "the [imperial] nations" who have kings and emperors who lord it over them. Throughout these dialogues Jesus sets the restoration of the people's dignity and independent social-political-economic life over against the practices and institutions of the exploitative wealthy rulers. And in every case he is drawing upon and creatively adapting the Israelite cultural tradition, especially the Mosaic covenant that articulated what Scott calls the "moral economy" under the exclusive rule of God.

Twenty-five years ago, Werner Kelber, in a telling critique of the print-culture assumptions of Rudolf Bultmann's form critical approach, pointed out that the Jesus teachings that survived were what resonated with the people.[13] In his reflections on the hidden transcript, Scott offers a way of appreciating the concrete situation in which this happened and a way of explaining why certain Jesus teachings survived: because they expressed collective indignation and restored people's dignity. In particular, Scott brings into focus the emotional energy that lies behind and finds expression in Jesus' teachings, which both resonate with long-standing Israelite traditions of resistance to oppressive power and bring creative new developments of traditional Israelite prophetic forms and principles. Adapting Scott's reflections on the hidden transcript to the teachings of Jesus enables us to discern a whole area of political resistance in between quiescence and revolt, and to discern that many much-discussed teachings of Jesus can be seen as aspects of resistance to domination.

The teachings of Jesus, however, form only part of the activities in which Jesus engaged and only part of the effects and significance of his activities that resulted in ongoing Jesus movements. Scott's reflections on other forms of popular political resistance also illuminate these other aspects of Jesus' overall conflict with the rulers, as portrayed in the gospel sources.

The Politics of Disguise and Anonymity: Jesus' Campaign in Galilee and Beyond

On occasion, groups of subordinated people move their continuing struggle against domination beyond the confines of their specially sequestered sites into "a politics of disguise and anonymity that takes place in public view but is designed to have double meaning or to shield the identity of the actors" (18–19). One of the principal modes of the politics of anonymity is rumor. Rumor travels in a process of elaboration in which it is adapted to the hopes and fears of those who hear it and retell it (145). Scott provides several illustrations that are suggestive for the Gospel of Mark and, through Mark, for Jesus and the movement around him. Prior to the French Revolution, when the king finally summoned the *Estates Général* for the first time since 1614, the peasants eagerly anticipated their imminent liberation. According to contemporary sources, they went home from assemblies called to elect representatives and to draw up their concerns believing that they were now at last free from tithes and feudal dues and that the king wished everyone to be equal, with no more bishops and lords (145–46). "In the [Caribbean] slave rebellions in the late eighteenth and early nineteenth centuries, there was a fairly consistent belief that the king or British officials had set slaves free and that the whites were keeping the word from them" (147). The many parallels from Russian serfs, Indian untouchables, and cargo cults among peoples overwhelmed by Western conquest, says Scott, "are too striking to ignore." Believing that God or the authorities had granted their dreams, "vulnerable groups express their hidden aspirations in public in a way that both enables them to avoid individual responsibility and aligns them with some higher power" (148).

Scott's list of parallels can be expanded from cases of peasant movements in first century Palestine. The first that immediately come to mind are the prophetic movements led by Theudas and "the Egyptian" in mid-century Judea, both of which involved large numbers of Judean peasants and a remarkable collective anticipation of divine deliverance, judging from the hostile accounts of Josephus. In a popular movement significant enough that it was remembered in tandem with the revolt against the tribute led by Judas of Galilee (Acts 5:36), Theudas "persuaded most of the common people to take their possessions and follow him to the Jordan River, saying that at his command the river would be divided . . ." (*Ant.* 20.97-98). "The Egyptian false-prophet" led "the mass of the common

people [about thirty-thousand] to go with him to the Mount of Olives, just opposite the city, from where, at his command, the walls of Jerusalem would fall down
[and the Roman garrison overpowered]" (*Ant.* 20.169-71, compare with *J.W.*
2.261-63). That the Roman governors sent out "a cavalry unit" and "heavily armed
Roman troops" to slaughter hundreds of these evidently non-violent seekers of
deliverance may be another indication of their numbers and an indication of how
far the rumor of imminent deliverance had spread among the Judean peasantry.
These collective anticipations of God's new acts of deliverance were clearly resonating with the Judean peasants' hidden transcript—the popular memory of the
"little tradition" of Moses and Joshua leading the people across the water (the Red
Sea and the Jordan) into their wilderness preparation for the entry into their land
and of Joshua's leading the miraculous battle against Jericho. As Scott comments,
"a powerful and suppressed desire for relief from the burdens of subordination
seems not only to infuse the autonomous religious life of the oppressed but also to
strongly color their interpretation of events" (147).

New Testament scholars have labeled these movements as "apocalyptic" or
their leaders as "sign prophets."[14] The latter label says too little, while the former is
much too broad and synthetic a concept. The principal sources for the broad general concept of apocalypticism used for late second temple Palestinian materials
are the literary products of Judean scribal circles. I have cautioned elsewhere about
presuming that elite scribal literature can be used to project popular thinking and
action.[15] Compared with the synthetic modern scholarly construct of apocalyptic,
Scott's discussion of hidden transcript gets us more deeply into the motives and the
dynamics of dignity and indignity, of oppression and subordination and resentment. The popular prophetic movements are not the apocalypticism expressed
in literary apocalypses, but peasant yearning or desire touched off by a symbol or
reports of an event. "A powerful and suppressed desire for relief from the burdens
of subordination seems not only to infuse the autonomous religious life of the
oppressed but also to strongly color their interpretation of events" (147).

Another ancient Palestinian collective action in which rumor must have
shaped events according to popular interests was the massive strike by Galilean
peasants over the emperor Gaius's plan to place an image of himself in the Jerusalem Temple. There is no reason to believe that Galileans peasants would have
had any reason to defend the sanctity of the Temple itself, one of the principal political-economic-religious institutions of domination to which they were
partially subjected. But the rumor of the impending invasion of their territory
by a huge Roman military expedition, the effects of which they knew only too
well from previous Roman military slaughter, enslavement, and devastation,
apparently motivated them to take collective action. Saying "we will die sooner
than violate our laws" (according to Josephus), they refused to plant their crops.
Herodian officials and the Roman legate of Syria knew exactly what the result

would be: "there would be a harvest of banditry, because the requirement of the tribute could not be met" (*Ant.* 18.261-74).

The occurrence of several other Judean and Galilean popular movements in which the spread of rumor of anticipated divine deliverance (or impending invasion) makes all the more intriguing the Gospel of Mark's portrayal of the rapidly widening popular response to Jesus' preaching of the kingdom of God and manifestation of God's enabling power in exorcisms and healings. Jesus came to Galilee, proclaiming "the time is fulfilled, and the kingdom of God is at hand." (Mark 1:15) He summoned disciples to assist in his mission, taught and performed exorcisms and healings in village assemblies and houses. His fame quickly spread throughout Galilee, crowds of increasing size gathered around and soon expanded into "a great multitude" and "great numbers" from Judea, Idumea to the south, and even from the region around Tyre and Sidon to the north (Mark 1:27-28, 32-33, 37-39, 45; 2:1-2, 13; 3:7-10, 20; 5:20-21, 24; 6:33, 54-56). People came bearing their friends and relatives for healing. A woman who had been hemorrhaging for twelve years touched him from behind and was instantly healed, not by his word or action, but through her own trust (faith) that power was working through him. In several motifs in the story, such as the appointment of the Twelve as representative figures and Jesus' acts of power as a new Moses (sea crossings and wilderness feedings) and new Elijah (healings), Mark indicates that Jesus was spearheading a renewal of Israel based in its village communities, a renewal that expanded into nearby regions to include other villagers as well.

Mark's portrayal of Jesus' mission in Galilee and beyond thus resembles other peasant movements that spread through rumor. These were movements where subordinated people's long-suppressed yearning for liberation, which had been cultivated in their hidden transcript, suddenly, in response to a rumor or a prophet's promise and miraculous actions, burst forth in rapidly spreading collective anticipation that the hour of deliverance was at hand. Earlier generations of critical New Testament scholars, reacting against the naïve assumption that the Gospel of Mark constituted a reliable historical record from which to reconstruct the history of Jesus' ministry—and finally assimilating the historical skepticism of Enlightenment reason—rejected Mark's narrative as historically worthless framing and much of the contents of Mark as historically worthless miracle stories and mythology. Indeed, the Markan framing, along with miraculous stories, was seen as an obstacle to historical reconstruction. Critical scholars focused mainly on the sayings of Jesus, which ostensibly offered greater possibilities for establishing at least some authentic fragments of Jesus' teaching. For the last century liberal scholarship has presented Jesus as primarily a teacher, lately even stripped of prophetic judgment and reduced to a sage or a Cynic-like philosopher. It is hardly considered that Jesus himself was connected with a movement—that was what the disciples founded in response to the resurrection faith. While still dismissing the value of particular healing or exorcism stories as historical information, scholars have come to believe that Jesus did perform healings and perhaps even exorcisms. But that is usually consigned to a separate, less important chapter in Jesus books, which focus on his sayings. It has been almost impossible to discern how Jesus' healings and exorcisms fit together with his teaching about the kingdom of God, except in a very general way as apparent manifestations of the kingdom that he preached as imminent.

Scott's presentation of the politics of disguise and anonymity as one of the modes of popular resistance to domination offers comparative material as a helpful model on which we can re-imagine, as components of a larger picture, the Jesus materials that atomizing analysis of Jesus as teacher has rejected. For example, parallel to belief among Caribbean slaves that the distant British king had set them free, Jesus' preaching that the kingdom of God was at hand and its manifestation in exorcisms touched off a movement of people who believed that God was liberating them from domination by the Romans and their client rulers (148). Perhaps Mark knows what he is talking about after all, given how similar his narrative is to many other historical cases of rapidly spreading popular movements that Scott cites as "too striking to ignore." Mark's narrative turns out to be remarkable for its historical verisimilitude.

This seems to open the possibility of taking Mark's narrative seriously as a historical source, but in a way very different from its naïve nineteenth-century use as a direct historical record for a sequence of events. The sequence of episodes in Mark has been narratively plotted by Mark's composers and performers. But the artfully composed narrative represents the way such a prophetic figure's message of God's imminent action and his manifestation of that action in healings and exorcisms would have resonated with the people on the basis of their shared hidden discourse of indignation and yearning.

We cannot understand Jesus except in the context of the movement of the people who responded to and interacted with him. Scott's exposition of the hidden transcript enables us to appreciate how that interaction worked on the basis of Israelite popular tradition in the context of Galilean villages. The hidden transcript, however, does not always remain confined to the secure sites in which it is regularly cultivated. Subjected peasants' indignation overflows the borders of their villages in other forms of popular politics, usually in various forms of disguise and anonymity. Mark presents a story of considerable historical verisimilitude of how Jesus' preaching and healing touched off a seemingly spontaneous movement of renewal that generated divinely inspired popular power opposed to and threatening to the dominant rulers and their representatives. Mark does not provide evidence for any particular healing or exorcism or speech before a Galilean village assembly—nor does it matter that we establish historical verification for any particular incident and the way it actually happened. But Mark does provide a credible account of the relationship between Jesus' proclamation of the kingdom, his practice of healing and exorcism, and the resulting renewal of personal life and village community in Galilee. By thus creatively adapting the central scripts and patterns of popular Israelite cultural tradition, Mark's Jesus brings political expression of the hidden transcript to public expression and public view.

Jesus' Bold Declaration of the Hidden Transcript in the Face of Power

The standard liberal approach to Jesus, focusing on atomized sayings of Jesus, grouping them into topics like artifacts in museum display cases, tends not to ask questions of historical significance and historical explanation. Martin Luther did not simply write up some theses, but nailed them to the church door—and was brought to trial where he firmly declared his stand. Martin Luther King did not simply make some memorable statements, but led marches in the face of municipal and state police, their attack dogs, water hoses, and truncheons—and was eventually assassinated. Modern western interpreters construct a Jesus who was politically innocuous. He is confined largely to cultural-religious affairs. His sayings were pithy and counter-cultural, and the table fellowship he shared was inclusive.[16] Any of his declarations or actions that might seem politically challenging are effectively de-politicized, either cleaned up (the obstructive prophetic demonstration against the Temple was only a "cleansing") or blunted (rendering unto God and Caesar reduced to church versus state). But Jesus would have had little historical impact, and no one would have remembered those sayings or continued the table fellowship, had he not carried out some public confrontation of the rulers and ruling institutions in Jerusalem—and been executed as an insurrectionary, crucified by the Romans. This is both suggested and can be explained by Scott's exposition of the fourth variety of the popular politics of resistance, the public declaration of the hidden transcript in the face of power.

Jesus' confrontation with the rulers in Jerusalem, perhaps mainly his condemnation of the Temple and high priests and compounded by his crucifixion, appears to have been the breakthrough event that led to the sudden expansion of the movement he had inaugurated in Galilee, ensuring that he became a significant historical figure. The expanding movement, in turn, did not merely remember his teachings and deeds, but perpetuated, cultivated, and consolidated his speech and program of societal renewal.

The breakthrough that consolidated his mission and energized the expansion of his movements was the result of a conjunction of factors. Because of the methodological individualism of New Testament studies and its focus on meaning abstracted from political context, it is important to learn from social-political historians the significance of structural factors. Jesus' and his followers' pilgrimage to Jerusalem juxtaposes the prophetic spokesperson and catalyst of an Israelite peasant movement from Galilee with the lavishly rebuilt Temple and high priesthood, the ruling institutions that had taken over and ruled that distant district for a hundred years prior to the lifetime of Jesus. In Scott's terms, they were a spokesperson of the subjugated versus the dominant ruling institution and rulers. Scott, however, insists on including key factors often ignored by social scientists as well as humanists—the emotional dynamics of domination and subjugation. The indignities imposed by domination induce in the subjugated a deep-running indignation that has not only produced a certain oppositional ideology, but an oppositional tone or mood of some intensity, the expression of which is ordinarily blocked by the potentially coercive power of the dominant. Because that indignation desires expression, however, a spokesperson's bold defiance of the dominant can transform the collective indignation into an excitement and energy that drives events; a political breakthrough can escalate rapidly into a significant movement. Such charismatic acts, says Scott, "gain their social force by virtue of their roots in the hidden transcript of a subordinate group" (203).

"The moment when the dissent of the hidden transcript crosses the threshold to open resistance is always a politically charged occasion" (207). The "politically charged occasion" in Jesus' case, moreover, was itself the politically and religiously charged occasion of Passover. We should remind ourselves that we cannot simply read a public declaration of the hidden transcript directly off of the Markan or other gospel text. Mark, the Gospel of John, and Q must all apparently be taken as hidden transcripts, although they portray forays by Jesus into public declaration of prophetic condemnations of the dominant. Generations of previous criticism of gospel accounts of Jesus' face-off with the Judean and Roman rulers in Jerusalem have resulted in critical consensus on a number of related matters: that Jesus and some followers did go, at Passover time, to Jerusalem where he carried out a demonstration and prophetic statement of destruction against the Temple, was arrested, apparently by betrayal, tried before a high priestly court, sentenced by Pilate, and crucified by the Romans. As we know from Josephus' account of a major riot and massacre under the governor Cumanus, the celebration of liberation from foreign rulers at Passover was carried out literally under the watchful eye of Roman troops posted on the Temple porticoes to intimidate the celebrants. As Scott's material suggests, however, such intimidation also effectively evoked indignation, which would have been all the more intense at such a moment of celebration of God's previous action in liberating the people from foreign rule.

The various aspects of the moment of breakthrough, which were inseparable in the event, can be pulled apart only momentarily for analysis. The energy generated by the event results from "the sense of personal release, satisfaction, pride, and elation" experienced in the moment of public challenge to domination, the moment when someone speaks truth instead of submissive lies and equivocation (208). Scott suggests that there is a double release that corresponds to a double frustration involved in subordination. In addition to the release of finally resisting rather than submitting to domination, there is the release of finally being able to express the response initially choked back to avoid repressive consequences (213).

Given the methodological individualism of American New Testament studies in particular, we should take special note of Scott's point that the breakthrough act of defiance must be public in order to have any impact (214–15). The individual and collective loss of dignity of the subordinated is a public loss in which they must continually kowtow to power, including, in ancient Judea and Galilee, the established ritualized mechanisms by which their produce is expropriated and their community and family life disintegrated, as well as the periodic predatory actions in which the Herodian and priestly aristocracy engaged. If his prophecies or demonstration against the Temple are included at all in the data base for the historical Jesus, they are often pictured as the statements of an individual prophetic reformer or as mere symbolic gestures. Yet whatever his precise action, which took place in *the* public space of the city, it did have a public impact, which is why the Jerusalem rulers needed to crack down and the Roman governor needed to make an example of him. The impact of his action derived from its having been a public defiance that matched the people's public humiliation.

Besides being public, Jesus' breakthrough act of defiance took the cultural form of "a public breaking of an established ritual of public subordination" (215). As specialists on the original establishment of the second temple have more consistently explained in recent decades, the Jerusalem temple-state was from its origin the local face of the imperial order (established by the Persian regime and perpetuated by the Ptolemies, Seleucids, and the Romans), as well as the institutionalized means by which the goods of the Judeans and other peoples were expropriated by the Jerusalem aristocracy (articulated in Ezra and Nehemiah). But the cultural form was that of a Temple and sacred priesthood that mediated between the people and "the God who is in Jerusalem" (Ezra 1:3). By the time of Jesus, Herod had dramatically expanded and rebuilt the Temple-complex in grand Hellenistic style as one of the wonders of the Roman imperial world, augmenting its already considerable sacred aura, at least in the minds of those who performed the public rituals of order and obedience.[17] As we know from severe criticism of the Temple and incumbent high priests even among scribal circles who were politically and economically dependent on the temple-state, opposition was strong even while compliance was forthcoming (for example, sharp criticism of the "Wicked Priest" and the incumbent Jerusalem priesthood in several the Dead Sea Scrolls, and the protest against the Roman eagle erected over one gate (*J.W.* 1.648-55; *Ant.* 17.149-67). For Jesus to utter a prophetic condemnation of the super-sacred institution of supposed hoary antiquity and to conduct some sort of disruptive demonstration in the courtyard of the Temple would have been the utmost in acts of profanation and blasphemy.[18] The witnesses at his trial in Mark's portrayal may have been false, but the charge was right on target. "The successful public breaking of a taboo imposed by the dominant. . . is an extremely efficient means of encouraging a conflagration of defiance" (215). Whatever he did and said in the Temple, Jesus' demonstration was far more ominous than the typical form of peasant or slave defiance such as refusing to salute or bow one's head.

Further, Jesus' public act of defiance had such evocative power because it was an irrevocable step. It was a direct, blatant challenge not only to the sacred power base of the rulers of Jerusalem but to the Roman imperial order represented by the golden Roman eagle that Herod the Great had erected above the principal gate and the daily sacrifices to Rome and the emperor conducted at the altar (*J.W.* 1.648-55; 2.197, 409). There was no going back, no withdrawal again to confinement in the villages of Galilee. In such an act of defiance, "even if it is beaten back and driven underground, something irrevocable has nonetheless occurred" (215). Even when the stories of Jesus' Temple demonstration and his prophecies and parable against the high priests were consolidated back into the hidden transcript of the gospel tradition behind Mark, something irrevocable had occurred that helped motivate the expansion of the renewal of Israel over against the temple-state that Jesus had inaugurated in his program of preaching the kingdom and manifesting it in healings and exorcisms. His action in the Temple was a breakthrough event.

As Scott explains, however, to more fully understand such breakthrough acts of defiance we must be able to discern how they arise from and derive their power from their relation with the hidden transcript that has long been cultivated in the secure sites of the subordinated (214). Jesus' prophecy against the Temple and prophetic demonstration in the Temple did not come out of the blue. From the previous and subsequent outbursts of popular protest against the high priesthood by Galileans and Judeans mentioned by Josephus[19] and reflections of Galilean laxity in rendering dues to the Temple in later rabbinic literature (*m. Ned.* 2:4; *t. Sanh.* 2:2; 2:2; *y. Sanh.* 1.18d; *y. Ma'asa. S.* 5.56b) we can deduce that a great deal of resentment against these ruling institutions festered in village communities. Galilean laxity on tithes and other dues, for example, suggests the kinds of hidden forms of resistance to domination that Scott documents for other peasantries. Jesus' preaching and healing in Galilean and other villages, moreover, had focused and articulated the resentment against the ruling institutions in Jerusalem. Many of the typical stories from Jesus traditions that made it into Mark or Q give expression to popular indignation at the Temple, priesthood, and their representatives. Jesus teaches with power and authority on behalf of the people in a way that the scribes had never done (Mark 1:22-28). Jesus heals or "makes clean" the "leper" in a way that does not require offering to the Temple (Mark 1:40-45). In his healing, Jesus mediates God's forgiveness of sins in sharp contrast to the Temple-based system that emphasizes sin in order to enhance motivation for recourse to its services as indispensable for salvation (Mark 2:2-12). Jesus insists that local family and village resources be deployed for local family subsistence in accordance with the covenantal commandment of God ("Honor father and mother") instead of being siphoned in support of the Temple (*korban*) as urged by the Pharisees (Mark 7:1-13).

The cumulative impact of all these stories is to indicate that Jesus' program for the renewal of Israel in the local village communities was pointedly over against the Jerusalem ruling institutions long before he made any move toward a confrontation in the capital city. That is, popular indignation against the Temple and high priesthood was focused and articulated in the special development of the Galilean villagers' hidden transcript spearheaded by Jesus' mission. There was no occasion for a dramatic declaration of that indignation so long as he remained in Galilee. The cultivation of that indignation in the Galilean hidden transcript, however, accounts for the latent energy that was suddenly released by Jesus' bold condemnation of the Temple in the very center of that sacred public stage. One might say that Jesus' confrontation in Jerusalem was already well rehearsed in his distinctive development of the hidden transcript. But rather than diminish the effect of the breakthrough, it enhanced it because it had been keenly anticipated by a movement already in the making.

A further and closely related aspect of Jesus' breakthrough is illuminated by Scott's distinction, borrowing the terms of Levi-Strauss, between relatively "raw" and relatively "cooked" declarations of defiance. As represented in the Gospel of Mark, Jesus' declaration of the hidden transcript on the public stage was not an impulsive expression of blind fury, but a measured symbolic action and a formal prophetic pronouncement. "Cooked declarations are more likely to be nuanced and elaborate because they arise under circumstances in which there is a good deal of offstage freedom among subordinate groups, allowing them to share a rich and deep hidden transcript. In a sense. . . [it] already has a quasi-public existence" (216). In the relatively secure sites of Galilean villages, which were historically not under regular surveillance by the Pharisees or Herodians (contrary to the picture of Mark 2–3, 7), Jesus had plenty of opportunity to voice condemnation of the Temple and high priests (as suggested just above). Because Galilean, Judean, and

Samaritan villagers had long cultivated versions of Israelite "little tradition" (to utilize another concept that Scott utilized earlier[20] to illuminate peasant "protest and profanation"), moreover, Jesus could draw upon the forms and themes of Israelite prophetic lore. His lament over the impending destruction and desolation of the ruling house of Jerusalem takes the traditional form of a prophetic lament, as evident in Amos 5:2-3. In Mark's account of the demonstration in the temple, not only does Jesus cite Jeremiah's famous prophecy of the original Temple's destruction in punishment for violating the covenantal commandments (Jeremiah 7 and 26), but his action is patterned after prophetic symbolic actions (Isaiah 20; Jeremiah 27–28). Israelite tradition thus provided forms of protest and condemnation that already carried ominous denotations of divine judgment. And it gave the breakthrough declaration of condemnation all the more resonance with the people, who were rooted in this prophetic tradition.

Scott's discussion of the "public declaration of the hidden transcript," finally, illuminates more precisely how the concept of charisma can be used to understand (or misused to misunderstand) Jesus as movement leader. Jesus' development of the hidden transcript constituted and prepared "the social production of charisma." Charisma has often been adduced to explain the significance of Jesus. Insofar as the concept was taken in its popular sense of an unusual quality possessed by or divinely bestowed upon a leader, however, it served simply to further mystify Jesus. And insofar as charisma is an abstract concept, without any particular context and cultural content, it does nothing to illuminate Jesus in particular, but only dissolved him into a trans-historical class of figures. Sensing the distortion and mystification in application to Melanesian cargo cults and other such resistance movements, Peter Worsley[21] carefully explained how the concept is relational, the people who project their desires or yearnings onto a leader or a leader's message in a crisis situation being as important as the figure who speaks their mind and leads their action in that intolerable situation. Recognizing the importance of the hidden transcript as the basis on which a breakthrough of defiance takes place and empowers people to wider protest and even wider development of a movement both restores the relational dynamics at the center of the concept of charisma and the cultural specificity of charisma.

Periodically in his discussion of the hidden transcript, Scott finds a telling example in the character of Mrs. Poyser, who in exasperation finally spoke her mind to Squire Donnithorne in George Eliot's novel Adam Bede. In speaking truth to power, "the role of heroine in this case is to a large extent scripted in advance offstage by all members of the subordinate group, and the individual who fills that role is that one who somehow—through anger, courage, a sense of responsibility, or indignation—summons the wherewithal to speak on behalf of others" (222).

With respect to Jesus of Nazareth in ancient Palestine, this is an understatement. Jesus was challenging not a single squire but the whole political-economic-religious dominant order. And Jesus' prophetic condemnation of the Temple was far more "cooked," a well-planned performance more than a sudden outburst. Jesus, moreover, was adapting a well-known cultural script deeply embedded in the Israelite popular tradition in which the people were rooted. He was not only the new Moses or Elijah, but the new Amos or Jeremiah who dared march directly into the Temple courtyard and pronounce God's condemnation. The charismatic charge of those earlier prophetic breakthroughs carried over onto Jesus action in the Temple and its resonance with the people. Jesus not only wills the general will so that he speaks for the crowd of pilgrims in Jerusalem and other Galilean and Judean villagers. He also, again with Amos and Jeremiah, speaks out the indignation of all those earlier generations of Israelite peasants. His speech and symbolic prophetic action resonate with Israelite tradition which has compounded and given particular cultural form to the hidden transcript of his Galilean and other followers. The specific contents and dynamics of the charismatic relation between Jesus and his movement was "the shared discourse of the hidden transcript created and ripened in the nooks and crannies" of the Galilean village communities where they were free to rehearse their indignation (223). That is what underlies and explains the instantaneous mutuality that comes to expression in Jesus' breakthrough.

In "the highly charged atmosphere created by the open declaration" of defiance, "a subordinate group learns. . . that they may now, more safely, venture open defiance" (222). The last several episodes in Mark's narrative may seem to contradict this in the case of Jesus' followers. "They were afraid!" Mark, however, has his own distinctive agenda in having the twelve all abandon Jesus, in addition to the betrayal and denial by some.[22] It is now commonly sensed that Mark is summoning the hearers of his gospel back to Galilee (where Jesus has preceded them) to continue the movement. Thereafter, in every performance of the gospel, particularly in Jesus' bold declaration of defiance, his followers were emboldened to continue the movement. Every performance of Q speeches, particularly the woes against the Pharisees and the prophetic lament over the Jerusalem ruling house, was a repeat performance of Jesus' breakthrough. Jesus' breakthrough act in Jerusalem was thus the decisive event that led to the rapid expansion of his movement through Palestine and beyond, "a crystallization of public action that is astonishingly rapid" (223). *It is only when this hidden transcript is openly declared that subordinates can fully recognize the full extent to which their claims, their dreams, their anger is shared by other subordinates with whom they have not been in direct touch"* (223, italics Scott's).

Toward the end of his discussion of public declaration, Scott comments on the relation between the hidden transcript that develops in sequestered sites over a period of time and the public breakthroughs that ignite wider resistance, that the process "is more one of recognizing close relatives of one's hidden transcript rather than of filling essentially empty heads with novel ideas" (223). This comment brings us full circle to where we started, with the recognition that Scott's discussion of the hidden transcript enables us to move from the revelation model of Jesus as a religious teacher of individuals to a relational model of the historical Jesus as communicating with other Galileans in a crisis situation on the basis of their shared Israelite tradition—and pursuing several interrelated forms of popular political discourse that express the people's dignity as well as indignation.

Chapter Ten

Moral Economy and Renewal Movement in Q

T he speeches of Jesus that appear parallel in the Gospels of Matthew and Luke, but not in Mark—known as Q (*Quelle*, Source)—offer perhaps our earliest access to the mission of Jesus, according to at least a partial scholarly consensus. Until recently, much of the analysis of these speeches, working on the individualistic assumptions of modern Western culture, has understood Q as a collection of individual sayings. Taking these sayings out of both literary and social contexts, some interpreters attributed their transmission to itinerant radicals who had abandoned normal social life to pursue a "countercultural" lifestyle. Somewhat of a consensus is emerging recently among North American interpreters, however, that Q arose from and was addressed to a movement in Galilee in mid-first century C.E.[1] Further critical analysis of the interrelation of Q and its political-economic circumstances, drawing on a wide range of comparative and theoretical studies along with all available textual and material evidence, is of crucial importance for fuller appreciation of the message it delivers.

Important early analysis of Jesus' teachings attributed to Q discerned that in both Matthew and Luke it appeared in clusters of sayings largely in the same order.[2] Interpreters nevertheless treated the material as individual sayings. Discovery of the *Gospel of Thomas*, which is organized according to single or double sayings of Jesus, and which also displays many parallels to sayings in Q, appeared to confirm the understanding of Q as a sayings collection. In a close analysis of the composition of Q, John Kloppenborg concluded that Q took the form of clusters of sayings, that is short discourses or speeches or *chreiai*.[3] Many interpreters of Q nevertheless persisted in treating the material as individual sayings, even labelling Q as a "Sayings Gospel." The International Q Project constructed a critical edition, saying by saying, without much attention to how a cluster of several sayings formed a discourse with an inherent structure. Even Kloppenborg's composition criticism began from a classification of individual sayings according to "sapiential" vs. "apocalyptic." The elaborate hypothesis that Q was composed in layers, an original "sapiential" (wisdom) stratum to which was added a secondary "apocalyptic" or judgmental stratum, was constructed on the basis of this classification of individual sayings. This stratigraphy of Q that figures prominently in recent North American discussion of Q, has not proven persuasive to European interpreters. Yet, whether based on the hypothesis of different strata (American) or not (European), most discussions of themes or issues or theology in Q has proceeded from analysis of individual sayings, not by analysis of clusters of sayings or discourses.[4]

Since Kloppenborg's pioneering composition criticism, however, further analyses have confirmed and strengthened his conclusion that Q, as evident through its incorporation into Matthew and Luke, had the "literary" structure of a sequence of speeches by Jesus on a series of issues such as mission or prayer or woes against the Pharisees (Q 10:2-16; 11:2-4, 9-13; 11:39-52, respectively).[5] One might even say that a consensus may be forming in this respect.[6] As in any verbal communication, the function and meaning of any particular component saying of a speech in Q depends on its literary context. The implication of the recognition that Q consisted of a series of speeches, not a collection of sayings, is that those larger and smaller speeches, not individual sayings, were the units of communication, intelligibility, and meaning. Particular speeches, moreover, must be understood in the context of the whole sequence of speeches. Recognizing that Q takes the form of a sequence of speeches recited in a particular social context makes a considerable difference in how the materials are analyzed and interpreted.

In this connection the work of James C. Scott offers considerable stimulation and assistance to interpreters of Q. His programmatic early article, "Protest and Profanation: Agrarian Revolt and the Little Tradition,"[7] has important implications for how the Q discourses are understood their broader historical context. Scott's first book, *The Moral Economy of the Peasant,*[8] presents highly suggestive comparative material and a theoretical framework for understanding Q speeches in the inseparably political-economic and cultural-moral dynamics of peasantries subject to the disintegrative impact of outside forces. His second major book, *Weapons of the Weak: Everyday Forms of Peasant Resistance,*[9] pioneers exploration of the more subtle and hidden ways in which peasants resist the various forms of domination that their landlords and rulers impose. Finally, Scott's *Domination and the Arts of Resistance: Hidden Transcripts,*[10] in which many of the implications of his earlier research and reflection come together, is of considerable importance for the way we assess and use our sources in historical reconstruction and textual interpretation—including the social location and social stance of Q itself.

Popular versus Elite Israelite Tradition

Recognition of the difference between elite and popular culture is essential for more precise investigation of the social context of Jesus' speeches in Q. Not only was society in ancient Palestine and surrounding areas in the Roman Empire divided politically-economically between rulers and ruled, taxers and taxed. It was divided culturally as well between a scribal elite supported by the ruling families and the vast majority of people, the peasants, including fishing people and some non-farming craftspeople as well as free-holding and tenant agrarians living in village communities. The standard conceptual apparatus of New Testament studies has been dominated by synthetic essentialist and modern scholarly categories, often in dichotomous pairs, such as Jewish versus Hellenistic or Judaism versus Christianity or sapiential versus apocalyptic. These synthetic constructs have, in effect, blocked discernment of the differences between elite and popular culture and channeled investigations into theological issues and the emergence of one religion, Christianity, from another, Judaism. It was simply assumed that Q originated in an essentialist Jewish culture. Hence if a Q saying seemed different, then it must somehow have been against the standard Jewish cultural conventions, in other words, unconventional or counter-cultural.[11]

The fields of New Testament studies and Jewish history, however, are beginning to recognize the difference, and indeed conflict, between the Herodian rulers, priestly aristocracy, and leading Pharisees, on the one hand, and the Judean and Galilean people, on the other. This conflict figures prominently in the histories of Josephus and other sources. Analysis of some of the popular movements that took action against the established order, moreover, indicated that they were fairly clearly informed by Israelite traditions of resistance to oppressive rulers.[12] These movements suggested that there must have been competing versions of Israelite tradition, one version serving to authorize the established order, and the other serving to authorize resistance.

The early work of James C. Scott was instrumental in the framing and investigation of such issues well before implications were drawn for interpretation of Q. Besides having read widely in historical and ethnographic studies of various peasant societies, Scott had done extensive field work in Malaysian villages where peasants were struggling with the impact of outside forces on their traditional economy and culture. Robert Redfield and other anthropologists had established a basic distinction between the "great tradition" and the "little tradition" to distinguish the interrelated lines of culture carried by the urban elite and ordinary people in the countryside, respectively.[13] Focusing on agrarian societies in "Protest and Profanation" (to which the pages in this section refer), Scott believes that "more or less in keeping with Redfield's concepts, we may define the little tradition as 'the distinctive patterns of belief and behavior which are valued by the peasantry of an agrarian society'; the great tradition is the corresponding patterns among the society's elite" (8). The great tradition was sometimes and to a certain degree written, whereas the little tradition was almost always cultivated orally. Scott widened the focus from mainly religion, ritual, and myth to issues of economic organization and political authority and added the word *valued*, since much peasant behavior may be coerced and not a normative aspect of peasants' own culture. Scott also found in the "little tradition" far more than simply "a parochial version of cosmopolitan forms and values."

There are differences between elite and popular culture even in modern society, with its highly effective integrative mechanisms in the mass media. Even more then in ancient societies, in the absence of these integrative factors, popular attitudes and understandings were likely to diverge more strikingly from elite beliefs and the variety of beliefs *among* ordinary people was also likely to be greater (7). Indeed, one can discern "what amounts to 'a shadow society'—a pattern of structural, stylistic, and normative opposition to the politico-religious tradition of the ruling elites" (4). "The material and symbolic hegemony normally exercised by ruling institutions does not preclude, but rather engenders, a set of contrary values which represent in their entirety a kind of 'shadow society'" (19). In some societies the folk culture functions, "both in form and content, as a symbolic criticism of elite values and beliefs. . . . Under certain circumstances. . . such forms of symbolic conflict may become manifest and amount to a political or religious mobilization of the little tradition" (12).

This distinction between the "little tradition" and the "great tradition" and its implications for study of Jesus and the Gospels in historical context have gradually worked their way into New Testament scholarship, even into interpretation of Q, mostly on the basis of Scott's programmatic comparative article. This basic distinction was helpful in explaining the popular Judean, Samaritan, and Galilean messianic and prophetic movements in late second temple times that appeared to be informed by Israelite traditions of popular kings such as Saul, David, and Jehu, and prophetic leaders such as Moses and Elijah.[14] As Scott comments, "the little tradition achieves historical visibility only at those moments when it becomes mobilized into dissident movements which pose a direct threat to ruling elites" (240). The "little tradition" concept is implicit throughout my treatment of Jesus and the Jesus movements, and explicit at certain points.[15] The distinction has since been used for popular movements by some and for Jesus and gospel materials by others.[16] The distinction played an important role in my tentative explanation of Galilean culture that resulted from a regional history different from that of Jerusalem and Judea.[17] I drew heavily on Scott's article in attempting to come to grips with the prominent appearance of Israelite traditions in Q discourses, particularly insofar as these traditions are clearly contested.[18] And Kloppenborg Verbin offered a qualified acceptance of Scott's treatment of the "little tradition" for the interpretation of what he sees as the "main redaction of Q."[19]

I have previously carried out a more extensive survey of Israelite "little tradition" in Q informed by Scott's article, along with analysis of Israelite popular tradition in particular Q speeches.[20] From that fuller discussion, a few examples can illustrate how the Q speeches differ significantly from the scribal elite in their version and use of Israelite tradition. In the penitential prayers in Nehemiah 9 and Baruch 1–3, the restored Jerusalem elite confess their ancestors' disobedience to the Mosaic covenant and rejection of the prophets in petitioning God to restore their fortunes more fully. They seem confident in the continuing validity (for themselves) of God's unconditional promise to Abraham. By contrast, the woes against the Pharisees in Q pronounce God's irrevocable indictment against the Jerusalem elite for having killed the prophets (Q 11:47-48, 49-51), denouncing the elite's building of tombs in honor of the very prophets killed by their ancestors. One of the next Q speech fragments pronounces God's judgment against the Jerusalem ruling house for having killed the prophets (13:34-35). And at two points in the Q sequence of speeches, John the Baptist or Jesus announces God's condemnation for presuming to find security in their Abrahamic lineage and pedigree (3:9; 13:28-29). The image of the restoration of Israel in the final speech in Q (22:28-30) has the people headed simply by twelve representative figures, symbolic of the twelve tribes. Superficially this resembles the parallel images of the restoration in the Psalm of Solomon 17 and the Community Rule of the Qumran community (1QS 8:1-3). But the renewal is far more egalitarian and non-hierarchical compared with these scribal-priestly texts, which have either three priests ranked above the twelve tribal representatives (1QS), or have a scribe-like Messiah, Son of David, carry out an imperial triumph over the foreign oppressors and then preside over the people (Ps Sol 17). Rather than multiply illustrations we can make several general observations about how Scott's distinction of the popular from the elite tradition illuminates the Q speeches in social context on the basis of the fuller earlier analysis.

First, both in terms of their occurrence in several Q discourses and by comparison with biblical materials and contemporary Judean texts such as certain Dead Sea Scrolls, particular themes are strikingly prominent in Q, some previously given little attention in Q studies: renewal of Israel (Q 3:7-9, 16-17; 7:18-35; 9:57—10:16; 11:2-4; 22:28-30), covenant, covenant law, and covenant renewal (6:20-49; 11:2-4; 12:22-31; 16:16-18), and prophets and prophetic forms (3:7-9, 16-17; 7:18-35; 9:57—10:16; 11:39-52; 13:28-29, 34-35).

Second, by comparison with Judean texts produced by scribal circles, differences are apparent between Q's versions and uses of Israelite traditions and the scribal texts' versions and uses. Those differences correlate with differences in social location.

Third, it is evident that some of those cultural traditions operative both in Q and in contemporary scribal literature were of broader scope than the verses or lines that we usually consider (given the standard scholarly focus on individual sayings)—for example, broader patterns of covenant renewal, series of prophetic woes, and prophetic roles. For us to recognize such broader patterns may require a conscious effort to counteract the influence of modern print culture that resulted in the printing of individual verses of the scripture in separate sentences or paragraphs (as in the King James Bible).[21]

Fourth, differences between elite culture, as evident in certain scribal literature, such as the Dead Sea Scrolls, and the popular culture that comes to articulation in Q (and Mark), accounts for distinctive expressions found in Q speeches more appropriately than standard older interpretative concepts such as the dichotomies between Jewish and Christian and cultural or conventional versus countercultural or unconventional.

Finally, recognition of the eclectic character of popular culture should make us cautious in our reception and analysis of Q materials. For what appears to us as eclectic elements that do not fit our conception of sayings or discourses may have been part of an eclectic popular culture, not the result of deliberate editing by an editor or redactor.

Moral Economy and Renewal Movement in Q

James C. Scott's broad purpose in *The Moral Economy of the Peasant* was to explain the occurrence of peasant revolts—in twentieth century Southeast Asia and more generally, as he read widely in studies of particular instances and comparative studies of peasant revolts. He found unsatisfactory previous approaches to peasants as individual actors with particular goals and previous explanations of the motivation of popular rebellion, as rooted in the quantitative degree of exploitation or in relative deprivation or in the "J" curve of rising expectations. Scott laid out an alternative theory, which appears applicable also to popular movements such as that evident in the sequence of Jesus speeches known as Q.

In bringing the work of Scott to bear on the Jesus speeches in Q, we are broadening consideration of the movement that produced and found expression in this—from previous focus on social context and social formation. Perhaps because of the modern Western habit of thinking of Jesus and his followers mainly in religious terms it has been difficult to conceive of movements of Jesus' followers as engaged in *politics*. This reluctance to think of Jesus and his movements in political terms has been reinforced, perhaps, by the kind of social scientific studies previously brought to bear on Jesus and gospel traditions as rooted in the Galilean peasantry. In *The Politics of Aristocratic Empires*, for example, John Kautsky argues that the genuinely political actions and decisions that determine peasants' lives are taken in aristocratic circles well above the level at which peasants operate in their village communities.[22] In contrast to the social banditry in Galilee and Judea, which Hobsbawm would label as "pre-political," however, the popular prophetic and messianic movements that appear to provide the closest parallels to the movements spearheaded by Jesus of Nazareth were taking political initiatives, actions to which the official political-military measures were reactions.[23] It could easily be said that in first century Palestine, peasant movements and protests were the principal political forces driving historical events.[24] The theory that Scott develops in *Moral Economy of the Peasant* can help us understand where the Jesus movement that comes to expression in Q fits in the historical dynamics of Roman-dominated Judea and Galilee of the first century C.E. Further illumination of that Jesus movement and its expressions in Q can be gained from Scott's subsequent research and reflection on more hidden and everyday forms of peasant resistance in *Weapons of the Weak*.

Scott's theory of the complex combination of factors that leads to peasant revolts can be summarized in six steps—with apologies to Scott for oversimplification—and then applied to the Jesus movement evident in Q in the same six steps (all references in this section not otherwise indicated are to Scott's *Moral Economy*). In the application of Scott to Q below, I am presupposing my previous analyses of the political-economic-religious structure and situation in Galilee (on the basis of extra-gospel sources)[25] and the application of that analysis to the origin of Jesus movements.[26]

Moral Economy and Popular Revolt among Various Peasantries

1. *Right to subsistence*: In close examination of southeast Asian peasant societies and more general historical and ethnographic studies, Scott discerned what he called the "moral economy" of the peasantry. Obliged by custom and often by force to meet the demands for their products by lords, landlords, the state, and creditors, peasant families are faced annually with the problem of feeding themselves (vii, 2–3). Besides its physiological dimension of enough calories to reproduce the producers, moreover, subsistence has social and cultural implications. "In order to be a fully functioning member of village society, a household needs a certain level of resources to discharge its necessary ceremonial and social obligations. . . . To fall below this level is not only to risk starvation. It is to suffer a profound loss of standing within the community and perhaps to fall into a permanent situation of dependence" (9). Peasantries develop a common sense of their right to minimum subsistence, which is a matter of social-economic

justice. Scott's emphasis on economic rights and a sense of social participation or failure recognizes that peasants, like elites, have a sense of the moral structure of their society and a political consciousness. Peasants judge others as morally responsible for their predicament and act to claim their rights when they are violated (189).

2. *Principles and mechanisms to protect the right to subsistence*: Precapitalist village communities, says Scott, were organized around maintaining subsistence for their constituent households and minimizing the risk to which they were exposed by their obligations for taxes, rents, weather, and so forth. Peasantries developed principles of reciprocity, mechanisms of redistribution, and other social arrangements to assure subsistence to the members of village communities (5–6, 9, 176). Central to the moral standards of the village community was a crude notion of equality. The possession of a minimum of land necessary for support of the family and the performance of essential social tasks was basic to the village sense of justice. The basic principles of this peasant moral economy usually had some sort of religious sanction, usually deeply rooted in popular tradition (10). Peasant religion tends to differ from that of the dominant classes precisely on its stress on these principles of justice. Village egalitarianism does not hold that all families should be equal, but insists that all should have a living. Among pre-capitalist peasantries where villagers remained in control of local community affairs, they maintained certain mechanisms whereby contributions of the better-off kept the weakest from going under. The pressures of community opinion enforced adherence to such mechanisms by the better-positioned families. In Andalusia, for example, "the idea that he who has must give to him who has not is not only a precept of religion, but a moral imperative of the pueblo".[27] Villagers studied by Scott, like those in many cross-cultural studies, offer "a living normative model of equity and justice. . . . a peasant view of decent social relations" (40–43). The fundamental right to subsistence that tended to be observed in pre-capitalist village communities thus provided the moral principle to which the poor might appeal, whether to their neighbors or in dealings with their lords and rulers (176–77).

3. *Criteria by which peasants judge claims on their produce*: Recognition of this moral economy among peasantries leads to a different approach to the occurrence of revolts and resistance movements. Instead of looking for the percentage or amount of the peasant product taken by lords or the state, we must begin with peasants' traditionally grounded belief in their fundamental right to subsistence and then examine peasants' relationships to other villagers, to elites, and to the state with regard precisely to this economic right (5). "This moral principle forms the standard against which claims to the surplus by landlords and the state are evaluated. . . . The test for the peasant is more likely to be 'what is left' than 'how much is taken'" (7, 19, 31). "The moral economy of the subsistence ethic can be clearly seen in the themes of peasant protest. . . ." Two themes prevailed: first,

claim on peasant incomes by landlords, moneylenders, or the state were never legitimate when they infringed on what was judged to be the minimal culturally defined subsistence level; and second, the *product* of the land should be distributed in such a way that all were guaranteed a subsistence living (10). Scott has thus arrived at a much more precise sense of the basis of peasant politics and, given the rarity of peasant protest and especially peasant revolt despite the ubiquity of intense exploitation, at a better understanding of why and when protests and revolts occur.

4. *Exacerbated conditions that lead to sense of indignation*: Political-economic transformations under modern colonial practices, including the transformation of land and labor into commodities, tended to violate the moral economy and threaten the subsistence rights of peasants, sometimes in ways that led to the conditions susceptible to peasant revolts (3–4, 9, 196). In Southeast Asia "colonial regimes were likely to press even harder in a slump so as to maintain their own revenue. . . . In the midst of a booming export economy, new fortunes for indigenous landowners, officeholders, and moneylenders, there was also growing rural indebtedness and poverty and an increasing tempo of peasant unrest. . . . The explanation. . . [is] new insecurities of subsistence income to which the poorer sector was exposed" (10). The experience of the Southeast Asian peasantry with the fiscal practices of the colonial state is analogous in many respects to the experience of the European peasantry, where taxation was the most prominent single issue in the large-scale rebellions during the European state-making of the sixteenth to nineteenth centuries (96).

5. *Factors that lead to organized resistance or revolt*: Given the increasing violation of the moral economy of the peasantry by escalating exploitation resulting from transformative effects of the state and a new economic system, Scott finds that certain factors tend to lead to revolt or non-revolt. One of the most important is the state's power of repression (195). "Tangible and painful memories of repression must have a chilling effect on peasants who contemplate even minor acts of resistance" (226). Another key factor is derived from the central role of economic security for the peasantry. Peasants may resist most seriously at the thresholds where they are threatened with loss of their self-sufficiency as smallholders, that is, where they "might lose the land that gives them their fairly autonomous subsistence... and they face having to become dependent clients. A second threshold occurs when the subsistence guarantees within dependency collapse" (39). These thresholds also have a cultural dimension insofar as they involve minimal cultural decencies, such as caring for elderly parents and crucial rituals, as well as subsistence economic resources (177–78). The ability of village communities to adjust to deteriorating conditions and to protect their component members, however, can delay the crossing of that first threshold (194). Scott found the social strength of this moral economy and its traditional mechanisms that protected the

village poor varied from village to village and region to region. "It was strongest in areas where traditional village forms were well developed and not shattered by colonialism. . . . It is precisely in areas where the village is most autonomous and cohesive that subsistence guarantees are the strongest" (40–41). On the other hand, similarly cohesive social composition with strong communal traditions and few sharp internal divisions can make some peasantries inherently more prone to insurrection. A less differentiated peasantry will experience economic shocks in a relatively more uniform fashion insofar as its members share more or less the same economic circumstances. Communitarian structures, moreover, have a greater capacity for collective action. It is easier for the peasants to organize if an existing structure of local cooperation has remained intact. In such communities, their "little tradition" is a ready-made source of motivation for collective action. "The more communal a village structure, the easier it is for it to collectively defend its interests" (201–2).

6. *Renewal of village community as alternative social order*: Finally, as Scott points out, even "false starts" to revolts and social-religious movements (such as Hoa Hao and Cao Dai in southern Vietnam and Iglesia Ni Cristo in the Philippines) can often reinforce the bonds between peasants and serve, paradoxically, as an alternative, a prelude, and a stimulus to revolt (207, 219–20). Evidence of nascent symbolic withdrawal can be found in movements among those who are exploited yet with little prospect of revolt. The views or grievances evident in a social-religious movement provide a telling indication of the degree to which they identify with or oppose the values of the elite (231). Even a religious movement whose orientation might seem otherworldly often articulates sharp criticism of the existing order and an alternative symbolic universe that contains seeds of potential social-political disruption. Such movements can also cultivate inter-village communications and alliances along with the newly articulated dissatisfaction with current conditions that anticipate more explosive future events (237). "Since peasants' freedom to define and elaborate their own culture is almost always greater than their capacity to remake society, it is to their culture that we must look to discover how much their moral universe diverges from that of the elite. . . . This symbolic refuge is not simply a source of solace, an escape. It represents an alternative moral universe in embryo—a dissident subculture, which helps unite its members as a human community" (238, 240).

Moral Economy and the Israelite Renewal Movement Evident in Q

1–2. *Right to subsistence and mechanisms to protect it*: Reading Scott's *Moral Economy of the Peasant* might be more compelling at first glance to those of us who also deal with the Hebrew Bible than to those who deal only with the

Synoptic Gospels. The Mosaic covenant in Exodus 20, the covenant law code in Exodus 21–23, and many provisions in the Deuteronomic code and the Holiness Code (especially Lev 25) are immediately intelligible as articulations of the moral economy of ancient Israelite peasants. The special provisions included in various Mosaic covenantal codes—exhortation to lend liberally to a needy neighbor, gleaning, prohibition of interest, sabbatical rest of the land, sabbatical release of debts and debt-slaves, redemption of land by the next of kin—constituted the social mechanisms by which Israelite villagers attempted to keep each member household economically viable. It is also evident that the prophet Micah was referring to one of those mechanisms in Micah 2:5—the periodic redistribution of communal land. Underlying all of these provisions, of course, was the principle that the land belonged ultimately to Yahweh and had been parceled out as a gift to each family or lineage as its own inheritance (Lev 25:23). A story such as that about Naboth's vineyard in 1 Kings 21 indicates that Israelite kings were put on notice that the peasantry as well as their prophetic spokespersons, such as Elijah, had a clear sense of their social-economic rights.

Most of the social mechanisms mentioned in Israelite law codes were designed to keep the land, the basis of subsistence, in those lineages. Subsistence rights and the broader moral economy of the peasantry were thus deeply rooted in Israelite tradition. Judging from elite sources such as Josephus, moreover, at least some of these social-legal mechanisms to protect the subsistence rights of peasants were still practiced in late second temple times. The sabbatical rest for the land was still observed, apparently sanctioned by the temple-state, in early Roman times and the sabbatical cancellation of debts was still practiced, as evidenced in the *prosbul* devised by Hillel to circumvent it. If some of these social-legal mechanisms were still officially observed and discussed, then almost certainly they were still alive among the Judean and Galilean villages, in the "little tradition."

This should lead us to take much more seriously the references and allusions to traditional Israelite covenantal laws and teachings in Q speeches. But before proceeding to examination of key speeches in Q, we should take note of the awkward situation we are in as would-be historians of the ancient Israelite "little tradition" with regard to our sources and how we use them. It is evident from a combination of archaeological and textual evidence that the fundamental social form in ancient Israelite society was the peasant village. It is equally evident from the content of the laws in the Covenant Code and the later Deuteronomic and Holiness Codes that the provisions and mechanisms such as liberal lending, prohibition of interest, and sabbatical release of debts applied mainly to relations among villagers, that is, to the moral economy of the peasant. Yet our sources all belong to the Jerusalemite "great tradition" of literature edited by scribes serving the temple-state. In using these sources, therefore, we must take into account the interests of the scribal elite as representatives of the temple-state aristocracy. Hence we cannot read the "little tradition" or the moral economy of the Israelite peasant directly out of the written texts that derived from the elite. We can only extrapolate and project on the basis of those written texts, with critical awareness of its particular interests.

When we come to Jesus' speeches in Q, we are apparently dealing with texts derived from the "little" or popular tradition.[28] That these speeches do not quote, but rather seem to allude, to laws in the Covenant Code (Exod 21–23) is probably one key indication of their popular derivation. They have not been conformed to the written texts of the "great tradition" by subsequence generations of scribal copyists. Given the limited sources, there are only two ways in which we as historians can discern that the Q speeches may be alluding to, derived from, or expressions of the Israelite popular tradition and covenantal principles of Israelite moral economy. One is by comparison with what we project onto earlier generations of Israelite villagers from the law codes that are extant only in the written texts of the Jerusalemite "great tradition," that is, what later became the biblical texts. The other is by comparison with the texts discovered at Qumran, produced by a scribal community more or less contemporary with the Q speeches.

Several of the speeches in Q articulate the concerns of the moral economy of the peasantry rooted in the Mosaic covenant, its principles and mechanisms. Most elaborate is the covenant renewal speech in Q 6:20-49. Q scholars tend to focus on individual Q sayings as artifacts isolated from their context and to interpret them according to modern scholarly categories, such as "sapiential." As noted in chapter 2, however, it is clear that the "love your enemies" section of the speech in 6:27-36 not only alludes in numerous ways to traditional Mosaic covenantal teaching, but is a continuation of that tradition. Most obvious perhaps are the comparisons between Q 6:27 and Leviticus 19:17-18, between Q 6:29 and Exodus 22:25-26 and Deuteronomy 24:10-13 (compare with Amos 2:8), and between Q 6:36 and Leviticus 19:2.[29] That the broader framework of the speech is a renewal of Mosaic covenant can be seen from comparison with covenantal texts in Exodus 20, Joshua 24, and the contemporary covenant renewal texts from Qumran, in the Community Rule (1QS 1–4) and the Damascus Rule (CD).[30] The "love your enemies" section of Jesus' covenant speech thus focuses on local economic relations that are disintegrating into mutual hostility. Jesus' renewed covenantal teaching calls basically for a return to the mutuality that will maintain the component family units of villages as viable members of those village communities: "Love your enemies, do good, and lend," not harassing each other for previous debts, and coming to each others' aid in times of difficult circumstances. Those are the basic principles of the moral economy in any number of different peasant cultures, according to Scott's cross-cultural studies.

Two other Q speeches also focus on concern for basic subsistence in peasant households: the Lord's Prayer in Q 11:2-4, 9-13, and the exhortation in Q 12:22-31 about single-minded pursuit of the kingdom of God, which constitutes the theme linking the Q speeches as a whole series. In the Lord's Prayer, people of the Q communities petition God for maintenance of their subsistence bread and cancellation of their debilitating debts that make them vulnerable to creditors, even to loss of their ancestral land. The petition for cancellation of debts, with its clear allusion to and basis in Israelite covenantal tradition, includes the principle of mutual-cancellation of debts by villagers: "cancel our debts as we herewith cancel those of our debtors." That is a renewal of one of the key Israelite social mechanisms by which households were to be kept viable in the village community, the cancellation of debts (known from all of the covenant law codes and subsistence-maintenance mechanisms, Exodus 21–23, Deuteronomy, and Leviticus 25). The point of the exhortation in Q 12:22-31 is apparently that if community members will only focus on the general goal of the renewal of Israel (the kingdom of God) then subsistence will not be a problem, presumably because of the renewed spirit of mutuality among members of the village community. It is surely significant that Matthew understood that this exhortation belonged together with the explicitly covenantal teachings on Q 6:27-36, such that he included it in his version of the covenantal renewal speech in Matthew 5–7 that has the same overall structure as Q 6:20-49.

The same covenantal concern for subsistence is articulated in two other Q speeches that mock the opulence and exploitative practices of the rulers and their representatives. The rhetoric in Q 7:18-35 mocks Herod Antipas, the Roman client ruler in Galilee, for his luxurious lifestyle of soft raiment and a fancy palace—all based on the products of peasant labor. And the (covenantal prophetic!) woes against the Pharisees in Q 11:39-52 indict them for pressing the peasants to tithe rigorously from their scarce resources and for not using their scribal authority to alleviate the burdens of those who are heavy laden with taxes and tithes.[31]

This reading of these Q speeches as statements of concern about the moral economy of ancient Palestinian and Syrian villagers is further supported by several parallels elsewhere in the teaching of Jesus. Matthew includes Jesus' parable about cancellation of debts in Matthew 18:23-33 that parallels the petition on debts in Q 11:2-4, and Mark has Jesus address the same problem in conversation with the wealthy young man in Mark 10:17-22 in an explicitly covenantal context that insists on the principle of non-exploitation among community members. We also happen to have evidence from a generation before and a generation after Jesus' activity in Galilee, and the early development of Q discourses, that concern about unjust taxes and indebtedness to wealthy creditors, in other words, basic threats to their subsistence, could drive the peasantry to protest and revolt. According to Josephus' accounts, the popular messianic movements just after Herod's death attacked royal fortresses and storehouses in order to "take back" the goods that had been seized and taken there (*Ant.* 17.271-76). And one of the first actions of the insurrection in Jerusalem in 66 C.E. was to burn the archives in order to destroy the records and to prevent recovery of debts (*J.W.* 2.427).

3. *Criteria by which peasants judge claims on their produce*: Were we to follow Scott's distinctive approach to peasant protest and revolt as rooted in the people's right to subsistence, we would no longer seek to establish the percentage or absolute amount of taxation, but rather look for the factors that combined to threaten their subsistence. Moreover, once we have learned from Scott's *Weapons of the Weak* about peasants' hidden forms of resistance such as sequestering produce from the tax collectors, which render the official rate of taxation functionally irrelevant, we are forced to devise a more subtle and nuanced approach anyhow. Also, more directly pertinent to interpretation of Q, if its speeches were addressed to and supposedly resonated with Galilean and other common people, then we must take into account not just their poverty and indebtedness, but both the social-cultural meaning of the threat to their subsistence and their indignation at the injustice of their circumstances. Both the blessings and woes that begin the covenant renewal discourse in Q 6:20-49 and the speech addressed to anxiety about subsistence in Q 12:22-31 appear directly to address the discouragement and self-doubt that poor indebted villagers might feel about their failure as members of the community. The prophetic declarations of woes against the Pharisees in Q 11:39-52 and condemnation of the Jerusalem ruling house in Q 13:34-35 (and the not-so-veiled commentary on Antipas in Q 7:24-25), as well as the blessings and woes in Q 6:20-26, appear to articulate their indignation.

4. *Exacerbated conditions that lead to sense of indignation*: As Scott points out, despite high levels of exploitation, peasants have seldom mounted outright revolt. But both in 4 B.C.E. after the death of Herod and again in 66 C.E., widespread revolt erupted among the Galilean and Judean peasantry. In between emerged the Jesus movements, one of which produced Q. With Scott's more nuanced approach, we can look for how the new order imposed by Rome through client kings was impacting the Galilean and Judean peasantry. Different from but corresponding to the dramatic changes that accompanied the introduction of the capitalist system under colonial rule of nineteenth and twentieth century peasantries, Roman imperial rule brought dramatic and relatively sudden changes that seriously impacted peasants in Palestine. Prior to the Roman conquest, there was one layer of rulers, the Jerusalem temple-state. When the Romans imposed Herod as king, and he in turn retained the high priestly and Temple apparatus, the peasant producers suddenly came under multiple layers of rulers and demands on their produce.

The rigorous collection of taxes under Antipas may have been an even more decisive factor in the origin and spread of a Jesus movement in Galilee. Under earlier empires and even under Rome prior to Antipas, Galilee had been ruled and taxed by distant rulers. One can imagine that under regimes ruling from a distance Galilean peasants may well have deployed some of those hidden forms of resistance that Scott discusses, such as sequestering crops and paying only part of taxation. Given the less-than-rigorous apparatus in modern Malaysia, "the official collection of the Islamic tithe in paddy is only a small fraction of what is legally due, thanks to a network of complicity and misrepresentation"[32] When the Romans assigned Antipas to rule Galilee, however, he immediately rebuilt Sepphoris in the center of western Galilee as his capital and within twenty years built a new capital city, Tiberias, on the lake. From these capital cities conveniently located with commanding surveillance over and immediate access to every village in Galilee, tax collection was suddenly more rigorous and hidden forms of popular resistance less effective. The presence of their rulers directly on the scene in Galilee must have become a major factor in the increasing pressure on Galilean peasant subsistence.[33]

Like the booming economy under modern colonial regimes, the booming economy of the new Roman imperial order in Palestine—Herod's lavishly rebuilt Temple and newly founded cities in honor of the emperor, the high priestly families newly built mansions in the New City in Jerusalem, the burgeoning estates of Herodian families in NW Judea, and Herod Antipas' spanking new cities in Galilee[34]—coincided with increasing poverty among peasant producers. And similar to the increase in rulers' demands that aggravated peasant conditions in early modern times in Europe, the suddenly unchallengeable political-economic power of the Roman client regimes of the Herodians and Jerusalem temple-state ratchetted up the pressure on ancient Palestinian peasants.

5. *Factors that lead to organized resistance or revolt*: Scott's generalizations based on a fairly wide selection of comparative materials are particularly suggestive for historians of early Roman Palestine and students of the Jesus movements, including the one connected with Q. It has to be striking, given the infrequency of widespread peasant revolt generally, that Galileans and Judeans put up a fierce resistance to Herod's conquest of his kingdom in 40–37 B.C.E., then revolted when the tyrant died in 4 B.C.E., and mounted an even more widespread revolt again in 66–70 C.E. Similarly striking is the seeming quiescence of the people during the reign of Herod the Great and again under Antipas and the early Roman governors. Striking, finally, is the emergence of the Jesus movements more or less midway between the increasingly tightened new Roman-imperial order in Galilee under Herod and Antipas, and the steadily expanding unrest in the 60s and the outbreak of the great revolt in 66, that is, as the Galilean peasantry began to feel the economic pressures of demands by multiple layers of rulers.

The principal factor in all of these revolts or movements was the new and continuing economic pressure on the Galilean and Judean peasantry that had such a strong tradition of independent rule deeply rooted in Israelite popular tradition. Surveys of the location and circumstances of large royal estates in Palestine[35] suggest that they were still concentrated mainly in the Great Plain, the rich agricultural lowland between Samaria and Galilee, and in the king's mountain country northwest of Jerusalem. They were apparently spreading, however, indicating that some peasants were losing control of their land and becoming dependent share-croppers or worse via the usual debt-mechanisms. That Herodian officers of Agrippa II in Tiberias still had their estates beyond the Jordan suggests that despite the intense economic exploitation of Herod Antipas earlier in the century and their difficult economic circumstances addressed in Jesus' speeches (6:20-21; 11:2-4; 12:22-31), Galilean peasants had not yet been reduced to dependency. Yet the concern of Jesus movements with debt as well as poverty and hunger and the outbreak of widespread revolt in 66 all suggest that the new pressures were pushing the Galilean and Judean peasants toward the first threshold delineated by Scott. That is, in the Jesus movement addressed in the Q speeches, we can see peasants threatened with loss of their traditional lands and semi-independence, motivated by indignation at the violation of their subsistence rights, responding to the call to renew their traditional mutuality and solidarity in resistance to the pressures and incursions of their rulers. There would be little point in the admonitions to lend and otherwise engage in mutual economic support in Q 6:27-36 if the addressees, having already become mostly dependents, were at the second threshold of absentee landlords withdrawing their guarantees of minimal security for share-croppers.

6. *Renewal of village community as an alternative social order*: Scott's comments that traditional communal structures of peasant villages that have not decisively disintegrated from the pressures of outside forces can function both as a factor contributing to revolt and a factor deterring revolt is highly suggestive for Jesus movements such as the one linked with Q. On the one hand, the people living in an intact communal village structure can more easily mount cooperative action rooted in their "little tradition" and communal structure. On the other hand, the more communal structures enable the villagers to redistribute the pressures so as to avoid or postpone subsistence crises. Suggestive in the same direction are Scott's observations about how a "false start" or a religious movement may serve as prelude to revolt. Both of Scott's observations point to the possible effects of the Jesus movement and its interaction with other Galilean people.

Again, if we assume that Q consisted of speeches addressed to ordinary people and was not simply a device for preserving Jesus' sayings, then discourses such as Q 6:20-49; 11:2-4, 9-13; 12:22-31 were concerned with people threatened with poverty, hunger, and debt. These speeches encouraged them to respond to God's bringing the kingdom with mutual caring and renewed cooperation in their communities. Indeed, since we may project that these discourses must have resonated with audiences or they would not have been perpetuated, they would have fostered and reinforced horizontal bonds among community members. If other Q speeches resonated similarly with Galileans, we can imagine that Q 7:18-35; 12:2-12; 11:39-52 and 13:28-29, 34-35 helped solidify their dissent from the values represented by Antipas, the Jerusalem rulers, and their scribal and Pharisaic representatives. "While folk culture is not coordinated in the formal sense, it often achieves a 'climate of opinion' which, in other more institutionalized societies, would require a public relations campaign. The striking thing about peasant society is the extent to which a whole range of complex activities. . . are coordinated by networks of understanding and practice. . . . No formal organizations are created because none are required [given the communal village structures]."[36] That is, Jesus or the Q performers did not have to organize new communities.

Virtually all of the speeches in Q articulated an alternative symbolic universe of Galilean Israelites focusing on the kingdom of God, which weaves through the sequence of discourses like a thematic red thread. That is, in terms of Scott's concept of moral economy, Jesus' speeches in Q crystallize and renew a "moral universe that diverges from that of the elite." Scott's exploration of how peasant politics are rooted in this moral economy thus provides a new vision for the historical imagination of biblical interpreters. Scott provides an alternative to the old debate about whether Jesus and his movements, like certain contemporary popular movements in Palestine, constituted what was in effect a revolt, or were absolutely anti-revolutionary. Approaching Q discourses with the help of Scott's moral economy might lead to the conclusion that, in their time, Jesus' speeches must have supplied cultural dissent, an alternative symbolic universe, and social links among the oppressed. The sequence of speeches in Q represented "an alternative moral universe in embryo—a dissident subculture, which help[ed] unite its members as a human community and as a community of values" (238).

Oral Performance of the Not-So-Hidden "Hidden Transcript" of Q

Scott's more theoretical work, *Domination and the Arts of Resistance*, enables us to discern how oral performance of Q speeches may have provided both an ideology and motivation for the communities of the movement that heard them performed. He had noted earlier that in some popular movements religion and politics become joined in a utopian vision of a revolutionary new order. A religious charter can become the basis for more far reaching revolution-ary goals.[37] Such an observation provides an overarching perspective from which to comprehend how the Q discourses in 6:20-49; 7:18-35; 11:2-4; 12:22-31; and 22:28-30 might have resonated with their audiences. To focus on the covenant speech analyzed in chapter 3, the communities of a movement that regularly cel-ebrated a renewal of the Mosaic covenant as a charter for community sharing and solidarity may well have understood that as a revolutionary new order in which the tables were turned, the poor enjoying the benefits of the kingdom while the rich were dethroned from their power and privilege. This seems all the more likely when we notice that other speeches in Q also condemn the wealthy in the ruling house in Jerusalem and their Pharisaic retainers (Q 13:34-35; 11:39-52).

Scott further observed that "ideology. . . may often be experienced by peas-ants. . . as a kind of magic charm, an esoteric religious knowledge that is capable, by itself, of transforming the world."[38] This observation takes us well beyond the attempt, some decades ago, by Norman Perrin and others, to use the concept of "tensive symbol" to understand the phrase "the kingdom of God." We must be careful not to over-interpret. But perhaps we should take seriously the possibil-ity that, if audiences of Q speeches heard "blessed are you poor, for yours is the kingdom of God" as a declaration of God's new action of deliverance and "seek first the kingdom of God and all these things [food, clothing, shelter] will be added" as an exhortation, then they, in response, would have been motivated almost magically, as it were, to "love your enemies, do good and lend" and not to worry about their threatened subsistence, since the world was obviously being transformed! Ironically for New Testament scholars, Scott reminds us to take religion and magic seriously as symbols at work in popular culture subject to high degrees of stress and distress.

Besides resonating with the hearers by metonymically referencing Israelite popular tradition, the Q speeches resonated with hearers as a no-longer-so-hid-den transcript. As noted in chapter 8, Scott's insights into usually unrecognized modes of popular politics, including the hidden transcript and the jolting pub-lic declaration of that hidden transcript, enable us to discern the character of the speeches in Q as communication (all references in the following paragraphs are to Scott's *Domination and the Arts of Resistance*). On the one hand, the Q speeches were clearly performed among communities of a Jesus movement, that is, among the subordinated, and not in public where the dominant would have been listening. That is why Jesus could condemn the Jerusalem ruling house and its Pharisaic retainers in no uncertain terms (Q 11:39-52; 13:28-29, 34-35) and not be apprehended and executed immediately. On the other hand, precisely these Q speeches represent Jesus as speaking truth to power. In these Q dis-courses Jesus is again brought to voice declaring the hidden transcript directly in the hearing and in the face of the dominant.

Cultivating the hidden transcript in safe sites, says Scott, creates a discourse of dignity, negation, and justice (114). This seems to be a principle function of some of Jesus' speeches in Q, such as 12:22-31. And this is surely one of the functions of most Q speeches. Just as Brer Rabbit stories lent a sense of pride and satisfaction to slave audiences (164), so Jesus' covenantal admonitions in Q 6:27-42 would have lent a similar sense to ancient Galilean audiences called to respond to God's gift of the kingdom. The beatitudes and woes, the covenantal blessings and curses, like the "symbolic reversals of folk religion," constitute the equivalent of a radical counter-ideology. Both "are aimed at negating the public symbolism of ideological domination" (199). As Scott comments about the counter-ideology contained in the hidden transcript, so the proclamation of the kingdom of God and renewed covenant in Q 6:20-49, along with the Lord's Prayer and the discourse in 7:18-35, presented a counter-ideology that enabled people to resist their rulers and their pressures that were threatening to disintegrate their family and village community lives.

But Q speeches performed in village communities went beyond the usual hidden transcript. They represented Jesus as proclaiming that God's decisive action in establishing the kingdom was already underway and proceeding with utter certainty. Insofar as they presented Jesus as having already declared the coming of the kingdom and the attendant condemnation of the rulers directly in the face of power, moreover, the Q speeches instilled in their hearers a confidence in the immanent realization of a revolutionary new social order of justice and sufficiency, in the apparent absence of their rulers whom God has condemned.

Just as "the hidden transcript is continually pressing against the limit of what is permitted on stage" (196), in potential resistance of the subordinated to the dominant, even more does Q's presentation of Jesus as declaring the agenda and resentment of the people push against and expand the limit of what is permitted. This is partly because "it is only when this hidden transcript is openly declared [as in the Q speeches] that subordinates can fully recognize the full extent to which their claims, their dreams, their anger is shared by other subordinates with whom they have not been in direct touch" (223). That we have the Q speeches of Jesus in at all must mean that they resonated with people in such a way that the movement expanded and these speeches themselves lived to tell about it.

Conclusion
Jesus and the Gospels in Context

As we have seen, recent research is undermining some of the assumptions on which standard study of the Gospels previously depended. We can recognize now that there were no stable written texts of Mark, Matthew, Luke, or John in late antiquity. The written texts were "unstable," that is, they kept developing, in part because any texts in antiquity, whether written down or not, were generally recited or "performed" before groups of people. Oral communication was predominant, even in literate circles.

We are also coming to recognize that Mark and the other Gospels were not mere "strings of beads," individual sayings and little stories that first circulated independently and only subsequently were collected, strung as it were end to end, in such a way that the modern scholar, preacher, or Bible-study group can separate them again today for close examination and interpretation. Rather, the Gospels were sustained narratives, with plots and subplots. Moreover, the "text" underlying Matthew and Luke, commonly called "Q," was not a mere collection of sayings, but a sequence of short speeches.

There is thus a kind of unreality, as well as an utter anachronism, to the standard old approach to the Gospels, in which we (a) focused on individual Jesus sayings or little stories about Jesus' actions as if such sacred artifacts had meaning in themselves, (b) sought to "establish" the "text" as precisely as possible, and (c) set about to determine the meaning of words and phrases. Insofar as the Gospels were sustained narratives, the smaller sayings and stories that made them up were mere text-fragments, components of larger sustained stories and speeches. The particular wording of the component "episodes" of a Gospel thus mattered very little. Most important was the overall story, the dominant plot of a Gospel (as well as the subplots and conflicts that complicated it).

Since they were performed in communities, the Gospels or their component speeches did not have meaning in themselves, but resonated with hearers in an immediate social context. Performed Gospels had certain effects, they did various kinds of "work," in a community of hearers, as it referenced the social memory or cultural tradition that the performer, text, and audience shared. To appreciate and understand the Gospels, therefore, we modern readers must not only attempt to appreciate the dynamics of oral performance, but become acquainted with the cultural tradition (or "social memory") that both the text and the audience shared, predominantly the Israelite tradition of the Galilean and Judean people. Otherwise, we simply won't "get it"!

When we read (or better, hear) the Gospel of Mark as a whole story, it is evident that the dominant conflict is between the Roman and Jerusalem rulers and the peoples they rule in Galilee, Judea, and nearby areas. (The same is true in Matthew and Luke, as well as in contemporary sources such as Josephus' histories.) In the main plot of Mark, Jesus leads a renewal of the people of Israel, in Galilee and beyond, against the Roman rulers and their clients in Jerusalem. Contemporary sources such as the histories of Josephus indicate that other, similar movements emerged among the Judean and Galilean people. The distinctively Israelite forms of those other popular movements leads us to recognize that a popular version of Israelite tradition was alive among Judean and Galilean villagers, parallel to the "little tradition" that may be contrasted with the "great tradition" in many agrarian societies.

The conflict between popular Israelite tradition and the "official" or elite scribal Judean tradition of the temple-state in Jerusalem enables us to understand the conflict between Jesus and the Pharisees without reverting to the old opposition of Jesus versus "Judaism" and "the Law." Parallels from social memory studies enable us to recognize that cultural tradition moves along in distinctive patterns. In Israelite popular tradition, those patterns featured the Mosaic covenant that guided social-economic interaction in village communities and informed prophetic criticism and condemnation of oppressive rulers, foreign and domestic. Recognizing the operation of these patterns in the overall narrative and component episodes and speeches of the Gospels enables us to appreciate how the renewal of Israel, which Mark and Q represent as Jesus' agenda, may have been one of the principal effects of the Gospels as well.

One consequence of understanding the Gospels as performances is that we come to understand the historical Jesus as "embedded" in the Gospels, or rather in the movements that produced and used the Gospels. He cannot be extricated from the network of relations by which he came to be thus embedded. This has important implications for how we proceed in investigating the historical Jesus. The standard approach must virtually be stood on its head. First, instead of trying to isolate individual sayings or "aphorisms" from their supposedly secondary literary context in order to determine their earliest or most original form, or trying to determine their authenticity (as judged by criteria such as their dissimilarity from earlier "Jewish" teachings or later "Christian" additions), the research discussed especially in chapters 3 through 7 suggests that we must start with whole stories, as with Mark, or sequences of speeches, as with Q.

Second, instead of taking textual sources more or less at face value, we will seek to offer a critical analysis of their social location and political agenda in terms of the determinative factors in people's circumstances, attitudes, and actions. It now seems clear that, for the most part, the Gospels and Gospel tradition were deeply rooted in Israelite popular tradition, while the Judean texts most often used for comparison with the Gospels were products of elite scribal circles. The latter cannot be used as a direct source for the attitudes of the ordinary people who were the principal participants in the movements focused on Jesus and other popular prophets and messiahs.

To illustrate the difference these first two principles can make, we can focus on one of the major debates about the historical Jesus in the last century: the construction, first popularized by Albert Schweitzer, of Jesus as caught up in an "apocalyptic" worldview, expecting (as Rudolf Bultmann would later put it) a "cosmic catastrophe." Variations on an "apocalyptic" Jesus are still widely propounded today. The principal alternative view prominent recently among political and theological liberals constructs Jesus as a wisdom teacher, a sage who resembled vagabond Cynic philosophers in Hellenistic cities. These scholarly constructs, however, have more to do with modern scholarship than with Jesus in his own context. They have been developed from elite sources, particularly Judean scribal literature produced by professional intellectuals. But Jesus does not appear to have been a professional intellectual. And the sources offer no evidence of the scribal instruction of artisans or peasants through which Jesus might have learned to think and speak like the scribes who produced the visions in Daniel or the instructional speeches in Sirach. Equally problematic, scholars constructed Jesus as *either* apocalyptic *or* sapiential by classifying individual Jesus-sayings as being one or the other. But neither apocalyptic visions such as those in Daniel nor instructional wisdom speeches such as those in Sirach communicate in individual sayings. The categorization of sayings as either "apocalyptic" or "sapiential" is a product of modern scholarship, but is not attested in ancient Judean texts.

Third, far from searching for Jesus as an isolated individual, as if he were floating above ordinary social relations, engagement, and communication, we will look rather for how he was embedded in social relations and circumstances. No one exists apart from a network of relationships, but a historically significant figure is especially a product of those relationships, being intimately involved with specific historical circumstances, social roles (including political offices), social movements, and significant events. In the case of Jesus in particular, our sources—the Gospels—were precisely the products of popular movements in response to social roles and circumstances. Here the people's history of Galilee and Judea in which Jesus emerged and the popular social memory on which he drew offer indispensable resources for investigation of Jesus-in-relational-context.

For all his biases, Josephus provides just enough examples of popular prophetic and messianic movements to enable us to discern distinctive social forms of people's resistance to the Roman imperial order in Judea and Galilee. Here are the distinctively Israelite "frames" of social memory and the leadership roles that Jesus-in-movement could adapt in spearheading a village-based renewal of Israel. Q speeches offer several examples of Jesus speaking (and acting) as a prophet like Moses (or Elijah), and Mark provides a rich narrative of Jesus acting the role of a prophet like Moses *and* Elijah—the prophetic founder and renewer of Israel, respectively. The Gospel of Mark also represents Jesus as highly ambivalent about being seen in the role of a popular messiah like the young David; the Q speeches offer *no* representation of Jesus in the role of popular messiah.

Prominent cultural patterns could be important to a leader and a movement in an even deeper way. Such was surely the Mosaic covenant, which provided principles for local social-economic interaction. The covenant renewal speech in Q 6:20-49, investigated more closely in chapter 3, and the somewhat parallel covenantal dialogues in Mark, covered along with Q 6 in chapter 2, suggest that covenant renewal may have constituted the very center of the renewal of Israel in the agenda of Jesus-in-movement. Many of the aspects of the "moral economy" evident in other Q speeches seem to specify or revolve around this village-based renewal of covenant.

Fourth, in contrast to standard assumptions that religion and politics are separate realms—assumptions that predetermine the judgment that if a figure like Jesus did not actively rebel against the established Roman imperial order, he must have accepted it—the work of James C. Scott enables us to discern the more subtle forms taken by popular politics. Our exploration of people's history has made clear that the principal division in ancient Judea and Galilee and surrounding areas was not between "Jews" and "Gentiles," but between the rulers (the Romans and their local clients) and subject peoples. This makes it possible to appreciate how Jesus and his movements could have cultivated a "well-cooked" "hidden transcript" in the semi-autonomous village communities of Galilee and nearby areas (chapter 8). Moreover, Jesus' renewal of the Mosaic covenant, which stood at the center of the traditional Israelite "moral economy" and was deeply embedded in popular social memory, suggests that what was being cultivated in those sequestered village communities was more than a "hidden transcript" of collective indignation. The comparative material presented by Scott enables us to appreciate how, rooted in the principles of the traditional Israelite moral economy, Jesus and his followers responded to the increasingly oppressive circumstances of Roman imperial rule by generating nothing less than a renewal of Israelite society in village communities (chapter 10).

Fifth, in contrast to the standard picture, often projected on the basis of Mark and the other Gospels, of Jesus as a solitary teacher who went to the cross as a solitary martyr, we see a figure embedded in social relationships rooted in Israelite tradition. The comparative study of other popular movements and their leaders enable us to posit both an intensively cultivated "hidden transcript" of resistance and, growing out of it, Jesus' bold confrontation of the Jerusalem and Roman rulers, which resulted in his execution *as a rebel leader.* His execution became the moment that crystallized the subsequent expansion of the Jesus movement (chapter 9). This understanding of Jesus' crucifixion has everything to do with Jesus having come to play a well-known role and script (a "frame" in Israelite social memory). In the understanding of his followers Jesus had appeared as a prophet leading a renewal of Israel (like Moses, Joshua, Elijah, and his near contemporaries Theudas and others)—and had shared the fate of popular prophets. Prophets, after all, confronted oppressive rulers. Jesus, leading his followers, did precisely this at the Passover festival that celebrated Israel's liberation from oppressive foreign rule. He "spoke truth to power," although not necessarily in just the way Mark narrates. We see him doing so in the Q speeches as well. Moreover, both Mark and Q, along with the later Gospels, represent his followers—that is, the Jesus movements—as continuing Jesus' renewal program under threat of arrest and execution (Mark's open ending; the community that generated Q self-consciously acting as prophetic imitators of Jesus and previous prophets). Not only was Jesus vindicated, according to these sources, but he promised that those who maintain solidarity with the movement would also be vindicated.

Finally, rather than treating the Gospels as mere containers of potential "data," it seems that investigators of the historical Jesus must become bona fide Gospel scholars, pursuing the full range of approaches to the Gospels, the sources in which an irreducibly relational Jesus is embedded. This would mean much more work to do. But they would at least be starting from their principal sources in the only ways that we have access to them: as they first resonated with hearers by drawing on Israelite social memory in order to catalyze the reordering of social life in particular historical contexts.

Appendix: Q Speeches

Moral Economy and Renewal Movement in Q

Introduction

"Q" has traditionally been understood as a collection of the sayings of Jesus. Recently it has even been dubbed a "Sayings Gospel," and compared with the sayings collected in the Gnostic *Gospel of Thomas*. Recent "composition criticism" of Q by North American and South African scholars, however, enables us to recognize that the sayings are not separate. They are rather grouped in "clusters" that form short speeches.[1] When we imagine these speeches in their original social context, we can recognize that they address major issues and concerns of communities of Jesus-loyalists, such as the renewal of covenantal community, the sending out of envoys, prayer, exorcism, how to speak when hauled into court, and anxiety about economic subsistence.[2] The Gospel of Luke has simply taken over those speeches and grouped them more or less end to end, interspersed with other materials, while the Gospel of Matthew has combined them into larger speeches, while still keeping them in more or less the same order as they stand in Luke. (It has become standard to refer to Q materials according to their appearance in Luke.)

Pursuing the standard practice of "establishing the text," one of the foundations of biblical studies deeply rooted in the assumptions and practices of print culture, scholars of the International Q Project reconstructed a written text of "the Sayings Gospel" saying by saying ("verse" by "verse") from the parallels in Matthew and Luke.[3] The result is useful insofar as it gives us the best compromise among scholars' judgments as to the "original" written text supposedly used by Matthew and Luke. In this scholarly reconstruction, however, the speeches or "clusters" of sayings that (still) appear in Matthew and Luke disappear, along with their broader "literary" context in those Gospels.

As explained in chap 3 above, when we bring comparative studies of oral performance to bear on Q speeches, they appear in the lines and stanzas of orally performed poetry. Readers with an elementary acquaintance with Hebrew or Aramaic poetry can recognize that the Greek sentences and clauses in Q speeches reflect the Semitic poetic syntax of parallel lines of two, three, or four words each, with prefixes and suffixes. It is a standard assumption that Jesus and his first followers in Galilee spoke Aramaic, supposedly the dominant language among ordinary people there. The speeches of Q may well reflect an earlier and/ or parallel Aramaic version. While some of the repetition of words and sounds in Aramaic were surely "lost in translation" into the Greek, it is remarkable how much the Greek of the Q speeches repeats words, sounds, and even phrases in parallel poetic lines, very much like orally performed poetry in other cultures. And while most of these characteristics of oral performance are lost in translation into English, it is remarkable how many persist.

How to represent an *orally* performed text in the *visual* medium of print is a problem, perhaps one with no satisfactory solution – especially for those who have little or no acquaintance with either Greek or Aramaic. This appendix nevertheless attempts to represent at least some of the features of the orally performed Q speeches, that is, (ironically) to represent the oral medium in the print medium. The lines and "stanzas" of several Q speeches in literal translation are blocked in measured verse to show visually some of the repetitions of sounds, words, even phrases, and the combinations of words in Greek and English that represent words with prefixes and suffixes in Aramaic.[4] There are inescapable inadequacies in any visual representation of oral-aural communication one or two translations removed from the communication between "Jesus" and early Greek- or Aramaic–speaking communities. Readers can nevertheless use their imaginations to "hear" these speeches. Laying out the speeches in "stanzas" and lines (e.g., A.1, 2, 3; B.1, 2 etc.) should enable the imaginative reader-hearers to appreciate the steps in the rhetoric or argument and the parallelism of lines, the fundamental "patterning" features of these poetic speeches in (Aramaic and) Greek. Among the other features to look for and then to imagine in oral-aural communication are the overall speech and its subject and structure, and the repetition of words, phrases, verb forms, word-endings, and simple sounds.

This appendix presents not a complete text of Q but only those speeches that are discussed or referred to prominently in chapters 2, 3, 5, 6, and 10 above.[5] In some of these the parallel texts in Matthew and Luke are close, often identical, for much of the speech. In others, where the particular wording in Matthew and Luke diverges, only the shape and gist of the speech is clear enough for approximation in English paraphrase.

The translation/paraphrase presented below generally follows the gist of the International Q Project text,[6] with secondary reliance on the translation by John Kloppenborg in *Q Parallels*.[7] Interested scholars and students will benefit greatly by consulting the parallel Greek texts of Matthew and Luke, along with other "parallels," as laid out in *Q Parallels*. Since any such "parallels" or compromise between the Matthean and Lukan texts involve abstraction, of course, most helpful would be consultation of the parallel Matthean and Lukan versions of Q speeches in a Greek or English Synopsis of the Gospels.

We do not know how Q may have begun. But the short speech by John the Baptist in Q 3:7-9, 16-17 would have provided a fitting introduction to the speeches of Jesus that follow. And the testing of Jesus in the wilderness (Q 4:1-13) would have been appropriate to the Moses- and Elijah-like prophet who delivers the ensuing speeches.

Q 6:20-49 Covenant Renewal

Step I:

1. Blessed are	the poor	for yours is	kingdom of God.
2. Blessed are	those who hunger,	for you shall be filled.	
3. Blessed are	those who mourn,	for you shall laugh.	
4. Blessed are	you when	they reproach	you
		and speak evil	against you
		on account of	the son of man.
5. Rejoice and	be glad		
for your reward	is great	in heaven.	
For so	they did	to the prophets	[before you].
1. Woe	to those who are rich,	you have received your consolation.	
2. Woe	to those who are full,	for you shall go hungry.	
3. Woe	to those who laugh,	for you shall mourn.	
4. Woe	when all people	speak well	of you.
5. For so	they did	to the false prophets.	

Step II:

1. Love	the enemies	of you(rs),
2. {Do good	to those who hate	you.
3. Bless	those who curse	you,}
4. Pray	for those who abuse	you.

1. To the one who strikes you	on the cheek	turn	also the other.
2. And [from the one who takes]	your coat	[offer]	also the tunic.
3. To the one who asks from you	give,		
4. And from the one who bor- rows	do not ask back.		
1. And as you wish	that people	would do	to you,
2. thus		do	to them.
1. And if you love	those who love	you,	what credit is that to you?
	For even the toll- collectors	do the same.	
2. And if you do good to	those who do good to you,	what credit is that to you?	
	For even the [other] peoples	do the same.	
3. {and if you lend	to those from whom	you hope to receive,	what credit is that to you?
	Even . . . lend to . . .}		
1. But love	your enemies,	and do good,	and lend,
and your reward	will be	great.	
2. And you will become	sons	of your Father,	
for he is	kind	to the ungrateful	and the evil.
3. Be	merciful,	as your Father	is merciful.

Step III:

1. And do not judge		and you will not be judged	
[for with the judgement	you judge	you will be judged,]	

2. for with the measure	you measure	it will be measured to you.	
1. Can a blind person	guide	a blind person?	
Will not both	fall	into a pit?	
2. A disciple	is not above	his teacher	
but everyone well trained	will be like	his teacher.	
1. Why do you see	the speck	in the eye	of your brother,
but	the log	in your own eye	you do not notice?
2. How [can you say]	to your brother,		
"Let me remove	the speck	from your eye,"	
and behold,	there is a log	in your own eye?	
3. Hypocrite!			
Remove first	the log	from your own eye,	
and then you will see (clearly)			
to cast out	the speck	from the eye	of your brother.

Step IV:

1. There is no	sound tree	which bears	bad fruit,
nor again	a bad tree	which bears	sound fruit.
2. For from the fruit	a tree	is known:	
they do not gather	figs	from thorns,	
or	grapes	from a bramble bush.	
1. The good man	from the good treasure	brings forth	good (things).
The evil man	from the evil (treasure)	brings forth	evil (things).
2. For from an overflow	of the heart	speaks	the mouth.

Step V:

1. Why	do you call me,	"lord, lord,"
And	not do	what I tell you?
1. Every one	who hears my words	and does them
2. is like	a man	
who built	his house	upon the rock.
3. And the rain came down	and the river beat upon	that house,
and it did not fall,	for it had been founded	upon the rock.
1. And everyone	who hears my words,	and does not do them.
2. is like	a man	
who built	his house	upon the sand.
3. And the rain came down	and the river beat upon	that house,
and it fell	and its fall was	great.

Q may have included the dialogue between Jesus and the centurion about healing the latter's boy or servant in Q 7:1, 6-9.

Q 7:18-35 The Coming / Presence of the Kingdom of God in Jesus' Actions

Step I:

1. John,	sending	his disciples,	said to him
Are you	the one to come,	or should we expect	another?
And answering	he said to him:		
Go	announce to John	what you hear	and see:
2. the blind	see,	and the lame	walk,
the lepers	are cleansed	and the deaf	hear,
the dead	are raised	and the poor	evangelized.
3. And blessed is	whoever is not offended	by me.	

Step II:

[and when they had left]

1. He [Jesus] began	to say	to the crowds	concerning John:
2. What did you go out	into the wilderness	to see?	
A reed	by the wind	shaken?	
3. But what	did you go out	to see?	
A man	in finery	appareled?	
4. Behold,	those in finery	are in the houses	of kings.
But what	did you go out	to see?	
A prophet?			
Yes!	I tell you,		
And more than	a prophet!		
1. This is the one	about whom	it has been written:	
2. Behold, I send	my messenger	before your face	
Who shall prepare	your way	before you.	
3. I tell you:			
There has not arisen	among those born of women	anyone greater than John.	
Yet the least	in the kingdom of God	is greater than he!	

Step III:

1. To what	shall I compare	this generation?	
They are like	children	seated	in the square,
Addressing	one another:		
We piped for you	and you did not dance,		
We wailed	and you did not mourn.		
1. For John came	neither eating	nor drinking,	
and you said:	"he has a demon."		
2. The son of man came	eating	and drinking,	
and you said:	"'Behold,		

a man	gluttonous	and drunk,
a friend of	toll-collectors	and sinners.'"
3. Thus wisdom	is justified	by her works.

Q 9:57—10:16 Sending Out Envoys

Prologue: A Prophet and His Envoys

1. And someone said:

| I will follow you wherever | you go. |

2. And Jesus said to him:

The foxes	have	dens
and the birds	of the sky	lodgings,
but the son of man	has no place	to lay	the head.

1. And another said to him:

| Lord, | permit me | first |
| to go | and bury | my father. |

2. But he said to him,

| Follow me | and leave | the dead |
| | to bury | their own dead. |

1. And another said:

| I will follow you, | Lord, | but first |
| permit me | to say farewell | to those at my home. |

2. But Jesus said to him:

| No one who puts | his hand | to the plow |
| and looks back | is fit | for the kingdom of God. |

The Sending and Instruction of Envoys

1. The harvest	is great	but the workers	are few.
2. So ask	the lord	of	the harvest
to send	workers	into his harvest.

1. Behold,	I [myself] send	you	
as lambs	in the midst of	wolves.	
2. Do not carry	a copper	or a purse	or sandals
and do not greet	anyone.		

[Note, Q 10:5-6 is reconstructed from Matt 10:12-13]

1. If you	enter	a house	
and if	the house	is worthy,	
let come	your peace	upon it.	
2. But if	it is not	worthy,	
your peace	to you	let it return.	
3. {And in this	house	remain,}	
{? eating	? and drinking}	[what they provide,]	
for worthy	is the worker	of his/her wage.	
1. Into whatever town	you enter,	{and they receive you,}	
heal	[those in it]	who are sick	
and say [to them]			
has come	upon you	the kingdom of God.	
2. Into whatever [town	you enter	and] they do not receive you	
as you depart	[out of that	town]	
shake off	the dust	from your feet.	
3. I tell you			
For the Sodomites	on that	day	
it will be more tolerable	than for that	town.	
1. Woe to you,	Chorazin!	Woe to you,	Bethsaida!
2. Because if	in Tyre and Sidon	had happened	
the wonders	which happened	in you	
already	in sackcloth and ashes	they would have repented.	
3. Indeed	in Tyre and Sidon	more tolerable	
it will be	in the judgement	than for you.	

4. And you,	Capernaum!		
Way up	to the heaven	will you be lifted?	
Down	to hades	you will be cast!	
1. Whoever receives	you	receives	me,
and whoever receives	me	receives	the one who sent me.

It is conceivable that the praise of the Father in Q 10:21-22 and the blessing of the hearers in Q 10:23-24 belonged together and/or formed part of a larger speech, perhaps together with the Lord's Prayer in Q 11:2-4 and exhortation to pray in 11:9-13.

Q 11:2-4, 9-11 Prayer

Pray:

1. Father,			
Let your name	be sanctified,		
let your kingdom	come.		
2. Our bread	for the day	give us	today
3. And release	for us	the debts	of ours
just as also	we	release	those indebted to us.
4. And do not	lead	us	into the test.
1. I tell you:			
Ask	and it will be given	to you,	
seek	and you will find,		
knock	and it will be opened	to you.	
2. For everyone	who asks	receives,	
and the one	who seeks	finds,	
and to the one	who knocks	it will be opened	to you.
1. Which person	is there	of you,	
if his son	asks	for bread,	
will give	him	a stone?	

2. Or if he	asks	for a fish,
will give	him	a snake?
1. If you	who are evil	know
to give	good gifts	to your children,
2. how much more	will the father	from heaven
give	good (thing)s	to those who ask him.

Q 11:14-20 (-26) In Jesus' Exorcism of Demons the Kingdom of God Is Come

Dialogue:

1. He was casting out	a demon	that was mute.	
The mute	spoke,	and the crowds	marveled.
2. Some (the Pharisees) said:			
'By Beelzebul	the prince	of demons	
	he casts out	demons.'	
1. Knowing	their thoughts	he said	to them:
Every kingdom	divided against itself	is laid waste,	
And every house	divided against itself	collapses.	
2. And if Satan	against himself	is divided	
how	will stand	his kingdom?	
3. But if I	by Beelzebul	cast out	the demons
your sons	by what	do they cast out?	
Therefore	they	will be	your judges.
3. But if	by the finger of God	I cast out	the demons
then has come	upon you	the kingdom of God.	

Warning:

1. Whoever is not	with me	is against me	
And whoever does not gather	with me	scatters.	
1. When	an unclean spirit	goes out	from a man,
it goes through	arid places	seeking a resting place	and does not find it.
2. He says:			
I will return	to my place	from whence	I came.
And moving in	he finds	it swept	and put in order.
3. Then he goes	and brings	seven other spirits	more evil than himself
And they enter	and dwell	there.	
4. And becomes	the last state	of that man	worse than the first.

The appeal to the examples of "the Queen of the South" and "the people of Nineveh arising at the judgment in Q 11:29-32 form a coherent, if brief, speech about "something greater" being here." It is difficult to discern how the sayings about the lamp in Q 11:33, 34-36 may have belonged to any sort of "cluster" in Q.

Q 11:39-52 Woes against the Pharisees[8]

1. Woe to you	Pharisees!		
For you purify	the outside	of the cup	and the dish
But inside	you are full	of extortion	and rapacity.
{First purify	the inside	that the outside	may be pure.}
2. Woe to you	Pharisees!		
For you tithe	mint	and dill	and cumin
and neglect	justice and mercy	and faithfulness.	
These	you ought to do	without neglecting	the others.
3. Woe to you	Pharisees!		
For you love	the prime seats	in the assemblies	
	and salutations	in the squares.	

4. Woe to you	Pharisees!		
(Lk) For you are like	graves	unmarked	
And men	who walk over them	do not know it.	
(Mt) For you are like	whitewashed	tombs	
which outside	appear	beautiful	
but within	are full of	dead bones	[and all impurity].
5. Woe to you	law-experts!		
For you load	people	with burdens	hard to bear
But you	with your finger	will not move	the burdens.
6. Woe to you	law-experts!		
(Lk) For you have taken away	the key	of knowledge.	
(Mt) For you lock	the kingdom of God	before the people.	
For you yourselves	do not enter	and you prevent	those trying to enter.
7. Woe to you	law-experts!		
For you build	the graves	of the prophets,	
but your fathers	killed	them.	
Thus	you witness	against yourselves,	
that you are the sons	of those who killed	the prophets.	
1. Therefore	the wisdom of God	said:	
I will send them	prophets	and scribes,	
some of whom	they will kill	and persecute.	
2. Thus/ so that	from this genera-tion	will be required	
the blood	of all the prophets	that has been shed	upon the earth,
from the blood	of Abel	to the blood	of Zechariah

whom you murdered	between	the altar	and the temple.
3. Yes I tell you:	it shall be required	of this generation.	

Q 12:2-12 Bold Confession when Brought to Trial

1. Nothing is covered	which will not	be revealed	
and (is) hidden	which will not	be made known.	
2. When I tell you	in the darkness	speak	in the light,
and what you hear	in your ear	proclaim	upon the house-tops.
1. And do not fear	those who kill	the body	
but (who) the soul	are not able	to kill.	
2. Fear	rather	the one able	
both soul and body	to destroy	in Gehenna.	
1. Are not two	sparrows	sold for	an *asserios?*
And one of them	will not fall	to earth	without God.
2. Even the hairs	of your head	all	have been numbered.
Do not fear,	you	are worth more	than many sparrows.
1. Every one	who confesses	me	before people,
also the son of man	will confess	him/her	before the angels of God.
2. But whoever	denies	me	before people,
	will be denied	before the angels of God.	
1. And whoever	speaks a word against the son of man	will be forgiven;	
2. but whoever	blasphemes against	the holy spirit	will not be forgiven

1. When you	are delivered up	do not be anxious about	what you will say;
2. for {it will be given	to you}	in that hour	what you will say.

Q 12:22-32 Anxiety about Subsistence and Single-minded Pursuit of the Kingdom

Therefore I tell you:

1. Do not be anxious	about life,	what you shall eat,	
	nor about body,	what you shall put on.	
2. Is not life	more than	food,	
and the body	(more than)	clothing?	
1. {Look at}	the ravens;		
they neither sow	nor reap		
2. and yet God	feeds	them.	
Are you not	of more value than	the birds?	
1. And who of you	by being anxious	is able	
to add	to his life-span	a {single} cubit?	
1. And why are you anxious	about clothing?		
Consider the lilies,			
they neither toil	nor spin.		
2. Yet I tell you,			
even Solomon	in all his glory	was not arrayed	like one of these.
3. But if the grass	in the field,	which is there today	
and tomorrow	is thrown	into the oven,	
4. God	clothes	thus,	
{will he not} much more	(clothe) you,	persons of little faith?	

1. [Therefore] do not be anxious,	saying,		
What shall we eat?	or What shall we drink?	or What shall we wear?	
2. For all these things	the (other) peoples	seek;	
for your Father	knows that	you need them.	
1. But seek	his	kingdom,	
and these things	shall be added to you.		
2. {Do not fear	little	flock,	
for the Father	is pleased	to give you	the kingdom.}

After the saying about where one's treasure is in Q 12:33-34, another speech may be discernible in the saying about how unexpected will be the coming of "the son of humanity" in Q 12:39-40 and the parable illustrating the (un)faithful steward in 12:42-46. It is more difficult to detect how the sequence of sayings in Q 12:49-59 may have comprised (part of) a (larger) speech. The parables of the mustard seen and the leaven were evidently grouped together in Q 13:18-21.

Prophetic Oracle against Jerusalem Rulers

1. [Many] shall come	from the east	and the west	
and recline	with Abraham	and Isaac and Jacob	in the kingdom of God.
2. {And the sons	of the kingdom}	will be cast out,	
and there will be	weeping	and gnashing	of teeth.
1. Jerusalem,	Jerusalem!		
2. Killing	the prophets		
and stoning	those sent to you!		
3. How often	did I want	to gather	your children
in the same way	as a hen (gathers)	her brood	under her wings,

4. and you	did not want (it).		
1. Behold	forsaken to you	is your house!	
2. I tell you:			
You will not see me	until {it comes when}	you say,	
"Blessed	is the one who comes	in the name	of the Lord."

The parable of the great supper in Q 14:16-24 could well have formed part of a single speech with Q 13:29-28, 34-35.

The remaining fragments of Q, from 14:26 to 17:5-6, include sayings about hating parents and taking up one's cross, savorless salt, not serving two masters, violence and the kingdom, the endurance of the law, divorce being equivalent to adultery, forgiveness, and faith. Q 17:23-37 appears to be another speech, focused on the judgment ("the day of the son of humanity"). The parable of the talents appears to have been in Q (19:11-27). And Q 22:28-30, perhaps originally the concluding lines of a speech, forms a fitting ending for the whole sequence of speeches that evidently comprised Q.

Notes

Introduction

[1] See further my earlier assessment of the state of the field of New Testament studies, "Innovation in Search of Reorientation: New Testament Studies Rediscovering its Subject Matter," *JAAR* 62 (1994), 1127-66.

[2] E. P. Sanders, *Judaism: Practice and Belief 63BCE – 66CE* (Philadelphia: Trinity International, 1992).

[3] For these and other popular protests, see Richard A. Horsley, *Jesus and the Spiral of Violence* (San Francisco: Harper and Row, 1987; Minneapolis: Fortress Press, 1993), chap 4.

[4] For these and other comments on or evidence derived from the Gospel of Mark, see further my *Hearing the Whole Story: The Politics of Plot in Mark's Gospel* (Louisville: Westminster John Knox, 2001).

[5] The pioneer in exploration of orality and literacy in the Gospels is Werner Kelber, *The Oral and Written Gospel* (Philadelphia: Fortress Press, 1983). Other important early probes were Paul J. Achtemeier, "Omne Verbum Sonat: The New Testament and the Oral Environment of Late Western Antiquity," *JBL* 109 (1990), 3–27; Pieter J. J. Botha, "Greco-Roman Literacy as Setting for New Testament Writings," *Neotestamentica* 26 (1992): 742–59.

[6] On Mark, see the many articles by Joanna Dewey, most recently "The Survival of Mark's Gospel: A Good Story," *JBL* 123 (2004) 495-507; and Pieter J. J. Botha, "Mark's Story as Oral-Traditional Literature: Rethinking the Transmission of Some Traditions about Jesus," *Hervormde Teologiese Studies* 47 (1991): 304–334.

[7] For example, on Q, John S. Kloppenborg Verbin, *Excavating Q: The History and Setting of the Sayings Gospel* (Minneapolis: Fortress Press, 2000).

[8] Since they were viewed as scriptural statements of truth and used as proof-texts in the construction of theological doctrines, early modern translations, such as the King James Version, printed each statement as a separate verse. More recent translations designed for reading in Sunday services, such as the New Revised Standard Version and the Jerusalem Bible, are divided instead into scriptural lessons, paragraph by paragraph.

[9] David C. Parker, *The Living Text of the Gospels* (Cambridge: Cambridge University Press, 1997). Eldon Jay Epp, "The Oxyrhynchus New Testament Papyri: 'Not Without Honor in their Hometown,'" *JBL* 123 (2004) 15-35; Kim Haines-Eitzen, *Guardian of Letters: Literacy, Power, and the Transmitters of Early Christian Literature* (Oxford: Oxford University Press, 2000), 106-11.

[10] William V. Harris, *Ancient Literacy* (Cambridge, Mass.: Harvard University Press, 1989); Catherine Hezser, *Jewish Literacy in Roman Palestine* (Tuebingen: Mohr/ Siebeck, 2001).

[11] This happens to come from Burton L. Mack, *A Myth of Innocence: Mark and Christian Origins* (Philadelphia: Fortress Press, 1988), 322-23, but it expresses a standard operating assumption in the field and could have been written by any number of us, who cannot but project our own scholarly self-image onto the texts we labor to interpret.

[12] Richard Bauckham, *Jesus and the Eywitnesses* (Grand Rapids, Mich.: Eerdmans, 2006).

[13] Oscar Cullmann, *Jesus and the Revolutionaries* (New York: Harper & Row, 1970); Martin Hengel, *Was Jesus a Revolutionist?* (Philadelphia: Fortress Press, 1971); *Victory over Violence* (Philadelphia: Fortress Press, 1973).

[14] On itinerant charismatics, see Gerd Theissen, *Sociology of Early Palestinian Christianity* (Philadelphia: Fortress Press, 1978); cf. Richard A. Horsley, *Sociology and the Jesus Movement* (New York: Crossroad, 1989); on Jesus as a Cynic, John Dominic Crossan, *The Historical Jesus: The Life of a Mediterranean Jewish Peasant* (San Francisco: HarperCollins, 1991); Burton L. Mack, *The Lost Gospel: The Book of Q and Christian Origins* (San Francisco: HarperSanFrancisco, 1993); and numerous articles in response.

[15] In such comments I am drawing on analysis in my previous studies of Q or Mark or Jesus: *Whoever Hears You Hears Me: Prophets, Performance, and Tradition in Q* (with Jonathan Draper; Harrisburg, Pa.: Trinity International, 1999); *Hearing the Whole Story*; and *Jesus and Empire: The Kingdom of God and the New World Disorder* (Minneapolis: Fortress Press, 2003).

[16] See further Horsley, *Jesus and Empire*, chap 4.

[17] Of direct significance for Jesus and the Gospels are Horsley, "Popular Messianic Movements around the Time of Jesus," *CBQ* 46 (1984): 471-93; "'Like One of the Prophets of Old':Two Types of Popular Prophets at the Time of Jesus," *CBQ* 47 (1985): 435-63; and *Bandits, Prophets, and Messiahs* (with John Hanson; Minneapolis: Winston, 1985; Harrisburg: Trinity International, 1999).

[18] For example, in *The Historical Jesus*, Crossan simply takes over the leaders and movements described in *Bandits, Prophets, and Messiahs* in part two on the historical context of Jesus; for NT Introductions, see Dennis Duling, *The New Testament: History, Literature, and Social Context* (Toronto: Thomson Wadsworth, 2002); and *Russell Pregeant, Engaging the New Testament* (Minneapolis: Fortress Press, 1995).

[19] For example, Cullmann, *Jesus and the Revolutionaries*; Martin Hengel, *Die Zeloten* (Leiden: Brill, 1961); Hengel, *Victory over Violence*.

[20] I then discovered that James C. Scott had similarly borrowed, and brilliantly explored, this concept in ways that are very suggestive for study of Jesus and the Gospels. At least a few highly regarded scholars of Jesus and the Gospels, such as Crossan (*The Historical Jesus*), Burton Mack (*A Myth of Innocence*), and John Kloppenborg (*Excavating Q*), have taken over and adapted this concept or its equivalent.

[21] See the cautionary comments in Horsley, *Jesus and the Spiral of Violence*, chap 5. Although they both adopted the concept of the "little tradition" (or at least the distinction between elite and popular culture), both Crossan and Mack continue to use elite texts such as the *Psalms of Solomon* and the treatises of Philo as direct sources for popular attitudes and views. Note that the whole ongoing debate about whether Jesus' teaching (or Gospels and pieces of the Gospels) was "apocalyptic" or "sapiential" was based on fragments of elite texts, all products and expressions of scribal circles. See Richard Horsley, *Scribes, Visionaries, and the Politics of Second Temple Judea* (Louisville: Westminster John Knox, 2007).

[22] Scott's reflections on the "official transcript" and the "hidden transcript" can help us develop some subtlety. See chap 8 below.

[23] In perspective, analysis, and conceptualization, the reconstruction of the history, politics, and local community life in my *Galilee: History, Politics, People* (Harrisburg, Pa.: Trinity International, 1995; and *Archaeology, History, and Society in Galilee* (Harrisburg, Pa.: Trinity International, 1996) are significantly different from books and articles that provide additional details to the standard older portrayal of "Judaism."

[24] Surveys in Harris, *Ancient Literacy*; Susan Niditch, *Oral World and Written Word* (Louisville: Westminster John Knox, 1996); Horsley, *Scribes, Visionaries and the Politics of Second Temple Judea*, chap 5.

[25] Hezser, *Jewish Literacy in Roman Palestine*.

[26] See survey in David Carr, *Writing on the Tablet of the Heart* (Oxford: Oxford University Press, 2005); Horsley, *Scribes, Visionaries and the Politics of Second Temple Judea*.

[27] Memory figured strongly already in Kelber's *Oral and Written Gospel*. He has explored the importance of cultural memory for the composition and appreciation of the Gospels in a whole series of significant recent articles. He calls attention to the centrality of Memory and the *ars memoriae* as the mediator of western culture (or any culture) from classical Greece through the Middle Ages—until it was "forgotten" in modern times. See many of the essays that explore the implication of Kelber's work in *Performing the Gospel: Orality, Memory, and Mark* , ed. Horsley, Draper, and Foley (Minneapolis: Fortress Press, 2006).

[28] And see now the essays (and bibliography), to which Kelber responds, in Alan Kirk and Tom Thatcher, *Memory, Tradition, and Text: Uses of the Past in Early Christianity*, Semeia Studies 52 (Atlanta: Society of Biblical Literature, 2005).

[29] Horsley, "Popular Messianic Movements," and "Like One of the Prophets."

[30] See the provisional reflections in Horsley, *Hearing the Whole Story*, chap 10.

[31] This relational and contextual approach, implicit in most of my work on the Gospels and Jesus in the last twenty years, is sketched explicitly in Horsley, *Jesus and Empire*, chap 3.

Chapter 1: "People's History" and Gospel Studies

[1] As David Sabean concluded in his important study of seventeenth-century peasants, *Power in the Blood: Popular Culture and Village Discourse in Early Modern Germany* (Cambridge: Cambridge University Press, 1984), ordinary people were every bit as much involved as their landlords and rulers in the great issues of history: justice, responsibility, community, vision, faith, and political communication. They may have been exploited. But they were not supine. They engaged actively and creatively in the political dynamics that determined their lives.

[2] Eric J. Hobsbawm, "History From Below—Some Reflections," in Frederick Krantz, ed., *History from Below: Studies in Popular Protest and Popular Ideology in Honour of George Rude* (Montreal: Concordia University Press, 1985), 72; Jim Sharpe, "History from Below," in Peter Burke, ed., *New Perspectives on Historical Writing* (University Park: University of Pennsylvania Press, 1992), 24–41.

[3] Adapted from Peter Burke, "Overture: the New History, its Past and Future," in Peter Burke, ed., *New Perspectives on Historical Writing*, 1–23, especially 3.

[4] Pioneers in the study of peoples history and popular culture have recognized that, despite the many mediating social and cultural factors that developed during the dramatic transition from

feudal medieval to capitalist modern political economic structures, "the polarities of elite and popular, dominant and subordinate, between powerful and powerless, us and them are so evident in the sources that we cannot ignore them." (Bob Scribner, "Is a History of Popular Culture Possible?" *History of European Ideas* 10/2 [1989]: 184.) Those polarities were more extreme in the Roman Empire, the context of Christian origins.

[5] Scribner, "History of Popular Culture;" Peter Burke, *Popular Culture in Early Modern Europe* (New York: Harper & Row, 1981); and especially James C. Scott, *Domination and the Arts of Resistance* (New Haven, Conn.: Yale University Press, 1990), which is applied to New Testament materials by the essays in Richard A. Horsley, ed., *Hidden Transcripts and the Arts of Resistance* Semeia Studies 48 (Atlanta: Society of Biblical Literature, 2004).

[6] William V. Harris, *Ancient Literacy* (Cambridge, Mass.: Harvard University Press, 1989).

[7] Catherine Hezser, *Jewish Literacy in Roman Palestine* (Tübingen: Mohr Siebeck, 2001).

[8] Richard A. Horsley, *Jesus and the Spiral of Violence: Popular Jewish Resistance in Roman Palestine* (Minneapolis: Fortress Press, 1993 [1987]), 129–31.

[9] Eugene C. Ulrich, *The Dead Sea Scrolls and the Origins of the Bible* (Grand Rapids, Mich.: Eerdmans, 1999).

[10] Hezser, *Jewish Literacy*. Martin Jaffee, *Torah in the Mouth: Writing and Oral Tradition in Palestinian Judaism, 200 B.C.E.–400 C.E.* (Oxford: Oxford University Press, 2001), argues that even in scribal circles, the scriptural "texts" were inscribed in memory as much as on the scrolls deposited in the temple or in the possession of the scribes themselves.

[11] Richard A. Horsley, *Galilee: History, Politics, People* (Valley Forge, Pa.: Trinity International, 1995), chaps 2 and 6.

[12] Ibid., 144–57.

[13] Horsley, *Jesus and the Spiral of Violence,* chap 5; on particular differences, see Richard A. Horsley with Jonathan A. Draper, *Whoever Hears You Hears Me: Prophets, Performance, and Tradition in Q* (Harrisville Pa.: Trinity International, 1999), chap 5.

[14] As the extraordinary people's historian Eric Hobsbawm points out, "most sources for grassroots history have only been recognized because someone has asked a question and then prospected desperately around for some way of answering it. We cannot be positivists, believing that the questions and the answers arise naturally out of the study of the material. There is generally no material until our questions have revealed it." ("History from Below," 66).

[15] Richard A. Horsley with John S. Hanson, *Bandits, Prophets, and Messiahs* (Harrisburg, Pa.: Trinity International, 1999 [1985]).

[16] Antoinette Clark Wire, *Holy Lives, Holy Deaths: A Close Hearing of Early Jewish Storytellers* (Leiden: Brill, 2002), esp chap 3; Richard A. Horsley, *The Liberation of Christmas* (New York: Crossroad, 1989).

[17] Elisabeth Schüssler Fiorenza, *In Memory of Her: A Feminist Theological Reconstruction of Christian Origins* (New York: Crossroad, 1983).

[18] Scribner, "History of Popular Culture," 181.

[19] Hence beyond Gerhard Lenski, *Power and Privilege: A Theory of Social Stratification* (New York: McGraw-Hill, 1966) to John H. Kautsky, *The Politics of Aristocratic Empires* (Chapel Hill: University of North Carolina Press, 1982).

[20] On Galilee and Judea, see further Horsley, *Galilee;* and David Fiensy, *The Social History of Palestine in the Herodian Period* (Lewiston, N.Y.: Mellen, 1991).

[21] Explored suggestively by Scott, *Domination and the Arts of Resistance*; see further chaps 8–10 below.

Chapter 2: Jesus Movements and the Renewal of Israel

[1] See further Richard A. Horsley with John S. Hanson, *Bandits, Prophets, and Messiahs: Popular Movements in the Time of Jesus* (Harrisburg, Pa.: Trinity International, 1999), chap 1; and on the Pharisees, etc., in the Judean temple-state, see Horsley, *Sociology and the Jesus Movement* (New York: Crossroad, 1989), 72-75; and Anthony J Saldarini, *Pharisees, Scribes, and Sadducees in Palestinian Society* (Wilmington, Del.: Glazier, 1988).

[2] Discussed more extensively in Richard A. Horsley, *Jesus and the Spiral of Violence: Popular Jewish Resistance in Roman Palestine* (Minneapolis: Fortress Press, 1993 [1987]), esp chaps 2 and 4.

[3] Compared with studies of protests by modern urban crowds in Horsley, *Jesus and the Spiral of Violence*, 90–99.

[4] Examined critically in Richard A. Horsley, "Popular Messianic Movements around the Time of Jesus," *CBQ* 46 (1984): 471–93; "'Like One of the Prophets of Old': Two Types of Popular Prophets at the Time of Jesus," *CBQ* 47 (1985): 435–63; "Popular Prophetic Movements at the Time of Jesus, Their Principal Features and Social Origins," *JSNT* 26 (1986): 3–27; and, more accessibly, in Horsley, *Bandits, Prophets, and Messiahs.*

[5] See further my *Jesus and Empire: The Kingdom of God and the New World Disorder* (Minneapolis: Fortress Press, 2003), chap 3.

[6] The following discussion of Jesus movements draws heavily on my recent treatments of Q and Mark in *Whoever Hears You Hears Me: Prophets, Performance, and Tradition in Q* (with Jonathan Draper; Harrisburg, Pa.: Trinity International, 1999), and *Hearing the Whole Story: The Politics of Plot in Mark's Gospel* (Louisville, Ky.: Westminster John Knox, 2001).

[7] Fuller critical examination in *Whoever Hears You Hears Me* and *Hearing the Whole Story.*

[8] More fully analyzed and discussed in Richard A. Horsley, *Galilee: History, Politics, People* (Valley Forge, Pa.: Trinity International, 1995); and *Archaeology, History, and Society in Galilee* (Harrisburg, Pa.: Trinity International, 1996).

[9] See especially James C. Scott, "Protest and Profanation: Agrarian Revolt and the Little Tradition," *Theory and Society* 4 (1977): 3–38, 211–45.

[10] Horsley, *Galilee*, 147-57.

[11] On the Herodian estates in western Judea, see David Fiensy, *The Social History of Palestine in the Herodian Period* (Lewiston, N.Y.: Mellen, 1991), 32–43; on the question of land-tenure and royal estates in Judea and Galilee in historical political-economic context, see Horsley, *Galilee*, chap 9.

[12] Summary of evidence and analysis in Horsley, *Galilee*, chap 10. Most of the buildings that archaeologists label as "synagogues" date to late antiquity. This suggests that village communities were not constructing such buildings yet at the time of Jesus and his movements.

[13] Fuller analysis of the mission discourses in *Whoever Hears You Hears Me*, chap 10.

[14] Building of a movement by sending envoys to work in village communities sounds similar to the activities of at least two known organizations, Der Bundshuh and Der Arme Konrad, which sent delegates to towns up and down the Rhine valley in the decade prior to the Peasants' War of

1524–5 in southwest Germany. See Peter Blickle, *The Revolution of 1525: The German Peasants' War From a New Perspective* (Baltimore: Johns Hopkins University Press, 1977).

[15] On the fishing enterprise under Herod Antipas, see K. C. Hanson, "The Galileans Fishing Economy and the Jesus Tradition," *Biblical Theology Bulletin* 27 (1997): 99–111.

[16] Horsley, *Galilee*, 147–57.

[17] The following discussion draws upon the fuller analysis in *Whoever Hears You Hears Me*, chap 9, and *Hearing the Whole Story*, chap 8.

[18] James C. Scott, *The Moral Economy of the Peasant* (New Haven, Conn.: Yale University Press, 1976), applied to Q speeches in chap 10 below.

Chapter 3: Oral Performance and Tradition in "Q"

[1] Vincent Taylor, "The Original Order of Q" in *New Testament Essays: Studies in Memory of T. W. Manson,* ed. A. J. B. Higgins (Manchester: Manchester University Press, 1959), 95–118.

[2] John S. Kloppenborg, *The Formation of Q* (Philadelphia: Fortress Press, 1987).

[3] Richard A. Horsley "Q and Jesus: Assumptions, approaches, and Analyses" *Semeia* 55 (1991): 175–209; Alan Kirk, *The Composition of the Sayings Source* (Leiden: Brill, 1998); Richard A. Horsley and Jonathan A. Draper, *Whoever Hears You Hears Me: Prophets, Perfomances and Tradition in Q* (Harrisburg, Pa.: Trinity International, 1999), 61–93; James Robinson, Paul Hoffman, and John S. Kloppenborg, eds., *The Critical Edition of Q* (Minneapolis: Fortress Press, 2000), lxii–lxvi.

[4] Developed further in Horsley and Draper, *Whoever Hears You Hears Me.*

[5] Such as William V. Harris, *Ancient Literacy* (Cambridge, Mass.: Harvard University Press, 1989); Susan Niditch, *Oral World and Written Word* (Louisville, Ky.: Westminster/John Knox, 1996); John Achtemeier, "*Omnes verbum somnat*: The New Testament and the Oral Environment of Late Western Antiquity," *JBL* 109 (1990): 3–27; Pieter J. J. Botha, "Greco-Roman Literacy as Setting for New Testament Writings," *Neot* 26 (1992): 206.

[6] Werner Kelber, *The Oral And Written Gospel* (Philadelphia: Fortress Press, 1983).

[7] Pieter Botha, "Mark's Story as Oral Traditional Literature: Rethinking the Transmission of Some Traditions about Jesus," *Hervormde Teologiese Studies* 47 (1991): 304–31; Joanna Dewey, "Oral Methods of Structuring Narrative in Mark," *Interpretation* 53 (1989): 32–44.

[8] For example, Horsley and Draper, *Whoever Hears You Hears Me*, chap 6.

[9] See especially Catherine Hezser, *Jewish Literacy in Roman Palestine* (Tübingen: Mohr Siebeck, 2001); Hannah M. Cotton "The Rabbis and the Documents" in *Jews in a Greco-Roman World*, ed. Martin Goodman (Oxford: Oxford University Press, 1998), 167–79; Michael Satlow, "Reconsidering the Rabbinic *ketubbah* Payment" in *The Jewish Family in Antiquity*, ed. Shaye J. D. Cohen, BJS 289 (Atlanta: Scholars, 1993), 133–51.

[10] Hezser, *Jewish Literacy*, 111–112, 297–99.

[11] Cotton, "The Rabbis and the Documents," 178.

[12] Satlow, "Reconsidering the Rabbinic *ketubbah* Payment," 133ff.

[13] Naphtali Lewis, ed., "Greek Papyri" in *The Documents form the Bar Kokhba Period in the Cave of Letters,* Judean Desert Studies 2 (Jerusalem: Israel Exploration Society, Hebrew University of Jerusalem, Shrine of the Book, 1989): 22–24.

[14] Martin Goodman, "Babatha's Story" *Journal of Roman Studies* 81 (1991): 72.

[15] Hezser, *Jewish Literacy,* 111–113.

[16] Ibid., 117.

[17] Ibid., 118–26.

[18] Ibid., 123–24.

[19] Ibid., 124–25.

[20] M. T. Clanchy, *From Memory to Written Record: England, 1066–1307* (London: Arnold; Cambridge, Mass.: Harvard University Press, 1979).

[21] Harris, *Ancient Literacy,* 198–200.

[22] Rosalind Thomas, *Oral Tradition and Written Record in Classical Athens* (Cambridge: Cambridge University Press, 1989), 41–43; Harris, *Ancient Literacy,* 68–72

[23] Clanchy, *From Memory to Written Record,* 232.

[24] Greg Woolf, "Literacy," *Cambridge Ancient History* 11 (2001): 877.

[25] Werner Kelber, "Jesus and Tradition: Words in Time, Words in Space," *Semeia* 65 (1994): 140.

[26] Ibid., 144.

[27] Ibid., 145.

[28] Ibid., 149.

[29] Ibid., 155.

[30] Daniel Boyarin, "Placing Reading: Ancient Israel and Medieval Europe" in *The Ethnography of Reading,* ed. Jonathan Boyarin (Berkeley and Los Angeles: University of California Press, 1993), 13.

[31] Ibid., 15.

[32] Ibid., 15.

[33] Ibid., 17.

[34] William Scott Green, "Writing with Scripture: The Rabbinic Uses of the Hebrew Bible" in *Writing with Scripture: The Authority and Uses of the Hebrew Bible in the Torah of Formative Judaism,* ed. Jacob Neusner (Minneapolis: Fortress Press, 1989), 14–15.

[35] Ibid., 14–15.

[36] Martin Jaffee, *Torah in the Mouth* (Oxford: Oxford University Press, 2001), 16.

[37] Martin Jaffee, "The Oral-Cultural Context of the Talmud Yerushalmi: Greco-Roman Rhetorical Paideia, Discipleship, and the Concept of Oral Torah" in *The Talmud Yerushalmi and Graeco-Roman Culture I,* ed. Peter Schaefer (Tübingen: Mohr Siebeck, 1998), 53.

[38] John Miles Foley, *Immanent Art: From Structure to Meaning in Traditional Oral Epic* (Bloomington: Indiana University Press, 1991); *The Singer of Tales in Performance* (Bloomington: Indiana University Press, 1995); *How to Read an Oral Poem* (Urbana: University of Illinois Press, 2002).

[39] Horsley and Draper, *Whoever Hears You Hears Me.*

[40] D. C. Parker, *The Living Text of the Gospels* (Cambridge: Cambridge University Press, 1997).

[41] Foley, *How to Read an Oral Poem.*

[42] Foley *The Singer of Tales*; Horsley and Draper, *Whoever Hears You Hears Me,* 160–74.

[43] Kirk, *Composition of the Sayings Source*; Horsley and Draper, *Whoever Hears You Hears Me,* 83–93, 166–68.

[44] Horsley and Draper, *Whoever Hears You Hears Me,* 168–70.

[45] Foley, *Immanent Art*; Foley, *The Singer of Tales*; Horsley and Draper, *Whoever Hears You Hears Me*, 170–74, Richard A. Horsley, *Hearing the Whole Story: The Politics of Plot in Mark's Gospel* (Louisville, Ky.: Westminster John Knox, 2001), chap 3.

[46] Kelber, "Jesus and Tradition," esp 152–59.

[47] John S. Kloppenborg Verbin, *Excavating Q* (Minneapolis: Fortress Press, 2000).

[48] Eugene Ulrich, *The Dead Sea Scrolls and the Origins of the Bible* (Grand Rapids, Mich.: Eerdmans, 1999).

[49] Hezser, *Jewish Literacy*.

[50] Ibid.

[51] Richard A. Horsley, *Galilee: History, Politics, People* (Valley Forge, Pa.: Trinity International, 1995); Richard A. Horsley, *Archeology, History, and Society in Galilee: The Social Context of Jesus and the Rabbis* (Valley Forge, Pa.: Trinity International, 1996).

[52] James C. Scott "Protest and Profanation: Agrarian Revolt and the Little Tradition," *Theology and Society* 4 (1977).

[53] Ulrich, *The Dead Sea Scrolls*.

[54] Horsley, "The Language(s) of the Kingdom; From Aramaic to Greek, Galilee to Syria, Oral to Oral-Written," paper delivered at the Conference on "Orality, Literacy, and Diversity" at the University of Zululand, October 2004. Publication forthcoming.

[55] Horsley and Draper, *Whoever Hears You Hears Me*, chap 10.

[56] Christopher M. Tuckett, *Q and the History of Early Christianity* (Edinburgh: T&T Clark, 1996).

[57] John S. Kloppenborg, *The Formation of Q* (Philadelphia: Fortress Press, 1987).

[58] Ibid.; Kirk, *Composition of Sayings Source*.

[59] Horsley and Draper, *Whoever Hears You Hears Me*.

[60] Ibid., 210–5.

[61] Richard Bauman, *Verbal Art as Performance* (Prospect Heights, Ill.: Waveland, 1977); Dell Hymes, *"In Vain I Tried to Tell You": Essays in Native American Ethnopoetics* (Philadelphia: University of Pennsylvania Press, 1981).

[62] Richard A. Horsley, *Jesus and the Spiral of Violence: Popular Jewish Resistance in Roman Palestine* (Minneapolis: Fortress Press, 1995), chap 9.

[63] Horsley and Draper, *Whoever Hears You Hears Me*, chap 9.

[64] Klaus Baltzer, *The Covenant Formulary* (Philadelphia: Fortress Press, 1971).

Chapter 4: Understanding Mark as Oral Performance

[1] William V. Harris, *Ancient Literacy* (Cambridge, Mass.: Harvard University Press, 1989), here especially 114; 264; 13, 22; cf. Mary Beard, ed., *Literacy in the Roman World* (Ann Arbor: Journal of Roman Archaeology, 1991).

[2] H. C. Youtie, "Petaus, fils de Petaus, ou le scribe qui ne savait pas ecrire," *Chronique d'Egypte* 81 (1966): 127–443; "*Aggrammatos*: As Aspect of Greek Society in Egypt," *Harvard Studies in Classical Philology* 75 (1971): 161–176; Harris, *Ancient Literacy*, 202, 277, 280–281.

[3] Harris, *Ancient Literacy*, 248–253.

[4] Ibid., 198–199, 201.

[5] See, for example, Martin Hengel, *Judaism and Hellenism* (Philadelphia: Fortress Press, 1974), 1.78–83; and S. Safrai, "Education and the Study of the Torah" in *The Jewish People in the First Century (Compendia Rerum Iudaicarum ad Novum Testamentum*; sec. I.2) ed. S. Safrai and Menahem Stern (Philadelphia: Fortress Press, 1976), 2.945–70.

[6] Harry Y. Gamble, *Books and Readers in the Early Church* (New Haven, Conn.: Yale University Press, 1995), 7.

[7] Compare Martin Goodman, *State and Society in Roman Galilee, A.D. 132–212* (Totowa, N.J.: Rowman and Allanheld, 1983), 72, whose discussion of "education" (71–81) does not appear to apply to village culture. See rather Catherine Hezser, *Jewish Literacy in Roman Palestine* (Tüebingen: Mohr Siebeck, 2001).

[8] Meir Bar-Ilan, "Illiteracy in the Land of Israel in the First Century C.E.," *Essays in the Social Scientific Study of Judaism and Jewish Society*, ed. Simcha Fishbane and Stuart Schoenfeld (Hoboken, N.J.: KTAV, 1992), 46–61; Hezser, *Jewish Literacy*.

[9] Rosalind Thomas, *Literacy and Orality in Ancient Greece* (Cambridge: Cambridge University Press, 1992), 102–103, 120–123.

[10] Thomas, *Literacy and Orality*, 118, 123–24; and J. Herrington, *Poetry into Drama: Early Tragedy and the Greek Poetic Tradition* (Berkeley & Los Angeles: University of California Press, 1985).

[11] Pierre Hadot, "Forms of Life and Forms of Discourse in Ancient Philosophy," *Critical Inquiry* 16 (1990): 497–8.

[12] Paul Achtemeier, "*Omnes verbum sonat*: The New Testament and the Oral Environment of Late Western Antiquity," *JBL* 109 (1990): 26–27; Pieter J. J. Botha, "Greco-Roman Literacy as a Setting for New Testament writings," Neotestamentica 26 (1992): 742-59.

[13] Thomas, *Literacy and Orality*, 48–50, 122–123.

[14] Harris, *Ancient Literacy*, 223–228.

[15] Compare the thesis of Mary Ann Tolbert, *Sowing the Gospel: Mark's World in Literary-Historical Perspective* (Minneapolis: Fortress Press, 1989), 59–79.

[16] By analogy with the *Didache:* "there is nothing in this *didache* that the reader does not already know." Ian Henderson, "*Didache* and Orality in synoptic Comparison," *JBL* 111 (1992): 292.

[17] Martin S. Jaffee, "Writing and Rabbinic Oral Tradition: On Mishnaic Narrative, Lists, and Mnemonics," *Journal of Jewish Thought and Philosophy* 4 (1994): 143–44.

[18] Vernon K. Robbins, "Oral, Rhetorical, and Literary Cultures," *Semeia* 65 (1994): 79.

[19] On the cultivation of popular Israelite tradition among Galilean and other villagers, see further Richard A. Horsley, *Galilee: History, Politics, People* (Harrisburg, Pa.: Trinity International, 1995), 148–156, 245–251; and in Horsley and Jonathan Draper, *Whoever Hears You Hears Me* (Harrisburg, Pa.: Trinity International, 1995) 98–122, 135–150.

[20] Richard A. Horsley, "Popular Messianic Movements around the Time of Jesus," *Catholic Biblical Quarterly* 46 (1984): 471–93; "'Like One of the Prophets of Old': Two Types of Popular Prophets at the Time of Jesus." *Catholic Biblical Quarterly* 47 (1985): 435–63.

[21] Horsley, *Galilee*, 152–155.

[22] Thomas, *Orality and Literacy*.

[23] Horsley and Draper, *Whoever Hears You Hears Me*, 140–144.

[24] Rudolf Bultmann, *The History of the Synoptic Tradition* (Oxford: Blackwell, 1963), 6.

[25] E. P. Sanders, *The Tendencies of the Synoptic Tradition* (SNTSMS 9; Cambrige: Cambridge University Press, 1969). See the discussion in Werner Kelber, *The Oral and Written Gospel* (Philadelphia: Fortress Press, 1983), 6, 8.

[26] Kelber, *The Oral and Written Gospel.*

[27] Walter J. Ong, S. J., *Interfaces of the Word* (Ithaca, N.Y.: Cornell University Press, 1977); *Orality and Literacy* (New York: Routledge, 1982).

[28] Joanna Dewey, "Oral Methods of Structuring Narrative in Mark," *Interpretation* 53 (1989): 32–44; "Mark as Aural Narrative: Structures as Clues to Undersanding," *Sewanee Theological Review* 36 (1992): 45–56.

[29] Ong, *Orality and Literacy*, 37–49; Eric Havelock, "Oral Composition in the Oedipus Tyrannus of Sophocles," *New Literary History* 16 (1984): 175–97; and *Preface to Plato* (Cambridge, Mass.: Harvard University Press, 1963).

[30] Joanna Dewey, "The Gospel of Mark as an Oral-Aural Event: Implications for Interpretation." in *The New Literary Criticism and the New Testament*, ed. Elizabeth Struthers Malbon and Edgar V. Mcknight (JSNTSup 19; Sheffield: Sheffield Academic, 1994), 148–57; "Mark as Aural Narrative," 48–50; and most recently, "The Survival of Mark's Gospel: A Good Story?" *JBL* 123 (2004): 495–507.

[31] Dewey, "Oral Methods," 34–38; drawing on Havelock, *Preface to Plato.*

[32] Dewey, "The Gospel of Mark as Oral-Aural Event."

[33] Ibid., 154–56.

[34] Kelber, *Oral and Written Gospel*, 30, 80.

[35] Pieter J. J. Botha, "Mark's Story as Oral-Traditional Literature: Rethinking the Transmission of Some Traditions about Jesus," *Hervormde Teologiese Studies* 47 (1991): 316.

[36] Ibid., 307.

[37] Ibid., 309, 317–22.

[38] Ibid., 318.

[39] Ibid., 306.

[40] Werner Kelber, "Introduction" in *Oral and Written Gospel* (Bloomington: University of Indiana Press, 1997), xxiii. On social memory, see further chaps 5, 6, and 7 below.

[41] The following is based on John Miles Foley, *Immanent Art: From Structure to Meaning in Traditional Oral Epic* (Bloomington: Indiana University Press, 1991); and *Singer of Tales in Performance* (Bloomington: Indiana University Press, 1995); and to M. A. K. Halliday, *Language as Social Semiotic: The Social Interpretation of Language and Meaning* (London: Edward Arnold, 1978).

[42] Kelber, *Oral and Written Gospel*, chap 2.

[43] Whitney Shiner, *Proclaiming the Gospel: First-Century Performance of Mark* (Harrisburg, Pa.: Trinity International, 2003).

[44] David Rhoads' performance of Mark is available from SELECT, online or at 1-614-235-4136.

[45] A link to the Network of Biblical Storytellers can be found at www.biblicalperformancecriticism.org.

[46] On Homeric epic and Bosnian and Serbian epic singers, see Albert Lord's classic book, *Singer of Tales* (Cambridge, Mass.: Harvard University Press, 1960).

[47] Very suggestive analysis of Native American storytelling has been done by Dell Hymes, "Discovering Oral Performance and Measured Verse in American Indian Narrative," reprinted in *"In Vain I Tried to Tell You": Essays in Native American Ethnopoetics* (Philadelphia: University of Pennsylvania Press, 1981), 79–141.

[48] Havelock, *Preface to Plato*, 180.

[49] Kelber, *Oral and Written Gospel*, 65.

[50] Ong, *Orality and Literacy*, 34.

[51] Havelock, "Oral Composition," 182.

[52] Ibid., 183.

[53] Ong, *Orality and Literacy*, 34.

[54] Walter J. Ong, S.J., *Interfaces of the Word* (Ithaca, N.Y.: Cornell University Press, 1977), 282.

Chapter 5: Social Memory and Gospel Traditions

[1] Werner Kelber, "The Case of the Gospels: Memory's Desire and the Limits of Historical Criticism," *Oral Tradition* 17 (2002): 55–86.

[2] Alan Kirk and Tom Thatcher, *Memory, Tradition and Text: Uses of the Past in Early Christianity* (Atlanta: Society of Biblical Literature, 2005).

[3] Jeffrey K. Olick and Joyce Robbins, "Social Memory Studies: From 'Collective Memory' to the Historical Sociology of Mnemonic Practices." *Annual Review of Sociology* 24 (1998): 106.

[4] Edward W. Said, *Orientalism* (New York: Random House, 1978).

[5] Eugene Ulrich, *The Dead Sea Scrolls and the Origins of the Bible* (Grand Rapids, Mich.: Eerdmans, 1999); D. C. Parker, *The Living Text of the Gospels* (Cambridge: Cambridge University Press, 1997).

[6] Werner Kelber, *The Oral and Written Gospel* (Philadelphia: Fortress Press, 1983).

[7] Catherine Hezser, *Jewish Literacy in Roman Palestine* (Tübingen: Mohr Siebeck, 2001).

[8] Richard A. Horsley, *Hearing the Whole Story: The Politics of Plot in Mark's Gospel* (Louisville, Ky.: Westminster John Knox, 2001).

[9] Martin Jaffee, *Torah in the Mouth* (Oxford: Oxford University Press, 2001); Richard A. Horsley, *Scribes, Visionaries, and the Politics of Second Temple Judea* (Louisville, Ky.: Westminster John Knox, 2007).

[10] Richard A. Horsley and Jonathan A. Draper, *Whoever Hears You Hears Me: Prophets, Performance and Tradition in Q* (Harrisburg, Pa.: Trinity International, 1999); Horsley, *Hearing the Whole Story*.

[11] Richard A. Horsley, *Jesus and the Spiral of Violence: Popular Jewish Resistance in Roman Palestine* (Minneapolis: Fortress Press, 1995).

[12] Kelber, *The Oral and Written Gospel*, chap 1.

[13] Jeffrey Prager, *Presenting the Past: Psychoanalysis and the Sociology of Misremembering* (Cambridge, Mass.: Harvard University Press, 1998). 70–71; Alan Kirk, *The Composition of the Sayings Source* (Leiden: Brill, 1998), 4.

[14] Maurice Halbwachs, *On Collective Memory* (1992), 173, 53; Kirk, *The Composition of the Sayings Source*, (Leidon: Brill, 1998), 3mb.

[15] Gérard Namer, *Mémoire et société* (Paris: Méridiens Lincksick, 1987), 154–55; James Fentress and Chris Wickham, *Social Memory* (Oxford: Blackwell, 1992), 73.

[16] David Lowenthal, *The Past is a Foreign Country* (Cambridge and New York: Cambridge University Press, 1985), 204.

[17] Parker, *The Living Text of the Gospels.*

[18] Jan Assmann, *Religion und kulturelles Gedächtnis: zehn Studien* (Münch: C. H. Beck, 2000), 53, 127; Jan Assmann, *Das kulturelle Gedächtnis: Schrift, Erinnerung und politische Indentität in frühen Hochkulturen* (Münch: C. H. Beck, 1992),141–42; Jan Assmann, "Collective Memory and Cultural Identity" *New German Critique* 65 (1995): 132.

[19] Parker, *The Living Text of the Gospels.*

[20] More fully documented and argued in Horsley and Draper, *Whoever Hears You Hears Me*; and Horsley, *Hearing the Whole Story.*

[21] Richard A. Horsley, "Popular Messianic Movements around the Time of Jesus," *Catholic Biblical Quarterly* 46 (1984): 471–95; Richard A. Horsley, "The High Priests and Politics in Roman Palestine," *Journal for the Study of Judaism* 17 (1986): 23–55; Richard A. Horsley with John S. Hanson, *Bandits Prophets and Messiahs: Popular Movements in the Time of Jesus* (San Francisco: Harper and Row, 1985).

[22] Yael Zerubavel, *Recovered Roots: Collective Memory and the Making of Israeli National Tradition* (Chicago: University of Chicago, 1995), 4–7, as summarized by Kirk, "Social and Cultural Memory" in Kirk and Thatcher *Memory, Tradition and Text,* 5.

[23] Edward S. Casey, *Remembering: A Phenomenological Study* (Bloomington: Indiana University Press, 1987), 291.

[24] Barry Schwartz, "The Social Context of Commemoration: A Study in Collective Memory," *Social Forces* 61 (1982): 377.

[25] W. Lloyd Warner, *The Living and the Dead: A Study of the Symbolic Life of Americans* (New Haven, Conn.: Yale University Press, 1959), 268.

[26] Kirk, *The Composition of the Sayings Source,* 15m; Fentress and Wickham, *Social Memory,* 51; Paul Connerton, *How Societies Remember* (Cambridge: Cambridge University Press, 1989), 2; Barry Schwartz, *Abraham Lincoln and the Forge of National Memory* (Chicago: University of Chicago, 2000), 225–230; Zerubavel, *Recovered Roots,* 229; Casey, *Remembering,* 284–85; Peter Burke, "History as Social Memory" in *Memory: History, Culture and the Mind,* ed. Thomas Butler (Oxford: Blackwell, 1989), 103; Roy Rosenzweig and David Thelen, *The Presence of the Past: Popular Uses of History in American Life* (New York: Columbia University Press, 1998), 68.

[27] George A. Bonanno, "Remembering and Psychotherapy," *Psychotherapy* 27 (1990): 177–82; Prager, *Presenting the Past,* 200–209.

[28] Barry Schwartz, "Frame Image: Towards a Semiotics of Collective Memory" *Semiotica* 121 (1998): 1.

[29] Ibid., 8.

[30] See also Yosef Hayim Yerushalmi, *Zakhor: Jewish History and Jewish Memory* (Seattle: University of Washington Press, 1982), 36–39.

[31] Fentress and Wickham, *Social Memory,* chap 3.

[32] Mary Hegland, "Two Images of Husain: Accommodation and Revolution in an Iranian Village" in *Religion and Politics in Iran: Shiism from Quietism to Revolution,* ed. Nikki R. Keddie (New Haven, Conn.: Yale University Press, 1981); Jan Hjärpe, "La commemoration religieuse comme légitimation politique dans le monde muselman contemporain" in *La commemoration,* ed. Philippe Gignoux (Louvain and Paris: Peeters, 1988); Richard A. Horsley, *Religion and Empire: People, Power, an the Life of the Spirit* (Minneapolis: Fortress Press, 2003), chap 3.

[33] See further chap 7 below.

[34] John Bodnar, *Remaking America: Public Memory, Commemoration, and Patriotism in the Twentieth Century* (Princeton, N.J.: Princeton University Press, 1992), 15.

[35] Benedict Anderson, *Imagined Communities: Reflections on the Origin and Spread of Nationalism* (rev. ed.; London: Verso, 1991).

[36] Eric Hobsbawm and Terence Ranger, eds., *The Invention of Tradition* (London and New York: Cambridge University Press, 1983).

[37] Horsley, *Hearing the Whole Story.*

[38] Schwartz, *Abraham Lincoln,* 204; Schwartz, "Frame Image," 23.

[39] James C. Scott, "Protest and Profanation: Agrarian Revolt and the Little Tradition," *Theory and Society* 4 (1977): 1–38, 211–46.

[40] Richard A. Horsley, "'Like One of the Prophets of Old': Two Types of Popular Prophets at the Time of Jesus," *Catholic Biblical Quarterly* 47 (1985): 435–63; Horsley, *Hearing the Whole Story.*

[41] James C. Scott, *Domination and the Arts of Resistance: Hidden Transcripts* (New Haven: Yale University Press, 1990).

[42] Richard A. Horsley, ed., *Hidden Transcripts and the Arts of Resistance: Applying the Work of James C Scott to Jesus and Paul* (Atlanta: Society of Biblical Literature, 2004); Richard A. Horsley, ed., *Oral Performance, Popular Tradition and Hidden Transcript in Q* (Atlanta: Society of Biblical Literature, 2006); and chaps 8, 9, 10 below.

Chapter 6: Patterns in the Social Memory of Jesus and Friends

[1] Paul Connerton, *How Societies Remember* (Cambridge: Cambridge University Press, 1989), 6.

[2] Werner Kelber, "The Case of the Gospels: Memory's Desire and the Limits of Historical Criticism," *Oral Tradition* 17 (2002): 55–86.

[3] Alan Kirk and Tom Thatcher, *Memory, Tradition and Text: Uses of the Past in Early Christianity* (Semeia Studies 52; Atlanta: Society of Biblical Literature, 2005.

[4] For example, see Richard A. Horsley, "'Like One of the Prophets of Old': Two Types of Popular Prophets at the Time of Jesus" *Catholic Biblical Quarterly* 47 (1985): 435–63; Richard A. Horsley, *Jesus and the Spiral of Violence: Popular Jewish Resistance in Roman Palestine* (Minneapolis: Fortress Press, 1995); Richard A. Horsley, *Galilee: History, Politics, People* (Valley Forge, Pa.: Trinity International, 1995).

[5] Horsley, *Galilee.*

[6] For example, Werner Kelber *Mark's Story of Jesus* (Philadelphia: Fortress Press, 1979); Richard A. Horsley, *Hearing the Whole Story: The Politics of Plot in Mark's Gospel* (Louisville, Ky.: Westminster John Knox, 2001).

[7] Alan Kirk, *The Composition of the Sayings Source* (Leiden: Brill, 1998); Richard A. Horsley and Jonathan A. Draper, *Whoever Hears You Hears Me: Prophets, Performance, and Tradition in Q* (Harrisburg, Pa.: Trinity International, 1999).

[8] Eugene Ulrich, *The Dead Sea Scrolls and the Origins of the Bible* (Grand Rapids, Mich.: Eerdmans, 1999).

[9] William V. Harris, *Ancient Literacy* (Cambridge, Mass.: Harvard University Press, 1989); Catherine Hezser, *Jewish Literacy in Roman Palestine* (Tübingen: Mohr Siebeck, 2001).

[10] Martin Jaffee, *Torah in the Mouth* (Oxford: Oxford University Press, 2001).

[11] Horsley and Draper, *Whoever Hears You Hears Me*; Horsley, *Hearing the Whole Story*; William R. Herzog II, *Jesus, Justice and the Reign of God* (Louisville, Ky.: Westminster John Knox, 2000).

[12] Horsley, "The Language(s) of the Kingdom; From Aramaic to Greek, Galilee to Syria, Oral to Oral-Written," paper delivered at the Conference on "Orality, Literacy, and Diversity" at the University of Zululand, October 2004. Publication forthcoming.

[13] Jocelyn Penny Small, *Wax Tablets of the Mind: Cognitive Studies of Memory and Literacy in Classical Antiquity* (London: Routledge, 1997).

[14] John Miles Foley, *The Singer of Tales in Performance* (Bloomington: Indiana University Press, 1995); John Miles Foley, *How to Read an Oral Poem* (Urbana: University of Illinois Press, 2002); Horsley and Draper, *Whoever Hears You Hears Me*; Horsley, *Hearing the Whole Story*.

[15] Werner Kelber, "Jesus and Tradition: Words in Time, Words in Space" *Semeia* 64 (1994): 139–67.

[16] John Dominic Crossan, *Historical Jesus: The Life of a Mediterranean Jewish Peasant* (San Francisco: HarperCollins, 1991).

[17] John Dominic Crossan, *The Birth of Christianity* (San Francisco: HarperCollins, 1998).

[18] Werner Kelber, *The Oral and Written Gospel* (Philadelphia: Fortress Press, 1983).

[19] James Fentress and Chris Wickham, *Social Memory* (Oxford: Blackwell, 1992), 2–5.

[20] Ibid., 6–7.

[21] Maurice Halbwachs, *The Collective Memory* (New York: Harper & Row, 1980); Maurice Halbwacks, *On Collective Memory* (Chicago: University of Chicago Press, 1992).

[22] Frederic C. Bartlett, *Remembering: A Study in Experimental and Social Psychology* (Cambridge, Cambridge University Press, 1964).

[23] Crossan, *The Birth of Christianity*.

[24] Fentress and Wickham, *Social Memory*, 45.

[25] Ibid., 25.

[26] Peter Burke, "History as Social Memory" in *Memory: History, Culture and the Mind,* ed. Thomas Butler (Oxford: Blackwell, 1989), 98.

[27] Fentress and Wickham, *Social Memory*, 68.

[28] Crossan, *Historical Jesus*, Burton Mack, *The Lost Gospel: The Book of Q and Christian Origins* (San Francisco: HarperOne, 1993).

[29] Connerton, *How Societies Remember,* 6.

[30] Fentress and Wickham, *Social Memory*, 24.

[31] Foley, *The Singer of Tales*.

[32] Fentress and Wickham, *Social Memory*, 47.

[33] Burke, "History as Social Memory," 99.

[34] Ibid., 100.

[35] Ibid., 107.

[36] Ibid., 106–107.

[37] Fentress and Wickham, *Social Memory*, 127.

[38] Connerton, *How Societies Remember*, 15.

[39] Crossan, *The Birth of Christianity*, 78–79.

[40] Crossan, *Historical Jesus*.

[41] Foley, *Singer of Tales in Performance*; Horsley and Draper, *Whoever Hears You Hears Me*.

[42] Jaffee, *Torah in the Mouth*.

[43] Richard A. Horsley "Popular Messianic Movements around the Time of Jesus" *CBQ* 46 (1984): 471–93; Horsley "Like One of the Prophets of Old."

[44] Connerton, *How Societies Remember*, 19.

[45] Horsley and Draper, *However Hears You Hears Me*; Horsley, *Hearing the Whole Story*.

[46] Kirk, *The Composition of the Sayings Source*, 18; compare with Barry Schwartz, *Abraham Lincoln and the Forge of National Memory* (Chicago: University of Chicago Press, 2000), 225–30; Edward S. Casey, *Remembering: A Phenomenological Study* (Bloomington: Indiana University Press, 1987), 150–53.

[47] Klaus Baltzer, *The Covenant Formulary* (Philadelphia: Fortress Press, 1971).

[48] Horsley and Draper, *However Hears You Hears Me*, chap 9.

[49] Horsley, *Hearing the Whole Story*.

[50] Ibid.

[51] Kirk, *The Composition of the Sayings Source*, 19.

[52] Fentress and Wickham, *Social Memory*, 51.

[53] Barry Schwartz, "Frame Image: Towards a Semiotics of Collective Memory," *Semiotica* 121 (1998): 8.

[54] Burton L. Mack, *A Myth of Innocence: Mark and Christian Origins* (Philadelphia: Fortress Press, 1988).

[55] Kelber, *The Oral and Written Gospel*, chap 2.

[56] Schwartz, "Frame Image," 8.

[57] Fentress and Wickham, "Social Memory," 59.

[58] Crossan, in *Historical Jesus*, of course suggests that Galilee was "cosmopolitan," including influence from Cynic philosophy.

[59] Mack, *A Myth of Innocence*, 322–23.

Chapter 7: Popular Memory and Cultural Patterns in Mark

[1] See especially Werner Kelber, *Mark's Story of Jesus* (Philadelphia: Fortress Press, 1979); *The Oral and Written Gospel* (Philadelphia: Fortress Press, 1983); "Memory's Desire and the Limits of Historical Criticism," *Oral Tradition* 17 (2002): 55-86.

[2] More fully explained in Richard A. Horsley, *Hearing the Whole Story: The Politics of Plot in Mark's Gospel* (Louisville: Westminster John Knox, 2001); and Horsley and Jonathan A. Draper,

Whoever Hears You Hears Me: Prophets, Performance, and Tradition in Q (Harrisburg, Pa.: Trinity International, 1999), especially chap 7. See further chap 4 above.

[3] Werner Kelber, "Jesus and Tradition: Words in Time and Words in Space" *Semeia* 65 (1994): 159.

[4] The standard modern scholarly assumption is stated explicitly by Burton Mack, *A Myth of Innocence: Mark and Christian Origins* (Philadelphia: Fortress Press, 1988), 321–23: "Mark was a scholar. A reader of texts and a writer of texts. . . . Mark's gospel was composed at a desk in a scholar's study lined with texts." Recent research on the limited literacy and availability of scrolls in antiquity make this appear as an anachronistic projection of modern scholarly print culture.

[5] As explained in Horsley and Draper, *Whoever Hears You Hears Me,* 140–44; and Horsley, *Hearing the Whole Story,* 231–35.

[6] Eugene Ulrich, *The Dead Sea Scrolls and the Origins of the Bible* (Grand Rapids, Mich.: Eerdmans, 1999).

[7] Martin Jaffee, *Torah in the Mouth: Writing and Oral Tradition in Palestinian Judaism, 200BCE—400CE* (Oxford: Oxford University Press, 2000).

[8] James C. Scott, "Protest and Profanation: Agrarian Revolt and the Little Tradition," *Theory and Society* 4 (1977): 3–32, 159–210, here p 8; applied to Jesus and Gospel materials in Horsley and Draper, *Whoever Hears You Hears* Me, esp chap 5; Horsley, *Hearing the Whole Story;* and Richard A. Horsley, ed., *Hidden Transcripts and the Arts of Resistance: Applying the Work of James C. Scott to Jesus and Paul* (Semeia Studies; Atlanta: Society of Biblical Literature, 2004).

[9] Scott, "Protest and Profanation," 9.

[10] Scott, "Protest and Profanation," 18.

[11] Jan Assmann, *Das kulturelle Gedächtnis: Schrift, Erinnerung, und politische Identität in frühen Hochkulturen* (Munich: Beck, 1992), 72–80, 294–97; Kirk, "Social and Cultural Memory" in *Memory, Tradition, and Text,* 17.

[12] John Bodnar, *Remaking America: Public Memory, Commemoration, and Patriotism in the Twentieth Century* (Princeton, N.J.: Princeton University Press, 1992); Michael Schudson, *Watergate in American Memory: How We Remember, Forget, and Reconstruct the Past* (New York: Basic, 1992); Jeffrey K. Olick, "Collective Memory: The Two Cultures," *Sociological Theory* 17 (1999): 337–38.

[13] Jeffrey K. Olick, "Social Memory Studies: From 'Collective Memory' to the Historical Sociology of Mnemonic Practices," *Annual Review of Sociology* 24 (1998): 126–27.

[14] See, for example, George Mendenhall, "The Covenant Forms in Israelite Tradition," *BA* 17 (1954): 50–76; Delbert Hillers, *Covenant: The History of a Biblical Idea* (Baltimore: Johns Hopkins University Press, 1969).

[15] Klaus Baltzer, *The Covenant Formulary* (Philadelphia: Fortress Press, 1971).

[16] Horsley and Draper, *Whoever Hears You Hears Me*, chap 9.

[17] Horsley, *Hearing the Whole Story*, chap 8.

[18] See further Richard A. Horsley, "Popular Messianic Movements Around the Time of Jesus," *CBQ* 46 (1984): 471–95.

[19] Fuller discussion and documentation in Richard A. Horsley, "'Like One of the Prophets of Old': Two Types of Popular Prophets at the Time of Jesus," *CBQ* 47 (1985): 435–63; and "Popular

Prophetic Movements at the Time of Jesus, Their Principal Features and Social Origins," *JSNT* 26 (1986): 3–27.

[20] Fuller analysis and argument in Horsley, *Hearing the Whole Story*, chap 10.

[21] Assmann, *Das kulturelle Gedächtnis*, 30.

[22] Kirk, "Social and Cultural Memory," 7, 11.

[23] See the studies of Philippe Joutard, *La Legend des Camisards* (Paris, 1977); and G. Lewis, "A Cevenol Community in Crisis: The Mystery of 'l'homme a moustache,'" *Past and Present* 109 (1985): 144–75; social memory analysis, James Fentress and Chris Wickham, *Social Memory* (Oxford: Blackwell, 1992) 87–114.

[24] Fentress and Wickham, *Social Memory*, 92.

[25] Ibid., 88.

[26] Ibid.

[27] Kirk, "Social and Cultural Memory," 15; Fentress and Wickham, *Social Memory,* 51; Michael Schudson, "The Presence in the Past versus the Past in the Present," *Communication* 11 (1989): 112; Yael Zerubavel, *Recovered Roots: Collective Memory and the Making of Israeli National Tradition* (Chicago: University of Chicago Press, 1995), 229.

[28] Kirk, "Social and Cultural Memory," 17; citing Schudson, "Presence of the Past. . . ," 111; Roy Rosensweig and David Thelen, *The Presence of the Past: Popular Uses of History in American Life* (New York: Columbia University Press, 1998), 75; Fentress and Wickham, *Social Memory,* 108–9.

Chapter 8: *"Hidden Transcripts" and the "Arts of Resistance"*

[1] James C. Scott "Protest and Profanation: Agrarian Revolt and the Little Tradition," *Theory and Society* 4 (1977).

[2] John Dominic Crossan, *The Historical Jesus: The Life of a Mediterranean Jewish Peasant* (San Francisco: HarperCollins, 1991); John Dominic Crossan, *The Birth of Christianity* (San Francisco: HarperCollins, 1998); Richard A. Horsley with John S. Hanson, *Bandits, Prophets and Messiahs: Popular Movements in the Time of Jesus* (San Francisco: Harper and Row, 1985); Richard A. Horsley, *Jesus and the Spiral of Violence* (Minneapolis: Fortress Press 1995); Horsley, *Sociology and the Jesus Movement* (New York: Crossroad, 1989); Horsley, *Jesus and Empire: The Kingdom of God and the New World Disorder* (Minneapolis: Fortress, 2003); Horsley and Jonathan A. Draper *Whoever Hears You Hears Me: Prophets, Performance, and Tradition in Q* (Harrisburg, Pa.: Trinity International, 1999).

[3] James C. Scott, *The Moral Economy of the Peasant* (New Haven, Conn.: Yale University Press, 1976).

[4] James C. Scott, *Weapons of the Weak* (New Haven, Conn.: Yale University Press, 1985).

[5] Crossan, *The Birth of Christianity*; Horsley, *Jesus and the Spiral of Violence*; Horsley and Draper, *Whoever Hears You Hears Me*; William R. Herzog II, *Jesus, Justice and the Reign of God* (Louisville, Ky.: Westminster John Knox, 2000).

[6] James C. Scott, *Domination and the Arts of Resistance: Hidden Transcripts* (New Haven, Conn.: Yale University Press, 1990).

[7] Martin Goodman, *The Ruling Class of Judea* (Cambridge: Cambridge University Press, 1987); Richard A. Horsley, "The High Priests and Politics in Roman Palestine," *Journal for the Study of Judaism* 17 (1986): 23–55.

[8] Susan P. Mattern, *Rome and the Enemy: Imperial Strategy in the Principate* (Berkeley: University of California Press, 1999).

[9] For example, E. P. Sanders, *Judaism: Practice and Belief 63B.C.E.–66 C.E.* (Philadelphia: Trinity International, 1992).

[10] For example, Sean Freyne, *Galilee from Alexander the Great to Hadrian* (Wilmington, Del: Glazier, 1980).

[11] Rudolf Bultmann, *The History of the Synoptic Tradition* (Oxford: Blackwell, 1963); Martin Dibelius, *From Tradition to Gospel* (New York: Scribners, n.d.).

[12] For example, Scott, "Protest and Profanation"; Herzog, *Jesus, Justice and the Reign of God*; Horsley and Draper, *Whoever Hears You Hears Me*; Horsley *Hearing the Whole Story: The Politics of Plot in Mark's Gospel* (Louisville, Ky.: Westminster/John Knox 2001); John S. Kloppenborg, *Excavating Q* (Minneapolis: Fortress Press, 2000).

[13] Ranajit Guha, "On Some Aspects of the Historiography of Colonial India" in *Subaltern Studies 1* (Delhi: Oxford University Press, 1988).

[14] Richard A. Horsley, "Religion and Other Products of Empire," *Journal of the American Academy of Religion* 71 (2003): 13–44.

Chapter 9: Jesus and the Arts of Resistance

[1] See further Richard A. Horsley, *Jesus and Empire: The Kingdom of God and the New World Disorder* (Minneapolis: Fortress Press, 2003), chap 3.

[2] M. A. K. Halliday, *Language as Social Semiotic* (Baltimore: University Park, 1978).

[3] Richard A. Horsley, *Hearing the Whole Story: The Politics of Plot in Mark's Gospel* (Louisville, Ky.: Westminster John Knox, 2001), chap 10.

[4] Richard A. Horsley, "Jesus and Galilee: The Contingencies of a Renewal Movement" in *Galilee Through the Centuries*, ed. Eric M. Meyers (Winona Lake, Ind.: Eisenbrauns, 1999); Horsley, *Hearing the Whole Story*; Richard A. Horsley and Jonathan A. Draper, *Whoever Hears You Hears Me: Prophets, Performance, and Tradition in Q* (Harrisburg, Pa.: Trinity International, 1999).

[5] James C. Scott, *Domination and the Arts of Resistance* (New Haven, Conn.: Yale Univeristy Press, 1990).

[6] Horsley and Draper, *Whoever Hears You Hears Me*, chap 5.

[7] Ibid.; Horsley, *Hearing the Whole Story*.

[8] Richard A. Horsley, *Galilee: History, Politics, People* (Valley Forge, Pa.: Trinity International, 1995).

[9] John S. Kloppenborg, *The Formation of Q* (Philadelphia: Fortress Press, 1987); James M. Robinson, Paul Hoffmann, and John S. Kloppenborg, "Introduction" in *The Critical Edition of Q* (Minneapolis: Fortress Press, 2000); Richard A. Horsley, "Q and Jesus: Assumptions, Approaches, and Analyses," *Semeia* 55 (1991): 175–209; Horsley and Draper, *Whoever Hears You Hears Me*, chap 4.

[10] Richard A. Horsley, "'Like One of the Prophets of Old': Two Types of Popular Prophets at the Time of Jesus," *Catholic Biblical Quarterly* 47 (1985): 435–63, Richard A. Horsley, "Popular Prophetic Movements at the Time of Jesus, Their Principle Features and Social Origins," *Journal for the Study of the New Testament* 26 (1986): 3–27.

[11] Klaus Baltzer, *The Covenant Formulary* (Philadelphia: Fortress Press, 1971); Horsley and Draper, *Whoever Hears You Hears Me,* chap 9; and chap 3 above.

[12] Richard A. Horsley, *Jesus and the Spiral of Violence: Popular Jewish Resistance in Roman Palestine* (San Francisco: Harper and Row, 1987; Minneapolis: Fortress, 1995), 255–75; see also James C. Scott, *The Moral Economy of the Peasant* (New Haven, Conn.: Yale University Press, 1976).

[13] Werner Kelber, *The Oral and Written Gospel* (Philadelphia: Fortress Press, 1983), chap 1.

[14] John Dominic Crossan, *The Historical Jesus: The Life of a Mediterranean Jewish Peasant* (San Francisco: HarperCollins, 1991); P. W. Barnett, "The Jewish Sign Prophets—A.D. 40–70: Their Intentions and Origins," *New Testament Studies* 27 (1980–81): 679–97.

[15] Horsley, *Jesus and the Spiral of Violence,* 140–43.

[16] Crossan, *The Historical Jesus*; Burton L. Mack, *The Lost Gospel* (San Francisco: HarperCollins, 1993).

[17] Josephus, *J.W.* 1.401; Josephus *Ant.* 17.162; Peter Richardson, *Herod: King of the Jews and Friend of the Romans* (Columbia: University of South Carolina Press, 1996), 245–49.

[18] James C. Scott, "Protest and Profanation: Agrarian Revolt and the Little Tradition," *Theory and Society* 4 (1977): 1–38, 211–46.

[19] Horsley, *Jesus and the Spiral of Violence,* 33–43, 90–99.

[20] Scott, "Protest and Profanation."

[21] Peter Worsley, *The Trumpet Shall Sound* (New York: Schocken, 1956).

[22] Werner Kelber, *Mark's Story of Jesus* (Philadelphia: Fortress Press, 1979); Horsley, *Hearing the Whole Story.*

Chapter 10: Moral Economy and Renewal Movement in Q

[1] William E. Arnal, *Jesus and the Village Scribe: Galilean Conflicts and the Setting of Q* (Minneapolis: Fortress Press, 2001); Richard A. Horsley and Jonathan A. Draper, *Whoever Hears You Hears Me* (Harrisburg, Pa.: Trinity International, 1999) John S. Kloppenborg, *Excavating Q: The History and Setting of the Sayings Gospel* (Minneapolis: Fortress Press, 2000).

[2] Vincent Taylor, "The Original Order of Q" in *New Testament Essays: Studies in Memory or T. W. Manson,* ed. A. J. B. Higgins (Manchester: Manchester University Press), 95–118.

[3] John S. Kloppenborg, *The Formation of Q: Trajectories in Ancient Wisdom Collections* (Philadelphia: Fortress Press, 1987).

[4] Kloppenborg, *Excavating Q*; Arnal, *Jesus and the Village Scribe.*

[5] Richard A. Horsley, "Q and Jesus: Assumptions, Approaches, and Analyses," *Semeia* 55 (1991): 175-209; Alan Kirk, *The Composition of the Sayings Source* (Leiden: Brill, 1998); Horsley and Draper, *Whoever Hears You Hears Me,* 61–93.

[6] James M. Robinson, Paul Hoffman, and John S. Kloppenborg, eds., *The Criticial Edition of Q* (Minneapolis: Fortress Press, 2000) lxii–lxvi.

[7] James C. Scott, "Protest and Profanation: Agrarian Revolt and the Little Tradition," *Theory and Society* 4 (1977).

[8] James C. Scott, *The Moral Economy of the Peasant: Rebellion and Subsistence in Southeast Asia* (New Haven, Conn.: Yale University Press, 1976).

[9] James C. Scott, *Weapons of the Weak: Everyday Forms of Peasant Resistance* (New Haven, Conn.: Yale Univeristy Press, 1985).

[10] James C. Scott, *Domination and the Arts of Resistance: Hidden Transcripts* (New Haven, Conn.: Yale University Press, 1990).

[11] Burton L. Mack, *The Lost Gospel: The Book of Q and Christian Origins* (San Francisco: HarperSanFrancisco, 1993); Kloppenborg, *The Formation of Q.*

[12] Richard A. Horsley, "Popular Messianic Movements around the Time of Jesus," *CBQ* 46 (1984): 471–93; Richard A. Horsley, "'Like One of the Prophets of Old': Two Types of Popular Prophets at the Time of Jesus," *CBQ* 47 (1985): 435–63.

[13] Robert Redfield, *Peasant Society and Culture* (Chicago: University of Chicago Press, 1956).

[14] Horsley, "Popular Messianic Movements"; Horsley, "Like One of the Prophets of Old."

[15] Richard A. Horsley, *Jesus and the Spiral of Violence: Popular Jewish Resistance in Roman Palestine* (Minneapolis: Fortress Press, 1995), esp chap 5; Richard A. Horsley, *Sociology and the Jesus Movement* (New York: Crossroad, 1989), chaps 6–7.

[16] Such as Burton L. Mack, *A Myth of Innocence: Mark and Christian Origins* (Philadelphia: Fortress Press, 1988); and John Dominic Crossan, *The Historical Jesus: The Life of a Mediterranean Jewish Peasant* (San Francisco: HarperCollins, 1991).

[17] Richard A. Horsley, *Galilee: History, Politics, People* (Valley Forge, Pa.: Trinity International, 1995), esp chaps 2 and 6.

[18] Horsley and Draper, *However Hears You Hears Me,* 99–122.

[19] Kloppenborg, *Excavating Q,* 206–208.

[20] Horsley and Draper, *However Hears You Hears Me,* 104–122, and chaps 9–13.

[21] See Werner Kelber, "Jesus and Tradition: Words in Time, Words in Space," *Semeia* 65 (1994): 139–67.

[22] John H. Kautsky, *The Politics of Aristocratic Empires* (Chapel Hill: University of North Carolina Press, 1982).

[23] Horsley, "Popular Messianic Movements"; Horsley, "Like One of the Prophets of Old."

[24] Richard A. Horsley, "High Priests and the Politics of Roman Palestine," *Journal for the Study of Judaism* 17 (1986): 23–55.

[25] Horsley, *Galilee*; Richard A. Horsley *Archaeology, History, and Society in Galilee: The Social Context of Jesus and the Rabbis* (Harrisburg, Pa.: Trinity International, 1996).

[26] Richard A. Horsley, "Jesus and Galilee: The Contingencies of a Renewal Movement" in *Galilee Through the Centuries* (Winona Lake, Ind.: Eisenbrauns, 1999), 57–74.

[27] Julian Pitt-Rivers, *The Fate of Shechem* (Cambridge: Cambridge University Press, 1977), 62.

[28] Scott, "Protest and Profanation"; Horsley and Draper, *Whoever Hears You Hears Me,* chap 5.

[29] Richard A. Horsley, "The High Priests and Politics in Roman Palestine," *Journal for the Study of Judaism* 17 (1986): 23–55; Horsley, *Jesus and the Spiral of Violence,* 255–73.

[30] Horsley and Draper, *Whoever Hears You Hears Me,* chap 9.

[31] Ibid., 285–291.

[32] Scott, *Weapons of the Weak,* 31.

[33] On Antipas' regime and newly built cities as a key factor in the emergence of the Jesus movements see further Horsley, "Jesus and Galilee."

[34] Horsley, *Galilee,* chap 7.

[35] Shimon Applebaum, "Judea as a Roman Province: The Countryside as a Political and Economic Factor," *ANRW* 2.8 (1977): 386–95; David Fiensy, *The Social History of Palestine in the Herodian Period* (Lewiston, N.Y.: Mellen, 1991) and Horsley, *Galilee,* chap 9.

[36] Scott, *Weapons of the Weak,* 300–1.

[37] Scott, "Protest and Profanation," 225.

[38] Ibid., 220.

Appendix

[1] John S. Kloppenborg, *The Formation of Q* (Philadelphia: Fortress, 1987); Alan Kirk, *The Composition of the Sayings Source* (Leiden: Brill, 1998); Richard A. Horsley and Jonathan A Draper, *Whoever Hears You Hears Me* (Harrisburg: Trinity Press International, 1999).

[2] Horsley, *Whoever Hears You Hears Me,* chap 4.

[3] James M. Robinson, Paul Hoffmann, and John S. Kloppenborg, eds. *The Critical Edition of Q.* (Hermeneia; Minneapolis: Fortress, 2000).

[4] Those interested in how the Greek text "looks" blocked for oral performance can consult the transliterations printed in *Whoever Hears You Hears Me.*

[5] My earlier analysis and discussion of the oral performance of most of these speeches in historical context can be found in the chapters of *Whoever Hears You Hears Me*; for an earlier analysis and discussion of Q/Luke 11:39-52, see Richard Horsley, "Social Conflict in the Synoptic Sayings Source Q," pp 37-52 in *Conflict and Invention; Literary, Rhetorical, and Social Studies on the Sayings Gospel Q* , ed. John S. Kloppenborg (Valley Forge: Trinity Press International, 1995).

[6] Most accessible is James M. Robinson et. al., *The Sayings Gospel Q in Greek and English* (Minneapolis: Fortress Press, 2002).

[7] John S. Kloppenborg, *Q Parallels: Synopsis, Critical Notes, and Concordance* (Sonoma, CA: Polebridge Press, 1988).

[8] It is particularly difficult to discern the sequence as well as the wording of these "woes against the Pharisees," partly because Matthew (in chap 23) has greatly expanded on the Q speech. Both in the rhetoric of the speech and in the traditional prophetic form that it follows, the declaration of punishment in Q/Luke 11:49-51 would presumably have come at the end. This suggests that the woe in Luke 11:52 // Matt 23:13 would have been earlier in the sequence, perhaps in the order represented in Matthew 23, between Q/Lk 11:46 // Matt 23:4 and Q/Lk 11:47 // Matt 23:29. It is also difficult to discern the precise addressees of the woes. But since "scribes" and "Pharisees" are closely associated in Judean texts as well as the Gospels (many Pharisees may have been scribes, but not all scribes were Pharisees), and since the Pharisees were known as experts on the laws of the Judeans (mentioned repeatedly in Josephus' histories), the terms may have been more or less interchangeable. (I translate *nomoi* with "law-experts," following Josephus accounts of the Pharisees, since "lawyers" is misleading because of its modern associations.)

Acknowledgments

The essays in this volume are adapted from earlier publications and papers as follows:

Chapter 1 is an abridgement of "Unearthing a People's History," pages 1–20 in *Christian Origins,* A People's History of Christianity, vol. 1, ed. Richard A. Horsley (Minneapolis: Fortress Press, 2005), 1–20.

Chapter 2 is from "Jesus Movements and the Renewal of Israel," *Christian Origins*, 23–46.

Chapter 3 is a revision of paragraphs from the "Introduction," pages 2–3, 6–7, 11–12, and "Performance and Tradition: The Covenant Speech in Q," pages 43–70 in *Oral Performance, Popular Tradition, and Hidden Transcript in Q,* Semeia Studies 60, ed. Richard A. Horsley (Atlanta: Society of Biblical Literature, 2006). Copyright © Society of Biblical Literature. Used by permission.

Chapter 4 is based on lectures and workshops on the Gospel of Mark as a complete story and oral performance.

Chapter 5 is a revision of a paper for the Mapping Memory Group at the 2005 SBL Annual Meeting (previously unpublished).

Chapter 6 is adapted from "Prominent Patterns in the Social Memory of Jesus and Friends," pages 57–78 in *Memory, Tradition, and Text: Uses of the Past in Early Christianity,* Semeia Studies 52, ed. Alan Kirk and Tom Thatcher (Atlanta: Society of Biblical Literature, 2005). Copyright © Society of Biblical Literature. Used by permission.

Chapter 7 is adapted from "A Prophet Like Moses and Elijah: Popular Memory and Cultural Patterns in Mark," pages 166-190 in *Performing the Gospel: Orality, Memory, and Mark*, ed. Richard A.Horsley, Jonathan A. Draper, and John Miles Foley (Minneapolis: Fortress Press, 2006).

Chapter 8 is an abridgement and revision of the "Introduction," pages 1–26 in *Hidden Transcripts and the Arts of Resistance: Applying the Work of James C. Scott to Jesus and Paul*, Semeia Studies 48, ed. Richard A. Horsley (Atlanta:

Society of Biblical Literature, 2004). Copyright © Society of Biblical Literature. Used by permission.

Chapter 9 is a [minor] revision of "The Politics of Disguise and Public Declaration of the Hidden Transcript: Broadening Our Approach to the Historical Jesus," pages 61–80 in *Hidden Transcripts and the Arts of Resistance: Applying the Work of James C. Scott to Jesus and Paul*, Semeia Studies 48, ed. Richard A. Horsley (Atlanta: Society of Biblical Literature, 2004). Copyright © Society of Biblical Literature. Used by permission.

Chapter 10 is an abridgement and revision of paragraphs of the "Introduction," pages 3–6, and "Moral Economy and Renewal Movement in Q," pages 143–157 in *Oral Performance, Popular Tradition, and Hidden Transcripts in Q*, Semeia Studies 60, ed. Richard A. Horsley (Atlanta: Society of Biblical Literature, 2006). Copyright © Society of Biblical Literature. Used by permission.

INDEX